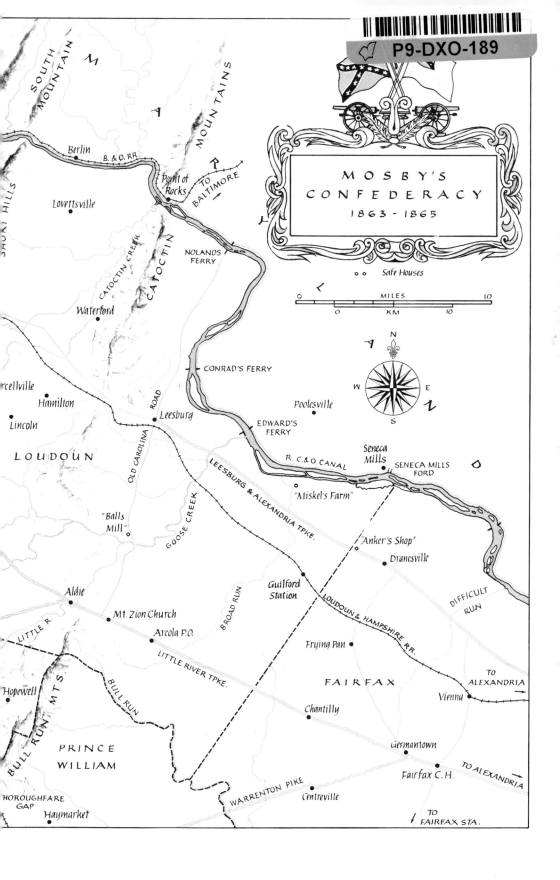

MOSBY'S CONFEDERACY 1863 - 1865

∘ ∘   Safe Houses

MILES

KM

N

SOUTH MOUNTAIN

M
O
U
N
T
A
I
N
S

SHORT HILLS

Berlin

B. & O. RR.

Point of Rocks

TO BALTIMORE

Lovettsville

CATOCTIN CREEK

CATOCTIN

NOLANDS FERRY

Waterford

CONRAD'S FERRY

Poolesville

rcellville

Hamilton

Leesburg

EDWARD'S FERRY

Lincoln

OLD CAROLINA ROAD

LOUDOUN

Seneca Mills

SENECA MILLS FORD

R. C. & O. CANAL

LEESBURG & ALEXANDRIA TPKE.

"Miskel's Farm"

"Balls Mill"

GOOSE CREEK

"Anker's Shop"

Dranesville

DIFFICULT RUN

Aldie

Mt. Zion Church

Arcola P.O.

BROAD RUN

Guilford Station

LOUDOUN & HAMPSHIRE RR.

LITTLE R.

LITTLE RIVER TPKE.

Frying Pan

FAIRFAX

TO ALEXANDRIA

Hopewell

BULL RUN MTS.

BULL RUN

Chantilly

Vienna

Germantown

PRINCE WILLIAM

TO ALEXANDRIA

Fairfax C.H.

HOROUGHFARE GAP

Haymarket

WARRENTON PIKE

Centreville

TO FAIRFAX STA.

Also by Jeffry D. Wert

From Winchester to Cedar Creek:
The Shenandoah Campaign of 1864

MOSBY'S RANGERS

JEFFRY D. WERT

SIMON AND SCHUSTER

NEW YORK LONDON TORONTO SYDNEY

TOKYO SINGAPORE

Simon and Schuster
Simon & Schuster Building
Rockefeller Center
1230 Avenue of the Americas
New York, New York 10020

SIMON AND SCHUSTER and colophon are
registered trademarks of Simon & Schuster Inc.

DESIGNED BY BARBARA MARKS
Manufactured in the United States of America

10   9   8   7   6   5   4   3   2   1

Library of Congress Cataloging in
Publication Data
Wert, Jeffry D.
Mosby's Rangers / Jeffry D. Wert.
p.   cm.
Includes bibliographical references and index.
1. Confederate States of America. Virginia
Cavalry Battlion, Forty-third—History.   2.
Virginia—History—Civil War, 1861–1865—
Regimental histories.   3. United States—
History—Civil War, 1861–1865—Regimental
histories.   I. Title.
E581.6 43rd.W47   1990
973.7'455—dc20   90-37917
                                         CIP

ISBN 0-671-67360-2

To Gloria,

with love

CONTENTS

PREFACE

 In January 1863 Confederate Major General J. E. B. Stuart, with the approval of General Robert E. Lee, detailed one of Stuart's best scouts, John Singleton Mosby, and fifteen men to operate within Union lines in northern Virginia. From this original nucleus, the unit evolved into the 43rd Battalion of Virginia Cavalry or Mosby's Partisan Rangers. During a span of roughly twenty-eight months, the 43rd Battalion was a matchless body of guerrillas, in turn becoming probably the most renowned combat unit of the Civil War.

Under Mosby's brilliant leadership, the Rangers were a constant presence in northern Virginia, striking daily in daylight and in darkness at Union outposts, pickets, wagon trains, troop detachments, headquarters and railroads. The Confederates attacked without warning and then disappeared. They seemed to relish the combat, fighting with a bravado that instilled both fear and hatred in their foes. Although they appeared as warriors of an earlier age, the struggle between them and their opponents was brutal, deadly warfare.

By the Civil War's conclusion, in April 1865, the Rangers stood unvanquished. All Federal counteroperations against them had failed and, once the principal armies of the Confederacy had surrendered or had been brought to bay, Mosby disbanded his command instead of accepting terms of surrender. Such a choice fit both Mosby and the men he led.

This book is a history of the 43rd Battalion of Virginia Cavalry, of John Mosby and the men who shared his mission with him for over two years. It is a recounting of their famous command—of its organization, membership, mode of operations, raids and exploits. It is also a reexamination, the first modern study, utilizing both unpublished and published sources, of Mosby's Rangers and their record. It presents the story of hard young men engaged in a hard war, a conflict shorn of romantic illusions by the staggering carnage.

Although the 43rd Battalion belonged to one man—John Singleton Mosby—he shares these pages with the youthful daredevils who rode by his side. An extraordinary officer, Mosby led by example and by the imposition of his will, and was the soul of the command. While any history of the battalion must have Mosby at center stage, he was surrounded by a remarkable group of officers and enlisted men. With him on scouts and on raids were men such as Adolphus "Dolly" Richards, William and Samuel Chapman, Richard Montjoy, James "Big Yankee" Ames, John Russell, Harry Hatcher, William Smith, Fount Beattie, William Thomas Turner and numerous others cut from a similar cloth. Mosby's story is also theirs.

Altogether, over 1,900 men belonged to the battalion. Throughout the unit's existence, recruits came in weekly, attracted by the glamour and successes, the lack of regulations and routine found in the regular army, the opportunity for many to be near home and the acquisition of plunder, which the members divided equally among themselves. They were overwhelmingly Virginians and Marylanders, with several dozen from other Confederate states. If they would not or could not adapt to Mosby's discipline and standards, Mosby sent them to the Army of Northern Virginia.

The fortunes and fate of the Rangers were also shared by the civilians who sheltered and fed Mosby's men, warning them of Union troops in the area and hiding them within their homes. When Mosby began his operations in early 1863, he chose the strategically important section of Virginia in the counties of Fauquier and Loudoun in the Piedmont region east of the Blue Ridge Mountains as his base. The area soon became known as "Mosby's Confederacy" and, from its farms, villages and woodlots, the Rangers rode forth until the end.

Without the support of the sympathetic populace, the 43rd Battalion could not have functioned as a guerrilla command. But the people of Fauquier and Loudoun soon learned that their efforts on behalf of the Rangers brought a price. Many saw their homes and livelihoods reduced to ashes, and their husbands and fathers placed in Union prisons. It is their story, too, and this book relates the sacrifices and the joys of life in "Mosby's Confederacy."

Finally, good military history requires balance, an integration of both sides' movements and actions into the narrative. Ranger operations usually resulted in Federal counteroperations, and these efforts by the Rangers' opponents are described in the book. Tough veteran Union cavalry regiments were assigned the temporary duty of opposing the Confederates and, although the Northerners ultimately failed, they proved to be worthy foes. They fought, bled and died in the same fields, woodlots and roadbeds as did the Rangers.

When John Mosby disbanded his command on a spring day in 1865, the men rode away from their final rendezvous with a legacy unequaled by other similar units of the war and with a historical fascination that transcends time. To retell their story frankly and without the veneer of romance is to do them and their foes justice. In the end, they were nothing more than men caught in a vicious war who tried to do their duty. That is reason enough to honor them and to recount their lives as Mosby's Rangers.

ACKNOWLEDGMENTS

 Many people have contributed to the research and writing of this book. They have generously shared with me their time, advice, knowledge and friendship, earning my gratitude and respect. Their efforts on my behalf have added measurably to the quality of my work. The responsibility, however, for errors contained within belongs solely to the author.

I wish to extend a special thank-you to the overworked and selfless professionals at the following libraries and institutions: William R. Perkins Library, Duke University, Durham, NC; Robert W. Woodruff Library, Emory University, Atlanta, GA; Handley Library, Winchester, VA; Library of Congress, Washington, DC; Maryland Historical Society, Baltimore, MD; Massachusetts Historical Society, Boston, MA; Middleburg Library, Middleburg, VA; National Archives, Washington, DC; Prince William County Library, Manassas, VA; Sky Meadows State Park, Paris, VA; Thomas Balch Library, Leesburg, VA; United States Army Military History Institute, Carlisle Barracks, PA; Bentley Historical Library, University of Michigan, Ann Arbor, MI; Alderman Library, University of Virginia, Charlottesville, VA; Virginia Historical Society, Richmond, VA; Preston Library, Virginia Military Institute, Lexington, VA.

Others deserve particular recognition for their contribution to my book:

Mary Morris, curator and archivist at the Clarke County Historical Association, Berryville, VA, and the Warren Heritage Society,

Front Royal, VA, for her tireless search for material on Mosby's Rangers and for exceeding the call of duty on my behalf.

Robert K. Krick, Historian, Fredericksburg and Spotsylvania National Military Park, and the foremost authority on the Army of Northern Virginia, for sharing with me his material on Mosby's Rangers.

Allan Tischler of Star Tannery, VA, a fellow Civil War historian and a friend, for tracking down sources on Ranger operations in the Shenandoah Valley.

Dennis E. Frye, Staff Historian, Harpers Ferry National Historic Park and Civil War scholar, for conducting me over the grounds of Loudoun Heights and for reading my chapter on that engagement, offering insight and criticisms in that ever friendly manner of his.

John Gott of Alexandria, VA, for sharing with me his family's version of the events of December 21, 1864, when John S. Mosby was seriously wounded in the home of Ludwell Lake, Mr. Gott's great-grandfather.

James Ewell Brown Stuart, IV, Director of the General Stuart–Colonel Mosby Museum, American Historical Foundation, Richmond, VA, for offering to me and my wife gracious hospitality and special assistance during our research at his institution.

Ronald Grove of Centre Hall, PA, for introducing me to the workings of a .44 caliber Army Colt revolver and for his friendship.

John Divine of Leesburg, VA, a Civil War historian and the epitome of a gentleman, for making my trip with him through "Mosby's Confederacy" one of the most unforgettable days of my life.

Robert Gottlieb, Vice President, William Morris Agency, New York, NY, and my agent, for his advice, concern and efforts on behalf of me and my family.

Bob Bender, Vice President and Senior Editor, Simon & Schuster, for accepting my idea, sharing the journey with me and making this a better book.

Jason and Natalie Wert, our children, for their patience, understanding and love, and for the pride they have given me as a father.

Finally, Gloria Wert, my wife and best friend, for her assistance with the research, for typing every word of the manuscript and for her love and support through over two decades together. Without her, this book would not be.

J. D. W.
Centre Hall, PA

PROLOGUE

It was an unlikely day for warriors. A slate of clouds and a late winter's drizzle portended miserable conditions. For the Confederate horsemen riding toward Dover Mill, west of Aldie in Loudoun County, Virginia, the weather mattered little. Orders had summoned them for a rendezvous on this afternoon, March 8, 1863, and they were coming.

The riders, twenty-nine in number, arrived in clusters, by twos, by threes, by fours. Roughly half of them were regular cavalrymen from the 1st Virginia regiment assigned to special duty in this section of the Old Dominion. The others had attached themselves during the preceding weeks to the unofficial command. Some of the latter had previous military experience; a few just possessed the exuberance of youth for adventure.

When they met, the talk must have centered upon the work ahead of them. No one among the group knew the destination, but that was the norm for the command. Frequently during the past several weeks, they had gathered at a designated site, spurred eastward toward Union lines south of Washington, DC, and attacked picket posts, troop detachments or wagon trains. Then, with prisoners and booty in tow, they returned to the farming country of Loudoun and Fauquier counties and dispersed to hiding places until summoned again.

These irregular operations were under the command of Lieutenant John Singleton Mosby, a wisp of a man who seemingly feared no one. He and his men had done well so far, but the command remained little more than an irritant—a pack of horse thieves—to Federal authorities in northern Virginia. This night's work would alter that perception.

About sundown, the thirty Confederates mounted, filed into a column and proceeded eastward on the Little River Turnpike, which ran from Aldie to Alexandria. Mosby rode in front with Private James F. "Big Yankee" Ames, a deserter from the 5th New York Cavalry who had joined Mosby about ten days earlier. From Ames, from his own reconnaissances, from the interrogation of Federal prisoners and from information supplied by civilians, Mosby learned, as he wrote later, "all the interior arrangements of their camps." He intended to penetrate Union lines, not attack them. His target was Federal headquarters at Fairfax Court House, specifically Colonel Percy Wyndham.[1]

Wyndham commanded a Federal cavalry brigade outside of the nation's capital. Mosby's forays had so frustrated and angered Wyndham that he called Mosby a horse thief and threatened to burn the village of Middleburg, the alleged center of Mosby's command. Mosby, who personalized warfare, decided that "I would put a stop to his talk by gobbling him up in bed and sending him off to Richmond."[2]

Mosby, as usual, kept the destination secret until the Southerners were on the move. He then revealed the plan to Ames as the pair rode together. The lieutenant expected to cover the twenty-five miles between Dover Mill and Fairfax Court House by midnight, entering the village from the south or east as circumstances dictated. Ames's role, as Mosby explained it, was to lead the column of horsemen undetected through the Union picket lines, which stretched from Dranesville, through Centreville to Alexandria. The Federal lines were like a knotted blue cord, with each knot an enemy outpost or garrison. Ames had to sever the cord between two knots.[3]

As the Confederates approached Chantilly, north of Centreville, Mosby and Ames led them off the Little River Turnpike and into the countryside. The pace of the march slowed as the rain and melting snow turned the fields into mud. The night was pitch dark, but Ames directed the column between the flickering Union campfires to the Warrenton Turnpike, where the raiders turned northward toward Fairfax. If a sentry challenged the horsemen in the blackness, Ames answered, "Fifth New York Cavalry." It was, as Mosby related, "pretty easy" for the Rebels to pass by the picket posts.[4]

Approximately a mile and a half from their destination, the riders veered eastward, swinging around the infantry camps of Vermont troops. Each Confederate now knew the target. The march had been slow and tiring because of the weather and the intense darkness. Nearly half of the men had lost their way in a pine forest between Chantilly and Centreville. It took perhaps an hour or more for the column to be reunited. When they finally entered Fairfax, it was two o'clock on the morning of the ninth, two hours behind Mosby's schedule.

The Confederates, coming in on the road from the railroad station, halted at the courthouse square. "Big Yankee" Ames and Walter Frankland, a former infantryman, grabbed a sentinel at a hotel which was being used as a hospital. Others collared a few more guards, who surrendered without resistance. Mosby quickly toured the village and returned to the square. Giving orders in whispers, he sent details to take the horse stables and various buildings and to cut the telegraph wires. Mosby, with most of the men, hurried to Wyndham's headquarters, a house belonging to a man named Murray. When the Rebels arrived and entered the house, Murray informed Mosby that his information was wrong: the Union colonel resided in a Judge Thomas's home at the other end of town.[5]

Returning to the courthouse square, Mosby sent Ames and a squad to the Thomas residence. The detail found Captain Augustus Barker, 5th New York Cavalry, Ames's former commander, and R. B. Wardner, an Austrian baron. One of the captives informed the Confederates that Wyndham was spending the night in the capital. The quarry had eluded the raiders.[6]

The other details, meanwhile, herded their prisoners and horses into the square. Joe Nelson brought Robert Weitbrecht, a telegraph operator, and an orderly to Mosby, who interrogated the pair. Weitbrecht told the Confederates that Brigadier General Edwin H. Stoughton, commander of the Vermont infantry brigade, had his headquarters at the brick home of Dr. William Presley Gunnell on the outskirts of the town. Mosby, with Weitbrecht and the orderly and five of his men, proceeded to the Gunnell house.[7]

While George Whitescarver and Welt Hatcher guarded the horses and the Yankees, Mosby, Nelson, William Hunter and Frank Williams walked to the front door. One of them knocked on the door, which brought a head out of a second-story window. The occupant growled, wanting to know the reason for the intrusion. "Fifth New York. With a dispatch for General Stoughton," was the reply. The Confederates heard the Yankee, a Lieutenant Prentiss of Stoughton's staff, come down the stairs. When Prentiss opened the door, Mosby grabbed him by his nightshirt, and the Rebels shoved through the passageway.[8]

Mosby, dressed in the uniform of a Confederate captain, forced Prentiss to lead him to the general's room. The Federals had evidently enjoyed themselves earlier that night as uncorked champagne bottles lay in the rooms. The twenty-four-year-old Stoughton had a reputation as a drinker and womanizer. In a nearby tent he kept a twenty-year-old woman from Cambridge, Massachusetts, named Annie Jones, an honorary major on Stoughton's staff.[9]

The four raiders found the brigadier asleep in bed. Mosby, according to his memoirs, removed the bedcovers, lifted Stoughton's nightshirt and unceremoniously spanked his bare behind. Other accounts, however, have Mosby shaking the young Vermonter. Regardless, Stoughton groggily asked who was present.

"General, did you ever hear of Mosby?" asked the Confederate lieutenant.

"Yes, have you caught him?" Stoughton responded.

"I am Mosby," came the reply. "Stuart's cavalry has possession of the Court House; be quick and dress."[10]

Astonished by the words, Stoughton rose from the bed and inquired if Confederate cavalry General Fitzhugh Lee was with the Rebels. Mosby lied, saying that Lee was present. The brigadier then requested that he be taken to Lee, for they had been classmates at West Point. Mosby consented and ordered the captive to dress quickly. But Stoughton—"He had a reputation of being a gallant soldier, but a fop," Mosby wrote later—dressed slowly and fastidiously before a mirror. Losing his patience, Mosby had two of his men assist the officer while the third guarded Prentiss. Finally, the captors hurried the two Federals downstairs and out the front door. As they were leaving the house, Frank Williams handed Stoughton his watch, which the officer had overlooked as he dressed.[11]

Back at the square, the other details had finished their work and had regrouped. It was nearly 3:30 A.M., and Mosby led them out on the road to the station. Scores of Yankees prowled around the square. "All was panic and confusion," Mosby stated. "Each man was in search of a safe hiding-place."[12]

The column of horsemen covered barely a few hundred feet when a man shouted at them from a second-story window.

"Halt!" he demanded. "The horses need rest! I will not allow them to be taken out! What the devil is the matter!"

When no one responded to his words, the Federal bellowed:

"I am commander of the cavalry here and this must be stopped!"

At this point, Colonel Robert Johnstone of the 5th New York Cavalry realized that it was Rebels beneath the window. Mosby, in turn, sent Joe Nelson and Welt Hatcher through the front door. In the hallway, the pair encountered Mrs. Johnstone, who tried to stall the pursuers. The still naked colonel, meanwhile, had exited through the back door and concealed himself beneath an outhouse in the yard. When Nelson and Hatcher returned empty-handed, the Confederates spurred southward and out of Fairfax Court House. Reportedly, Mrs. Johnstone later that morning refused her husband's embrace until he bathed.[13]

Mosby exited as he had entered in order to deceive any pursuit parties. Roughly one-half of a mile from the village the Southerners abandoned the roadway, plunging into the countryside. Difficulties mounted as the column became strung out because of the darkness and the captured men and horses. A number of Yankees escaped, disappearing into the night. When the Confederates struck the Warrenton Pike, Mosby gave William Hunter—"I looked to him more than to any of the men to aid me in accomplishing my design," Mosby said of the twenty-year-old Virginian—command of the column with orders to move at a fast trot and to keep it closed up. Mosby, with Joe Nelson, trailed as a rear guard.[14]

Once again, as they had done on the way in, the raiders skirted Federal camps north of Centreville. If they were to be detected, it would be along this sector, but the sentries, if they heard the horses, mistook them for a Union cavalry patrol. Mosby and Nelson, with a stint of hard riding, overtook the column at this point. They soon reached the final obstacle, a flooded Cub Run, which necessitated the swimming across by men and beasts. "Captain," a dripping wet Stoughton allegedly said to Mosby, "this is the first bad treatment I have received at your hands."[15]

After the crossing, Mosby and George Slater rode ahead as scouts. The column followed, across Bull Run at Sudley Ford and on to the battlefield where Northerners and Southerners bloodied each other in July 1861 and again in August 1862. Faint rays of a rising sun revealed corpses washed out of their shallow graves by winter rains. The sight and the stench served as reminders of war's costs.[16]

Mosby, still in the lead with Slater, ascended the Brawner farm hill at Groveton, where Thomas J. "Stonewall" Jackson's troops slugged it out with Federals the previous August. The lieutenant, looking eastward toward a risen sun, saw white-tented Union camps seven miles away. Below him, Hunter and the column were spurring up the hillside; no Yankee pursuers dogged their rear. It was a moment Mosby never forgot. To him, it seemed as though the sun "never shone with such splendor before. I was safe."[17]

He and his twenty-nine men had accomplished, by his own admission, "an impossibility," a feat he never duplicated, "one of those things a man can do only once in a lifetime." The raiders had bagged a Union general, two captains, thirty enlisted men and fifty-eight horses by riding into and out of a garrisoned village without firing a shot or losing a man. War offered incalculable moments—the long sleep to many; a morning's sunrise, made sweeter by victory, to but a few.[18]

For the spare lieutenant and his youthful daredevils this winter morning was but a beginning. Time and again during the next two years, they appeared, as if risen from the soil of the Old Dominion, attacking Yankee troops, wagon trains and railroads. Numbers of them fell maimed or dead, numbers more ended the war in Northern prisons, but still others joined the command. They would become the 43rd Battalion of Virginia Cavalry, a matchless command of partisan rangers who ruled a section of northern Virginia known as "Mosby's Confederacy." Fame followed the Stoughton raid; romance and legend enshrouded their exploits by the Civil War's conclusion.

John Singleton Mosby created the battalion, recruited and disciplined its members, planned their raids, led them in the roughest of fights and, in the end, refused to surrender them. Union generals such as Ulysses S. Grant, Philip Sheridan, Winfield Scott Hancock, Joseph Hooker, George Custer and Wesley Merritt formulated plans or led troops into combat against Mosby. None, however, succeeded in the elimination of his partisan command. He had no rival as a guerrilla officer during the conflict.

But as on that day on the Brawner hillside, Mosby never stood alone. That morning there were William Hunter, James Ames, Joe Nelson, Walter Frankland, John Scott, Welt Hatcher, John Underwood, George Whitescarver, Frank Williams, George Slater, Daniel

Thomas, William Thomas Turner, Edward Hurst and others with him. On future days "Dolly" Richards, William Smith, the Chapmans—William and Samuel—Fountain Beattie, John Russell, John Alexander, James Williamson, John Munson, Harry Hatcher and hundreds more followed him into combat. They were Mosby's Rangers.

Chapter 1

THE
MAN
AND
THE
MISSION

 "I was so depressed at parting with my wife and children that I scarcely spoke a word," wrote John Mosby of his entry into Confederate service in May 1861. He was a reluctant soldier. Few who saw him or knew him could have anticipated his future military success and renown. But the mettle of the man had been already fused. John Mosby spent a lifetime leaning into the winds. The gale of civil war found him prepared.[1]

John Singleton Mosby was born at Edgemont, the farm of his maternal grandfather, James McLaurine, in Powhatan County, Virginia, on December 6, 1833. His parents were Alfred D. and Virginia McLaurine Mosby. When John was five or six years old, the family moved to a farm outside of Charlottesville. There Alfred Mosby prospered. He owned slaves and saw to the education of his two sons and seven daughters, one of whom died in infancy.[2]

John's education began in a country schoolhouse in Nelson County before the family moved from Edgemont. Following the resettlement in Albemarle County, he continued his studies at a small schoolhouse near the family farm. At age ten, John transferred to a school in Charlottesville. An avid learner, he rode a horse or walked the four miles, rarely missing a day's schooling. Unlike boys of his age, he disliked the athletic activities of recess; "I always had a literary taste."[3]

On October 3, 1850, John enrolled as a student at the University of Virginia in Charlottesville. During his first year he excelled in Latin, Greek and English while scoring poorly in mathematics. Chronic illnesses, however, plagued him throughout the term. In addition, in the spring of 1851 Mosby broke a gunstock over the head of Constable George Slaughter during a melee in the town and was fined ten dollars.[4]

Mosby, a thoughtful young man with a penetrating mind, continued to show excellence in the languages and literature during his second and third years at the university. Mathematics still baffled him, but he added chemistry and moral philosophy to his course work. More frequently, during 1852–1853, he gravitated into the social life offered by the community. It was in this latter milieu that Mosby revealed those traits which made him the future leader of men at war.[5]

Sometime during 1852 or early 1853 Mosby apparently met George Turpin, the son of a Charlottesville tavernkeeper, and burly town bully. In March 1853, Turpin disparaged Mosby in some remarks to mutual acquaintances. When the college student learned of Turpin's words, he sent the townsman a note, asking him to explain the matter. Such a message from a frail-looking nineteen-year-old enraged Turpin, who went to Mosby's boardinghouse to seek a confrontation. As Turpin ascended the stairway to an upper floor, Mosby stood at the top, leveled a pistol and squeezed the trigger. Turpin collapsed in the hallway, the bullet having entered his mouth, lodging in the neck.[6]

Charlottesville authorities arrested Mosby and confined him in the local jail. While few townsfolk liked Turpin, the assailant had nearly killed an unarmed man. Mosby was arraigned before Judge

Richard H. Field on May 16, charged with "malicious shooting" and "unlawful shooting."[7]

The trial lasted five days, with one day off for the Sabbath. William J. Robertson, an able lawyer, prosecuted for the state. Two local attorneys represented the defendant; Turpin's personality and record abetted the defense's case. He had earlier nearly killed one man with a rock and sliced another with a pocket knife. He also publicly threatened Mosby before the incident. The key area of dispute in the testimony centered upon which of the two men advanced first against the other. If Turpin moved toward Mosby, the latter's action could be construed as self-defense.[8]

The jury began deliberations on Tuesday, May 24. Late that afternoon the members returned to the courtroom, informing Judge Field that they had failed to reach a decision. He returned them to the jury room for a reconsideration. Finally, the next day the jury found Mosby not guilty of "malicious shooting," but guilty of "unlawful shooting." The panel sentenced him to one year in the local jail and the payment of a 500-dollar fine. On the thirtieth Judge Field formally sentenced the youth.[9]

Mosby served nearly seven months of his one-year sentence. From the time of his conviction, family and friends used political influence to obtain a pardon. Governor Joseph Johnson, after reviewing the evidence, pardoned him on December 21, 1853, fifteen days after his twentieth birthday. Mosby walked out of the Charlottesville jail two days later. The state legislature also rescinded the fine. The incident, including the trial and conviction, so affected Mosby that he never wrote about it in his later memoirs.[10]

During his incarceration, Mosby began the study of law, having borrowed a copy of Blackstone's *Commentaries* from his prosecutor, William Robertson. Upon his release, he continued the training in Robertson's law offices. He was admitted to the bar several months later and opened his practice in Howardsville in Albemarle County. There he met Pauline Clarke, daughter of Beverly J. Clarke, a former United States congressman and diplomat from Franklin, Kentucky. The couple was married in a Roman Catholic ceremony in Nashville, Tennessee, on December 30, 1857.[11]

The newlyweds relocated to Bristol, Virginia, during the next year. Mosby was the first lawyer to open a practice in the community. He did well as an attorney, and Pauline gave birth to a daughter, May Virginia, and a son, Beverly. As the nation began its dissolution into civil war, Mosby opposed the secession of the Lower South states following the election of Abraham Lincoln in November 1860. He reluctantly joined a militia company, the Washington Mounted Rifles, during the winter of 1861. When Virginia seceded in April, after the firing upon Fort Sumter in the harbor of Charleston, South Carolina, the Washington Mounted Rifles marched eastward to join the burgeoning Confederate forces in the Old Dominion.[12]

The cavalry unit was organized as Company D, 1st Virginia Cavalry, with William E. "Grumble" Jones as captain. Jones, who had formed the company, was a cantankerous, eccentric former West Pointer and regular army officer. Colonel of the 1st Virginia Cavalry was James Ewell Brown "Jeb" Stuart. Under Stuart, the regiment saw its initial combat in the conflict's first major engagement at the Battle of Bull Run or Manassas on July 21, 1861.[13]

Mosby, a private, subsequently wrote in his memoirs of his first battle. He recalled the foreboding he felt the night before, but he added that "nothing afterwards occurred in my military career that gives me more satisfaction to remember." Captain Jones previously had selected Mosby and five others to receive six Colt pistols given to the company. When Stuart ordered Jones to conduct a reconnaissance across Bull Run Creek on the morning of the twenty-first, the captain assigned the task to the six men. The group splashed across the creek, entered a woodlot but found no Yankees. While the battle raged during the remainder of the day, Mosby's squadron remained as bystanders. The next day he wrote to Pauline: "I was in the fight."[14]

While Jones saw promise in Mosby, others who knew him at this time thought otherwise. "There was nothing about him then to indicate what he was to be," argued William Blackford, a member of the regiment and a future aide of Stuart. "He was rather a slouchy rider, and did not seem to take any interest in military duties. He had been but seldom at our drills before starting, and we all thought he was rather an indifferent soldier."[15]

Mosby cared little for the routine of military life and the boredom. "I preferred being on the outposts," he admitted. From the summer of 1861 until the spring of 1862 he served constantly along the picket line. Scouting and vedette duty suited his restless nature.[16]

But "Grumble" Jones, who succeeded Stuart as colonel of the 1st Virginia Cavalry, had increasing regard for the lawyer's talents. When in January 1862 Mosby applied for a six-day furlough, Jones approved it, endorsing the request by noting that the private had been "in the most active dangerous duty rendering brilliant service." On February 14, the colonel installed Mosby as the regiment's adjutant. He was appointed to the rank of first lieutenant on April 2.[17]

"The duties are very light," Mosby informed Pauline of the adjutant's post. Nevertheless, he disliked the paperwork and the regulations required of the position. "I remember the few weeks I served as an adjutant," he wrote in his memoirs, "with less satisfaction than any other portion of my life as a soldier." When Fitzhugh Lee, an officer Mosby detested personally, replaced Jones as colonel of the 1st Virginia, Mosby resigned as adjutant and also resigned his commission as lieutenant on April 23.[18]

While Mosby had served as regimental adjutant, he had conducted some scouting operations for Jeb Stuart, now cavalry commander of the Confederate Army of the Potomac. When Mosby resigned, Stuart attached the Virginian to his staff. Although the new aide had no commission, Stuart referred to him as a lieutenant. The appointment began the most important association of Mosby's military career. Stuart "made me all that I was in the war, but for his friendship I would never have been heard of," Mosby stated in a postwar letter. The flamboyant cavalry commander, Mosby added in another letter, was "the best friend I ever had."[19]

Jeb Stuart was twenty-nine years old—ten months older than Mosby—in the spring of 1862. A brigadier general because of his performance at First Bull Run, he had already demonstrated those qualities which would make him one of the finest cavalry commanders of the war. An able organizer, a superb intelligence and reconnaissance officer, Stuart came to have no rival as a horse officer in Virginia. He possessed ambition, courage, daring and a relish for the pageantry of warfare. Although deeply religious, he enjoyed life, and his headquarters was noted for its liveliness and camaraderie. What Stuart saw in Mosby were the shared traits of intelligence, boldness and resourcefulness.

The first significant service Mosby rendered for Stuart came in June 1862. Major General George B. McClellan's Union Army of the Potomac had advanced to within six miles of Richmond, Virginia, the Confederate capital. Opposing McClellan's bluecoated forces was the Army of Northern Virginia, under the command of General Robert E. Lee. The Confederate commander ordered Stuart to gather solid information on McClellan's dispositions. Stuart, in turn, directed Mosby to conduct a scout within Union lines.

Mosby, with four men, entered Federal lines on what he told Pauline was "the grandest scout of the War." He discovered that McClellan's right flank north of the Chickahominy River was unprotected and reported to Stuart that the cavalry could ride around the entire Union army. Stuart listened and directed Mosby to prepare a written statement and sign it. Stuart then carried the document to army headquarters, where he and Lee discussed the merits before Lee granted approval. Two days later, on June 12, Stuart departed with approximately 1,200 troopers and rode around McClellan's army in a four-day raid which insured the dashing cavalryman's reputation. Mosby rode in the forefront throughout the raid, prowling along roads, scouting for Federal units.[20]

A month later, after McClellan's army had been driven eastward down the Virginia Peninsula, Stuart sent Mosby, with a note of introduction, to Thomas J. "Stonewall" Jackson, stationed at Gordonsville. Mosby, Stuart informed Jackson in the message, "is bold, daring, intelligent and discreet. The information he may obtain and transmit to you may be relied upon, and I have no doubt that he will soon give additional proofs of his value."[21]

Mosby traveled by horseback to Beaver Dam Station, where he planned to finish the trip by railroad. As he waited on the platform for the cars on July 20, a Yankee cavalry patrol swept into the station, capturing him and several other Confederates. He was sent to Washington and placed in the Old Capitol Prison. His captors had found Stuart's note, the contents of which revealed clearly the value of the prisoner to the Confederate general. Federal authorities, however, exchanged Mosby within ten days for Lieutenant C. A. Bayard of the 5th Wisconsin. It was a decision the officials would regret.[22]

Upon his release, Mosby returned to duty with Stuart. He participated in the summer and autumn campaigns of Second Bull Run or Manassas in August, Antietam in September, Stuart's raid into Chambersburg, Pennsylvania, in October and Fredericksburg, Virginia, in December. Mosby frequently scouted alone or with a few comrades. When George McClellan relinquished command of the Army of the Potomac to Major General Ambrose Burnside and bid farewell to fellow officers at Rectortown, Virginia, in November, the Confederate scout witnessed the scene from behind nearby bushes. At year's end, Stuart raided behind Burnside's army in the region between Fredericksburg and Washington.[23]

Soon after this last raid, the Southern horsemen retreated into

Loudoun County for a few days' rest. Stuart and his staff found lodging on December 30 at "Oakham Farm," homestead of the Hamilton Rogers family, west of Aldie on the Little River Turnpike. The next morning Mosby met with Stuart in the general's bedroom. For some time Mosby had been mulling the idea of conducting guerrilla forays in Loudoun County during the winter months. "I did not want to rust away my life in camp," as he explained it later. Mosby requested a detail of men and permission to remain behind when the cavalry returned to winter quarters west of Fredericksburg.[24]

Stuart consented to the request. The general, according to another staff officer, had come "to repose unlimited confidence" in the lieutenant's resourcefulness and "relied implicitly upon him." Stuart must have regretted losing Mosby's services, if only temporarily, but Mosby expected to rejoin the cavalry when spring campaigning began. "At the time," recalled Mosby, "I had no idea of organizing an independent command. . . . I was indifferent to rank, and would have been as contented to be a lieutenant as a colonel."[25]

Later that day Stuart bid farewell to his hosts and clattered with his troops southward for Lee's army at Fredericksburg. Mosby and his detail of nine men most likely watched the columns of horsemen disappear beyond the horizon. It is unlikely that any of those passing by noticed the lieutenant who remained behind. At first glance John Mosby did not look like much of a warrior.

James Williamson first glimpsed Mosby in the spring of 1863 when he came as a recruit for the partisan command. Mosby's renown had fashioned Williamson's expectations. "I could scarcely believe," asserted Williamson, "that the slight figure before me could be that of the man who had won such military fame by his daring."[26]

Another volunteer, John Munson, remembered vividly his initial view of the guerrilla chieftain. Munson, with others, approached a farmhouse where some Confederates were gathered to inquire of the location of Mosby. When one of the men on the porch identified Mosby, Munson later stated that "the shock was something considerable. I beheld a small, plainly attired man, fair of complexion, slight but wiry, standing with his arms behind his back, talking quietly to one of his men. A military belt girded his waist, from which hung two Colt's army pistols.

"The visions of splendor and magnificence that had filled my mind swept away. The total absence of visible might, the lack of swagger, the quiet demeanor of the man, all contributed to my astonishment and chagrin. He did not even strut."[27]

If Mosby had strutted, in fact, he would have appeared like a bantam rooster. There was not much to the man physically. He stood five feet, seven or eight inches tall and weighed 128 pounds. When he stood, he had a slight stoop in his posture, which made him seem even shorter. By his own admission, he was "the frailest and most delicate man in the Company" when he enlisted in 1861. But, by the end of 1863, his thin frame had been toughened. Few, if any, of the men matched his endurance.[28]

Fair complexioned, with sandy-colored hair, Mosby was, by most accounts, not a handsome man. A Northern newspaperman who met him after the war reported that "he is nothing of the sort [handsome]. . . his face is very commonplace, and his light brown hair, worn unkempt, adds nothing to its attractiveness." One of his men described him as "hatchet-faced" with "a hawk-like nose." He remained clean-shaven until the final months of the war. His appearance, remarked John Esten Cooke, a member of Stuart's staff, was "wholly undistinguished."[29]

But Cooke and the hundreds of other men who crossed Mosby's path could not forget the eyes. They were blue, luminous, piercing, the most compelling element about the man. When the eyes flashed, thought Cooke, they "might have induced the opinion that there was something in the man, if it only had an opportunity to 'come out.' " Munson argued that Mosby's eyes and what they revealed were "the secret of the power over his men." "When he spoke," Munson added, "they flashed the punctuations of his sentence." And when men angered him, Mosby's glare chilled their spines. "I often watched him," Williamson remembered, "as he would stand intently gazing at a man—staring as though he were reading him through with those eyes, like a book."[30]

Mosby seldom revealed himself. What did "come out," he carefully modulated. He was a reserved, even tactiturn, individual. When he spoke, he did so in a low voice, slowly, distinctly, tersely; "there was no mistaking the meaning of his words," said Williamson. At times, however, Mosby could be quite talkative, his speech animated, the words shooting out as if discharged from a revolver. At other times, he seemed bothered to answer a question asked of him.[31]

He could be what an acquaintance said, "a disturbing companion." He was obstinate, cantankerous, ill-tempered, with a brusqueness to his demeanor. Scrupulously honest, Mosby cared neither for sentiment nor for pretense. There was a hard realism, even cynicism, to the man.[32]

The Virginian seldom occupied the middle ground—he was either for or against a man. Those whom he disliked saw the sharp edge of his personality; but those whom he liked knew him as a loyal, generous, witty friend and companion. Mosby possessed, in Williamson's words, a "rich vein of humor." Around a campfire or at a dinner table with friends, the reserve, the reticence gave way to camaraderie and laughter. No one who knew him, however, described Mosby as affable. There always seemed to be beneath the exterior a smoldering flame ready to blaze forth through the blue eyes at any moment.[33]

Beneath the exterior, to be sure, was a keen intellect. An acquaintance from Jeb Stuart's staff, John Esten Cooke, asserted that Mosby had "one of the most active, daring and penetrating minds of an epoch fruitful in such." He was a deep thinker and, when in thought, he had the habit of picking his teeth with a toothpick or small twig. While his raids on Union outposts and detachments might have had the appearance of spontaneity, nothing could be further from the truth. As a partisan commander, Mosby incessantly sifted, planned and calculated. He seldom spoke on a raid as he plotted in his mind the final details of the attack.[34]

A restless man—"he rarely sat still ten minutes," said Cooke—Mosby possessed untiring energy. He could spend hours in the saddle, scouting Union lines, gathering information from civilians. He studied, prepared and then struck. His tirelessness, his dauntlessness, his daring and his intellect made Mosby a formidable opponent. He worked at waging war.[35]

Mosby never rested, perhaps, because he never could. Warfare suited the man. Combat was an imperative, a ceaseless hunt for an opponent. He was, in the view of a biographer, an "aginner." Mosby tested the prevailing winds, found their direction, and faced them squarely. He chose a mission which would unleash a maelstorm in northern Virginia.[36]

It was Mosby who brought guerrilla warfare to that section of the embattled Old Dominion. When Mosby conferred with Stuart at Oakham, he outlined to the general a modest operation. "I thought," he later wrote, "I could make things lively during the winter months." He had no plans at the time to organize an independent partisan command, but his nine-man detail would be the beginning of twenty-eight months of raids, ambushes and attacks against Union forces in the region which stretched from the outskirts of Washington, across the Blue Ridge Mountains into the Shenandoah Valley and beyond the Potomac River into Maryland.[37]

No sector of Virginia held better opportunities for Confederate guerrilla operations than the area Mosby selected. When Confederate authorities designated Richmond as their nation's capital in May 1861, the hundred-mile stretch of the Old Dominion between that city and Washington, DC, became the battleground of the war in the East. The opposing armies bloodied each other across this landscape as campaign after campaign unfolded in 1861 and 1862—First Bull Run, Peninsula, Seven Days, Second Bull Run, Antietam and Fredericksburg. The war in Virginia was to be decided in this region and in the Shenandoah Valley, westward beyond the Blue Ridge Mountains.

Union forces in the East had the dual assignment of defending their capital and invading Confederate territory. Union advances overland from Washington to Richmond, or southward or up the Shenandoah Valley exposed their supply and communication lines to Southern raiders, either cavalry forces or guerrilla commands. Protection of those lines required detaching units from the invading forces. As the pressure on the lifelines of the Yankees increased, more troops were needed for guard duty along railroad lines or with wagon trains.

Mosby believed that an enemy's rear was the most vulnerable section of his lines. "A small force moving with celerity and threatening many points on a line can neutralize a hundred times its own number," he argued. "The line must be stronger at every point than the attacking force, else it is broken." Continuing, he wrote: "The military value of a partisan's work is not measured by the amount of property destroyed, or the number of men killed or captured, but by the number he keeps watching."[38]

Mosby's base of operations became the counties south and west of Washington, south of the Potomac River, and those at the western base of the Blue Ridge in the lower or northern end of the valley of Virginia. Stationing his men in the northern and western portion of Fauquier County and southern Loudoun County, he could strike eastward into the counties of Prince William, Fairfax or Culpeper or westward beyond the mountains into Jefferson, Frederick, Clarke and Warren counties. While some of his raids covered a wider swath, these counties remained the center of his activities. He could attack the defenses of Washington or assail Federal supply lines east or west of the Blue Ridge.

The terrain in this part of Virginia was conducive to guerrilla warfare. Hundreds of square miles of forested mountains, woodlots and hills interspersed with fertile farmlands. A single sentry on horseback, stationed on a knoll, could scan miles of territory for enemy units. Country lanes, edged with stone walls, and obscure trails provided a network for movement. Small towns and homes of planters and yeoman farmers provided places of refuge and a network of informants. It was a region of beauty—the Blue Ridge Mountains reaching toward the clouds, the lush soil of the Piedmont or "foot of the mountain" giving forth its abundance. A Yankee visitor admitted that it was "one of the loveliest countries in the world."[39]

Nature rendered it rich; war rendered it strategic. From the counties of Fauquier and Loudoun, Mosby stood across vital supply and communication links of invading Federal armies. His presence became a constant factor in the development of Union campaign strategy. By keeping numbers of Northern troops watching, Mosby's men drained the strength of the invaders. His mission, as he stated it, was "to weaken the armies invading Virginia by harassing their rear."[40]

So Mosby and his men rode from Fauquier and Loudoun, striking in the dark of night or in the glare of day, at unexpected places, in good weather and bad. It was warfare predicated upon speed, mobility and surprise attacks—the tactics of thrust before parry. Its nature, however, generated bitterness between antagonists. Hard men rode as guerrillas; hard men met them in combat. The cloak of romance that surrounds guerrilla activity could not conceal the killing and the maiming.

The man and the mission thus came together in a Virginia farmhouse on a winter's morning. John Mosby had found his niche in the struggle between his fellow countrymen. Outside the house, nine other men waited; Mosby's mission had become theirs.

Chapter 2

A
WILY
FOE

New Year's 1863 dawned with the promise of a bright winter's day in Virginia. Thousands in the state and tens of thousands more in the embattled nation probably took time for reflection. No longer did Americans see the glory of war, only its sacrifice and cost. The past year had shattered such romantic illusions as blood flowed in such places as Shiloh, Seven Pines, Gaines Mill, Malvern Hill, Cedar Mountain, South Mountain, Antietam and Fredericksburg. And still more killing loomed with the advent of another year.

Amanda Virginia "Tee" Edmonds, who lived at "Belle Grove," her family's farm outside of Paris, Fauquier County, Virginia, thought about the past and the future on this first of January. "Tee"

Edmonds was twenty-three years old, unmarried, with kinfolk in Confederate service. "I have never said or felt before that I was glad at the departure of the old year, but I am now," she confided in her journal. "The months do not pass speedily enough for I feel it is that much nearer peace. War's alarm is that much nearer being calmed. The past year has been one of pleasant memories, yet with them all was intermingled sadness and gloom for our Country's fate. Good-bye, fast fleet hours of winter away."[1]

Not far from "Tee" Edmonds, near Middleburg in Loudoun County, Catherine Barbara Broun, a wife and mother, thought more of the future than of the past. In her diary she scribbled under this day's date: "It is truly thrilling to write 1863 another year is passed with all its changing scenes and we now commence a new one. God only knows what we may have to endure during the present year. But he has promised 'his grace shall be sufficed.'"[2]

Uncertainty bred such contemplation and conviction. For Miss Edmonds and Mrs. Broun and their neighbors, war's presence had never been far away. Men in gray and in blue had come and gone, and returned. They watched their own in July 1861 scramble onto railroad cars bound for Manassas and Bull Run Creek. Then came the sound—the strange rumble of battle not heard before. A year later, in August 1862, some of them cheered as "Stonewall" Jackson and Robert E. Lee with their troops passed through on the roads leading back to Bull Run. They also read the newspapers and the letters, noting those friends and loved ones who would never return.

During those times when Confederate troops were not at hand, the Yankees came and stayed. For weeks at a time the Northerners— "Blue Devils," to Ida Dulany of Upperville—occupied parts of their counties, protecting the tracks of the important Orange and Alexandria Railroad. Blue-jacketed cavalrymen on patrol were almost a daily sight. The Federals treated them kindly much of the time, but the conflict was developing a hardness few yet perceived.[3]

The counties of Fauquier and Loudoun were a land of farms and farmers. In the shadows of the Blue Ridge, Catoctin and Bull Run mountains horses, cattle, sheep and swine fattened themselves in pastures and fields of corn, wheat and oats. Miles of stone walls, dividing neighbors' fields, gave a symmetry to the rich landscape. Stately large houses of stone, brick or clapboard crowned the numerous hills or nestled in the valleys between. Families such as the Edmunds, Brouns,

Dulanys, Hathaways, Carters, Blackwells, Rectors, Washingtons, Fletchers, Lakes, Tripletts, Rogerses, Skinners, Morgans, Richardses, Ashbys, Bakers and Shackletts harvested the soil's bounty. It was a land in which the Lord's grace was sufficed.[4]

Craftsmen and merchants shared in the abundance, selling their wares or services to the farmers. Blacksmiths, tanners, saddlers, wheelwrights, shoemakers; wagon, cart and carriage makers; bakers, tavernkeepers, hostelers, doctors, dentists and teachers contributed to the economic fabric of the counties. Dozens of water-powered mills—grist, lumber and woolen—dotted the countryside. Isham Keith and John Ambler's woolen mills at Waterloo in Fauquier were that county's largest employers, with twenty-six workers. Livelihoods and life-styles followed the rhythm of the seasons and their yields.[5]

Fauquier and Loudoun had almost identical populations, roughly 21,700 each in 1860. A key difference in the number of residents, however, was the proportion of whites to black slaves. The white population of Loudoun comprised 70 percent of the total, while Fauquier's whites were a minority, numbering only 48 percent. A large contingent of Quakers, located in the central part of Loudoun around Waterford, owned no slaves and accounted in part for the disparity in slaveholders between the two counties.[6]

The towns of Warrenton and Leesburg, the county seats of Fauquier and Loudoun, respectively, were the commercial centers of the region. Warrenton, with about 1,200 residents, boasted three hotels, two newspapers, fifteen stores, professional offices, an iron foundry and wooden sidewalks. A spur of the Orange and Alexandria Railroad ran from the town eight miles southeastward to Warrenton Junction and the main line of the railroad. None of the other villages in the county—Upperville, Salem, Paris, Rectortown, Markham and New Baltimore—equaled Warrenton in size or importance. Warrenton lay in the section known locally as "Lower Fauquier," while the other towns, except for New Baltimore, lay in "Upper Fauquier."[7]

Leesburg, like Warrenton, dominated its respective county. Located forty miles northwest of Washington and less than three miles south of the Potomac River, the town bustled with activity. It too was a center of commerce and government, with hotels, stores and professional offices. Middleburg, Aldie, Snickersville, Union, Waterford, Lovettsville and Hillsborough were some of the other villages scattered throughout the county. The Catoctin Mountains ran like a forested spine from the Potomac to Aldie, dividing the county through its center. The area between the Blue Ridge and the Catoctin locals called "Between the Hills." The one geographic feature shared by both counties was Goose Creek, or Gohangarestaw, meaning "river of swans" in an Indian language. Goose Creek, beginning in Fauquier, followed a convoluted path of fifty miles before entering the Potomac four miles northeast of Leesburg.[8]

When Virginia seceded from the Union in April 1861, the citizens of Fauquier and Loudoun embraced the Confederate cause. While the Quaker settlements in Loudoun voted against secession, the remaining sections of the counties endorsed it overwhelmingly. Their menfolk, in turn, formed companies, enlisted in the Confederate forces and went off to war. The course of the struggle and the periods of Federal occupation during 1861 and 1862 had not altered the residents' sympathies. The suffering and losses had only increased their resolve.[9]

With the advent of a new year, then, the people of Fauquier and Loudoun awaited the future. Perhaps most of them, like "Tee" Edmonds and Catherine Broun, welcomed 1863, but with misgivings and apprehension. On January 1, John Mosby and his Confederate cavalrymen came into their midst, bringing with them a mission and the future.

After Stuart departed from Oakham on the thirty-first, Mosby and his detail most likely rode into Upper Fauquier. His exact whereabouts during the early days of January cannot be established, but the Salem-Rectortown-Paris area became the center of his operations until the end of the war. He and his men dwelt in the surrounding farmhouses; many of his recruits came from the families in the area; and the civilians steadfastly supported his command. The numerous hills and knolls served as natural watchtowers; the nearby Blue Ridge Mountains and its spurs provided hideaways. To the east, a day's ride away, lay his target—the Union lines surrounding the capital.

The identities of the nine men with Mosby remain unknown. He almost certainly selected them and, most likely, they were members of the 1st Virginia Cavalry, his old regiment. With them on January 10, Mosby struck Yankee pickets near Herndon Station on the Alexandria, Loudoun and Hampshire Railroad. The attack was the only operation he conducted with the detail.[10]

A week later Mosby reported to Stuart at the latter's headquarters in the Fredericksburg area. Mosby requested a fifteen-man detail, with the assertion that he could make the Federal commander in

Fairfax County contract his lines. Stuart consented, directing Mosby to operate within enemy lines and to provide Stuart with reconnaissance reports. While these orders were evidently not written, Stuart and Robert E. Lee always provided Mosby with written instructions throughout his later service as an independent commander. With Stuart's approval and orders, Mosby departed on the eighteenth for Upper Fauquier with fifteen members of the 1st Virginia Cavalry. Brigadier General Fitzhugh Lee, in whose brigade the regiment served, temporarily detached the cavalrymen at Stuart's request.[11]

These fifteen men were the original nucleus of Mosby's Rangers. Each, in all likelihood, had been handpicked by Mosby. Twelve of them were native Virginians; three were Marylanders. The group included twenty-one-year-old Fountain Beattie, Mosby's former messmate and close friend who became, in Mosby's words, "my own most trusted lieutenant"; two brothers, Jasper and William Jones from Washington County; John Charles Buchanan; Christian Gall; twenty-year-old William L. Hunter; thirty-one-year-old Edward S. "Ned" Hurst; William Keyes; Benjamin Morgan; George Seibert; Charles Wheatley; John Wild; and the Marylanders: twenty-two-year-old George M. Slater, twenty-year-old Daniel L. Thomas, and William T. Turner.[12]

When the sixteen Confederates reached Upper Fauquier, Mosby dispersed the men with orders to meet him at Mount Zion Church, east of Aldie, on the twenty-eighth. During the next week, Mosby scouted Union lines in Fairfax County. He was systematic and methodical and preferred working alone. He probably searched for civilians who would supply him with information or act as guides.[13]

His reconnaissances revealed, as he stated later, "that here was a beautiful harvest to be gathered, and that the reapers were few." Union cavalry regiments, Mosby discovered, had camps or outposts at Centreville, Chantilly, Vienna, Dranesville and Occoquan. The mounted units were under the command of Colonel R. Butler Price, 2nd Pennsylvania Cavalry, and were a part of the defenses of Washington, Major General Samuel P. Heintzelman, commanding. The Yankee horsemen numbered roughly 3,300, organized into six regiments and two detachments. Mosby planned to end their "life of drowsy indolence."[14]

The Confederates rendezvoused at Mount Zion Church on Wednesday, the twenty-eighth. Mosby led them eastward on the Little River Turnpike, moving with caution. The day before, Yankee troopers had ridden into Middleburg and arrested seven or eight citizens. With Mosby in the column was John Underwood, a thirty-year-old resident of Fairfax County whom Mosby apparently met during the previous week and convinced to join. Underwood became the first recruit and proved to be an invaluable asset. He knew Fairfax, claimed one of the men, "better than the wild animals that roamed over it by night or by day." Mosby said that he was indebted to Underwood for the latter's "skill and intelligence for whatever success I had in the beginning of my partisan life. . . . He was equally at home threading his way through pines or leading a charge."[15]

By nightfall the Southerners halted near Chantilly. Ahead in the darkness was a party of Union vedettes, the mounted pickets of the 18th Pennsylvania Cavalry. Mosby deployed his men and, at a signal, they galloped forward into the astonished Federals. The raiders grabbed nine members of the Federal regiment with their mounts and arms. Then, as swiftly as they had appeared, the Rebels, with their prisoners, vanished into the night.[16]

Union officers, upon learning of the attack, ordered a pursuit. The following night 200 cavalrymen, under Colonel Percy Wyndham of the 5th New Jersey Cavalry, trotted into Middleburg. Mosby and Fount Beattie were asleep in the home of Lorman Chancellor when a black servant warned them. The pair gathered six others and charged into the rear of the Federal column as it retired from the town. In the melee the Confederates killed one Yankee and captured three others. But the Northerners nabbed Beattie, John Charles Buchanan and another when their horses fell during the chase. Federal authorities, however, released the trio within a few weeks.[17]

During the next week Mosby continued his raids on the enemy picket posts. Despite inclement weather, the Southerners brought in nineteen more Northerners, their horses and gear. Wyndham, infuriated by the attacks, once again chased the elusive Rebels. He laid a trap for the guerrillas, but Mosby charged into it, killing one Federal and seizing a dozen more, with "the balance running." Wyndham, a British soldier of fortune, threatened to burn Middleburg to the ground and torch the country between it and Fairfax Court House.[18]

On February 4, Mosby filed his first report to Stuart on his initial forays. The lieutenant summarized the number of captures and related his skirmishes with the mounted pursuers. "I have harassed them so much," Mosby concluded, "that they do not keep their pickets over a half a mile from camp."[19]

When Stuart received Mosby's report on the eighth, he replied: "I have heard with great gratification of your continued success and shall take pleasure in forwarding with my warm commendations your Report of your late operations, received this morning. I heartily wish you great and increasing success in the glorious career on which you have entered." The general forwarded the report to Lee, endorsing it "as additional proof of the prowess, daring, and efficiency of Mosby (without commission) and his bond of chosen spirits." Lee, in turn, added, "evidence of merit of Captain Mosby," before sending it to the War Department.[20]

The same day Mosby penned his report, February 4, he received a petition from several citizens of Middleburg. The gentlemen asked the Confederate raider to cease operations against the Union forces. They feared that Wyndham would carry out his threat to burn their community. Mosby responded that day:

> *I have just received your petition requesting me to discontinue my warfare on the Yankees because they have threatened to burn your town and destroy your property in retaliation for my acts. Not being yet prepared for any such degrading compromises with the Yankees, I unhesitatingly refuse to comply.*
>
> *My attacks on scouts, patrols, and pickets, which have provoked this threat, are sanctioned both by the customs of war and the practice of the enemy; and you are at liberty to inform them that no such clamor shall deter me from employing whatever legitimate weapon I can most efficiently use for their annoyance. I will say this to you, however, that it was through a misunderstanding of my orders that the prisoners were brought through your town to be paroled. I was myself several miles behind the guard that had them. As my men have never occupied your town, I cannot see what possible complicity can be between my acts and you.[21]*

While Mosby refused the request of the civilians, his activities moderated for most of February. Catherine Broun noted in her journal that the Confederates passed their farm on the night of the eleventh, but recorded nothing of prisoners or of seeing the band at other times that month. Mosby did not file another report to Stuart until the last day of the month. Federal parties, however, scoured the region, bagging six Rebels, who had gone to a dancing party in violation of Mosby's orders, on February 6. Their identities are unknown and they were evidently soon paroled and released.[22]

Mosby's command probably doubled in size during February. Recruits came in, attracted by the adventure and the spoils, which Confederate law and Mosby permitted the men to keep. Mosby "utilized every man who came to him," remarked a member. He received some dismounted cavalrymen from Stuart, accepted men on furlough or those too young for conscription and even took convalescents from a hospital in Middleburg. Some of the volunteers remained with the command; others returned to their regiments or to civilian life. The original members called the new men "conglomerates."[23]

A few of the conglomerates became some of Mosby's most reliable soldiers or officers in the future. Richard "Dick" Moran, a forty-one-year-old from Loudoun County, volunteered early in the month and would prove to be a ferocious fighter. Also from Loudoun came William Hibbs, a forty-five-year-old blacksmith with two sons in the Confederate army. Mosby eventually dubbed him "Major," and the nickname stuck. Hibbs, said a comrade, was "the most excitable of men." About the middle of the month Walter Frankland, George Whitescarver, Joseph Nelson and Frank Williams signed up. The quartet had planned to enlist in Colonel E. V. White's 35th Battalion of Virginia Cavalry, but a citizen living near Rectortown directed them to Mosby. Frankland and Whitescarver had been members of the 17th Virginia and, along with Nelson, were from Fauquier. Williams resided in Fairfax.[24]

During the final week of February James F. Ames, a member of the 5th New York Cavalry, walked into Fauquier County and inquired about Mosby. The deserter was brought to Mosby, who interrogated him. Ames, a large, muscular man, stated that he had abandoned the Union cause because of President Abraham Lincoln's Emancipation Proclamation which freed the slaves in Confederate territory as of January 1, 1863. Mosby remained skeptical. "At first I did not give him my full confidence," he wrote of the Yankee, "but accepted him on probation. Ames stood all the tests, and until he was killed I never had a more faithful follower."[25]

Neither Ames nor Frankland had a mount—a requirement for service with the command—when they joined. The New Yorker proposed to the Virginian that together they enter Ames's old camp and secure two horses. The pair started on February 28 in a heavy rain for Germantown, thirty miles distant. Arriving at midnight, Ames gained access to the camp by talking with sentries. The two guerrillas then walked to the stables, saddled two fine horses and departed unchallenged.[26]

John Underwood, who knew every obscure trail in Fairfax, also determined to steal some Yankee horseflesh. Crawling on his hands and knees with a cowbell around his neck, Underwood entered a Federal camp at Alexandria under the cover of darkness. He lashed five officers' horses together and then passed between the guard posts. When one of the victims discovered the theft and learned of the details, he allegedly ordered all cowbells removed from animals in a ten-mile area around the camp.[27]

Mosby brought the "conglomerates" together for their first raid on February 25. Twenty-seven men appeared at the rendezvous which had been ordered a week before. Departing late in the day, the Confederates reached a Union cavalry outpost two miles from Germantown at four o'clock on the morning of the twenty-sixth. The Federals, numbering roughly fifty under the command of a lieutenant, occupied a log house with the chinking removed for the use of their carbines. The Yankees, Mosby asserted, "ought to have held it against a greatly superior force, as they all had carbines." But, when the Rebels charged, the blue-jacketed troopers scrambled from the house, fleeing into the darkness. Mosby's men killed the lieutenant and three enlisted men, and captured five more, plus most of the horses.[28]

The attack on the outpost brought a response from the Federals. On March 2, 200 troopers of the 18th Pennsylvania Cavalry, under a Major Gilmer, entered Middleburg. The Pennsylvanians searched homes, arrested a handful of citizens and again threatened to burn the village. A female resident told Gilmer that "he might as well begin now for they had no more power to prevent Capt. Mosby than they could prevent them from coming."[29]

Departing from Middleburg, Gilmer's command rode eastward toward Aldie. As the Pennsylvanians cleared the latter town, Gilmer mistook a fifty-man detachment of the 1st Vermont Cavalry for Mosby's men. The major, who was drunk, ordered an immediate retreat. A panic-stricken scramble ensued until the Vermonters overtook their comrades and identified themselves. The Pennsylvanians informed Captain F. T. Huntoon that Mosby was not in Aldie. As Gilmer's men rode westward, Huntoon led his cavalrymen toward the town, halting at the brick gristmill at the eastern edge of Aldie to rest and feed the mounts.[30]

Mosby, meanwhile, had gathered approximately twenty-eight

men and entered Aldie from the western end. When he saw the dismounted Vermonters at the mill, he ordered an attack. The Confederates galloped down the roadway and into the midst of the startled Federals. Yells mingled with gunfire in a wild melee. Mosby's horse became so unmanageable that he leaped from the saddle and allowed it to run to the enemy. A Captain Woodward of the Vermonters was pinned beneath his fallen mount. One of the Confederates fired at him, and Woodward, using a small pocket pistol, wounded the assailant. Some of the Rebels, believing Woodward had surrendered before shooting their comrade, wanted to execute the officer. Mosby, who had witnessed the exchange of gunfire, interceded, and Woodward, along with Huntoon and fourteen enlisted men, were paroled. The sole Confederate casualty was the man shot by Woodward. When the residents of Middleburg learned of the rout, they poured, cheering, into the streets.[31]

"Gilmer's expedition into our territory," Mosby wrote, "had been so disastrous that the Union cavalry seemed to be content to stay in camp and let us alone." As a consequence, Mosby plotted the raid into Fairfax Court House to capture Percy Wyndham, which resulted in the seizure of Edwin Stoughton.[32]

Wyndham stuck in Mosby's craw. The Britisher's disparagement of the Confederates as a pack of horse thieves and his threats against civilians rankled the proud Mosby. Mosby never doubted the legitimacy of the warfare he was waging and Wyndham, with his remarks, slurred Mosby and his jealously guarded reputation. The Confederate also had scant respect for the Union officer's tactical abilities. Wyndham, Mosby asserted, "struck blindly around like the Cyclops in his cave, but nobody was hurt. The methodical tactics he had learned in European wars were of no more use to him than a suit of armor of the Middle Ages."[33]

The "Stoughton Raid" thus typified Mosby's interpretation of warfare. He had found a personal antagonist, a foe who had impugned his honor. The Virginian internalized the conflict and made it his own—"Mosby's War." Percy Wyndham was George Turpin clad in Union blue.

Praise for Mosby's raid began on the morning, March 9, 1863, that Mosby brought Stoughton and the other prisoners out of Fairfax Court House. From the Brawner farm, the raiders rode to Warrenton, where the people cheered as the column proceeded through the town. Mosby took Stoughton to the Beckham family home in Warrenton.

The Vermonter had been a West Point classmate of their son, Frank, and had visited with the Beckhams before the war. The family shared breakfast with Mosby and his prisoner.[34]

From Warrenton the mounted party continued to Stuart's headquarters at Culpeper Court House, arriving on the morning of the tenth. A cold rain was falling as Mosby, with Stoughton and the other Federal officers, walked into Fitzhugh Lee's headquarters. Mosby and Lee disliked each other and, as the group entered, Lee, the nephew of Robert E. Lee, was writing at a desk. A fire blazed in a fireplace as Mosby presented Stoughton to the brigadier. "If I had been an orderly who brought him a morning report," Mosby wrote of Lee's reception in a postwar letter, "he could not have treated me with more indifference. You would have thought from his manner that I had [not] done anything more than an ordinary matter of routine." Lee offered the dripping wet Mosby neither a chair nor a chance to warm himself before the fire. "It was plain that he was sorry for what I had done," added Mosby. Suppressing his anger, Mosby shook hands with the Federals and walked out of the house and into the rain.[35]

Stuart, however, could not have been more pleased with his subordinate. Mosby had telegraphed the general the day before about the captures. When they met at the Culpeper railroad station, Stuart handed the unofficial lieutenant a captain's commission of Virginia troops, signed by Governor John Letcher. Since no such organization existed, the form was blank. Stuart must have enjoyed the prank. Mosby did not, and indignantly told Stuart: "I want no recognition."[36]

But Mosby did want recognition, and it followed swiftly. On March 12 Stuart issued a special congratulatory order citing Mosby and his men for "boldness, skill, and success." Stuart called Stoughton's capture a feat "unparalleled in the war." The major general had the order read to every cavalry regiment in his command. That same day, Robert E. Lee wrote that "Mosby had covered himself with glory."[37]

Eleven days later, on the twenty-third, in Special Orders #82, Mosby was officially commissioned a captain. The appointment was dated March 19, to rank from March 15. The orders from Lee read: "The Genl Commdg is confident that this manifestation of the approbation of his superiors, will but serve to incite Captain Mosby to still greater efforts to advance the good of the cause in which we are engaged."[38]

The commanding general enclosed with the special order a letter which granted Mosby authority to organize a company. The letter, written by Lee's staff officer, Walter Taylor, instructed the officer that all troops enrolled in the company must be "mustered unconditionally into the Confederate service for and during the war." Taylor added: "Though you are to be its captain, the men will have the privilege of electing the lieutenants, as soon as its numbers reach the legal standard. You will report your progress from time to time, and, when the requisite number of men are enrolled, an officer will be designated to muster the company into the service."[39]

The "Stoughton Raid" was a turning point for Mosby and his command. In a winter's night he and his raiders achieved fame and official recognition. "There was nothing in boldness or originality which surpassed it during the entire war," a member somewhat immodestly wrote later of the exploit, "nor did anything reflect more credit on the little command or create any more notoriety than his [Stoughton's] capture." A new band of Southern heroes emerged in a nation hungry for such men.[40]

In the North, reaction to the capture of a Union brigadier general from his headquarters bed in the center of a garrisoned village on the outskirts of the capital combined disbelief with admiration for and fear of the perpetrators. When military authorities learned of the brazen raid, they responded swiftly. The Federal troops in the region were alerted—a Pennsylvania infantryman, encamped at Fairfax Station, described the scene in his camp as one of "turmoil." Three cavalry regiments—the 5th New York, 18th Pennsylvania and 1st West Virginia—scurried in pursuit but returned empty-handed.[41]

A sense of vulnerability now pervaded Union camps and headquarters. The sortie into their lines, according to one of Mosby's men, "taught the Federals that there was safety nowhere from this daring midnight raider." Department headquarters pulled in the outposts and also some units—the capture of Stoughton, an officer informed his mother, "probably scared the Generals"—and assigned Major General Julius Stahel to command of the department's cavalry forces. The concern for security, in fact, led to some surprising actions. The belief surfaced that President Lincoln or cabinet members might be the next target. Each night for weeks, consequently, troops removed the planks from the flooring of the Chain Bridge which linked the capital to Virginia across the Potomac River.[42]

Lincoln, however, viewed Mosby's exploit from a different perspective. With his wry sense of humor, Lincoln said that "he didn't mind the loss of the Brigadier as much as the horses."

"For," the commander-in-chief remarked, "I can make a much better General in five minutes, but the horses cost one hundred and twenty-five dollars apiece."[43]

Others held less charitable views of the embarrassing affair. The Washington *Evening Star* editorialized on March 9 that "there is a screw loose somewhere, and we need a larger force in front." A New York cavalryman argued that the Confederate foray "reflects very uncreditably upon some of our military leaders, while it shows how wily a foe we have to contend with." The trooper added that many Federals believed that Mosby could only have succeeded with the assistance of Southern sympathizers.[44]

Union officials endorsed the belief of civilian connivance in the operation. Four days after the capture of Stoughton, the Yankees arrested Antonia Ford of Fairfax Court House. Miss Ford, a blond, brown-eyed beauty in her early twenties, was the daughter of Edward R. Ford, a merchant in the town. An avowed supporter of the Confederacy, she knew both Stuart and Mosby and had supplied the general with information. A number of Stoughton's aides resided in the Ford household, and this gave the young woman opportunities for overhearing unguarded remarks. Antonia, however, had had nothing to do with Mosby's operation.[45]

The Federals placed Antonia, her father and other unnamed residents in Old Capitol Prison. Fitzhugh Lee, when he learned of Miss Ford's arrest, asked Mosby for a letter that would exonerate the woman. Mosby complied, but Antonia remained in prison for several months until she was released and sent through Confederate lines to Richmond. A year later, almost to the day of the raid, March 10, 1864, the beautiful Rebel married Union Major Joseph C. Willard, cofounder of the Willard Hotel in Washington and provost marshal in Fairfax Court House, who had secured her freedom.[46]

While the enemy implemented countermeasures and searched for scapegoats, Mosby resumed his raids. On March 16, with roughly fifty men, he struck two Yankee cavalry outposts. A detachment of horsemen, numbering about 200, pursued the Rebels. When the Northern troopers approached to within one hundred yards, Mosby wheeled his column around and charged. The Federal ranks dissolved into a panic-stricken mob. "It was more of a chase than a fight for 4 or 5 miles," Mosby reported to Stuart. The Southerners killed five, wounded a considerable number and captured thirty-six. The next day, near Herndon Station, the Southerners bagged a twenty-five-man picket post of the 1st Vermont Cavalry, the regiment of their victims at Aldie mill.[47]

A week later, on March 23, Mosby's "conglomerates" returned to Fairfax County to "do something." Near Chantilly they struck the vedettes of the 5th New York, James "Big Yankee" Ames's old regiment. The New Yorkers scattered on contact, racing eastward to their reserve picket post. The Federals counterattacked down the Little River Turnpike, driving the Rebels for three miles. At this point, Mosby dismounted his men, formed a line behind some fallen trees and fired into the oncoming column. The gunfire stalled the New Yorkers long enough for the Confederates to remount and charge. As had happened on the sixteenth, the Northerners fled in a wild horse race. In the forefront of the Southerners rode "Major" William Hibbs, "uncontrollable in his joy." Mosby's men bagged thirty-six New Yorkers and fifty horses. One of the mounts the captain presented to Hibbs as a reward for his conduct. The prisoners, instead of being paroled, were forwarded to Richmond. Lee had reversed the old policy, directing Stuart to send captives and deserters, under guard, to the capital.[48]

What had begun two months earlier, in Mosby's own words, "as though I was leading a forlorn hope," had evolved into an officially authorized command. Recruits kept coming in, and the citizens of Fauquier and Loudoun accepted the presence of the guerrillas. "Public sentiment seems now entirely changed," Mosby informed Stuart on March 16, "and I think it is the universal desire for me to remain." Fitz Lee still prodded Stuart for the return of his men, but the cavalry commander deferred a recall for at least another month.[49]

Finally, sometime during March, Pauline joined her husband. When she had last seen him, he was a private; now he was a renowned captain, the captor of a Union general. Mosby brought Pauline to the home of James and Elizabeth Hathaway located along a country lane roughly four miles north of the village of The Plains. The Hathaways' beautiful two-story brick house, built in 1850 and still standing, attested to the family's substance. The couple were both fifty years old and the parents of five children, who ranged in age from twenty-two to nine. Their land and personal wealth was placed at over $53,000 in 1860. The Hathaways belonged to the gentry of Fauquier.[50]

Pauline's welcomed presence could not deny the reality of the times, however. The war, the mission, the command, the enemy awaited. With the arrival of spring, Mosby's operations accelerated.

Chapter 3

FROM MISKEL'S TO GRAPEWOOD

 Thomas and Lydia Miskel farmed a section of Loudoun County where Broad Run emptied into the Potomac River. A young couple, with a son and a daughter, the Miskels toiled on land which had nourished Virginians for over a century. Their two-story L-shaped clapboard farmhouse dated from ca. 1750, with the wing added about 1810. Behind the house a hay barn provided storage for the harvests and shelter for the livestock.[1]

A road, following the course of Broad Run on its eastern edge, connected the Miskel place to the Leesburg Pike, roughly a mile to the south. For over two years the couple had heard the rumble of armies in motion. Most likely, soldiers in blue and in gray had passed by their doorstep or stopped for a drink or for a meal. They might have even seen war's grimness as wounded Yankees stumbled across their land after the two battles at Bull Run. But in most respects the Civil War had bypassed the Miskels—until the night of March 31, 1863.

About ten o'clock that night Captain John S. Mosby and between sixty-five and seventy Confederate horsemen bridled up before the Miskels' farmhouse. The Southerners had been in the saddle most of the day, covering forty miles, through snow and mud, and needed a place to sleep and some forage for the animals. Mosby had come to Loudoun, as he liked to say, to "flush something out" at Dranesville, but the Federals had withdrawn their outposts behind Difficult Run, precluding an attack by the guerrillas. Now, Mosby asked Tom and Lydia Miskel if he and his men could spend the night and feed their mounts. The couple consented to the request.[2]

The soldiers led their horses into the barnyard, where they fed the hungry beasts. A high wooden fence, with a gate that opened into a field, enclosed the area. A lane, bordered by two fences, ran from the barnyard to the road that led toward the Leesburg Pike. Most of the men bedded down in the hay barn, while a lone sentry stood watch in the barnyard. Mosby and a few others slept in the house. According to local tradition, the captain slept before the stone fireplace in the kitchen (which still warms today's owners).[3]

The return of Mosby's men to eastern Loudoun did not pass unnoticed or unreported. Later that night a woman entered Federal lines at Union Church and informed Major Charles F. Taggart of the 2nd Pennsylvania Cavalry of Mosby's presence at the Miskel farm. Taggart ordered Captain Henry C. Flint to take five companies, roughly 150 troopers, of the 1st Vermont Cavalry and "rout or capture" the Southerners. Twice before in the previous weeks these Vermonters had been victimized by the guerrillas and perhaps with this opportunity they could settle the accounts.[4]

Flint led his Green Mountain volunteers at midnight westward on the Leesburg Pike. Near the road leading to the Miskel farm, the Yankees halted briefly at a house owned by a man named Green. If Flint inquired about the location of Thomas Miskel's place, it remains unknown. But as the early light of April 1 brightened the sky, the Vermonters turned northward off the pike into the proper road. Broad Run gurgled to their left as the horsemen approached the farm site. Flint had already divided the column into two groups, with Captain George H. Bean commanding the rear section as a reserve for Flint's companies in the van. Just before the Yankees turned into the fenced lane to the farmhouse and barn, a Confederate horseman crossed in front of the column and spurred his mount toward the buildings.[5]

When the Federals had stopped at the Green place, one of Mosby's men, Dick Moran, was inside visiting with the family. Moran reacted quickly when the Vermonters departed. Saddling and mounting his horse, Moran rode across the fields to warn Mosby. He barely made it ahead of the oncoming enemy. Moran, described as "a warring Methodist with a voice of thunder," turned his horse into the lane and, waving his hat, shouted: "Mount your horses! The Yankees are coming!"[6]

Moran's warning indeed sounded like a thunderclap to the Rebels. The barnyard came "alive with excitement." Mosby, emerging from the house, rushed to his men, who were scrambling to saddle and mount their horses. The shouts of the charging Yankees mingled with the yells of the surprised guerrillas. When Mosby reached the enclosure, Harry Hatcher handed the reins of his mount to the captain. Roughly twenty other men were on horse as the blue-clad troopers surged toward the gate.[7]

"Never before or after," exclaimed a guerrilla, "had the federal troops such another chance to secure Mosby and wipe out his men." Miskel's fenced-in barnyard was "a perfect trap," but Flint adopted the wrong tactics. Instead of having the Vermonters dismount and use their carbines, the captain ordered a saber charge down the lane toward the gate. The Southerners had no weapons to match the carbines and to escape they would have had to ride through a gauntlet of rifle fire.[8]

So the Yankees, wielding sabers and pistols, drove toward the barnyard. As they closed on the gate, Flint, in the forefront, shouted: "shoot the d——d cowards." From within the yard, pistols exploded in response, and the Union officer died where he fell from the saddle with six bullets in his body. The fire from the Confederates stopped the attackers. Caught between the gate and the fences along the lane, the Federals panicked. At this point Mosby ordered a counterattack, and the Rebels burst through the gate, held by John Farrar, into the head of the jumbled column. A brief melee ensued until the Vermonters fled in "fearful" confusion. Those who could not escape surrendered. The victors pursued the broken remnants for several miles.[9]

In the lane and in the barnyard the dead lay with the maimed. Most of the bodies wore blue uniforms. Mosby lost only one killed— a Davis from Kentucky. Little else is known of the victim, except he was the first in the command to sacrifice his life for the mission. Three others fell wounded—Ned Hurst, William Keyes and R. A. Hart. Hurst and Keyes belonged to the original detachment of fifteen from the 1st Virginia Cavalry, while Hart, a member of Company H, 4th Virginia Cavalry, the "Black Horse Troop," was home on furlough in Fauquier County and rode along with the guerrillas.[10]

Casualties among the Vermonters Mosby reported as nine killed, fifteen wounded and eighty-two captured, along with ninety-five horses seized. Flint and Lieutenant C. A. Woodbury were among the killed, while three lieutenants suffered wounds and fell into Confederate hands. Mosby's men left the worst of the wounded Federals at Miskel's and took their three comrades to a hospital in Middleburg.[11]

Several of the Confederates, whom Mosby cited in his report, distinguished themselves in the fight. One of them was a new member of the unit, William H. Chapman of Fauquier. A former artilleryman and conscript officer, the twenty-two-year-old Chapman had joined with his younger brother, Samuel. In the action, the brothers shot seven Federals between them, William accounting for five. Harry Hatcher, during the pursuit, saved Dick Moran's life by gunning down a Yankee who was prepared to saber the "warring Methodist." Others who received Mosby's official praise were William Hunter, Tom Turner, John Wild, "Big Yankee" Ames and J. W. Sowers. Frank Williams, who had risen early and gone in search of breakfast, missed the combat but captured two Vermonters on his return ride.[12]

Mosby filed his report on the engagement at Miskel's on April 7. He admitted in it "that on this occasion I had not taken sufficient precautions to guard against surprise." The Rebels had been spared because of Flint's ineptitude. Robert E. Lee, however, praised the captain for the outcome and, with the approval of Confederate President Jefferson Davis, promoted Mosby to the rank of major, to date from March 26. In a span of two weeks, the partisan officer had advanced two grades in rank.[13]

To the Federals, Miskel's was another embarrassing defeat. "The whole affair," wrote a Vermonter, "was alike a mortification and an

exasperation to the whole command." Julius Stahel, the cavalry commander, blamed Flint and Bean, commanding the reserve, for the
disaster. "Had a proper disposition been made of our troops," the
major general reported, "Mosby could not by any possible means
have escaped." Continuing, Stahel asserted: "It is only to be ascribed
to the bad management on the part of the officers and the cowardice
of the men." Flint paid for the mistake with his life; Bean was dismissed from the service.[14]

Two days after the Miskel engagement Brigadier General Joseph
Copeland's cavalry brigade, composed of the 5th, 6th and 7th Michigan regiments, entered Middleburg. From the third through the sixth
the Yankees scoured the surrounding countryside, searching for the
guerrillas. "The country is again filled with Yanks," Catherine Broun
wrote in her journal, "now in every direction we look see squads
riding over the fields stealing every horse have had four different
squads here searched the stable brought out our old gray." In Middleburg the Wolverines stood all the male residents against a brick
wall. Broun noted a rumor that 300 citizens were sent to Washington
but only after their guards had removed all their money. The sweep
garnered only three partisans—Nimrod Ashby, Washington Garrison
and W. Rutledge.[15]

The Federal raid "terrified" the local citizens, according to Broun.
Another diarist, Edward Carter Turner of "Kinloch" in Fauquier,
believed that the Yankees would return again and again to protect
their camps and outposts in Fairfax. Turner, the father of Tom
Turner, one of Mosby's men, argued that "this being the case, the
people of this country will doubtless suffer much." His diary entry
on April 5 read: "Things are looking darker and darker for our unhappy and unprotected people." The owner of "Kinloch" opposed
Mosby's methods of war.[16]

Three weeks after Edward Turner penned that entry, darkness
came to "Kinloch." He learned that his son had been mortally
wounded on the twenty-fifth while on a scout toward Warrenton.
Young Turner, Walter Frankland and William Hunter had been surprised by a detachment of the 8th Illinois Cavalry at the home of
Charles Utterbach outside of the county seat. The three Rebels tried
to fight their way out, but a Yankee felled Turner with a bullet in
the lungs and Frankland and Hunter surrendered. Edward Turner
went to Utterbach's and brought his son home. On April 29, Tom

Turner died, nine days short of his twentieth birthday. Jeb Stuart had recommended the young soldier to Mosby with the endorsement: "Give him a chance."[17]

The grieving father sat down with his diary two days later. He had objected to his son's decision to become a partisan and now he was gone. The manner of Tom's death brought little comfort. "In the first place," Turner wrote, "I did not respect the service in which Mosby was engaged. Its object was mercenary rather than patriotic. A number of adventurous men, and I feared men of desperate character or doubtful characters, had united under Mosby for the purpose of making raids upon the enemy. In order to encourage them and to make them active, vigilant and dangerous, the Government allowed them the privilege, the extraordinary privilege, of retaining and converting to their own use all property they captured from the enemy. . . . I cared nothing for the glory others seemed to see in reckless feats and hair breadth escapes."[18]

The "darker" days Turner had predicted continued throughout the month. On April 27, 28 and 29, the Yankees returned to southern Loudoun and northern Fauquier. They seized every horse they could find and arrested all male citizens who had not fled. Squads searched houses, confiscating food. As had happened earlier in the month, Mosby's men vanished before the numerically superior Federals. Ida Dulany, living near Upperville, had heard often that the guerrillas protected them. But all she saw on these three days were roaming groups of enemy horsemen. She scoffed at the idea of security. "I fear it is just the reverse," she argued, "as every raid Moseby [sic] has made has produced a retaliating raid from the Yankees in which the citizens suffer severely. Moseby having always to get out of their way."[19]

Mosby could not openly oppose these Union excursions into the region. His men might gnaw at the edges of the forces, bagging a few stray Yankees, but he could not engage them in an open fight. The suffering inflicted upon the populace did not deter Mosby in the accomplishment of his objective, however. Even as stronger enemy units penetrated deeper into his base during April, the partisan officer acquired more recruits.

By the beginning of May roughly 125 men rode in the still unorganized company. Numbers of them were transient guerrillas, like the eight members of the 2nd South Carolina Cavalry sent into Fauquier on a horse detail. Others were regular army men home on furlough who chose temporary duty with the command. A large accretion occurred on April 20, when Lee assigned Captain William G. Brawner's Partisan Ranger Company to Mosby. Finally, recruits continued to enlist for various reasons. On one day during the month, for instance, seven volunteers—John H. Barnes, Frank Fox, Philip Lee, Thomas Lee, Charles Ratcliffe, James Williamson and Albert Wrenn—joined Mosby at Upperville. All were from either Fairfax County or the District of Columbia and had been arrested for their Southern sympathies. Upon their release from Old Capitol Prison, they sought Mosby as Federal authorities barred them from returning to their homes.[20]

Mosby needed the additional volunteers as his operations were redirected during the final week of April. The warm spring weather and the drying of roads meant a resumption of active campaigning in Virginia between the Union Army of the Potomac and the Confederate Army of Northern Virginia. Jeb Stuart, consequently, ordered Mosby on April 25 and 26 to reconnoiter in the Federal rear around Centreville and to strike the Orange and Alexandria Railroad in the vicinity of Warrenton Junction. The cavalry commander described the situation as a "splendid opportunity" for Mosby to "capture a train. . . . Information of the movements of large bodies is of the greatest importance to us now," concluded Stuart.[21]

The Yankees, as Stuart anticipated, began stirring. On April 27, the Federal army, now under Major General Joseph Hooker, abandoned their winter camps at Falmouth, across the Rappahannock River from Robert E. Lee's army at Fredericksburg, and marched up the river. For three days blue-clad infantrymen and artillerymen filled the roads that led to the upper fords of the Rappahannock. By nightfall of the twenty-ninth, much of Hooker's army lay encamped south of the river in an entangled area of woods and scrub brush known as the Wilderness. "Fighting Joe" Hooker in a skillful maneuver had brought his corps beyond Lee's left flank. The Confederate commander, dividing his outnumbered legions, confronted Hooker on May 1. For the next four days, around the crossroads village of Chancellorsville, the graycoats shattered Hooker's plans and inflicted a severe defeat on the Northerners. The Battle of Chancellorsville, however, cost Lee Stonewall Jackson, who was mortally wounded by his own troops.[22]

Hooker, as a part of the campaign, sent Major General George Stoneman and the cavalry on a raid behind Lee's lines. Stoneman, whose units had been guarding the Orange and Alexandria Railroad, departed from the Warrenton area on April 29. The thrust toward Richmond lasted until May 8, achieving only negligible results. The absence of Stoneman's cavalry, in fact, crippled Hooker in his movements against Lee.[23]

When Stoneman marched out on the twenty-ninth, the duty of guarding the single-track railroad fell to the cavalry division of Julius Stahel. Blockhouses and signal towers lined the rails which served as the major supply artery for Hooker's army. Pickets guarded the twenty bridges along the railroad, while Stahel's horsemen roamed daily between the blockhouses and spans.[24]

Stahel, perhaps in an effort to keep the guerrillas at bay, raided into southern Loudoun around Middleburg at the end of April. The Yankee cavalrymen confiscated from the civilians wagon loads of bacon, cotton and wool. At one house they found a cache of rifles, pistols and uniforms. They also arrested about two dozen male citizens, one of whom a party discovered beneath his house. When the Federals withdrew on May 1, numbers of slaves fled with them, taking their initial steps toward freedom.[25]

The next day Mosby, pursuant to Stuart's orders, gathered one hundred men, his largest force to date, and started for the Orange and Alexandria Railroad at Warrenton Junction. The Southerners entered Warrenton, where the residents welcomed and fed them. At nightfall the command bivouacked along the railroad spur midway between the county seat and the junction. The Northerners, guarding the rail intersection, had not learned of the reception given Mosby's men in Warrenton although they were stationed only eight miles away.[26]

The Confederates struck at six o'clock on the morning of May 3. The Union garrison, composed of roughly 300 members of the 1st West Virginia Cavalry, initially mistook the oncoming horsemen for fellow Yankees. When the West Virginians realized their mistake, they scattered into a house and outbuildings. The attackers, however, were momentarily delayed as their mounts bogged down in a miry stream. By the time the Rebels closed on the campsite, the Federals unleashed a "hot fire" from carbines and pistols.[27]

Mosby's men divided into parties as some charged the house, some rode toward the outbuildings and some rounded up the grazing horses. The Federals in the smaller structures surrendered after offering little resistance. Those in the dwelling, numbering about a

hundred, fought tenaciously. The Southerners circled the house, firing into the windows. With a few of his men wounded, Mosby
ordered Alfred Glascock to torch the house. Four other of the attackers, meanwhile, battered their way into the house. Samuel Chapman, Richard Montjoy, Harry Sweeting and John DeButts, with
pistols blazing, entered the first floor hallway. Chapman shouted to
those upstairs to surrender while Montjoy, Sweeting and DeButts
disarmed some defenders. In a room on their left the occupants continued their shooting. DeButts fired through the door, killing a West
Virginian. The other three then broke in the door and, amid a thick
smoke, accepted the surrender of the remaining Yankees. The four
guerrillas filed the prisoners outside, where their comrades were scattered across the camp grounds, corralling Federals and their mounts.[28]

Before the Confederates could reassemble, a squadron of the 5th
New York Cavalry came swirling down the road from Cedar Run,
where they had been encamped. When the gunfire erupted at the
junction, a Major Hammond of the regiment ordered the New Yorkers to horse and requested support from the 1st Vermont Cavalry
stationed nearby. The charge of the Empire State volunteers scattered
the guerrillas, who, abandoning their seizures, spurred toward Warrenton in a "precipitate flight." Mosby reported, "I used every endeavor to rally and form the men, but found it impossible, and there
was no alternative left me but retreat."[29]

The chase was vindication for the Yankees, and they took to it
with a fierceness. Most of the Confederate casualties occurred during
the headlong race as the New Yorkers shot down a dozen or more
of the fleeing Southerners. None of the accounts of the action detail
any resistance on the part of the Rebels—it was a rout from beginning
to end. The Federals abandoned the pursuit around Warrenton.[30]

Warrenton Junction was the worst defeat suffered by Mosby's
command to date. The Confederate major lost one man killed and
reported between fifteen and twenty wounded and/or captured. The
dead guerrilla was a man named Templeton, who reportedly had
served as a scout for Stonewall Jackson. Templeton had been boarding
at "Belle Grove," the home of diarist "Tee" Edmonds, while he rode
with Mosby. She described him as "a brave and useful man." A
Northerner who saw Templeton's body stated that he was wearing
a coat of "rust brown and pantaloons of butternut."[31]

Those wounded and/or captured included some of the best men
in the command. Seven of the nine guerrillas who suffered wounds

fell into Union hands. The brothers, Jasper and William Jones, members of the original fifteen, both were badly wounded and captured. William was paroled at a later date while Jasper, after recovering, was placed in a prison for over a year until he escaped on September 13, 1864. The other five who went down and were seized included the "warring Methodist," Dick Moran; Thomas W. T. Richards of Upperville, a former college student who had served in both the infantry and cavalry before joining Mosby; Sam Ducheane, a former captain in the renowned "Louisiana Tigers"; John W. Holmes and Robert S. Walker. Moran, Underwood and Richards were soon paroled; if Ducheane and Holmes were released, they evidently did not rejoin the command. The other two wounded men were T. M. Grigsby and Samuel Underwood, a brother of John. Both stayed on their horses and eluded the Federals.[32]

The New Yorkers and Vermonters overran another seven of the guerrillas, forcing them to surrender. This latter group of captives included Christian Gall and George Madison of the 1st Virginia Cavalry; Charles Edward Smith, a former member of the 6th Virginia Cavalry; eighteen-year-old Christopher C. Shaw; David L. Jones of Fredericksburg, who was not exchanged until March 3, 1864; William "Willie" Martin, who was destined for higher rank under Mosby; and "Major" William Hibbs. Except for Gall and Madison, the others returned to the command upon their releases.[33]

With the victory at Warrenton Junction, the Federals increased their sorties and raids into the guerrillas' bailiwick during the next two weeks. Stahel determined to eradicate the "Mosbyites," as the Yankees called their opponents. "Everything was in a state of excitement" in Upper Fauquier and southern Loudoun during these days in May. Men and boys herded livestock into the secluded spots in the mountains, and the women concealed valuables in the homes at the cry of "the Yankees are coming!"[34]

The resolve of the Northerners reflected their mounting dislike, even hatred, of the guerrillas. A New York cavalryman believed Mosby to be "an honorable and magnanimous foe," but that was a sentiment shared by few of his comrades. Another New Yorker called the Rebels "a sort of terror," while a member of the 1st Vermont Cavalry described the partisans as "our eternal torment." Washingtonians thought that the gray-clad raiders were "no better than highway robbers." A Michigander added that the guerrillas "had taught us to expect an enemy to fire at us from every bush or fence corner

on the road, and we were careful to keep a good lookout for Rebs."
But a Rhode Island volunteer captured well the frustrations of the
cavalrymen who opposed the Southerners when he wrote of them:
"to-day, swearing marauders; to-morrow, whining sufferers." "We
could only despise the skulking Mosby," he concluded.[35]

The initial Union operation against the "swearing marauders"
after Warrenton Junction occurred on May 5 and 6. The raiding force,
unlike previous commands, came from the west, from across the
Blue Ridge Mountains. Federal officers in the lower Shenandoah Valley sent a squadron of the 1st New York Cavalry and 400 members
of the 67th Pennsylvania Infantry across the mountain range. The
plan was to use the horsemen as bait to lure Mosby's men into an
ambush prepared by the foot soldiers.[36]

The New Yorkers and Pennsylvanians marched out of Berryville
in Clarke County on the morning of the fifth. They forded the Shenandoah River at Snicker's Ferry, with the infantrymen crossing in
skiffs. At nightfall the column encamped near or in Snicker's Gap.
On the morning of May 6, the Yankees passed through Snickersville,
where they captured a guerrilla, Rinaldo Hunt. By three o'clock in
the afternoon the cavalrymen, commanded by First Lieutenant Jesse
F. Wyckoff and Second Lieutenant William H. Boyd, Jr., made contact with Mosby's men at Blakeley's Grove between Bloomfield and
Upperville. The opponents engaged in some long-range skirmishing
that allowed the Pennsylvanians to deploy on both sides of the road
in the rear of the New Yorkers.[37]

Wyckoff, with the trap set, advanced toward the Southerners.
When the Rebels counterattacked, the New Yorkers turned and raced
toward the concealed infantrymen. Mosby's men spurred in pursuit,
firing their pistols at the retreating horsemen. But as Wyckoff's troopers galloped into the trap, the Pennsylvanians mistakenly unleashed
a volley, killing two cavalrymen and wounding both lieutenants.
"This was the most criminal and inexcusable blunder that I ever heard
of," growled one of the New Yorkers. The Confederates reined up
at the burst of gunfire; their losses amounted to one man, Robert
Gray, slightly wounded.[38]

A week later a hundred-man detachment of 1st New York Cavalry, under Captain William H. Boyd, Sr., returned to Loudoun
County. The raiding party reached Leesburg on the twelfth and bivouacked. From the county seat the Federals proceeded the next day
to Middleburg, where they captured James Gulick and George Mat-

thews. Mosby, meanwhile, had gathered approximately fifty men and they prowled along the edge of the column as the New Yorkers rode toward Upperville. Outside of the latter village, Boyd, dividing his command into two wings, charged the Confederates. The Yankees, according to one of them, collared about a dozen guerrillas in the attack. The records list Gulick and Matthews as captured on this date, but no one else. Mosby's men who wrote memoirs do not even mention this engagement. In all likelihood, all the New Yorkers had to show for their two-day expedition were the unfortunate Gulick and Matthews.[39]

The Union incursions took their toll on the Confederate command during May. In addition to the fourteen captured at Warrenton Junction and Hunt, Gulick and Matthews, Mosby lost another seventeen to Federal parties. Some of Stahel's cavalrymen nabbed John Barnes, Albert Wrenn and L. Taliafero and badly wounded John C. Buchanan in Upperville on the eighth, and seized Minor Thompson, John Green and J. R. Hutchinson in Aldie. In two more brushes with the 1st New York Cavalry at Berry's Ferry on the Shenandoah River on May 16 and 17, Joseph Nelson, Mortimer Page, Michael Trapp and John Young fell into Union hands. A week later, on the twenty-third, Northerners bagged Joshua Pool at Upperville and James Tillett at Manassas. Finally, Samuel Anderson, A. J. Brown, C. W. Selden, Joseph Smoot and James Wilson ended up in prison during the month.[40]

These losses were compounded by the recall of the detail from Fitzhugh Lee's brigade. The brigadier general, who opposed Mosby's operations, had been badgering Stuart for two months for the return of his troopers. Stuart finally relented and on May 13 directed Mosby in Special Order No. 88 "to return to their respective commands at once men belonging to General Fitzhugh Lees Brigade of Cavalry, heretofore detailed for service with him." Of the original fifteen-man detail, seven were transferred to Mosby's command; three—Jasper and William Jones and Christian Gall—occupied Union prisons; one, John Charles Buchanan, lay wounded; only Benjamin Morgan, George Seibert and Charles Wheatley returned unscathed to the 1st Virginia Cavalry.[41]

The status of the imprisoned guerrillas caused a minor controversy between the two opposing governments. During the first week of May, Union officials informed Robert Ould, Confederate agent of exchange, that a dozen of Mosby's men confined in Old Capitol Prison would not be exchanged for Federal prisoners because the Rebels were regarded as bushwhackers and guerrillas. "Mosby's command is in the Confederate service in every sense of the term," replied Ould on May 14. "He is regularly commissioned and his force is as strictly Confederate as any in our army." Authorities in Washington accepted Ould's statement and, on the nineteenth, exchanged the partisans. (Later, as the war progressed and Mosby's successes increased, Federal authorities retained any of his men who were captured in an attempt to weaken the command.)[42]

Despite the losses incurred during May, Mosby in obedience to Stuart's instructions continued his raids against the Orange and Alexandria Railroad. On the tenth the Southerners burned two bridges, shutting down the track for two days. Mosby refrained from attacking the heavily guarded supply trains because he lacked ammunition for his men's carbines. Consequently, he wrote to Stuart on May 19: "If you would let me have a mountain howitzer, I think I could use it with great effect, especially on the railroad trains. I have several experienced artillerists with me. The effect of such annoyance is to force the enemy to make heavy details to guard their communications."[43]

Stuart complied with the request within ten days. Mosby and forty-eight men rendezvoused at the J. Patterson farm south of Middleburg on the twenty-ninth. Before them squatted a bronze mountain howitzer made at the Tredegar Iron Works in Richmond the year before. "Some of the men," John Munson remarked, "thought it a bit too large to carry in a holster, but not big enough to be called a cannon." Mosby selected a crew for the howitzer, assigning Sam Chapman, a former member of the Dixie Virginia Battery, as commander. Seventeen-year-old George Turberville was detailed as driver of the two-horse team pulling the limber and cannon. Before the command departed on the raid, Chapman drilled the crew in the use of the new weapon.[44]

The Confederates marched southeastward from the Patterson farm later that day, crossing the Bull Run Mountains at Hopewell Gap and encamping for the night near the village of Greenwich. Well before daylight they were back in the saddle and arrived at a point on the Orange and Alexandria Railroad where the tracks rounded a curve and sliced through a cut on a downhill grade roughly a mile or so north of Catlett's Station. Chapman's crew unlimbered the howitzer on the bluff above the defile while details severed a telegraph wire and attached it to a loosened rail. Mosby intended to pull the rail from the track when a train approached.[45]

The raiders waited but a brief time until a fourteen-car supply train, loaded with rations, forage and mail, steamed toward the cut. As the engine neared the unsecured rail, however, it screeched to a halt. Mosby signaled Chapman, and the howitzer barked—its shot plowing into the engine's boiler. The Confederates swarmed down the bluff and toward the cars. On board a thirty-man detachment of the 15th Vermont Infantry, seeing the enemy, leaped off the cars and fled. Within minutes Mosby's men were rifling through the cars, grabbing oranges, lemons, leather and the mail bags. They found a newsboy with a broken leg and an injured fireman who were removed before the Rebels applied torches to the cars.[46]

Mosby remounted the command and started them on the road toward Greenwich. Three miles to the north along Kettle Run, troopers of the 5th New York Cavalry, 1st Vermont Cavalry and 7th Michigan Cavalry were scurrying into the saddle. When the Yankees heard the cannon fire, officers ordered detachments from each of the three regiments in pursuit. The New Yorkers, under a Captain Hasbrouck, led the column, trailed by the Vermonters and the Michiganders.[47]

Moving across country, Hasbrouck's cavalrymen overtook the guerrillas a few miles south of Greenwich. The Union captain, however, bridled up when he saw Mosby's men. Second Lieutenant Elmer Barker questioned Hasbrouck as to why he had halted. Hasbrouck responded that he would wait until support arrived. Angered by the captain's timidity, Barker shouted to the men to follow him, and the New Yorkers spurred after the Confederates.[48]

Mosby, meanwhile, deployed a rear guard and the howitzer at the entrance of the Grapewood Farm, home of Charles Green, two miles south of Greenwich. The gun crew placed the artillery piece on a knoll beside the farm lane, with its muzzle sweeping the old post road upon which the pursuers were coming. Fences lined both sides of the road, creating an avenue of fire for the Confederates. Mosby, Fountain Beattie, Bradford Smith Hoskins and a few others remained on horseback near the howitzer.[49]

When Barker's New Yorkers turned a bend in the post road, Chapman's crew met them with shellfire. The impetuous lieutenant exclaimed: "I think we can get that gun before they fire again." The

Yankees responded: "Let's go," and the cavalrymen surged up the roadbed. Pressed between the rails, the New Yorkers came on four abreast; dust and shouts rose into the air. Before them on the knoll stood Sam Chapman, a soldier who saw the handiwork of the Lord in such moments.[50]

Sam Chapman, from Page County, Virginia, was twenty-four years old, a former divinity student who had abandoned his study at the outbreak of the Civil War. His passion for the divine mixed easily with his fervor for combat. Chapman, said a compatriot, "considered that Mosby's men were organized for fighting purposes; that whenever Providence presented an opportunity for a fight it was his duty to embrace it and trust the Lord for consequences. So he incontinently pitched into what was in front of him."[51]

When the charging Federals closed to within ten yards, Chapman "pitched into" them. The howitzer roared, belching forth a sheet of grapeshot. The blast leveled the front rank of the column and part of the second. Three New Yorkers were killed and six wounded, including Barker with a mangled left thigh. The other Confederates opened fire with pistols, and the Northerners had had enough.[52]

The broken column rallied beyond the bend, where the detachment of the 1st Vermont Cavalry and some members of the 7th Michigan Cavalry had halted. Once the New Yorkers cleared the roadway, the Vermonters thundered toward the knoll. Chapman again waited until the horsemen were nearly upon him before discharging the howitzer. More Yankees tumbled into the dust but this time the others kept coming. Within seconds the Vermonters were among the gun crew and the rear guard.[53]

Hand-to-hand combat ensued. Chapman fell near his gun, his thigh ripped open by a Yankee bullet. Nearby, Richard P. Montjoy, a darkly handsome Mississippian, wrestled Sergeant E. R. Havens, 7th Michigan, to the ground. Before Montjoy could escape, however, other Federals overpowered him. They wanted to kill the prisoner, but Havens spared the Mississippian's life. The Vermonters also grabbed Fount Beattie as he tried extricating the howitzer. George Turberville escaped with the limber, and Mosby, who lost his hat and bruised his face when his frightened mount ran into a tree, eluded the Federals.[54]

Chapman, Montjoy and Beattie, although prisoners, would fight again, but not so Bradford Smith Hoskins. A native of Kent County, England, the thirty-year-old Hoskins had been a captain in the 44th

Royal Infantry during the Crimean War. He had recently crossed the Atlantic Ocean, found Jeb Stuart and volunteered. Stuart sent him to Mosby, and now he lay mortally wounded in a roadbed. The Federals carried Hoskins into the Green farmhouse, where the Britisher died. The Greens buried him in their family plot in the cemetery of the Greenwich Presbyterian Church which lay across the post road from the entrance to their farm. Years later the Hoskins family had a grave-stone erected. It remains there today, a sentry watching over a fallen soldier far from home.[55]

The Union cavalrymen returned in triumph to Kettle Run with the howitzers and Beattie and Montjoy. (The Yankees paroled the badly wounded Chapman on the field.) The officers forwarded the artillery piece to Fairfax Court House, where Stahel displayed it in front of his headquarters. The division commander then sent a con-gratulatory message to the regiments, offering "his grateful acknowl-edgements for the valuable service which you have rendered in routing the enemy and capturing their artillery in the fight of yes-terday."[56]

Although Stahel's campaign of eradication of Mosby's command had not succeeded, his operations during May had bloodied the Con-federates and had kept the vital Orange and Alexandria Railroad in service. The defeats inflicted upon the Rebels at Warrenton Junction and Grapewood Farm stood in contrast to Miskel's Farm and Aldie mill. While a Northern soldier might admit that duties against Mosby "were very trying," the Federals had fought well during the month. The raids into Mosby's base had netted prisoners and taught the civilians the costs that could accrue for their support of the guerrillas. Caution remained the hallmark of Union tactics, but the men in the saddles showed a grittiness that boded well for the future.[57]

A number of the Yankee horsemen, in fact, nearly seized the most important prize of all during May. Twice, while scouting, Mosby barely avoided capture. Returning alone through the Bull Run Moun-tains, the Confederate halted for a rest under a chestnut tree. Two Federals soon stumbled upon the prostrate officer and, drawing their pistols, demanded his surrender. Mosby quickly stood, deflected the two soldiers' pistols, drew his own and killed one of them. The other Northerner fled.[58]

Later in the month Mosby and "Big Yankee" Ames rode together on a scout. The pair had separated when seven Union cavalrymen, seeing a solitary Confederate horsemen, charged Mosby. He killed three, but the other four closed in with sabers. Using his pistols, Mosby fended off the thrusts until Ames came up and killed two more of the assailants. The other two Yankees spurred away.[59]

For Mosby and his command the action from Miskel's Farm to Grapewood Farm defined a period of transition. Much of the original detail had been recalled only to be replaced by "conglomerates." The development of the command had occurred without a pattern or a preconceived design during these two months. "The battalion that gradually grew up," Mosby wrote, "was a pure case of evolution." As the warmth of June settled over Virginia, the time had come for the formal organization of Mosby's Rangers.[60]

Chapter 4

MOSBY'S RANGERS

 Major John S. Mosby, James William Foster, William Thomas Turner, William L. Hunter and George H. Whitescarver rode into the village of Rector's Cross Roads (today, Atoka), Virginia, on June 10, 1863. The five Confederates halted at the stone house of Clinton Caleb Rector, dismounted and walked inside. The presence of Mosby and some of his men in the village probably elicited little curiosity. For five months the guerrillas had come and gone, passing through on their way to Middleburg or Upperville. Many times they had stopped at the Rector house, where they filled their canteens from the family's springhouse. Rector's Cross Roads was not much of a place, an unlikely site for what transpired on this day.[1]

Once inside the Rector home, Mosby sat down and signed the papers officially creating Company A of what would become the 43rd Battalion of Virginia Cavalry. The quartet of men with him served as witnesses. Mosby, who had not confided earlier to the four the reason he had brought them along, then informed Foster, Turner, Hunter and Whitescarver that they were the new officers of the company. The ceremony could not have taken too long for it was much like Mosby, secretive and unadorned.[2]

Mosby acted under the authority granted to him in the letters of Robert E. Lee and Jeb Stuart, dated March 23 and 25, respectively. Lee's instructions, written by his aide, Walter Taylor, and noted above, specified that Mosby could organize a company when he had obtained "the requisite number" of enrolled men. All members of the company, the orders read, must be "mustered unconditionally" into Confederate service for the duration of the conflict.[3]

Stuart's letter endorsed Lee's order and contained advice for his trusted friend and subordinate. "You will proceed to organize a band of permanent followers for the war," wrote the cavalry commander, "but by all means ignore the term 'Partisan Ranger.' It is in bad repute." Stuart favored the term "Mosby's Regulars," as that would be "a name of pride with friends and respectful trepidation with enemies." He added that Mosby should be watchful of deserters from the regular army and require evidence of honorable discharge. Mosby could select his own officers, "provided no unworthy man be so chosen." "As there is no time within which you are required to raise this command," admonished Stuart, "you ought to be very fastidious in choosing your men, and make them always stand the test of battle and temptation to neglect duty before acceptance." Finally, the general cautioned that Mosby "not have any established headquarters anywhere but 'in the saddle.' "[4]

Stuart's advice, particularly his concern over the term "Partisan Rangers," reflected Confederate ambivalence regarding the use of guerrilla or irregular warfare. The debate within the Southern nation over the legitimacy and effectiveness of that type of unit began at the struggle's outset and continued until the end. Early proposals by individuals to raise such commands met official disapproval. Jefferson Davis and generals such as Lee and Joseph Johnston disapproved of the formation of irregular forces. Johnston, when he commanded the army in Virginia, banished from his camps recruiters who were distributing handbills which urged soldiers to enlist in "local service."[5]

Guerrilla warfare, in the view of professionally trained soldiers like Jefferson Davis, Robert E. Lee, Joseph Johnston and others, sapped strength from regular forces and often resulted in undisciplined bands that roamed the countryside victimizing civilians and bringing reprisals from Union forces. Brigadier General Henry Heth, a district commander in Virginia, described such units as nothing more than "notorious thiefs and murderers, more ready to plunder friends than foes.... They do as they please go where they please." Irregular commands frequently were beyond the control of army, department or district commanders. The absence of regulations and the license to plunder attracted unsavory elements who cared neither for cause nor country.[6]

Military necessity, however, brought the implementation of guerrilla warfare. Confronting an onslaught of Union invaders, irregular bodies sprung up throughout the embattled South. Officers advertised in newspapers for volunteers. The government in Richmond eventually justified this type of fighting, asserting that members of these commands were "citizens of this Confederacy who have taken up arms to defend their homes and families." For Southerners, the defense of homeland and the desire for independence were in the tradition of their forefathers during the American Revolution, a struggle Rebels of the 1860s invoked as a model for their own. And to Southerners, one of the most renowned heroes of the conflict of the 1770s was Francis Marion, the "Swamp Fox," whose guerrilla band terrorized British and Loyalist troops in South Carolina.[7]

Confederate authorities, in the end, sanctioned the organization of partisan commands in order to give them legitimacy and to protect members who were captured by Union forces. As early as July 1861, Secretary of War Leroy Walker counseled that partisan units had to "conform strictly to the laws and usages of civilized nations." Walker also recommended that officers must be commissioned and paid by the government, an action which would ensure their safety upon capture.[8]

Walker's basic ideas were incorporated nine months later in April 1862 in a law enacted by the Confederate Congress for the creation of partisan ranger commands. The act, signed by Jefferson Davis on the twenty-first, authorized the chief executive "to commission such officers as he may deem proper with authority to form bands of partisan rangers, in companies, battalions, or regiments, either as infantry or cavalry." Officers and enlisted men of such units, the legislation declared, were equal to troops in the regular armies of the Confederacy and were subject to the Articles of War and Army Regulations. As an inducement for the raising of partisan commands, Congress allowed the members of the organizations payment for the "full value" of any "arms and munitions" seized from enemy units.[9]

The passage of legislation produced the desired results, but it neither silenced the debate over irregular service nor precluded modifications in the policy. By September 1862 six regiments, nine battalions and several companies of partisan rangers had been organized in eight states. Complaints about the units still deluged the government. In August the War Department limited the enlistments in the units by requiring a recommendation from a department commander before authorizing a command in the department and by prohibiting transfers from the regular service to partisan service. A few months later, on January 3, 1863, Secretary of War James Seddon reported to Davis: "The permanency of their engagements and their consequent inability to disband and reassemble at call precludes their usefulness as mere guerrillas, while the comparative independence of their military relations and the peculiar awards allowed them for captures induce much license and many irregularities. They have not infrequently excited more odium and done more damage with friends than enemies." The department, Seddon told Davis, was reluctant to disband those in service but had avoided the authorization of additional units. Finally, in June 1863, the War Department directed department commanders to combine partisan units into battalions or regiments in order to place "them under the same regulations as other soldiers in reference to their discipline, position, and movements."[10]

Thus, when Mosby signed the papers at the Rector home, he organized the company under the provisions of the April 1862 law and the directives from the War Department. The 43rd Battalion of Virginia Cavalry became a unit in the Army of Northern Virginia, subject to the orders of Lee and Stuart. It remained so throughout its existence.

The first duty Mosby executed after he formed the company was the selection of its officers. He had brought Foster, Turner, Hunter and Whitescarver with him to Rector's as witnesses and to inform them of their appointment, subject to election by members of Company A. Mosby, following Stuart's advice and his own standards, chose "no unworthy man" for either of the four officer positions.

Mosby picked James William Foster as captain of the company. A native of The Plains, Fauquier County, Foster had served as a private and sergeant in Company A, 7th Virginia Cavalry before joining Mosby in March 1863 while in Fauquier on a horse detail from his regiment. Known familiarly as "Willie," Foster was only nineteen years old in June 1863, when Mosby appointed him. Despite his youth, he was an imposing man, standing six feet, two inches, tall, with a dark complexion and brown eyes. Foster, like the other three officers, had proven his courage and skill in combat, or he would not have been Mosby's choice.[11]

The company's first lieutenant was one of the original detail from the 1st Virginia Cavalry, William Thomas Turner. A Marylander, Turner enlisted in Company K of the cavalry regiment in July 1861 along with others from his state. He was one of only three Marylanders who came with Mosby in January 1863.[12]

Second Lieutenant William L. Hunter was also one of the original fifteen. Hunter was twenty years old, a native Virginian from the Staunton area in the Shenandoah Valley. He had been captured in April 1863 and exchanged. At the time of the Stoughton Raid in March, Mosby regarded few, if any, of the men more highly than Hunter, who led the main body through Federal lines. But between that date and June, Mosby concluded that Foster and Turner deserved higher rank than Hunter.[13]

George A. Whitescarver from Fauquier served as the company's third lieutenant. Whitescarver had served as a private in Company K, 17th Virginia Infantry, and possibly in the 5th Virginia Cavalry. He had joined Mosby on February 25 and had participated in all the major raids after that date.[14]

From the Rector home, Mosby and the four officers traveled south out of the village to a woodland, where the other members of the command waited. They had been directed there by Mosby and had come in throughout the morning. Expectations must have spurred their ride as rumors abounded that Mosby was formally organizing them into a company. Roughly a hundred men stood among the trees on that day. Of that number, approximately thirty belonged to Captain William G. Brawner's company of partisan rangers. Brawner's unit would eventually be detached from Mosby and was not evidently enrolled in the 43rd Battalion. As for the others, enlistment papers for sixty of them exist in the Compiled Service Records in the National Archives. Since several known members of the command as of that date have no papers, the figure of seventy seems close to the correct number for the original enlistees of Company A.[15]

When Mosby met with the group, the men encircled the major. He knew well the faces around him and, when he spoke in that low voice of his, he confirmed what they had expected. It was a historic moment for many of them, a time from which some measured the achievements of a lifetime. No longer were they simply guerrillas or irregulars or "conglomerates," but partisan rangers, Mosby's Rangers. It would come to mean much.

Mosby then informed the Rangers that they had the right to elect their own officers. With that stated, he presented a slate, comprised of Foster, Turner, Hunter and Whitescarver, and accepted no other nominations. It was a practice Mosby continued throughout the command's existence—he selected the officers, and the men endorsed the choices with a vote. He gave them no other option. "In no other body of troops," wrote one of them, "were all the officers thus *unanimously* elected." His absolute control over the elections eventually caused grumbling within the ranks, but no one ever openly confronted the commander regarding Mosby's brand of democracy.[16]

From this beginning in a stand of timber south of Rector's Cross Roads, Company A expanded into the 43rd Battalion of Virginia Cavalry, comprised of several companies, and finally into a regiment, with two battalions of eight companies. The addition of hundreds of volunteers and the increasing frequency and size of Mosby's operations caused the growth of the command. What remains a matter of dispute and will probably never be answered with complete accuracy is how many men served in the 43rd Battalion and, of that number, what was the largest number of men available at one time for operations. What is certain, however, is that far more Rangers fought under Mosby than previously believed or stated.

Estimates of the number of members in the 43rd Battalion range from 800 to slightly over 1,000. In fact, the total number of Rangers far exceeded the higher figure. The basis for an accounting is the roster of the command in the Compiled Service Records in the National Archives. Confederate records, however, are notably less complete than those of Federal units, and Mosby's seems particularly so. While hundreds of enlistments papers, parole forms and papers completed by Union captors are contained in the records, hundreds more are not. Some of the records have just a clothing receipt for a member; others simply list a name, with or without rank and company. Nevertheless, the roster is the primary source and, by combining it with other sources, a reasonably accurate figure can be determined.

At least 1,900 men served in Mosby's command from January 1863 until April 1865. (The list published in the Appendix contains 1,902 names.) This number includes those who fought with Mosby before the official formation of Company A, those who probably never went on a raid but were enlisted members, those who were dismissed after a brief period of time and those who participated in a few raids and then quit the command. As the size and frequency of Mosby's operations increased—particularly during 1864—he had the manpower necessary for the execution of those forays. At the war's conclusion, Mosby had well over 700 men still in the command.[17]

A more difficult calculation is how many men rode with Mosby at any given time. The fluid nature of the membership makes this an almost impossible computation. Ranger John Munson asserted that the battalion never exceeded 350 members at any period during the war. But this is unquestionably low, for at least 779 Rangers received paroles in April and May 1865. Mosby, however, rarely gathered over 300 men for an operation because such a body of horsemen could not travel, except at night, without probable detection. What does seem clear is that Mosby had available a pool of manpower that far exceeded previous estimates.[18]

Virginians overwhelmingly filled the ranks of the battalion. While Mosby's reputation and successes attracted recruits from other states and countries, natives of the Old Dominion comprised between 80 and 90 percent of the command. Mosby, in turn, drew over a third of his Rangers from his base—the counties of Fauquier, Loudoun, Fairfax and Prince William. Of the non-Virginians in the unit, Marylanders were the largest contingent, far exceeding in numbers men from other Confederate states and the border states. These Southern sympathizers from The Old Line State joined Mosby because of the nearness of the battalion to their homes and the glamour associated with partisan warfare. Mosby also had a handful of recruits from Canada, England, Ireland and Scotland. Finally, a few Northerners from New York, New Jersey and Pennsylvania fought with Mosby.[19]

These men rode with Mosby for various reasons. Devotion to

the Confederate cause brought in some; personal convictions animated others; grievances harbored against Yankees drove a few; the
desire to serve near home lured many; and a relish for fighting attracted more. But nearly all were drawn to the battalion because of
an image. "Usually a young fellow who joined Mosby's Command,"
wrote John Munson, who walked from Richmond for ten days to
enlist in the battalion, "came to him with romantic ideas of the Partisan Ranger's existence. It was something vague in his mind. He was
ever on the look-out for its secrets and its inner working."[20]

"The true secret," Mosby claimed on why men joined him and
stayed, "was that it was a fascinating life and its attractions far more
than counterbalanced its hardships and dangers." The Rangers, living
with civilians or in secluded places, had no camp duties, none of the
routine and drudgery of regular army life. A Confederate compared
going from the regular service to partisan service with Mosby as "like
going from Hades to Elysium." Under Mosby, they could ride as
cavaliers, as knights from the pages of Walter Scott's popular novels
brought to life on the fields of Virginia. It was compelling stuff, the
mingling of chivalry and danger, "for which they were anxious
to fight and willing to make sacrifices." He called them his "Tam
O'Shanter Rebels" for the hero of Robert Burns's poem.[21]

It was warfare befitting young bloods. "What Mosby liked best
was youth," asserted Munson. When someone asked Mosby why he
recruited so many boyish warriors, he replied: "Why they are the
best soldiers I have. They haven't sense enough to know danger when
they see it, and will fight anything I tell them to." While a few dozen
Rangers were in their thirties and forties, most of them were teenagers
or men in their early twenties. The youngest member of the battalion
was Walter W. Faulkner who was fourteen years old when he enlisted
in July 1864. Many of the recruits, only slightly older than Faulkner,
ran away from home to ride with Mosby.[22]

Roughly 10 percent of the Rangers had served previously in Confederate forces. Mosby welcomed these veterans because they brought
experience and discipline to the battalion. Each, however, had to
provide Mosby with proof that he had been properly discharged from
the regular service. Mosby refused to accept deserters or to make his
command a refuge for them. "The discipline of the regular army,"
Munson wrote, "was a law unto Mosby that was never broken." He
aided conscript officers in the apprehension of deserters and of civilians eligible for military service. As the fortunes of the Confederacy

waned during the conflict's final year and desertions became epidemic in the armies, Mosby increased his efforts on behalf of the Conscript Bureau and held periodic rendezvous to ferret out runaways from Lee's army.[23]

The Rangers were, according to Munson, "as vain a lot of dandies as one would wish to see." Mosby encouraged "the men in their vanities" as they sought uniform coats with buff trimmings and hats with gold braid and ostrich plumes. Some, indeed, dressed with fastidiousness. Ranger Charles Landon Hall was so concerned with his appearance that he took the time to brush the dust off his uniform after an action. But the paintings of Mosby's men charging into battle, wearing plumed hats and scarlet-lined capes is an example of artistic license. Their uniforms generally meant "something gray," plain jackets and pants typical of a Confederate cavalryman. The trimmings, the braid, the capes were saved for special occasions—portraits, dances, those events which drew young, impressionable women. Vanity, more often than not, gave way to war's reality. They knew that a horseman dressed in a flowing red cape made a conspicuous target.[24]

Ranger John Hearn, by contrast, cut a figure of a different sort. An "uncouth" man, Hearn wore a ragged jacket frayed at the elbows, trousers too short for his legs and a pair of boots from which his toes protruded. He "looked every inch a clumsy clown in a sea of trouble," said a comrade.[25]

Mosby, a man noted for his own vanity, preferred neat, unadorned attire. When duty or orders sent him to Lee's army for a conference, he dressed in a uniform with the trimmings, a red-lined cape and plumed hat. "I have always believed," Munson argued, "that he did it for the purpose of impressing the regulars with the importance of his Partisan Rangers, in whom he had the greatest pride." On a raid, however, Mosby, like most of his men, left the fancy coats and accessories behind.[26]

Yankees accused the Rangers of wearing Federal uniforms or dressing as civilians to hide their identities and to give them the advantage of surprise. Mosby's men did not disguise themselves as Yankees, but wore the uniforms of Confederate soldiers. "I never was out of uniform or in disguise a minute during the war," asserted Mosby. During inclement or cold weather, the Confederates covered their uniforms with rubber blankets or captured Union overcoats. On a number of occasions, Northern cavalrymen mistook the bluecoated Rangers for comrades and were routed as a consequence.[27]

When a recruit joined the Rangers, he learned quickly that duty with Mosby could be exacting. The novice Ranger, said Munson, "took his lessons from some one or more old models, but he learned the first day of his enlistment that he must keep awake and fight. These were the two important first lessons." If a recruit failed to measure up, Mosby dismissed him for "inefficiency" or sent him, under guard, to the regular service.[28]

Mosby's "personality," asserted John Alexander, held the battalion together. "Between his command proper and himself," Alexander wrote, "there was a perfect rapport, and they delighted in working together." Ranger John Scott claimed that Mosby knew every member, his name, his appearance, his character, where he boarded and to what company he belonged. He had personal favorites among the Rangers, and they shared meals and beds with the commander. Mosby, however, based promotions upon merit, not favoritism. George H. Hart, a correspondent for the New York *Herald* who was captured by the Rangers, wrote later that "Mosby's men, such as I have seen, are intelligent beyond the average, and seem to revere their leader, who, to use their own words, can wear out any four of them by their labors."[29]

There was much more to the relationship between Mosby and his men than "a perfect rapport" and reverence, however. "Old Mose" or "our Mose," as the men called their commander, tolerated little misconduct. "Never an easy or indulgent officer," according to a man who served with him, Mosby brooked no opposition to his orders. An unidentified old Ranger told an acquaintance long after the war that "if you want to get along with Mosby, never disagree with him in anything. If he says black is white, you say 'Yes Sir' or keep quiet." Alexander had it right when he stated that Mosby's "personality" kept the Rangers in line, but it was more of the darker side of his makeup that ruled the young hotbloods.[30]

Alexander Hunter, a Confederate soldier from Fauquier, came to know Mosby and some of the Rangers. Hunter, with an objectivity not found in former Rangers, perhaps saw things as they were in the partisan command better than most. Hunter wrote: "His [Mosby's] power over his men was complete, but they did not love him. He had no magnetism; he was as cold as an iceberg, and to shake hands with him was like having the first symptoms of a congestive chill. He was positive, evidence of a self-centered man, and did not know what human sympathy was." Mosby, Hunter believed, was "a born soldier, a light cavalryman by instinct," but he was "cold, indifferent, and utterly selfish."[31]

Mosby's control had its limits. The youthful Rangers were an "undisciplined lot," admitted John Alexander. "I fear," he wrote, "that not all of them were model Sunday-school boys." They possessed a zest for life reflective of their ages and of the freedom they enjoyed away from parental influence. The civilians, with whom they lived, unquestionably moderated their behaviors. If a Ranger breached the line of proper behavior in regard to civilians, justice was swift and sure. But, with the men dispersed throughout dozens of square miles of Fauquier and Loudoun, Mosby's grasp extended only so far.[32]

Mosby expended much effort in keeping whiskey out of the hands of his men. He periodically sent squads throughout the region, destroying farmers' stills. The extent of whiskey drinking among the Rangers is difficult to assess. Memoirists such as Munson, Alexander, Scott, Crawford and Williamson avoided the subject. A Union prisoner of the Rangers later recounted a conversation he had with one of the partisans. The Southerner told the Yankee: "We had uproarious times when an invoice of whiskey happened to fall into our hands. Sometimes I've seen half the troop drunk for three days in the mountains, and Mosby storming like a pirate; but they minded him very little till the last drop was gone, and then all hands were ready for work again. He never touched liquor; coffee excited him just as whiskey will most men."[33]

The Ranger's boast to his captive has credence, particularly in regard to Mosby's relish for coffee. Mosby loved the brew, often riding miles out of his way to secure a cup from a family whom he knew had a pot full of the liquid. He would only drink the real thing, not the concoctions made from peanuts, beans or sweet potatoes which became prevalent in the beleaguered South. A black slave woman recalled that on one occasion she served him a cup of the sham coffee. Mosby tasted it, set the cup on the table and then knocked it over. Even when he went on a raid, Mosby carried a pouch of ground coffee with him.[34]

Mosby's temperance campaign, in all likelihood, failed. Whether or not the Rangers indulged in periodic binges in the swales of the Blue Ridge or Bull Run Mountains, remains inconclusive. They unquestionably drank alcohol at the homes of civilians with whom they resided and, when they rummaged through captured wagons, they grabbed probably every bottle of spirits they found. Had the battalion been composed of teetotalers, it would have been a unique command in the annals of the Civil War.

The behavior and decorum of the Rangers were governed to a considerable extent by their boarding with civilians. Many of them stayed at their parents' homes, and many others resided with family friends or distant relatives. These circumstances and the certainty of Mosby's wrath made the Rangers well-behaved guests. No account contains an incident of rape or murder. While a handful of the partisans contracted venereal disease, they most likely became infected while on leave in one of Richmond's flourishing brothels.[35]

Salem (today Marshall), Virginia, was the recognized center around which the Rangers boarded. Generally two or three men stayed with a family. These "safe houses" were all known to Mosby and, by 1864, nearly every one had a hiding place, entered into by a trapdoor, floorboards or secret wall panel. The families fed the boarders and their horses, and the grateful Rangers shared their supplies secured in a raid with the civilians. When an area became oversupplied with the Confederates, some of the men shifted to different quarters.[36]

When Federal raiding parties entered the region, the Rangers abandoned the homes for huts or "shebangs" in the woods and mountains. The "shebangs" were built of poles, covered with brush or cornstalks, with blankets stretched over a floor of dry leaves. One Ranger described his hut as "a comfortable lodging place." Some of the men slept under rock ledges or in fence corners until the Yankees departed. Ranger James Sinclair bunked in a graveyard. The makeshift shelters on the outcroppings of rocks provided comfort in warm weather but little during the winter months. "The greatest hardship of the service that I can recall," said John Alexander, "was spending a cold winter evening in the cheer of a glowing fire and brighter eyes and at bedtime riding a mile or more away to the chilling couches on the lee side of a big rock, or at best snuggled up under a straw rick."[37]

The "safe houses" served as residences, watchtowers and signal stations for the Rangers. When Mosby summoned the men to a meeting or rendezvous, couriers rode from farmhouse to farmhouse, relaying the news. On some occasions, a civilian acted as a signalman by hanging a pair of red flannel underwear in an upstairs window or dropping a blanket over a hayrick in the barnyard. Young boys were also sent scurrying from place to place with the messages.[38]

These methods could bring together at a designated place and time over one hundred men within a few hours. The rapid gathering of the partisans "gave a mystery and weirdness to our operations which were not without effect on the enemy," Alexander claimed. The rendezvous sites, according to John Scott, were "always selected with reference to the vicinity of a blacksmith's shop," if any member's horse needed the attention of the blacksmith. One shop, owned by a man named Hooper, outside of Middleburg, was a favored rendezvous location. If more Rangers assembled than Mosby required for the raid, he sent the surplus on a scout with an officer or back to their boardinghouses. When the operation had been completed, the guerrillas disbanded on their own, except for a detail, assigned by Mosby, for the disposition of any captured horses and prisoners.[39]

Mosby ordered a rendezvous after the receipt of intelligence from civilians or after a scout conducted by himself and/or a few of his men. Mosby had scouts out at all times along the Potomac River, in Fairfax County and in the Shenandoah Valley. He occasionally rode alone on a scout, but generally brought one or two Rangers with him. "Mosby was the fastest 'scouter' I ever knew," avowed Munson. "It was his constant care," added the Ranger, "not to take his men into any place that he could not bring them out." Once Mosby selected a target and formulated a plan, he drafted a message which appointed a time and place for a rendezvous. If circumstances warranted, he gave his men three days notice of a meeting.[40]

Two items were "indispensable" to the Rangers—horses and pistols. If a prospective recruit could not mount himself, he could not join the battalion. Nearly all the partisans owned two mounts, and many of them had more. Mosby had half a dozen at one time during the war, the care of which he assigned his black servant, Aaron Burton, a family slave who was with Mosby throughout his partisan career. They supplied themselves with the animals from local farmers in Fauquier and Loudoun, an area noted for its fine horseflesh, and from the capture of Union horses. The Rangers took excellent care of their mounts, because their lives depended upon the speed and endurance of the beasts. The men rode some of the finest thoroughbreds in the Old Dominion. A young girl, seeing some Rangers pass on horseback, wrote that one of the mounts "seemed to move on velvet slippers." The command sheltered the horses in farmers' barns or in corrals secluded in the mountains.[41]

The armament of the Rangers consisted of pistols, the ideal weapons for the type of combat in which they engaged. While a few of the men carried carbines for long-range skirmish shooting, all of the command were armed with handguns. Mosby, who required the weapon for each man, attributed his command's "efficiency as cavalry" to the use of pistols. He discarded the saber as obsolete and useless in cavalry fights. John Munson remembered seeing only one Ranger, Emory Pitts, use a saber, and Pitts did so to prod a Yankee out from under a wagon. "My men were as little impressed by a body of cavalry charging them with sabres," Mosby asserted, "as though they had been armed with cornstalks."[42]

The Rangers, almost to a man, used the six-shot, single action, .44 caliber Army Colt revolver. "I think," Mosby boasted after the war, "we did more than any other body of men to give the Colt pistol its great reputation." The men acquired the weapon from captive Yankee cavalrymen. The Union government purchased 127,156 Army Colts, at $13.75 per gun, during the conflict, making it the standard sidearm of its forces. The Rangers, in turn, like their compatriots in Confederate armies, relied upon their enemy to meet their supply needs.[43]

The Army Colt revolver, with a naval scene etched on the cylinder and a walnut stock, weighed two pounds, eleven ounces, and had an overall length of fourteen inches. Described as a "muzzleloader," the pistol was actually loaded through the cylinder. A man removed the cylinder by knocking out a pin. He then took the cartridges, made of skin gut or paper, tore the covering, separated the bullet, poured the powder into each chamber, and rammed the bullet into the powder. After loading the six chambers, he greased the head of each bullet to reduce sparks and to prevent the discharge of all the chambers at once. A brass percussion cap, containing a small charge of gunpowder, was placed in a notch at the rear of each chamber. When the hammer struck the cap, the charge ignited the powder and fired the bullet. A Ranger or Union cavalryman always had a loaded revolver when he started out on an operation.[44]

Mosby's men carried a brace of Colt pistols in two holsters. Many of them also had a pair of revolvers in saddle holsters or additional, loaded cylinders in their pockets. During combat if a Ranger needed to reload cylinders, he dismounted and sought cover. While the Confederates practiced frequently with their pistols and were decent marksmen, the Colt revolver was not a particularly accurate weapon;

it had a tendency to shoot high. In the close, swirling fighting typical of Ranger actions, however, the Colt was a deadly arm.[45]

The members of the battalion, thus armed and mounted, started forth from the rendezvous site on a raid. Each man carried a few sandwiches in his haversack for food, relying upon the generosity of civilians along the route for additional victuals. The Rangers called the inveigling for food from the locals "pie-rooting," because they most often were given pies. If the pie-rooting failed and the sandwiches were eaten, the men comforted themselves by smoking their pipes.[46]

When Mosby directed them forward, the Rangers filed into a column of fours, as scouts rode out to encircle the main body. "No special regulation" governed a man's place in the column; each one fell in at a convenient opening. The "dandies," as Alexander dubbed them, usually hurried to the front ranks, where they could impress onlookers as they sauntered past. Alexander also noted that the "dandies" seldom filled the front rank of a battle formation with the same alacrity shown on a march.[47]

The youthful Confederates while on the march acted with a "devil-may-care hilarity." John Munson said they were "as light-hearted as school boys at recess." They joked, sang, swapped stories and chased each other up and down the column. Mosby, if he had the operation's details finished to his satisfaction, also enjoyed the ride. He would send one of the men along the sets of fours with orders to bring George Kennon forward to "tell us a good lie." Kennon, a former captain in the "Louisiana Tigers," was regarded as the "biggest liar in command." Another, unidentified Ranger entertained his comrades by sticking his tongue out of his mouth for several minutes. He had been shot in the mouth and, when the wound healed, a ridge formed on top of his tongue. His friends paid him to display it and roared at the sight.[48]

The atmosphere in the ranks changed as the horsemen approached the target. Few in the column knew the purpose of the raid or its destination until Mosby halted them and issued orders for the attack. John Munson, who roomed in a farmhouse with Mosby on occasion, once asked his commander about the latter's reticence in sharing his plans with the men. "Munson," replied Mosby, "only three men in the Confederate army knew what I was doing or intended to do; they were Lee and Stuart and myself; so don't feel lonesome about it."[49]

The Rangers knew, however, that the final halt meant fighting, and fighting meant attacking, or in their parlance, "getting the bulge on" the Yankees. Mosby's tactics were governed by a simple rule: "If you are going to fight, then be the attacker. That is an old principle, and it is also my own principle." In a postwar letter he told Ranger John Russell much the same. "You know," he informed Russell, "it was never my tactics to stand still & receive a charge, but always make a countercharge." Mosby believed that the success of his operations was contingent upon surprise and the charge of his pistol-firing Rangers.[50]

Once, as a party of Rangers were duelling at long range with some Federals, Harry Hatcher, nicknamed "Deadly" by his comrades, told his officer: "If you are going to fight, fight; and if you are going to run, run; but quit this d——n nonsense." On another occasion, after Hatcher had been promoted to lieutenant, Mosby ordered him to make a demonstration with some of the men. Hatcher led the partisans forward in an attack that dislodged the Northerners from a fence row. When Hatcher reported back, Mosby questioned him about disobeying orders. "You told me to make a demonstration to get them from behind that fence, and if that didn't mean charge 'em, I don't know what it did mean." Most of the Rangers shared Hatcher's interpretation of combat.[51]

"I used to think it was glorious sport in those days," Munson wrote of the raids and combat. But that was the memories of an old man, years removed from those long minutes of introspection which gripped soldiers before they entered the bloody work of battle. John Alexander recalled such times before the signal was given. "While waiting in position for a fight," he declared, "I have known the best of them to sicken and tremble with nervousness, caused not so much I think by fears for themselves as anxiety about the work that was before them."[52]

When the attack signal finally came, the Rangers spurred forward in what was described as a "helter-skelter race" for the front. The nervousness and doubts were erased as the din of shouts and gunfire erupted. On they came, not in serried ranks, but in a wild swarm, gripped with the fervor of the assault, with their Colts blazing. "There is no thrill like that which strains the soul in the onward rush of battle," recounted Alexander, "no ecstasy on earth like that with which one sees the foe shiver, break, and run." Each daredevil was on his own as they closed in on the Yankee force.[53]

The combat was measured in minutes, not hours. During that

time span, "human life was cheap." The staccato of gunfire blended
into a roar. Ranger Jimmy Keith believed that his comrades "shoot
as much as a whole brigade when they go into action." It was grievous
work and, by the admission of one of them, "acts of cruelty were
sometimes committed" by the guerrillas. If the fighting went against
the Confederates, each member "worked out his own salvation" and
escaped "by his own particular path."[54]

Fighting was the test, the ultimate standard by which Mosby
judged the worth of a man in the battalion. If a Ranger failed that
accounting, he could be dismissed from the unit. The records and
the memoirs are silent about the punishment meted out to cowards,
except for an incident related by the slave woman who had served
Mosby the cup of bad coffee. She claimed that once while cooking
a meal for a party of Mosby's followers she saw a Ranger who had
been condemned for cowardice tied to a tree. The next morning four
guerrillas led the soldier away into nearby woods and returned later
without him. The veracity of the woman's account cannot be sub-
stantiated with other sources.[55]

If the attack by the Rangers succeeded and supplies were garnered,
Mosby divided the spoils among the members of the raiding party.
He never took any for himself, not even horses. He designated those
who could choose first, based upon their prowess in the charge. "This
system, by rewarding individual merit," A. E. "Dolly" Richards
commented, "encouraged a healthy rivalry among the men, and at
the same time removed all to leave the fight for plunder." Spoils or
plunder, John Scott argued, was the "cohesive force in the Ranger
service." Years later, the Rangers recalled specific raids in relation to
the amount of material harvested.[56]

When the raiding party returned to the confines of Upper Fauquier and southern Loudoun, Mosby dismissed them until the word
raced through the countryside for another rendezvous. As the command grew in membership and as the demands accelerated, groups
of Rangers, either on a scout or on a raid, were almost daily riding
forth. Mosby endeavored to exert constant pressure on the Federal
camps and lines of communication and gather reconnaissance information for Stuart and Lee. In his words, "I wanted to use and consume
the northern cavalry in hard work." That task fell to the Rangers—
young warriors, armed with Colt six-shooters, mounted on fine
horses, attired in "something gray," who could suddenly rise out of
the mists, like specters chasing a prey, and charge.[57]

Chapter 5

WAGON HUNTING

 The morning's first light silhou-
etted the horsemen as they waded
their mounts into the waters of
the Potomac River at Seneca Ford, ten miles upstream from Washington, DC. A long ride from Rector's Cross Roads, Virginia, had
brought them here, and they were hours behind schedule because a
guide had led the column of riders down a wrong road. The chatter,
the camaraderie of the previous afternoon, had subsided into the
silence of fatigue. At the head of the fording Confederates, John
Mosby probably bristled with anger over the guide's incompetence.
It had been less than a day since Mosby organized Company A and,
now leading it on its first raid after the formation, he had to attack
an enemy camp in the light of day, not in the dark of night as planned.[1]

The rendezvous in the woods south of Rector's Cross Roads, on June 10, 1863, had served two purposes—the official creation of the company and the gathering of the partisans for an operation. Mosby learned through his own reconnaissance or that of scouts that a camp of two companies of the 6th Michigan Cavalry at Seneca Mills, Maryland, was a promising target. The Confederate raiders had not struck across the Potomac, and Mosby grabbed the opportunity. As soon as he completed the details of the company's organization, the Rangers spurred northward toward Seneca Ford.

But the Federal cavalrymen had been forewarned of the Southerners' approach and, when the Rebels came into view, were prepared. Mosby had brought his men a long way, and he was not about to turn back without a testing. He ordered the charge, and the hundred Rangers plunged forward. The Union line flashed, but the attackers came on, breaking into the camp, and a hand-to-hand struggle ensued. Lieutenant George Whitescarver and Captain William G. Brawner died and Privates Alfred Glascock and William Hibbs fell in the exchange of gunfire. The Yankee ranks, however, splintered into pieces, and the Union troopers fled in a rout. The Rangers bagged seventeen prisoners and twenty-three horses, while killing seven of the enemy and wounding a dozen or more. The raiders then burned the tents, stores and equipment, before retiring into Virginia.[2]

Mosby accomplished his objective in the raid, but the loss of Brawner and Whitescarver was a high price for the seizure of the Yankees and horses. The fall of Brawner left his company of partisan rangers without a leader. The unit remained attached to Mosby's command for several months, but its role in operations during this period is unclear. Whitescarver had proven his worth to Mosby and was regarded as a promising officer. Mosby did not fill the vacancy in the rank until April 1864.[3]

The Rangers arrived back in Upper Fauquier and southern Loudoun late in the afternoon or early in the evening of June 11. They dispersed to their homes, with Mosby rejoining his wife, Pauline, at James Hathaway's house northeast of Salem. About eight o'clock that night a detachment of the 1st New York Cavalry, Captain William H. Boyd, Sr., commanding, clattered into Salem. The Yankees, coming from Berryville in the Shenandoah Valley, had been roaming the countryside since before daylight, moving from farmhouse to farmhouse, searching for Mosby's men. The Yankee net landed a few suspected guerrillas and approximately twenty horses.[4]

The New Yorkers came to Salem after an informant told them that Mosby and his wife were hiding at "Western View," the Hathaway home. While the main body halted in the village, Boyd sent Lieutenant Ezra H. Bailey and a detail to the residence. The Yankees bridled up before the brick house; Bailey directed some men toward the barn as he and two troopers walked to the front door. Inside, a light flickered as an occupant moved toward the entry. Bailey, knocking on the door, demanded that it be opened, and Elizabeth Hathaway complied.[5]

The trio of Yankees moved rapidly into the house. James Hathaway most likely had joined his wife by this time in the hallway. While the two enlisted men watched the couple, Bailey, carrying a light, searched each room on the first floor. He then ascended the stairs to the second story. He must have moved with caution and with a drawn pistol. In one bedroom he found Pauline Mosby, dressed in nightclothes. The Yankee officer discovered a pair of spurs on the floor but nothing else of Pauline's elusive husband. Returning to the main floor, Bailey ordered the fifty-year-old owner to dress himself as he was under arrest. Then, with the prisoner, the New Yorkers walked outside to the farm lane, where Sergeant Russell P. Forkery showed Bailey a sorrel mare he had found in the barn. Forkery kept the animal and named it "Lady Mosby." The Northerners remounted and disappeared into the darkness.[6]

In the upstairs bedroom Pauline Mosby opened a window, and her husband crawled back inside. When the New Yorkers first arrived, Mosby had bolted from the bed, hurriedly dressed, lifted the window and grabbed a limb of a large walnut tree next to the house. There he clung as Bailey talked to Pauline and found the spurs. Troopers prowled below the perch but never saw the Rebel. Today, the walnut tree remains, but the limb that had touched the brick house in 1863 is gone.[7]

The Union cavalrymen rode out of Salem on the morning of the twelfth, marching to Middleburg. There the troopers surprised and captured Ranger Charles McDonough, whom Munson described as a "brevet-outlaw," and discovered Captain James William Foster in a barbershop waiting his turn. In two days Company A lost its captain and a lieutenant. The New Yorkers, proceeding eastward to Aldie, grabbed Ranger George Turberville, the teenager who had escaped from the Yankees at Grapewood Farm with the artillery limber. From

Aldie, the horsemen continued through Loudoun and reentered Federal lines at Fairfax. It would be a long time before they learned how close they had come to seizing Mosby.[8]

Within days after Boyd's New Yorkers rode from the Middleburg/Aldie area, the war in Virginia came in force to Fauquier and Loudoun. Ranger operations were suspended as Union and Confederate cavalrymen duelled between the Blue Ridge and Bull Run mountains. Mosby, however, became a key participant in one of the most controversial aspects of the unfolding Gettysburg campaign.

On June 3, 4 and 5, infantry divisions of the Army of Northern Virginia abandoned their lines south of the Rappahannock River and marched northwestward. These troops were the first elements in what would be a floodtide in gray moving toward the Potomac River. After his victory at Chancellorsville in early May, Robert E. Lee secured permission from Jefferson Davis and the cabinet for a second invasion of Northern soil. Lee believed that such an offensive operation would relieve the Old Dominion of the ravages of war, offer Confederate troops the opportunity to garner much needed supplies and disrupt Federal operations in the East for the summer. Finally, a decisive battlefield defeat of his opponent in the North might end the conflict. Lee, with these objectives, directed his reforged legions toward Pennsylvania.

The movement consumed weeks. While the Confederates raced northward down the Shenandoah Valley, the Union Army of the Potomac advanced east of the Blue Ridge through Virginia's Piedmont. Major General Joseph Hooker, who had lost the strategic initiative to Lee, dispatched his cavalry corps toward the mountain barrier to locate the Confederate infantry and artillery units. Lee, in turn, posted Stuart's horsemen at the Blue Ridge's eastern base to seal the gaps. When the opposing forces met, combat ignited and flared.

Stuart's troopers filtered into Upper Fauquier and southern Loudoun on June 16 and 17. A week earlier, on the ninth, the mounted opponents had clashed at Brandy Station in the largest cavalry engagement of the war. The Federal units, directed by Major General Alfred Pleasonton, gave as good as they took in the fighting, which raged much of the day. The Southerners held the field in the end, but the Northerners had fought with tenacity they had not shown on previous fields. No longer, after Brandy Station, did the Confederate mounted arm possess the superiority it had in the conflict's first two years.

Stuart, whose reputation suffered in the Confederate press because of the engagement, arrived on the seventeenth at Middleburg, where he and his staff relaxed, entertaining civilians. To the east at Aldie, one of his brigades sparred with a Union brigade in a series of mounted charges and countercharges throughout much of the day. Near nightfall, the Southerners retired to within a mile of Middleburg. Stuart and his staff, however, were nearly gobbled up late in the afternoon when a solitary Federal regiment galloped into the village. Stuart hurried another brigade to Middleburg which drove out the Yankees and secured the area.[9]

The fighting subsided on June 18. That evening Mosby and three Rangers penetrated Pleasonton's lines around Aldie and captured a courier with dispatches from Hooker to his cavalry commander. Mosby then rode to Middleburg, where Stuart had remained during the day. Reporting to headquarters, Mosby delivered the intelligence find to Stuart. It was the kind of feat Stuart had come to expect from the partisan officer. The papers revealed that Pleasonton had his entire command of nearly 7,000 troopers concentrated near Aldie. Stuart's aides scurried forth with instructions for the Confederate units.[10]

Pleasonton, a bantam-sized, vain, ambitious man, had earlier proposed a novel scheme for securing the services of Mosby. "Ask the general," Pleasonton wrote to one of Hooker's officers, "how much of a bribe he can stand for Mosby's services. There is a chance for him, and just now he could do valuable service in the way of information as well as humbugging the enemy." Army headquarters approved, noting that Pleasonton should "not hesitate as to the matter of money." What "chance" Pleasonton had is unknown, but the plot evaporated. There is no evidence that a formal proposition was ever made to Mosby.[11]

Mosby, in fact, was back in the saddle for Stuart on the night of the twenty-first, leading a contingent of Rangers across the Bull Run Mountains. Early the next morning, the Rebels charged a small party of Union cavalry near a church, but were repulsed when enemy infantrymen, concealed around the building, unleashed a volley into the ranks of the attackers. Ranger Richard Montjoy had a finger severed in the gunfire; Charles Hall took a bullet in the shoulder; and J. N. Ballard had a leg bone splintered. When the Rangers reached the security of the mountains, a surgeon amputated Ballard's leg. Ballard rejoined the battalion the following winter outfitted with the artificial leg of Union Colonel Ulric Dahlgren, who was killed on March 2, 1864, in a raid against Richmond.[12]

Mosby, while the raiding party returned to the mountains, scouted through the columns of Union infantry en route for Maryland. Rain had been falling periodically since the twentieth, and Mosby had on a waterproof which concealed his uniform. He met Stuart at Rector's Cross Roads on the twenty-third, reporting that the Confederate cavalry could ride through Hooker's dispersed infantry corps and ford the Potomac between the Federal army and the capital. Mosby suggested that Stuart cross the river at Seneca Ford.[13]

Stuart ordered Mosby back across the mountains for a reconfirmation while forwarding the intelligence to Lee. The fighting between Stuart and Pleasonton, which flowed back and forth from Middleburg to Upperville, had ceased on the twenty-first, and the Southern general had been since that day exchanging messages with Lieutenant General James Longstreet, commander of the First Corps, and Lee, on his role during this phase of the campaign. Late on the night of June 23–24, a courier brought a letter from Lee to Stuart. The commanding general directed Stuart to march east or west of the mountains, cross the Potomac and "move on and feel the right" of Lieutenant General Richard S. Ewell's Second Corps, the vanguard of the Confederate invasion. The instructions were imprecise and discretionary.[14]

The Confederate horsemen prepared for the march throughout June 24. Mosby reported back and reiterated his belief that Stuart could slide between the Federal infantry corps. At 1:00 A.M. the next morning, Stuart and three brigades trotted out of Salem toward Thoroughfare Gap in the Bull Run Mountains. When the troopers reached the village of Haymarket, they found, instead of a clear path, a road clogged with Union infantrymen. Stuart swung the column in a wider arc, losing hours and miles at the outset. It was not until the night of June 27–28 that the cavalrymen forded the Potomac. Further delays ensued and by the time Stuart completed the ride around Hooker's army, Lee's units, without Stuart's reconnaisance reports, had stumbled into a major engagement at the southern Pennsylvania crossroads village of Gettysburg on July 1. The errant cavalry general reported to Lee on the afternoon of the second. It was the low point in the career of an otherwise excellent horse soldier.[15]

Mosby's intelligence reports contributed to Stuart's decision to interpret Lee's orders in the broadest sense. But Mosby could not have seen the march of all the Union corps and, by the time Stuart reached Haymarket, Mosby's information was outdated. This initial delay was compounded by debatable decisions Stuart made on the march. "Stuart's Ride" sparked a controversy almost immediately after the Confederate defeat which has endured to this day. For Mosby, the defense of his friend and superior became a crusade. After the war, Mosby penned numerous articles and a book, trying to absolve Stuart of blame for Gettysburg. The partisan officer carried the struggle with him to the grave.[16]

During this period of time Mosby's men, except for those detailed for scouting duties, disappeared into hiding places. "All of the citizens of Middleburg belong to or are implicated with Mosby," Hooker wrote to his cavalry officers and ordered a sweep of the region. Yankee patrols arrested all males they found and instructed the women to stay inside their homes. The Northerners collared seven Rangers.[17]

After the departure of the cavalry forces, Mosby gathered fifty men at noon on June 28. He intended to link up with Lee's invading army in Pennsylvania. Crossing the Blue Ridge at Snicker's Gap, the Rangers moved down the Shenandoah Valley, forded the Potomac at Hancock, Maryland, and entered Pennsylvania miles west of Lee's army, which was converging on Gettysburg. The partisans seized over 200 head of cattle, fifteen horses and a dozen blacks, before returning to Southern soil on or about July 1.[18]

During the next fortnight, as Lee's army recoiled from its defeat at Gettysburg, on July 1–3, and withdrew to Virginia, Mosby's command roamed into eastern Loudoun and western Fairfax. On July 13, twenty-seven Rangers, under Mosby, struck twenty-nine sutlers' wagons, overrunning the guards and encircling the entire train. Sutlers were civilian businessmen who sold a variety of merchandise—food, tobacco, cloth, cutlery, illegal alcohol, newspapers and books—to Federal soldiers. These Yankee peddlers were favorite targets of the Rangers. Their wagons were loaded and Mosby, instead of destroying them, started them toward Middleburg. The attack brought a pursuit by the 2nd Massachusetts Cavalry, which overtook the slow-moving caravan at Aldie. The outnumbered Rangers had no choice but to flee, and the Federal troopers retook the wagons and the prisoners. "If the boys could only have got home safely with those twenty-nine loaded wagons," John Munson asserted, "we could have opened a big department store in Mosby's Confederacy."[19]

Within a week of the attack on the sutlers, Mosby's base was "overrun with troops" from the Army of the Potomac. Lee's army had completed the crossing of the Potomac River on July 14 and had begun filing southward into the Shenandoah Valley. Five days later the Federal army, now under the command of Major General George G. Meade, reentered Virginia east of the Blue Ridge. As the Yankees edged southward, fighting erupted in the gaps of the mountains. Meade's troops probed through the defiles to locate the enemy, while Lee's veterans contested the thrusts to screen the main army. By the twenty-fourth, Meade began concentrating his corps around Warrenton as the Confederates occupied the Culpeper area south of the Rappahannock River. The opposing armies would stalk each other along the river until mid-September.[20]

The occupation of Fauquier and the heavy guard details along the Orange and Alexandria Railroad by the Yankees disrupted the pattern of much of Mosby's operations for the next two months. The Rangers gnawed at the edges of the Federal units, apprehending stragglers and patrols, and targeted wagon trains for attack. With Northern regiments and brigades scattered throughout the region, Mosby established a temporary base, dubbed "Camp Spindle." It was located north of Hopewell Gap in the Bull Run Mountains in eastern Fauquier, seven miles or so east of The Plains and roughly fifteen miles north of Warrenton. Here the Rebels pitched shelter tents for themselves and their captives, who could not be passed through Federal lines to Lee's army and on to the prison camps.[21]

Ranger James Williamson remembered that "our little band was darting in and out" during these weeks. The constant movement consumed horseflesh, and some of the partisans had to ride mules. To the occupying Yankees, however, the Rangers seemed to be everywhere. "They gave us more trouble than a whole brigade of confederate soldiers," a Pennsylvanian wrote of Mosby's men. The guerrillas, claimed another Northerner, "were very good file-closers for the Union army," reducing straggling within the Federal units. During July the Rangers seized 186 Union soldiers, 123 horses and mules, fifty sets of harness and arms and a dozen wagons.[22]

Mosby redirected the raids during the initial week of August, leading his men into Fairfax County against the long strings of wagons en route to Meade's army. The Rangers attacked sutler trains on

Thursday, the sixth, four miles west of Fairfax Court House, on Sunday, the ninth, near Goodling's Tavern east of Leesburg and, on Tuesday, the eleventh, near Annandale. Sometimes when the Confederates grabbed sutler wagons ("cracker outfits" to Yankees), they shared the goods with the captured escorts. "It was amusing to see," Munson stated, "the fiendish delight with which the boys in blue would go through their natural enemy. They always looked upon their own sutlers as robbers, and they never got a chance to get even with their foe except on occasions of this sort."[23]

Mosby's campaign against the wagon trains, however, elicited criticisms from Lee. The army commander, endorsing Mosby's report of August 4, wrote: "I greatly commend Major Mosby for his boldness and good management. I fear he exercises but little control over his men. He has latterly carried but too few on his expeditions, and his attention has been more directed toward the capture of wagons than military damage to the enemy." Stuart relayed Lee's concerns to Mosby.[24]

Two weeks later, on the eighteenth, Lee expanded his criticisms of the partisan command in a letter to Stuart. He once again noted that even though Mosby had "a large number of men," the major operated with small parties against wagon trains, not Meade's communications and outposts. "The capture and destruction of wagon trains," wrote Lee, "is advantageous, but the supply of the Federal Army is carried on by the railroad. If that should be injured, it would cause him to detach largely for its security, and thus weaken his main army." The commanding general added that he had received reports of Mosby's men selling captured goods. "This had better be attended to by others," Lee directed Stuart. Finally, Lee wanted all deserters who had reportedly joined the Rangers returned to the army. Lee believed Mosby knew nothing of the deserters but ordered Stuart to make him aware of the situation.[25]

If Stuart forwarded Lee's letter to Mosby and if Mosby responded, the records do not indicate. The occupation of Fauquier by Meade's troops disrupted Mosby's method of operations, limited his opportunities for strikes and forced him to move with smaller groups. Mosby had neither the artillery nor the sufficient numerical strength for raids against the railroad. Part of the command had to man Camp Spindle and to guard the prisoners at all times. The damage he inflicted upon the wagon trains had, as Lee correctly argued, little military value. But the attacks kept his command active and resupplied, and brought in prisoners. Stuart, by contrast, twice recommended Mosby for promotion during this period.[26]

The substance of Lee's other charges is difficult to ascertain. If the Rangers conducted a business in stolen goods, none of the members wrote of it. The market for such transactions would have been limited to western and northern Loudoun, for the Yankee presence in Fauquier would have precluded much of this activity in that county. Since the Rangers were not residing with the local people, they might have sold extra commodities to other families. That Mosby would have condoned the trade is questionable, as is his acceptance of deserters into the command. If he knew that a recruit had run away from the army, he would have sent him back when conditions allowed. He adhered to that policy throughout the existence of the battalion.

The warfare during these summer days exacted a toll from the partisan command. Between July 15 and August 20 at least twenty-one Rangers fell into Union hands. The Northerners captured nine in Rectortown on August 4 and 5, while the remaining dozen were lost in raids. None of the guerrillas were killed, and only Ranger James Hammond suffered a wound. The losses amounted to roughly a fifth of the unit.[27]

The losses incurred by the Rangers were caused largely by the counteroperations of a small brigade of Federal cavalry assigned to the defenses of Washington, DC. The mounted unit, composed of companies from the 2nd Massachusetts, the 13th New York and the 16th New York Cavalry, under the command of Colonel Charles Russell Lowell, were the same troopers who saved the wagons at Aldie on July 13, bagged the nine Rangers in Rectortown in early August and pursued the partisans when they hit the "cracker outfits" in Loudoun and Fairfax.[28]

Charles Russell Lowell, the brigade commander, was twenty-eight years old when he began his duties against Mosby's men. A member of the prominent Lowell family of Massachusetts, he was graduated first in the Harvard class of 1854 and was pursuing a career in iron making when the Civil War began. Lowell secured a commission of captain of cavalry and served through much of 1862 on the staff of George McClellan. After the Battle of Antietam in September, he returned to the Bay State and recruited and organized the 2nd Massachusetts Cavalry. Promoted to colonel in May 1863, Lowell soon thereafter assumed command of the brigade.[29]

Major Caspar Crowninshield, successor to Lowell in command of the regiment, knew him well and in August 1863, wrote home: "The Colonel & I get along very well together. He is a very brilliant man, but is to [sic] hasty in his judgements of men & things. And is so very ambitious, that he sacrifices everything for advancement."[30]

This drive of Lowell's for rank perhaps explained in part his dislike for the duty against the Rangers. He might have viewed it as an uncertain path to a brigadier's star. In his letters home during the summer Lowell described the assignment as "all in the day's work." He called Mosby "an old rat [who] has a great many holes," claiming that the partisan officer "is more keen to plunder than to murder, —he always runs when he can." He concluded: "I do not fancy the duty here, serving against bushwhackers. It brings me in contact with too many citizens, and sometimes with mothers and children."[31]

Crowninshield echoed Lowell's view of the onerous duty before the Federals. Trying to find the Rangers, Crowninshield told his mother, "is almost like hunting for a needle in a hay stack." He described one pursuit after the Rebels as a "long tramp after Mosby." Every day guards were detailed for the wagon trains, and the regiments enclosed their camps with stockade fences as protection against the Rangers. Crowninshield grumbled about a "general feeling of dissatisfaction" and about "disputes and jealousy among officers" within the 2nd Massachusetts, but added that "as a fighting Regt. I don't believe that there is a better one in the service."[32]

A test of the Bay Staters' combat prowess occurred on August 24, in the first real clash between the Yankees and the Rangers. A thirty-man detail of Company A, 2nd Massachusetts Cavalry was escorting a herd of one hundred horses from Alexandria to Centreville. When the Federals reached Billy Goodling's Tavern, ten miles out of Alexandria, they halted to water the animals. Mosby and thirty Rangers, meanwhile, were prowling around the area when they saw the enemy detachment. Mosby had brought his men into Fairfax to burn three bridges but decided instead to attack the horse detail. He split his force into two groups, assigning Lieutenant William Thomas Turner to hit the Yankee rear with fifteen men, while he and the other half struck the front.[33]

The Southerners charged "with a yell that terrified the Yankees and scattered them in all directions," in Mosby's words. Most of the blue-jacketed troopers scurried for cover around the tavern and opened fire with their carbines. The Federals were actually Californians, members of a hundred-man contingent who had traveled to the east coast the previous winter and formed Company A of Lowell's regiment. They called themselves the "California Battalion" and prided themselves on their toughness.[34]

The Californians' carbine fire ripped into Mosby's oncoming ranks. Ranger Joseph C. Calvert, a forty-one-year-old native of Upperville, took a bullet in the ankle, while Rangers Norment Smith and Charles Shriver were killed. Smith was, Mosby reported, a soldier "of great usefulness and of brilliant service." Shriver, a Marylander, was only seventeen years old when he died in front of Goodling's Tavern.[35]

More importantly, the Californians wounded Mosby, who was hit in the thigh and in the groin by two bullets. Mosby reeled in the saddle when struck, and one or two of his men assisted him into nearby woods, where Surgeon William Dunn examined him. The other attackers, seeing Mosby retire, pulled up and followed him into the trees. Before Mosby could order them back, all but a handful of the Federals escaped. Turner led the Confederates in pursuit and secured most of the horses.[36]

Mosby, despite the loss of blood and the pain, acted hurriedly, reforming the group, assigning guards for the horses and moving out before a pursuit force appeared. Darkness soon shielded the Rangers, who divided into small parties during the return march. Major Crowninshield followed with the 2nd Massachusetts Cavalry but only found a few horses which had been lost by the fleeing Southerners. In his report on the action, Mosby cited Turner and William R. Smith, brother of Norment, who was on detached duty from the 4th Virginia Cavalry. When Stuart learned of the fight at Goodling's Tavern, he praised Mosby for the latter's "boldness and skill."[37]

Mosby's wounds disabled him for nearly a month. While he recuperated at the family homestead in Albemarle County, Lieutenant Turner commanded the unit. During these weeks the Rangers continued their sorties against Union sutler wagons or, as Munson dubbed them, "a traveling retail general store." Handfuls of Rangers roamed across the countryside in "private scouting expeditions" for the wagons laden with goods. The operations, in Mosby's absence, had little military value. Plunder seemed to be the guiding motive.[38]

On September 16, Turner led a detachment of thirty men toward Warrenton. The bulk of Meade's army had departed the area during the previous three days, probing Lee's defenses along the Rapidan River. Lee had withdrawn his forces south of the stream after the departure of two of Longstreet's infantry divisions and an artillery battalion for Georgia. The armies remained stationary for the next few weeks, engaging in minor skirmishes across the river.[39]

The Rangers, finding the Federals on the march, circled Warrenton and by nightfall reached the village of Fayetteville, a few miles south of the county seat. In the town the Confederates located several sutler wagons parked beside a house. A few of them moved to the dwelling and, looking through a window, saw the Yankee peddlers and their infantry guards seated at tables drinking and playing cards. William Smith and John Puryear knocked on the door and, when a soldier opened it, they grabbed him and led their comrades through the doorway. Before the Northerners could react, the Rangers disarmed the lot. Within minutes the raiders were eating sardines, raisins, cakes, figs, cheese, chocolates, pickled onions, oysters and jelly, and washing the feast down with champagne, claret wine and beer. What they could not consume, they stuffed into sacks. Ranger Sewell Williams, who neither smoked nor gambled, took only cigars and decks of cards. By the time the Rebels departed with their prisoners and booty, many were sick from the food and drink.[40]

The attacks on the sutlers brought the usual response from the Federals. Cavalrymen made sweeps through the region, hunting for the guerrillas. The 1st Pennsylvania Cavalry conducted one of the searches on September 10 and 11, but returned empty-handed. A member of the regiment, writing home to his sister, attributed their failure to Mosby's network of informants. The Rangers, he said, "have too good a means of finding out our movements to get caught easily." The counterraids resulted in the capture of only five Rangers during the first three weeks of September.[41]

Mosby rejoined the command about September 20. During his return trip, he detoured to Richmond, where he conferred with Secretary of War James Seddon and secured a number of percussion torpedoes, explosive devices developed by Brigadier General Gabriel J. Rains which were forerunners of land mines. Mosby planned to use the torpedoes against Federal railroad trains. From the capital, Mosby journeyed to Lee's headquarters at Orange Court House. "Old General Lee," as Mosby told Pauline, was "very kind to me & expressed the greatest satisfaction at the conduct of my command."[42]

Operations against Union military targets resumed with the return of Mosby. On the twenty-first, he gathered a detachment of Rangers and started for the Orange and Alexandria Railroad, halting for the night near Warrenton Junction. The Southerners moved toward Bealeton Station the next morning and saw a wagon train loaded with a pontoon bridge en route for Meade's army. Mosby dispatched Horace Johnson with the information to Lee's headquarters while he split the detachment into two parties, leading one toward Auburn to the northwest and directing the other southwestward along the tracks. Union troops in heavy numbers patrolled the railway. The second group collided with a Yankee force at Madison Court House and lost seven members as prisoners to the Federals. Mosby's band garnered a few captives and a handful of horses, but the raid proved to be more costly than its worth, for the Confederates had not impeded operations on the railroad.[43]

A few days later Mosby took four men with him into Fairfax County. He planned to dispel the rumors of his death with the capture of Francis H. Pierpont, governor of West Virginia, whose temporary headquarters were located in Alexandria. After passing through Federal lines under the cover of darkness, the five Confederates bridled up before the governor's mansion. Mosby and his men entered the house only to learn that Pierpont, like Percy Wyndham, the Union cavalry officer whom Mosby had tried to capture in March, was spending the night in Washington. They then went to the residence of Colonel D. H. Dulany, Pierpont's military aide. Dulany, believing the party to be Federal scouts disguised in Confederate uniforms, welcomed them until he recognized his son French, who rode with Mosby. As they were preparing to leave, the disgruntled father told his son that he should take a pair of old shoes with him as the colonel reckoned shoes "were d——d scarce in the Confederacy." French, lifting his trouser leg, revealed to his father a fine pair of cavalry boots taken from a sutler and asked his captive "what he thought of that."[44]

The capture of Dulany, while not as notorious a feat as the seizure of Edwin Stoughton from his headquarters in Fairfax Court House on March 8–9, startled Union authorities. Mosby was not only alive, but still capable of penetrating to the doorsteps of the capital. He seemed ubiquitous, always somewhere out there. He was elusive, spectral, a ghost in Confederate gray. Mosby and the Rangers continued to haunt northern Virginia.

Chapter 6

AUTUMN
1863

 During the final days of September 1863 John Mosby stopped at the home of a Ferguson family somewhere in the Virginia Piedmont. As he dismounted and walked toward the house, Mrs. Ferguson greeted the renowned Confederate, asking if he wanted to see "Mosby." Before he could respond, the lady rushed inside and returned with a baby boy several months old. The proud mother then introduced Mosby Ashby Jackson Ferguson to the partisan officer. Just a short time before, near Alexandria, another mother had shown him *her* baby son named Mosby.[1]

Mosby wore fame well. He was, said a Ranger, "not without some jealousy for his own laurels." Vain, proud, sensitive, he enjoyed official and public approval of himself and his command. The daring nighttime entry into Alexandria to capture a governor served little military purpose, except to enhance his own notoriety and to embarrass the Union administration. The seizure of Colonel D. H. Dulany was but a sideshow to the main drama, however. And it was to the latter that Mosby turned his attention as the heat of summer gave way to the chill of autumn.[2]

"I am now fixing my trigger for several good things," Mosby informed Pauline, on October 1, 1863, in a letter which included the accounts of the two babies. Since he rejoined the command less than a fortnight ago, he had been in constant motion—scouting, leading a raid, nabbing Dulany. He was now "fixing my trigger" for a renewal of operations against the Orange and Alexandria Railroad, the lifeline of George Meade's Army of the Potomac deployed along the Rapidan River. Gone, temporarily at least, were the "private scouting expeditions" against sutlers favored by his men during his absence. With the coming of autumn and the return of Mosby, the Rangers were back on duty.[3]

Mosby's purpose at this time he reported to Richmond. "The military value of the species of warfare I have waged," he wrote, "is not measured by the number of prisoners and material of war captured from the enemy, but by the heavy detail it has already compelled him to make, and which I hope to make him increase, in order to guard his communications, and to that extent diminishing his aggressive strength."[4]

Mosby, in order to expedite his objectives and to improve the effectiveness of the command, organized a second company. While the exact number of men with him at that time cannot be ascertained with accuracy, it had to be roughly 150 horsemen. Such a contingent of men in one company weakened control of the officers. Thus on the same day he wrote to Pauline of "fixing my trigger," October 1, he held a rendezvous at Scuffleburg, a speck of a village located in a hollow of the Blue Ridge between Paris and Markham. Scuffleburg consisted of a blacksmith shop, a house and a wheelwright shop but was frequented by the Rangers because of its remote location. Yankee patrols seldom passed through the place.[5]

After the Rangers had arrived, Mosby formed them into a line and designated sixty men to step forward. He then directed the new members of Company B to vote for the slate of officers he presented. They complied, and it was done.[6]

The choice for captain of Company B was William R. Smith. A native of Fauquier County, "Billy" Smith had served as a lieutenant in Company H, 4th Virginia Cavalry, the Black Horse Troop, before joining Mosby during the previous summer. He had distinguished himself in the fight at Goodling's Tavern, where his brother Norment had been killed. Mosby regarded him highly, and Billy Smith, a man of courage and remarkable physical strength, proved himself worthy of that confidence.[7]

The company's three lieutenants, unlike Smith, had no prior military service before joining Mosby. First Lieutenant Franklin Williams, who stood only five feet, six inches, in height, was a twenty-six-year-old from Fairfax County and had been in the command since February. Second Lieutenant Albert "Ab" Wrenn also hailed from Fairfax and was a year younger than Williams. Wrenn, captured in April, had spent a few weeks in a Federal prison until exchanged. Third Lieutenant Robert Gray was a resident of Loudoun County and enlisted with Mosby during the unit's early weeks. All three of the new officers served capably in their posts, but none achieved higher rank.[8]

Mosby, in turn, appointed noncommissioned officers for Company B. The number of sergeants and corporals, according to the records, varied for each company. These differences may be attributed to the incompleteness of the documents or that Mosby only chose certain members of each company for the ranks. Company A, for instance, had five sergeants and four corporals while Company B's list named three sergeants—Horace Johnson, James W. Wrenn and Richard Dorsey Warfield. The disparity in the number of noncommissioned officers would continue with the formation of additional companies.[9]

Company B received orders, as did Company A, in June for a raid immediately after its organization. At noon on the second, Captain Smith met forty of his men at Salem. Proceeding southeastward, the Rangers approached Warrenton at dusk when a howling rainstorm blew in. Smith turned the column around, leading it to his home, where his mother and sister fed the wet, hungry Rebels. They stayed the night until daybreak, when Smith directed them to scatter, rest, and regroup later that afternoon at the residence of a man named Cross, located six miles from Warrenton.[10]

The members of Company B met Smith at the designated site at 4:00 P.M. Scouts fanned out in front as the main body rode slowly toward Warrenton. Smith halted at nightfall; the men fed themselves and their mounts and relaxed. At eleven o'clock they were in the saddle again, circling around the county seat. Three miles past the town the Confederates located a Yankee campsite of the crest of a hill. Smith, with William Chapman and Richard Montjoy, spurred toward the camp. As the trio neared the tents they dismounted and walked through the camp, counting roughly 250 Federals occupying the position.[11]

Smith, upon their return, described the situation to the men, telling them that "if you all go in, there will be a horse for each of you." Chapman and Montjoy argued for a frontal attack, but Smith overruled them. The Rangers skirted the Federal pickets and came in at the rear of the camp among the tents. When they closed to within ten yards, Smith shouted the charge. Before the Northerners could offer a defense, the thundering horsemen were among them. Ranger Sam Alexander, a short, round man who weighed 200 pounds, galloped in the forefront, yelling: "Give me your greenbacks! surrender!" All but a half dozen of the Yankees escaped in the darkness. The Southerners grabbed twenty-seven horses and suffered no casualties. Each man did not get a horse, but Company B achieved a modest success on its initial raid.[12]

Less than a week later, on the ninth, men from both companies met at Rector's Cross Roads. Mosby selected roughly forty men for the raid, issued instructions to Captain Billy Smith and Lieutenant William Thomas Turner and then rode away to scout. The Rangers followed, camping for the night in a stand of pine trees near Frying Pan in Fairfax County. Mosby returned about eleven o'clock and, like his men, slept for a few hours. Before daylight he was back in the saddle, taking Sergeant Dorsey Warfield, "Big Yankee" Ames, John Edmonds and John Munson with him. The five, moving through Federal lines, scouted as far as Falls Church, eight miles northwest of Alexandria on the Leesburg Pike.[13]

Smith and Turner, meanwhile, relocated their campsite to a thicket. The main party moved carefully as Yankee mounted patrols roamed the countryside and Union-sympathizing civilians would have reported the presence of Mosby's men to army officers. John Edmonds returned that evening with orders from Mosby for Smith and Turner's men to ride to Guilford Station, a stop on the Loudoun & Hampshire Railroad approximately four miles northwest of Frying Pan. Starting at ten o'clock, the Confederates reached Guilford three hours later, halted, fed corn to their mounts and bedded down for a few hours rest. Smith and Turner had them on the move again before sunrise, angling eastward along the Leesburg Pike to a point five miles from Alexandria. Here, in a pine forest, Mosby and the others found them.[14]

The daylight hours passed into the afternoon as the Rangers waited. Late in the day a wagon train, guarded by 150 Union troopers, approached. With the number of Yankee cavalrymen strung out among the wagons, Mosby could not attack the train as it creaked past. Finally, near the end of the caravan a wagon bogged down in a hole in the roadbed. The Rangers, advancing cautiously, surrounded two wagons. The raiders found between 150 and 200 pairs of cavalry boots and some food inside the vehicles. While the unsuspecting guards and other wagons proceeded westward, the Rangers loaded themselves down with the boots and food and then disappeared into the trees. Mosby, because of the Federal activity in the area, abandoned his plans for a night assault on an enemy camp and turned his men westward for their base. Dividing the plunder at a farmhouse in Loudoun, the Southerners returned to their own boarding places. Except for the boots, it was not much to show for a five-day raid, but they had not fired a shot.[15]

While Mosby and his party were on this foray, Lee's and Meade's armies began restirring along the Rapidan River. Lee, learning that Meade had detached two infantry corps to Tennessee, undertook an offensive operation with the purpose of turning Meade's right flank and driving toward Washington. The ensuing Bristoe Campaign, beginning on the ninth, lasted for twelve days. Meade reacted skillfully to Lee's advance, kept his units between the Rebels and the capital and bloodied a division of Lee's troops at Bristoe Station on the Orange and Alexandria Railroad. By the twentieth, Lee's army had withdrawn, occupying its old lines south of the Rappahannock River. The campaign exacted approximately 3,600 casualties but did little in altering the strategic situation in Virginia.[16]

Mosby's command, meanwhile, played no role in Lee's offensive. The raid of October 9–13 concluded before the Army of Northern Virginia pushed Meade's legions back to the Manassas area. From the evidence, the Rangers remained quiet as the two behemoths stalked each other along the tracks of the Orange and Alexandria. Diarist "Tee" Edmonds noted that on the fifteenth—Lee's and Meade's armies were facing each other along Bull Run Creek—

Mosby was at Middleburg, and every Ranger was "required to be at his post." But the accounts contain no information of a raid on this date. If Mosby had an opportunity of rendering service for Lee, it slipped by.[17]

Perhaps an explanation for Mosby's inactivity during the Bristoe Campaign was the presence of Union cavalry in the region. Mounted detachments came hunting, capturing two Rangers on the twelfth and two more three days later. One of those seized on the twelfth was William Dunn, the command's surgeon. Dunn had treated Mosby's wounds on August 24, and the Ranger commander thought highly of the doctor's skill. But Dunn wanted to be a warrior, not a healer. He was, said Mosby, "too fond of fighting. I wanted a surgeon that took more pride in curing than killing." Dunn and the other three were later exchanged.[18]

The Yankee horsemen most likely belonged to the brigade of Colonel Charles Russell Lowell. The duel between the two antagonists had never subsided since August. The contest had interludes, but it was always present, waiting to flare when contact ignited it. It was thrust, counterthrust, a sort of deadly minuet on horseback.

Lowell's troopers struck with an increasing frequency and with a new harshness. Late in September the Union horsemen, approaching Rector's Cross Roads, discovered the Rangers at a meeting of the command. The Yankees charged and the Confederates, surprised and unprepared, scattered across the countryside in what one of them called a "stampede" toward the mountains. Several days later another Federal detachment burned two mills and a farmhouse. Lowell had orders to destroy all houses that belonged to known supporters of Mosby. The Union colonel did not agree with the directive and wrote to Mosby that "it was not my intention to burn the houses of any men for simply belonging to his command; that houses would be burnt which were used as rendezvous." In a letter home at this time, Lowell stated that "Mosby is an honourable foe, and should be treated as such."[19]

While no major clash occurred between the foes during October, the counteroperations by the Northerners exacted a toll from the Rangers. In addition to the four guerrillas captured on the twelfth and fifteenth, the Yankees collared four more Rangers between the seventeenth and twenty-first. Then on the twenty-third, detachments from the 2nd Massachusetts Cavalry and the 1st D. C. Cavalry found five of Mosby's men on a scout in Fairfax County. The Rebels were betrayed by a civilian and, when the Federals attacked, they fought valiantly until overwhelmed. Ranger Charles Mason was killed in the exchange of gunfire, while three of his comrades—John H. Barnes, Robert Harrover and Thomas E. Stratton—surrendered. Only Lieutenant Frank Williams escaped.[20]

Despite these minor successes, the Federals did not cripple Mosby's command, and they knew it. Few in the cavalry brigade probably shared Lowell's view of the enemy as an "honourable foe." Duty against the Rangers was dangerous and unending. Handfuls of prisoners, captured sporadically, did not counterbalance their losses. It was not the kind of warfare many of them enlisted for in the army.

Lieutenant Colonel Henry S. Gansevoort, commander of the 13th New York, expressed well the sentiments of his regiment during these early autumn days. On October 1, from Centreville, he wrote: "In fact, the whole country, in our rear, front, and flanks is full of guerrillas. These chaps murder, steal, and disperse." A week later, from Fairfax Court House: "Here we are surrounded by the enemy. He makes frequent dashes here and there, surprising, capturing, and destroying. . . . They fight with desperation when attacked, but principally confine themselves to dashes here and there, and long pursuits of small bodies of our forces. The night does not know what the morning may disclose." Finally, on the eighteenth, Gansevoort, a twenty-seven-year-old former attorney, added: "The country is so thickly wooded, and the inhabitants so rebellious, that the enemy is exceedingly audacious."[21]

No matter how the Union cavalry responded, the Rangers frustrated their efforts. The Yankees were engaged in warfare with shadows and, as Gansevoort asserted, the darkness of night brought the unknown. The duty wore away men and horseflesh. They could kill, wound and capture their nemeses, arrest civilians and burn buildings, but always the gray-clad partisans returned. And the work continued.

Mounted patrols rode forth daily; companies guarded supply trains; heavy picket details rimmed the camps at night. The grinding tasks yielded small rewards—eight more Rangers fell into Yankee hands during the last days of October and the first two weeks of November. Reports came in of Ranger attacks on wagon trains near Gainesville and outside of Warrenton, but neither strike harvested much for the Confederates. Yankee cavalrymen, for instance, foiled

Mosby's plans to burn the wagons at Gainesville by their swift response to the gunfire. "Mosby's cake was all dough," boasted a
trooper.[22]

Ranger operations, in fact, abated throughout much of November. Mosby "has been very quiet of late & I hope he will continue
to," wrote Major Caspar Crowninshield of the 2nd Massachusetts
Cavalry on the ninth, "as it is very cold sleeping out with only an
overcoat on now." The reasons for the inactivity by the partisans
remain unclear. Lee's and Meade's armies had returned to the line of
the Rappahannock River, which reopened the Federal rear to forays
by the Rangers. While strong detachments protected the railroad,
wagons still rumbled southward toward Meade's camps. But the
Rangers, as noted above, hit only twice, and then without much
success.[23]

The Federals, by contrast, intensified their counteroperations
against Mosby's command. Overall direction of the campaign since
October had been under the authority of Major General Christopher
C. Augur, commander of the Department of Washington. Augur
was forty-two years old, a West Pointer and regular army officer
who had risen through brigade, division and corps command until
his appointment to the department. He retained the post until the
war's conclusion, and much of his attention focused on the Rangers.[24]

Shortly after he assumed command of the capital's defenses, Augur concocted a scheme for the capture of Mosby. He hired a detective, a man named Pardon Worsely, who posing as a sutler would
stray into Upper Fauquier and allow himself to be seized by the
guerrillas. Worsely, Augur believed, could gain the confidence of
Mosby by offering to trade merchandise and thus relay intelligence
to the Federals who could ambush the partisans. It was a harebrained
plan, conceived by a general new to the duty.[25]

Worsely and a female companion or "wife" soon came with the
wagon of trade goods. When some Rangers snared the easy target,
Worsely asked to be taken to Mosby. At the meeting, the bogus sutler
offered to supply the partisans with wares at fair prices. Mosby agreed
to the arrangement but never trusted the Yankee peddler. Worsely,
however, discovered that he had a prime market for Northern merchandise, and for weeks he traveled back and forth, dealing with the
Rangers. When Augur finally realized that he had been flimflammed
by Worsely, he had the detective arrested. Ranger John Munson recalled that he purchased for twenty dollars a big doll baby from

Worsely and, when he took it with him on a furlough to Richmond, the doll caused a mild sensation among the residents as it was the first such new toy in the capital since the war began.[26]

The department commander also adopted standard tactics against the partisans, ordering Lowell's horsemen on sweeps into the region. On November 20, Lowell, who had recently returned to duty with his bride, sent his old regiment, the 2nd Massachusetts Cavalry, and the 16th New York Cavalry to the Middleburg-Upperville area. The Bay Staters, according to Crowninshield, had had enough of their former commander and, said the major, "everyone prays that he may be made a Brigadier Gen. so that we may get rid of him." Crowninshield admitted that Lowell was "the most brilliant young man I have ever met with and he is as brave a little fellow as ever lived," but the brigade commander was "hasty, inconsiderate and has not very good judgement." Lowell, thought Crowninshield, was not "much of a soldier."[27]

These views Crowninshield confided to his mother and, like a good soldier, obeyed the orders of his superior. If the Bay Staters so thoroughly disliked Lowell and prayed for his promotion, it seemed not to affect their performance. For three days, from the twentieth to the twenty-second, two regiments combed the countryside between Aldie and Paris. The Yankees were guided by Charles Binns, a Ranger, who while drunk had "committed some acts of rascality for which Mosby ordered his arrest." Binns fled to Union lines and swore revenge. With Binns pointing out farmhouses that sheltered his former comrades, the Northerners rounded up twenty partisans. The Federals "had on the whole rather a good time," said Crowninshield, who complained only of the cold nights.[28]

The incursion might have garnered more Rangers had Mosby not taken seventy-five men with him on a raid against the Orange and Alexandria Railroad. Meeting at The Plains, the Rebels started at sunset on the twentieth, the same day the Yankees entered Fauquier. Jeb Stuart evidently suggested such a foray, as he sent one of his best scouts, Captain Frank Stringfellow, to accompany Mosby. With Brigadier General David McM. Gregg's cavalry division occupying Warrenton, Stringfellow led the partisans around the town, halting them for the night in a stand of timber. The Southerners, returning to the saddle at daybreak, proceeded to Bealeton Station, a railroad stop nine miles southeast of Warrenton. Mosby hid them in some woods and waited for a target.[29]

The weather was miserable, a cold autumn rain fell in torrents. The Rebels huddled beneath the barren limbs, watching the activity in a cavalry camp and an infantry camp pitched around the depot. The Yankee horsemen, the 1st Rhode Island Cavalry, erected a barricade of logs around their campsite, and at nightfall stretched telegraph wire across the entrance. Shortly after noon five wagons, escorted by thirty cavalrymen, approached the concealed Rangers. Mosby split the command in two, instructing Billy Smith and Company B to charge the rear while William Turner and Company A knifed into the front. Both companies, however, stormed from the woods at nearly the same point. The Federal troopers bolted at the sight of the oncoming Rebels and abandoned the wagons, which were laden with valuable medical supplies. Some of the Rangers chased the enemy until they reached an infantry picket line. But, with the alarm sounded, Mosby extricated his men, a few of whom gathered some of the stores before they rode away.[30]

The Confederates dispersed into smaller parties, with the majority of the men crossing the Bull Run Mountains and disbanding at Salem. Stringfellow, Adolphus E. "Dolly" Richards and Ludwell Knapp rode together, stopping for the night at the home of James K. Skinker, located six miles from Warrenton on the road to The Plains. The guests had finished their meal when they heard the hoofbeats of a mounted party. The Yankee pursuers shouted for the surrender of the men inside and, when no response came forth, they opened fire through the windows and doors. Inside, the terrified family cowered under cover; Templeton and Knapp scurried upstairs and concealed themselves under some loose floorboards in the attic. Richards, however, stumbled and fell on the stairs and, by the time he reached the upper level, the enemy was inside the house.[31]

Dolly Richards was as fearless and combative a man as any who rode with Mosby. He was not about to give it up without a fight. With both Colts in his hands, he leaped from a second story window into the yard. He began firing at once, driving two Federals to shelter, and sprinted away under a storm of gunfire. Richards walked a few miles, stopped at another farmhouse, where he borrowed a mount, and rode back toward Skinker's. When he found his pursuers for a second time, he duelled with them for a few minutes and finally spurred away. It was just a beginning for Dolly Richards.[32]

Stringfellow and Knapp escaped detection and rejoined their comrades the next day. Mosby, upon his return, learned of the treachery of Binns and the loss of twenty followers. Whether he admitted it or not, he had come up short. The command had not much to show for the month's operations, while the Federals continued to bleed the ranks with the captives.

Mosby had the Rangers in motion again four days later, on Thursday, November 26. Roughly 125 men reported for a rendezvous at Rectortown. Scouts had informed Mosby that Meade's army was marching across the Rappahannock against Lee's lines south of the river. (Meade's movement initiated the so-called Mine Run Campaign, which lasted six days and accomplished little.) Mosby, in turn, decided upon another strike on the railroad.[33]

Mosby pushed the column, and by late afternoon the Confederates reined up before Brandy Station, the site of the cavalry battle of the previous June. A park of white canvas–topped wagons covered a field beside the station. Nearby, clusters of infantrymen warmed themselves around fires, their rifles and ammunition belts stacked. Mosby waited until nightfall and then led his men into the rows of wagons. The Rangers persuaded the black teamsters to unhitch the teams at gunpoint. When the drivers finished, the partisans torched the vehicles. The flames brought the foot soldiers spilling out of their bivouacs and into ranks. As the Rangers galloped away, the infantrymen unleashed a volley. One bullet struck Mosby's horse, and another grazed the thigh of a Ranger. En route back, they captured a scouting detail of a dozen Yankee horsemen.[34]

The strength of the raiding party—125 men—indicated that Mosby had planned an attack on a railroad train but settled for the destruction of the wagons. The number also indicated that despite the losses incurred during the months of October and November— the Federals had captured approximately forty Rangers—recruits still flocked to the command. In fact, because of the enlistments, Mosby formed a third company.

The Rangers gathered at Rectortown on December 7. Mosby conducted the organizational meeting as he had the previous two—he presented a list of officers, allowed no further nominations and ordered a vote. The new members were also issued printed certificates of membership signed by Mosby. He had given members of Companies A and B their certificates weeks earlier, after he learned that Confederate deserters were passing themselves off as Rangers.[35]

Mosby selected William H. Chapman for the captaincy of the

company. Chapman was twenty-three years old, a native of Page
County, Virginia, and a former student at the University of Virginia.
When the war began, he enlisted as a lieutenant in an artillery battery,
was promoted to captain in December 1861 and commanded the unit
until its disbandment in October 1862. He then served as a conscript
officer in Fauquier until he and his brother, Samuel, joined Mosby
in the early days of the command.[36]

Chapman was a tall, darkly complexioned man, with black eyes
and black hair. The mother of a Ranger came to know Chapman and
said of him: "It seemed to me he knew everything." His previous
experience as a battery commander demonstrated his capacity for
leadership. And with his courage and intelligence, it was only a matter
of time before Mosby gave him authority and responsibility. Chapman was destined for more.[37]

Chapman's first lieutenant was Dolly Richards. Like his superior,
Richards was a native Virginian, a former college student and had
previous service. He had ridden with Turner Ashby's cavalry, rising
in rank from private to lieutenant, and had served on the staff of
William E. "Grumble" Jones until he apparently resigned his commission and volunteered for duty with Mosby. Richards had barely
turned nineteen years old when he became a partisan in May or June
1863.[38]

Dolly Richards impressed everyone who crossed his path. He
stood five feet, ten inches, tall, had a dark complexion—"swarthy-
looking," said a Yankee—and blue eyes. Comrades who saw him in
combat described him as "fearless," "self-possessed" and "active."
He had a sagacity that belied his age and a coolness in tight spots that
made him a deadly opponent. His one-man fight at the Skinker farmhouse perhaps had finally convinced Mosby that such a man deserved
a leadership post.[39]

He was also one of the command's "dandies." He possessed "ex-
quisite taste," a Ranger claimed. "His uniform was of the most unex-
ceptionable finish; his hat and feather were the most stylish in the
command." Richards stayed at his family's farm, "Green Garden,"
located two miles north of Upperville. Once, while he was at home
in the beautiful brick house which graced the crown of a knoll, a
Federal raiding party visited. While he hid under a trapdoor, the
Northerners found his uniform and took it with them. When the
troopers departed, he collected a few men and tracked the Yankees.
He overtook them at Paris, led the charge and, routing them, re-

covered his uniform. Dolly Richards was not a man to be fooled with.[40]

The second and third lieutenants of Company C were Frank Fox and Frank Yager, respectively. Fox resided in Fairfax County, enlisting as a Ranger in the spring of 1863. Yager, like the Chapman brothers, was a native of Page County, twenty-six years old in 1863, but without prior military service. Neither Yager nor Fox was cut from the same bolt of cloth as Chapman and Richards.[41]

Within a few days after the formation of Company C, Mosby held a rendezvous for the purpose of undertaking yet another raid against the Orange and Alexandria Railroad. While he had forced Meade and Augur to detail units for guard duty along the tracks, caused the fortification of stations and increased the frequency and strength of mounted patrols, Mosby had neither damaged the rail line nor disrupted the flow of the trains laden with supplies for Meade's army. The Ranger campaign, in most respects, had failed. The partisans possessed neither the strength nor the artillery to cripple seriously Meade's logistical tether. Although Stuart characterized Mosby's command as "ever vigilant, ever alert" during these days, the fact remained that the Rangers had not fulfilled Lee's wishes.[42]

The target of the operation was again Brandy Station and, once again, Mosby came away with little to show for it. The Rangers once more skirted Warrenton as Gregg's cavalry division remained posted in and around the village and halted near the depot. During the night and for most of the following day Mosby and others scouted the campsite, grabbing four luckless Yankees. On the second night a detachment of Rangers penetrated into the camp and hauled off a dozen Federals with their horses and gear. That was the extent of the seizures, and Mosby led them homeward. As they rode westward the weather turned bitterly cold.[43]

The frigid temperatures heralded a fortnight of early winter weather which lasted until the end of the month. It was a miserable mix—snow fell, followed by days of sunshine which thawed the white blanket, followed by nights of freezing temperatures which iced the ground. Travel on horseback was dangerous for both men and mounts, and military activity slowed. The Rangers enjoyed themselves before the fireplaces of their hosts. Their scouts still roamed daily, but Yankee detachments seldom appeared.[44]

Numbers of Rangers, including Mosby, gathered in Salem on Christmas Day. The festivities were hosted by Mrs. Jane Murray and a Dr. Bispham at their respective homes. Such activities did not pass unnoticed, and a spy or a civilian reported the parties to Union officers in Warrenton. Detachments from the 1st New Jersey and 3rd Pennsylvania Cavalry, with orders to disrupt the "frolic," rode forth. Ranger scouts, however, detected the Yankee column long before it arrived at the village, and their comrades scurried away, except for D. Grafton Carlisle and John W. Davis. This pair tarried for some reason and, when the Union cavalrymen entered Salem, it was too late for Carlisle and Davis. The Northerners searched the Murray and Bispham residences, found only the owners and their families, and departed.[45]

Mosby, ironically, rejected a similar foray by his own men. A female acquaintance of Ranger Richard Montjoy had informed him that officers of Gregg's division were preparing for a Christmas gala at the Warren Green Hotel. Members of the 8th Illinois Cavalry had decorated the hostelry, the community's finest, with holly, berries and hothouse roses. Regimental and national flags, unfurled, draped from the walls. It was to be a celebration befitting officers. And, in its small, symbolic way, it was a celebration that contrasted the wealth of the Union with the poverty of the Confederacy. No similar party was held in Warrenton on that day. So, too, in such disparity could the outcome of a war be measured.[46]

Before year's end Lowell's troopers came once more to southern Loudoun and Upper Fauquier. The Yankees belonged to the 2nd Massachusetts Cavalry, and they followed their favored route through Aldie and Middleburg. The horsemen nabbed four Rangers in the Middleburg area. These captives brought the total to roughly eighty-five of Mosby's men who fell into Union hands since August when Lowell's brigade began counteroperations against the Rangers. Other Federal units bagged some of those, but Lowell's men had garnered the majority.[47]

The Massachusetts regiment reported the capture of ten guerrillas, but the records list only four. The other six prisoners most likely were civilians, suspected of giving aid to the Rangers. Time and again, when the Federal cavalrymen came on a raid, they hauled away with them male citizens of the region. While Mosby's men could protect the populace, they could not shield them. The burning of a house and two barns in October was to be but a harbinger of a hard war made harder for those who lived in what became known as "Mosby's Confederacy." The residents' support sustained the Rangers but, as the war lengthened, the Virginians paid a dear price for such loyalty.

Chapter 7

LIFE
IN
MOSBY'S
CONFEDERACY

 Major General Henry Wager Halleck sat at the top of the Union military hierarchy in the fall of 1863. Since July 1862, when Abraham Lincoln had brought him from the Department of the Missouri to serve as general-in-chief, Halleck had overseen the Federal war effort from the capital. His responsibility encompassed departments and armies from the Mississippi River to the defenses of Washington. A man of demonstrated administrative ability and intellectual capacity, "Old Brains" Halleck, as he was dubbed, gave advice, issued orders and relayed the plans and ideas of the administration to officers in the field. Few matters pertinent to the conduct of the struggle did not pass across his desk.

From Halleck's office a stream of telegrams and letters went forth, containing his opinions and instructions on matters as diverse as the formulation of grand strategy for a campaign to the dispositions of units in the field. His concerns stretched from the capture of Vicksburg, Mississippi, the pursuit of Lee's army after Gettysburg and to the counteroperations against Mosby's Rangers. On this latter subject, Halleck had reached the limits of tolerance.

"Most of the difficulties are caused," Halleck asserted in an analysis of the success of Mosby's unit in a letter of October 28, 1863, "by the conduct of the pretended non-combatant inhabitants of the country. They pretend to act the part of neutrals, but do not. They give aid, shelter and concealment to guerrilla and robber bands like that of Mosby. . . . If these men carried on a legitimate warfare no complaint would be made." To Halleck, the supporters of the Rangers "forfeited their lives" by their actions when captured within Union lines. Halleck understood, as he added, why Yankee troopers "shoot them down when they can."[1]

Halleck was not alone in his assessment; it could be found among the rank and file of Union regiments who tangled with the Rangers and rode into Fauquier and Loudoun counties. "The feeling against the citizens of the surrounding countryside was very bitter," remarked a trooper of the 10th New York Cavalry. "It was generally believed that they were privy to the frequent murder of Union soldiers, if they were not the actual perpetrator of the crimes." An officer of the 1st Massachusetts Cavalry, in a similar vein, admitted that his outfit "can do nothing against this furtive population, soldiers to-day, farmers tomorrow, acquainted with every wood path, and finding friends in every house." The Bay Stater thought that the only solution was to "clear this county with fire and sword, and no mortal can do it in any way."[2]

This antipathy toward the civilian supporters of Mosby thus pervaded the Union chain of command, from the general-in-chief to the trooper in the saddle. The Northerners correctly understood that without the active cooperation of the residents of Fauquier and Loudoun the Rangers could not have continued in existence for a long time. When Mosby came to that section of Virginia, he made his mission theirs and gave shape to the people's lives for over two years. In no other region of the Old Dominion—and for that matter throughout much of the Confederacy—did the war take the character it did as in the region known as "Mosby's Confederacy." The story of Mosby's Rangers was, in the end, a shared saga.

Mosby's Confederacy, by some accounts, embraced the counties of Fauquier, Loudoun, Fairfax and Prince William. While the Rangers prowled constantly throughout the four counties and found friends, food and shelter in numerous houses, the heart of the "Confederacy" covered a smaller swath of the region. Mosby during the summer of 1864 actually prescribed the boundaries of his domain, confining his men within the limits. The "Confederacy," by Mosby's delineation, was a large triangle which began in the northwest at Snickersville at the eastern foot of Snicker's Gap in the Blue Ridge, ran southward along the mountains to Linden at the mouth of Manassas Gap, then turned eastward through Upper Fauquier to The Plains, along the Bull Run Mountains to Aldie, where its final side followed the Snicker's Gap Turnpike to Snickersville. The Confederacy encompassed roughly 125 square miles of land.[3]

When Mosby first began his operations in 1863 from the "Confederacy," the region was marked by its natural and man-made beauty and the intense devotion of the populace to the Southern cause. Even the Yankees admitted that nature favored this section of the Old Dominion. Union Major General John Sedgwick in the autumn of 1863 described it simply as "a beautiful country." Trooper Fred Corselius, a member of the 6th Michigan Cavalry, after passing through the area on a reconnaissance to Ashby's Gap in June 1863, remarked that "there were fine houses & farms & pretty villages & all the evidences of an abundant population." In such a region, Corselius believed, he and his comrades "will not starve."[4]

What also struck the Yankees whose duty brought them into the Confederacy was the hostility of the residents to them. Diarist Amanda "Tee" Edmonds called the enemy "black Devils," and she was not alone in such belief. Wherever the Federals roamed throughout the region, they found the locals to be, as a member of the 1st Pennsylvania Cavalry said, "nearly all secesh." "Every farmhouse in this section," a Massachusetts cavalryman claimed, "was a refuge for guerrillas, and every farmer was an *ally* of Mosby, and every farmer's son was with *him* or in the Confederate army."[5]

The people, according to a Confederate, "believed implicitly" in Mosby. The trust, the support were underlaid with the personal stakes many of the people had in the success and safety of the Rangers; or, as a young woman wrote, "We all had brothers cousins & lovers with Mosby, & each one thought of her own loved one" when they heard the gunshots and fighting nearby. The bond between the inhabitants and the Rangers went deep. If the residents did not have kinfolk in the command, many knew them personally, shared their food with them or concealed them from the "black Devils."[6]

The partisans, in turn, had an open door in all but a few of the homes throughout the Confederacy. "[There were] Few indeed, even among the poorest mountaineers," stated James Williamson, "who would refuse shelter and food to Mosby's Rangers." A Yankee, Joseph Schubert of the 1st New Jersey Cavalry, saw such hospitality firsthand. While a prisoner, Schubert and his captors stopped at a house for breakfast, for which Mosby paid twenty-five cents per man. "I think he had regular places to stop," Schubert wrote afterwards, "they all knew who he was and they would give him All the information about our men."[7]

Each Ranger, as noted previously, boarded with civilian families. Those who were native to the region stayed at their own homes as frequently as prudence and safety permitted. The nonnatives resided where they were welcomed and, as one of them said, lived "as a member of the family." While villages such as Salem, Rectortown, The Plains, Rector's Cross Roads, Aldie, Middleburg, Upperville, Paris and Markham served as rendezvous sites and offered entertainment and food for the young warriors, the Rangers generally chose the isolated farmhouses encircling the towns for their boarding places. The homes of farmers and planters offered remoteness, shelter and fodder for their mounts and an open countryside through which a Federal raiding party must approach.[8]

While any dwelling within the region could have had one or a handful of Rangers within, the majority of the command's members resided in the section which ran from Paris, through Upperville, Piedmont, Rectortown, Salem and The Plains to Middleburg. These villages and surrounding farms comprised the heart of Upper Fauquier and the center of "Mosby's Confederacy." The network of roads and obscure country paths coursing through this confined area linked each Ranger to his comrades and shortened the length of time required for the gathering of men for a raid or an emergency.

"Safe houses," as the Rangers called them, dotted the land outside these villages. The partisans could stop at the home of George Short, or James L. Adams, or William Hopper, or Samuel Craig, or Edwin Broun, or George McArty, or Widow Rutter, or Benjamin Shacklett or William Fletcher and find a meal, a bed or a friendly welcome.

Still, with so many houses open to them, Mosby and his men had favorite "safe houses," places where they were nearly in constant residence throughout the existence of the command. These selected homes belonged, in most cases, to the landed gentry of the region.[9]

The area outside of Paris offered the Rangers stately homes and a nearness to the concealing swales of the Blue Ridge Mountains. Paris, nestling at the foot of Ashby's Gap, was not much of a town— "a very forlorn village," to a Southerner and a "dirty little village" to a Northerner—consisting of approximately twenty houses, three stores and a hotel. Benjamin Adams owned the hotel, located at the eastern edge of the town, and he often entertained Rangers, who rode in at night from their nearby boarding places.[10]

Three houses lying south of Paris along the road to Markham were frequented by Rangers on an almost daily basis. "Belle Grove," the home of Betsey Edmonds and her daughter Amanda "Tee" and son Clement, was an imposing three-story house, located two miles south of Paris. Within sight of "Belle Grove," on a high knoll was "Mount Bleak," the residence of Abner and Mary Settle, brother and sister-in-law of Betsey Edmonds. "Mount Bleak"—today, Sky Meadows State Nature Park—was a beautiful stone house, with a clapboard wing. The Rangers built a signal station near "Mount Bleak" as the high ground offered a commanding view for miles in three directions. Farther down the road were the homes of Benjamin Triplett, called "Hill-and-Dale," and of Jamieson Ashby, where Mosby and his closest companions regularly visited.[11]

Several houses served as refuges for Rangers in the Upperville area. Five of the hosts had sons in Mosby's companies—Daniel Kerfoot, Benjamin Chappelair, Robert Bolling, Thomas Glascock of "Rose Hill" and Jesse Richards of "Green Garden." All were men of substance and personal wealth whose homes were some of the finest in the region. Also nearby, close to "Green Garden," was "Ayrshire," the residence of George S. Ayre. Mosby came often to "Ayrshire," which graced a knoll two miles northwest of Upperville.[12]

South of Upperville, a mile or so north of Piedmont was "Heartland," the home of Joseph Blackwell. Here with increasing frequency Mosby spent his time, until by late 1863 or early 1864 his men designated it "Mosby's Headquarters." Compared to other houses in the region, "Heartland" was small with only five rooms in the dwelling. The frame house, however, sat on the peak of a high hill, offering the inhabitants a commanding view of the surrounding countryside.

"Heartland" stood back from the road which ran between Upperville and Piedmont, giving additional seclusion from roaming Federal parties.[13]

The owner of "Heartland," Joseph Blackwell, became a favorite of Mosby and of a number of Rangers. Forty-three years old when Mosby met him, Blackwell was a squat, "very corpulent" man, who acquired the nickname "Chief" from his young boarders. John Munson and Johnny Edmonds, Blackwell's brother-in-law, bunked at "Heartland," and Munson recalled the friendliness of the family and the good meals served by Lucy Blackwell. The "Chief" badgered Mosby, according to Munson, to give him a uniform and the opportunity to participate in a raid. One operation into Maryland cured Blackwell of his martial dreams, however, and he never rode again with the Rangers. Despite this experience, Blackwell, wrote Munson, "wanted to command us." Mosby most likely laughed at the suggestion and ignored the pomposity of his host. Mosby enjoyed the man's company.[14]

The location of "Heartland" perhaps contributed in part to Mosby's selection of it as his headquarters. It lay roughly at a midway point. From Blackwell's Mosby could scan miles of territory. To the north and west the fields and woods stretched toward Upperville and Paris; to the south and east, Rectortown, then Salem and on to The Plains. Around these latter towns was the greatest concentration of farmhouses and planters' mansions favored by the Rangers.

Rectortown and Salem were the largest and most prosperous communities in Upper Fauquier. The Manassas Gap Railroad, coming westward from Manassas Junction, Gainesville and The Plains, passed through both on its route toward the Shenandoah Valley. Rectortown, about the size of Paris, benefited from the rail traffic, with Alfred Rector's warehouse the village's leading business. Salem, situated between Rectortown and The Plains, contained a population of about 300 residents, forty homes, five stores and an academy. The homes, the businesses, the churches of Salem lined its half-mile-long main street.[15]

The Rangers were a common sight in Rectortown, Salem and The Plains. They bought and traded merchandise, visited friends and kinfolk, found meals and held parties like the 1863 Christmas gathering in Salem. Mosby, on one occasion, was enjoying a supper at the home of A. J. Sampsell in Rectortown when a detachment of Union horsemen clattered into the village. Mosby quickly changed from his uniform into worn clothes while his host, sneaking outside, concealed the uniform under a big rock. The partisan officer eluded the Yankees and later secured his uniform.[16]

"Safe houses" encircled the three villages. In the Rectortown area, the Rangers found lodging at several preferred houses. Northeast of the town Ludwell Lake at "Lakeland" and Aquilla Glascock at "Rockburn" welcomed Rangers day or night. Both men had sons in the guerrilla command. Fire destroyed "Rockburn" in 1864 when the chimney overheated, and the Glascocks lived in a small house along nearby Goose Creek while their house underwent reconstruction.[17]

Southwest of "Lakeland" and "Rockburn" were the residences of two Rawlings families. "Flint Hill," owned by John Rawlings, served as the home of Rangers Phil Davis, Corbin Mercer and one named Gault. Rawlings's young son acted as a messenger for Mosby. Not far from "Flint Hill" was "Rawlingsdale," the home of John Douglas Rawlings. Mosby stopped often at "Rawlingsdale" to race captured horses against the farm's thoroughbreds. John Douglas Rawlings reportedly owned the fastest horses in the region, and Mosby and his men enjoyed the competition.[18]

The countryside outside of Salem held a similar number of dwellings frequented by the partisans. South of the town were W. Morgan's "Clover Hill" and J. A. Washington's "Waveland," a brick house which rested on the crest of a towering knoll. To the east lay "Meadow Grove," owned by a Mrs. Carter, and "Gardensdale," owned by Dr. R. E. Peyton. And to the north were Mrs. Ella Buckner Smith's "Ellerslie" and Richard Carter's "Glen Welby."[19]

"Glen Welby" was one of the most imposing mansions in the "Confederacy." Its owner was one of the region's wealthiest men, whose personal and property holdings were assessed at nearly $134,000 in 1860. "Glen Welby" reflected Carter's financial ranking, and Mosby stayed often with the family, using it as another headquarters. Carter was a neighbor of James Hathaway of "Western View" and, perhaps after his narrow escape at Hathaway's, Mosby spent more time at "Glen Welby." Regardless, Mosby seemed to enjoy the hospitality of "Glen Welby" more than any other place except Joseph Blackwell's "Heartland."[20]

"Avenel," located a few miles east of The Plains, rivaled "Glen Welby" in its beauty and substance. Owned by Robert Beverley, "Avenel" was a stately frame house with a stone wing. Mosby stopped there and Rangers boarded there; even Robert E. Lee, when operations brought him to the region, visited. The Beverleys were generous, gracious hosts, and "Avenel" and James Skinker's "Huntley," where Dolly Richards had fought his way out, were the favorite stopovers of the Rangers in The Plains area.[21]

From Paris to The Plains, from "Mount Bleak" to "Avenel," the Rangers found safety among loyal friends and relatives. Without these havens, without that loyalty and aid, the command could not have functioned as it did. The people's assistance was multifaceted and indispensable to the success of the partisans' mission.

Each "safe house," for example, possessed a hiding place for the Rangers. Mosby's men called them "*secret closets,*" and they varied from an underground passageway leading to the outside to a false wall panel in a room. When the cry "Yankees coming" was heard, the Rangers scrambled for one of the secret closets. Dolly Richards and companions hid between two walls at his father's house. At "Belle Grove," the Confederates crawled through a trapdoor in a closet which led to a three-foot-high cellar underneath the dining room floor. Eva Broun's house near Upperville had a trapdoor which opened into a cellar. At "Glen Welby," a Ranger could squeeze into the top of a "monstrous wardrobe," enter a trapdoor in the library floor, or crawl through a garret on to the tin roof and then slide down to the ground. Mosby allegedly used the latter route on one occasion. The residents concealed the trapdoors or loosened floorboards under carpets or oilcloths.[22]

If the alarm of "Yankees coming" had been given before the Federals appeared, the Rangers sprinted from the houses and galloped away. They and their hosts knew that if the Confederates were discovered at a residence, the owners faced incarceration and reprisal. The local folk consequently were always on alert, serving as a vast warning and intelligence network for the Rangers. Nearly every house in the region held either a spy or a messenger for the guerrilla command.

The network functioned at all times, day and night. The sightings of Federal units or rumors of the approach of Northerners—which one citizen groused were as "plenty as blackberries"—spurred the network into operation. A light placed in a certain window at night could be a signal; a woman waving a shawl or colorful garment could be another. A small boy, like the son of John Rawlings, walking or running across fields, aroused little suspicion. It was a web, seamless and unobtrusive, that ensnared any Yankee force that entered among its strands.[23]

Information garnered by the civilians about Union operations proved as invaluable to Mosby as the warning system. The tentacles of informants or spies extended well beyond the Confederacy into Lower Fauquier, Prince William, Loudoun and Fairfax counties and beyond the Blue Ridge into the lower or northern Shenandoah Valley. "Nothing could transpire in Warrenton during the day," wrote Ranger J. Marshall Crawford, "which we would not know at headquarters before twelve o'clock the same night."[24]

Crawford's assertion about informants in Warrenton held true for nearly any town within less than a day's ride from the Confederacy. Older men living in the villages were a rich source of intelligence for the Rangers. In Fairfax County, for instance, a local minister, Ovid A. Kinsolving, spied for Mosby, and Ben Halton, who sold goods in Union camps, forwarded information to the Rangers. In Berryville in the Shenandoah Valley, a physician served as the contact for Mosby's men. If a Ranger saw a light through the shutters of a window, he ran his riding whip or pistol across the slots, and the doctor came outside, relaying the information.[25]

The most reliable informants for Mosby, perhaps, were young women, who by their flirtations and cajolery extracted plans from Union officers. Mosby based a number of his raids on the intelligence supplied by them. Warrenton, a community "famous for its pretty girls," according to a Federal officer, had several Ranger spies, including Roberta Pollock and Annie Lucas, fiancée of Ranger Richard P. Montjoy. Miss Lucas kept her betrothed informed by relaying notes into the Confederacy. Miss Pollock, however, in the winter of 1864 overheard Yankees planning a surprise raid into the Confederacy. Returning to her home, she and a servant saddled two horses and rode forth into the night. The pair lost their way in the darkness, and a Ranger picket nearly shot them. But she succeeded and sounded the alarm.[26]

Another trusted feminine source for Mosby lived in Frying Pan in Fairfax County. Jeb Stuart introduced Laura Ratcliffe to Mosby in December 1862. Miss Ratcliffe, described as "a rather striking brunette," had supplied Stuart with information, and when Mosby began his partisan career, he contacted her. Within days she warned him of a Federal ambush prepared for the guerrillas at Frying Pan Baptist

Church, a small frame building with a circular pulpit north of Chan-tilly. (The church's odd name resulted from the first settlers' discovery of an old frying pan, discarded by Indians, on the site.) From that time onward Mosby utilized the intelligence she forwarded. The pair often communicated by placing letters under a large stone, dubbed "Mosby's Rock," near her home. Mosby's Rock became so familiar to the Rangers that Mosby used it as a rendezvous point when the raiders were in Fairfax County.[27]

The relationship between the residents of the Confederacy and the Rangers, however, extended well beyond the trapdoors, the sig-nals, the exchanged notes and the midnight rides. War, the people discovered, came with many faces.

To "Tee" Edmonds and the single young women like her, war had the look of romance, of strolls under a moonlit sky with dashing, handsome warriors. The nature of the circumstances—eligible, youthful men, who rode forth to risk their lives for a cause and who boarded with families who had daughters—fostered inevitable court-ships and flirtations. The Rangers were "charmers," in the admission of John Alexander, but he added that "indeed, they were just as much sinned against as sinning in this regard."[28]

"Tee" Edmonds's diary is a chronicle of the "sinning" between Mosby's men and the ladies. She wrote of card games, of "eating grapes, peaches, flirting," of real and imagined engagements, of lone-liness when Rangers were on a raid, of evenings spent with music and apple toddies, of dances, of "monkey doings," of tête-à-têtes, of a handsome Mississippian, Matthew Magner, with whom she became infatuated. Under the date of September 15, 1863, she confided: "I have become perfectly devoted to the society of the Rebels, too much so for my own happiness and too indifferent to females. Why should I not love them for their heroic valor and fortitude and some very pleasant, agreeable and fine company. I can look back when the war is over and recall some of the happiest moments of my life—yes, even amid the terrible war with all its sorrow and grief. I have spent many happy days full of change, variety and romance—excitement is the thing that suits my fancy."[29]

For all those times she had at "Belle Grove," such moments and "excitement" were found at numerous other houses. Friendships deepened into courtships; courtships into marriages. Several Rangers found their brides in the area. Not all of the relationships went smoothly, however. In late 1864, after the so-called "Greenback Raid" when the Rangers were flush with money, two of them ordered engagement rings from the North. When the rings arrived, they made their proposals of marriage. The young lady accepted both offers, and wore two identical rings on her finger. As for "Tee" Edmonds, her Mississippian returned home after the war, and she married another.[30]

The Rangers seemed to have been models of decorum with the women. John Scott argued that they were restrained by the "discipline of society." John Alexander believed that a Ranger's "standing and deportment as a soldier were public property," and each man's "sensitiveness to what those among whom he lived thought of him" resulted in a high *esprit de corps* among the partisans and in gentlemanly behavior. Mosby, asserted Alexander, used this "sensitiveness" to report a man's performance where it "would do the most good." Mosby, likewise, countenanced no breaches of proper conduct and, if he learned of a violation, he either reprimanded the offender or returned him to the regular army. The certainty and swiftness of Mosby's justice in such matters most likely chilled the ardor of a number of men. If serious transgressions occurred, the records, the memoirs, the diaries are mute.[31]

Mosby's authority in the Confederacy, in fact, embraced more than the 43rd Battalion. For two years he enforced the civil law in Upper Fauquier and southern Loudoun. The conflict had destroyed the governments and court systems of the counties and Mosby, with his training in law, stepped into the void in this section of the two counties. He regarded his powers as a "trust," according to Scott, with the Rangers performing the "duties of police as well as soldiers."[32]

Mosby acted as both judge and jury, a "civil power of unquestioned authority," in the words of one of his men. He ordinarily conducted hearings or a trial at a rendezvous with the men present as witnesses. He settled disputes between neighbors, ruled on complaints filed against his command for confiscation of property, and punished perpetrators of various crimes. He "detested red tape in every form," wrote a Ranger, meting out swift justice which "admitted of no appeal." Mosby's "word was law in that section," a Federal officer claimed, and the Yankee had it right.[33]

When strangers entered the Confederacy, they had to provide to Mosby evidence of their business. He and his men were merciless in their pursuit of horse and cattle thieves. Such thieves were usually deserters and "desperadoes" who operated from hiding places in the Blue Ridge and Bull Run Mountains. They became "a prevalent nuisance," and Mosby published an order which condemned all who were captured to execution. He also sent details of Rangers through the region with instructions to arrest all soldiers not on an approved leave from the army.[34]

The Ranger net also extended to distilleries. Mosby, said James Williamson, "was very active" in the search for and destruction of whiskey stills. While his men probably harbored mixed feelings towards Mosby's campaign against liquor making, he argued that he did so because of the scarcity of grain in the region. Details of Rangers roamed beyond the limits of the "Confederacy," into all of Loudoun and into Lower Fauquier in the hunt for distilleries.[35]

Mosby's exercise of military and civil power received the approval of the vast majority of the residents. He operated with fairness, and the Rangers protected the civilians from many of the scourges that plagued Southerners in other sections of the country. Edward Marshall of Markham wrote to the Richmond *Examiner* during Mosby's tenure, stating: "Old Fauquier was now under the reign of a king, who heard petitions, settled disputes, and by his justice and legal knowledge gained universal approbation, and that the section of the county had never during the memory of man been so cheaply and ably governed."[36]

While Mosby and the Rangers could protect the local folks, they could not spare them from the hardness of the struggle. The price exacted from the civilians for the support of the partisans was steep, and it increased as the war lengthened. The Civil War, like all major conflicts, generated new standards of acceptable conduct—the old measures were abandoned amid a mounting toll of blood and destruction. The United States slid into an abyss the crevices of which no one had foreseen in 1861. Few areas of the Confederacy were spared from this descent. The hard face of war also came to Mosby's Confederacy.

"It must be admitted," wrote a grandson of the "Glen Welby" Carters, "that many local people suffered from helping him [Mosby] or from being suspected of doing so." He argued that the Federals "were beside themselves with fury" at the audacity and effectiveness of Ranger operations. "In their fury," he concluded about the Northerners, "they wreaked their vengeance on any local citizens they felt to be in league with him."[37]

Evidence of the suffering was present by the summer and fall of 1863. While parts of Fauquier and Loudoun counties bore the scars of campaigns and occupations in the war's first two years, with the arrival of Mosby in early 1863, those wounds spread and were exacerbated. The "desolating hand of war," as a Yankee phrased it, was evident in the region by the summer. Union General John Sedgwick, writing in July 1863, noted that the land "has not been cultivated this year; fences all down, houses deserted." In Lower Fauquier and Warrenton, conditions were "truly deplorable, " said another Yankee, with civilians begging and buying food from the occupiers. The New York *Times* claimed in October that the residents of Fauquier "bordered on starvation."[38]

Within Mosby's Confederacy the situation and the destruction had not reached the proportions evident in Lower Fauquier at this time. But shortages of necessities and isolated cases of burned mills and barns still stalked the region. An ill wind blew across the area in the heat of 1863, a harbinger of darker days ahead.

Accounts conflict as to the extent of deprivation and scarcity of items within the Rangers' base. Some civilians fared better than others, with sufficient food which they shared with the partisans. Others report that they and neighbors subsisted on the barest necessities, lacking tea, coffee, sugar and milk. Nearly all indicated that medicine, clothing and shoes became increasingly difficult to obtain. Women eventually wore dresses made from captured Union cavalry overcoats.[39]

"Our chief circulating medium was 'booty and greenbacks,'" wrote a Ranger. A civilian added that "those who were fortunate enough to have greenbacks or tobacco would succeed in getting things." Mosby's men generously shared their spoils with the families, and those civilians with Federal money could purchase supplies from local merchants or travel to the North, particularly Baltimore, and buy goods. Yankee peddlers appeared occasionally in the region, offering their merchandise for sale. Union army authorities sold supplies to civilians who took an oath of allegiance to the Federal government. Few people in the region accepted the bargain.[40]

In the end, the presence of the Rangers in the region was a double-edged sword. Mosby's men ameliorated some hardships endured by the populace, bringing in booty and money from raids, sharing the surplus with the folk, plowing fields and harvesting crops, and patrolling against the undisciplined guerrillas who infested the mountains. Mosby's court of justice brought order out of disorder. But the constant threat of Federal incursions or occupation disrupted the patterns of life. Adult males feared imprisonment; women bided time in the silence of anxiety; churches stood nearly vacant of Sabbath worshippers.[41]

As 1863 gave way to 1864, the people of Mosby's Confederacy remained steadfast in their loyalty. The winter weather might bring some relief from Yankee raiding parties but, if "Old Mose" kept his men in the saddle and on the move, the "black Devils" were certain to come back. At least one Northern cavalryman, stationed in Warrenton, expected as much. Writing to his sister in Pennsylvania, the trooper stated: "we can spend the winter here very well if Old Moseby does not trouble us too much. We will have to chase him away I suppose every few days that will do to keep us in exercise."[42]

Chapter 8

BLOOD ON THE SNOW

 The winter of 1864 came early to northern Virginia, with the cold temperatures and snow blowing in by mid-December 1863. The arrival heralded weeks of bitter weather. Snow piled up; thermometers plummeted; winds howled. Operations by the major armies all but ceased as the troops huddled in their winter cabins.

The camps of George G. Meade's Army of the Potomac and Robert E. Lee's Army of Northern Virginia sprawled across the countryside north and south of the Rapidan River. The region had been a battleground since the Confederate retreat from Gettysburg in July. Infantry and artillery bivouacs rimmed the stream for miles while cavalry campsites squatted near the flanks. Separated by the Rapidan, the armies' fronts extended from the Piedmont region eastward toward Fredericksburg.

Meade's cavalry units were stationed along the upper Rapidan at Culpeper, Stevensburg, Brandy Station and Warrenton. The horsemen secured the army's right flank and protected the Orange and Alexandria Railroad, the Federal supply line. Despite the harsh weather, patrols and scouts went forth daily, taxing the endurance of men and beasts.[1]

Colonel John P. Taylor's brigade of Brigadier General David McM. Gregg's Second Cavalry Division occupied Warrenton. Taylor's six regiments had the assignment of opposing incursions by Mosby's Rangers. From December 1863 until spring campaigning resumed in April 1864, Taylor's men garrisoned the county seat and carried out counteroperations into "Mosby's Confederacy." In the view of a member of the 3rd Pennsylvania Cavalry the winter's duty against the Confederate partisans was "without doubt the most severe and trying" in his regiment's experience.[2]

Taylor's Federals converted Warrenton into an armed camp. Well manned sentry and picket posts encircled the village. A mile west of town on Water Mountain, the Yankees built a blockhouse and signal station protected by a heavy guard detachment. Buildings were converted to barracks and stables; fences and groves of trees disappeared for firewood. The town was a scene of desolation. By Gregg's order, citizens were confined to the town to prevent them from delivering messages to Mosby. Gregg reported that the residents were impoverished, and were requesting to purchase foodstuffs from the occupiers.[3]

From Warrenton the Union troopers marched into Mosby's Confederacy, combing the region for the guerrillas. Each patrol that rode out contained companies from one or more regiments. Most of the time the Yankees returned empty-handed. Captain Walter S. Newhall, 3rd Pennsylvania Cavalry, called the efforts "fruitless mud-raids." "I know the programme by heart," Newhall wrote home in December. "'Successful attack on wagon-trains; Mosby off with his plunder. Nobody hurt.' That's how it will be."[4]

Trooper Aaron B. Tompkins, 1st New Jersey Cavalry, described one operation by his unit in mid-January. Tompkins informed his mother: "the other day we was out on a scoute to a place that Mosby keepes him self I suppose that you know him fore you see him in the papers we get after him every once and a wile but he has got such good horses that we very seldom get eny of them they have there horses trained so that they can jump over a fence like a deer." He added, however, that the New Jersey men nabbed two guerrillas when their horses failed to leap a fence.[5]

Brief clashes occurred between the Union cavalrymen and the Rangers during the initial days of January. On the third, the 1st Maine and 1st Pennsylvania Cavalry, returning from a reconnaissance beyond the Blue Ridge Mountains, encountered a band of partisans at Salem and scattered them. The historian of the Maine regiment asserted later that they captured nine guerrillas, but the records and reports list none. A day later, Mosby struck back, sending twenty-five men of Company A, under Lieutenant William Thomas Turner, to Warrenton. Snow was a foot deep, and it was freezing cold with a bitter wind. Ranger William Walston lost four fingers to frostbite when he returned. But the conditions fostered surprise, and Turner's men bagged twenty-five prisoners and forty-five horses outside the village.[6]

Another detachment of Rangers, moving in during a snowstorm, attacked the picket post of the 3rd Pennsylvania Cavalry on the Sulphur Springs road on January 7. The Southerners charged about 4:00 A.M, dashing into the rear of the Federal position. The Pennsylvanians lost six wounded, including their captain, and eighteen captured, along with forty-three horses. The snowstorm muffled the sounds of gunfire, and the Rangers escaped without a pursuit force on their tracks.[7]

The attacks of January 4 and 7 indicated that regardless of the ferocity of the winter, the Rangers could be expected at any time. Mosby kept scouts out on a daily basis in order to locate weakness in the ring of Federal picket posts and guard details around Warrenton and along the railroad. His primary target remained the supply line from Washington to Meade's army, so in addition to the assaults on the Warrenton outposts, on most days a second group of Rangers hunted for a train of supply wagons. This method contributed in part to the Federal belief that the Rangers operated with "never ceasing activity" in the foul weather.[8]

Mosby undertook additional precautions in the "Confederacy" by assigning each company to patrol duty in the area. Company A established its sentries along the eastern sector below Middleburg; Company B guarded the northern approaches between Upperville and Bloomfield; and Company C, the southern roads from Salem to The Plains. Each company commander designated details, under the command of a sergeant or corporal, for specific days and nights.[9]

These Ranger sentry posts covered the most likely routes of Federal entry into the region. Mosby implemented this warning system because bad weather frequently kept civilians and their Ranger guests inside their houses. The Confederates were more vulnerable to capture and, without the assistance of the local folks, who could spread the word of a Yankee force in the neighborhood during the other times of the year, the Rangers drew the onerous duty, much like their comrades in the regular cavalry. When the weather was especially miserable, however, the sentries were evidently withdrawn in the belief that the Northerners would not be on the move during such times.[10]

Company B's sector from Upperville to Bloomfield included the main road from Harper's Ferry, where a Federal garrison was located. While a majority of the Union incursions into the Confederacy came from the east and the south out of Washington and Warrenton, troops from Harper's Ferry increased their raids against the Rangers with the advent of cold weather. The Yankees belonged to the 1st Maryland Cavalry, Potomac Home Brigade, known as Cole's Cavalry, after their commander, Major Henry A. Cole.[11]

Cole's Cavalry consisted of four companies recruited from Maryland and the southern tier of Pennsylvania in August 1861. The battalion had spent much of its time patrolling along the Potomac River and in the Shenandoah Valley. During the summer and fall of 1863, Cole's troopers occasionally entered Mosby's Confederacy but did not stay long and were little more than an annoyance to the Rangers. That pattern changed by the end of the year.[12]

The Union battalion operated from a base camp on Loudoun Heights, a partially cleared ridge across the Shenandoah River from Harper's Ferry. The village of Harper's Ferry lay at the bottom of a bowl at the confluence of the Shenandoah and Potomac Rivers. The government had established an armory and arsenal here decades before the Civil War. In October 1859 the abolitionist John Brown had led a small band of followers into town and seized the government buildings. Although Brown was captured, tried and executed, his raid inflamed the crisis which was mounting in the nation. When the war exploded eighteen months later, Harper's Ferry became a vital site for both sides. By January 1864 the Federal garrison in the town and outposts in the lower Shenandoah Valley numbered roughly 8,000 men, protecting the Baltimore & Ohio Railroad and the Chesapeake & Ohio Canal, which passed through the region.[13]

On January 1, 1864, eighty members of Cole's Cavalry, led by Captain A. N. Hunter, scouted into Mosby's Confederacy, passing through Upperville and proceeding toward Rectortown. Captain William R. "Billy" Smith had scheduled a rendezvous at Rectortown as Mosby was away in Fairfax County. When Hunter's party appeared, only a handful of Rangers had arrived for the meeting. They scattered when they saw the Federals, who quickly passed through on the road to Middleburg. Smith, meanwhile, gathered thirty-two men and pursued. Near Five Points, where five roads converged, the Rangers overtook the enemy column. Hunter managed to deploy his men before Smith ordered a charge. The Rangers galloped into the Federal ranks. When Hunter's horse was killed under him, his men panicked and raced toward Middleburg. "It was a regular Gilpin chase" after the Yankees, recalled a Rebel. Smith's men killed, wounded or captured fifty-seven of the Federals and corralled sixty horses.[14]

A week later Mosby was informed that Cole's camp on Loudoun Heights was vulnerable to an attack. The information came from Benjamin Franklin Stringfellow, who had attached himself to Mosby's command during the previous weeks. A native of Culpeper County, Virginia, Stringfellow was a thin blond man, twenty-three years old, who, like Mosby, had become a favorite of Jeb Stuart. He and Mosby, said one of Stuart's staff officers, were "two of the best scouts in either army." Stringfellow had received permission to ride temporarily with Mosby and, when such a reliable scout forwarded information, Mosby had to act.[15]

Mosby ordered a rendezvous, and approximately one hundred Rangers met at Upperville at noon on Saturday, January 9. The column of men rode northwestward through snow one described as "quite deep." The chill of the afternoon indicated that the night was to be intensely cold. About 8:00 P.M. Mosby halted the command at the home of Ranger Henry Heaton in Woodgrove, in Loudoun County. The men ate some food, warmed themselves before the Heaton fireplace and fed their mounts.[16]

They were back in the saddles by ten o'clock, moving almost due north to Hillsborough, where the road from that town led to Cole's camp on Loudoun Heights, which formed the northern end of the Blue Ridge. The pace of the march was slow under a starlit sky and plummeting temperatures. The men rode with the reins between their teeth to keep their hands warm. When their feet started to numb from the freezing temperatures, they dismounted and walked beside their mounts. Many of them probably wore captured Union overcoats over their uniforms, but the heavy garments were not enough. It was an ordeal many did not soon forget.[17]

Beyond Hillsborough, as the Rangers filed down the narrow valley between the Blue Ridge and Short Hill to the east, they met Stringfellow and his small scouting party. Stringfellow outlined for Mosby the layout of the Federal camp, estimating Cole's strength at 300 by the number of tents which sprawled along the foot of Loudoun Heights west of the Hillsborough road. Cole's headquarters were in a house at the northern end or rear of the camp. The Federals had posted pickets on the Hillsborough road where a bridge crossed a small stream, roughly a mile or so south of the campsite. Stringfellow's report provided, in Mosby's words, "exact information," and the Confederate commander was confident of success if the attackers were not detected before the assault.[18]

When the Rangers closed to within a mile of the pickets at the small bridge, Mosby led them off the road to the right into the wooded expanse of Short Hill. The riders shifted into a single file, following a path along the base of the slope. The deep cold still numbed their hands and feet, but they stayed on horseback. Descending the northern slope of the ridge, the Rangers reached the southern bank of the Potomac, turned westward and proceeded to the foot of Loudoun Heights. Across the river on Maryland Heights the campfires of Union troops sparkled in the crisp winter night. Mosby halted the column at the entrance to a ravine; the men dismounted and then continued up the ascent on foot. They most likely welcomed the climb as the walk stimulated what must have been nearly frozen feet.[19]

The Confederates halted a second time about 200 yards from the rear of the Federal camp, where Mosby gave Stringfellow a squad of ten men and instructions to seize Cole's headquarters when he heard the gunfire of the main attack. "On reaching this point without creating any alarm," Mosby reported, "I deemed that a crisis had passed and the capture of the camp of the enemy a certainty." Mosby, with the majority of the men, then rode up the slope of the ridge, stopping at a point opposite the camp on the eastern side of the Hillsborough road. Mosby closed the column, filed the men into an attack rank and prepared to give the signal. "The camp was buried in profound sleep," he added in his report, "there was not a sentinel awake." It was 4:30 A.M., January 10; moonlight still bathed the ground.[20]

Suddenly, to the right in the direction of where Stringfellow's squad was posted, gunfire erupted, and horsemen—"yelling and shooting," as one of the men with Mosby described them—galloped into the rear of the camp. The oncoming riders were Stringfellow's men, but Mosby mistook them for a Federal party which had discovered the attack, and he signaled the charge. The Rangers and their mounts plunged down the ridge and crossed the road into the campsite. Mosby's men, believing like their commander that Stringfellow's squad were Yankees, began firing at the party. One Ranger emptied his six-shot Colt at Stringfellow but missed. It was a wild, confusing melee for a few minutes before the Rangers realized the mistake.[21]

The confusion within the attackers' ranks gave the Federals a few precious minutes to rally. "No one who has not experienced a night attack from an enemy," argued a Marylander with Cole, "can form the slightest conception of the feelings of one awakened in the dead of night with the din of shots and yells coming from those thirsting for your blood." The Northerners had been sleeping with their weapons for several nights and, when the Rangers duelled with each other, Cole's men, grabbing their pistols and carbines, scrambled behind bushes and trees among the tents. Many had nothing on but their underclothing.[22]

"Every man was for himself," remembered a Federal. It was still dark and neither side could distinguish the faces or uniform colors of the other. A number of Yankees shouted: "shoot every soldier on horseback," and their volleys were directed at the mounted fighters. One of Cole's men heard a Ranger respond: "Give the d——d Yankees sons-of-b—— no quarter." As soon as the Southerner finished the challenge, he tumbled from the saddle.[23]

The initial Union volley caught the Rangers in the open ground along the road. The "rebels were easy targets because no one else was on horseback," claimed a Northerner. One bullet struck First Lieutenant William Thomas Turner of Company A. When he was hit, Turner toppled into the arms of Ranger Walter Frankland, saying, "I am shot." "Fighting Tom," as the men called him, had been a member of the original detail of fifteen, a Marylander who had joined the Confederate cause. According to a comrade, he was "brave and courageous," an absolutely composed fighter in combat. But as

Frankland led him to the rear on his horse, "Fighting Tom" Turner's life was oozing away, marked by blood on the snow.[24]

Somewhere else in the nasty battle—"it was a perfect hell," according to a Yankee—Ranger John Robinson lay dead. Robinson was a Scotsman, a former officer in the British army whom his comrades called "Captain." When he fell no one knew for certain, but it no longer mattered. He had come to a foreign land to die.[25]

Four other Rangers were either dead on the ground or dying. The gunfire cut down William Owens, a Ranger named Yates, William H. Turner and Charlie Paxson. Owens and Yates were killed; Turner and Paxson, mortally wounded. Owens rode in Stringfellow's party and was probably killed by a comrade. Turner, like "Fighting Tom," was a Marylander, while Paxson was from Loudoun County. Little is known about Yates, except his surname and place of death.[26]

When Paxson fell in the combat, Captain "Billy" Smith spurred to his assistance. As the commander of Company B reached Paxson, an enemy trooper from behind a tent fired. Smith reeled in the saddle, and "Champ," his horse, bolted with fright. Captain William H. Chapman of Company C reined in "Champ," dismounted and laid Smith on the ground. Chapman saw that the wound was fatal and most likely bid farewell to the fallen officer, whom another Ranger described as "no ordinary man."[27]

By this stage in the action Mosby had ordered a withdrawal. The Rangers, he said, retired in "good order," bringing out six captives and between fifty and sixty horses. But before the retreat order was given, some of the Confederates broke into a retreat. Ranger William E. Colston, while trying to rally the fleeing men, was shot down. Colston was a twenty-four-year-old Marylander who had served in the 21st Virginia and 1st Maryland Infantry. Permanently disabled in June 1862, he volunteered as an aide to Major General Isaac Trimble during the Gettysburg Campaign. When Trimble was wounded and captured in the battle, Colston joined Mosby upon the army's return to Virginia. He was the third Marylander with Mosby to lose his life on Loudoun Heights.[28]

The Confederates followed the Hillsborough road. A short distance from Cole's camp, they halted at the home of Levi Waters and carried "Fighting Tom" Turner inside. The family tended to the wounds, but there was no hope. Turner died at the Waters residence on January 15 and was buried in the Hillsborough Cemetery.[29]

Before the retreat resumed, Mosby sent Chapman and Richard

Montjoy, under a flag of truce, back into the Federal camp. The pair of Rangers, speaking for Mosby, offered to exchange their six prisoners for the dead and mortally wounded Confederates. Cole or another officer rejected the request, and Chapman and Montjoy rode away. As they passed through, they saw the body of Billy Smith; it had been stripped to his underwear, and a watch that was a gift from his wife was missing.[30]

"My loss was severe," Mosby stated in his report on the fight. He lost four killed, four mortally wounded, five wounded and one captured. Those wounded included Fount Beattie, who had his horse killed under him and took a bullet in the leg, and William Mosby, younger brother of the major. Willie Mosby was eighteen years old when he had enlisted in his brother's command in the fall of 1863. His wound was slight. The captured partisan was Leonard Brown, a thirty-three-year-old miller from Fauquier County.[31]

The losses had a deep effect upon the Rangers. One member of the raiding party described the return march as "a gloomy one." "A sad and sullen silence pervaded our ranks," he continued, "and found expression in every countenance. . . . Even the Major, though he usually appeared cold and unyielding, could not conceal his disappointment and keen regret at the result of this enterprise. He knew and felt that he had suffered a loss which could not well be repaired."[32]

The death of Billy Smith and the fatal wounding of Tom Turner caused much of the despair. The pair were "universal favorites" among the men, J. Marshall Crawford stated, adding that the members of Company B "idolized" Smith, who was "brave and generous to a fault." James Williamson wrote later that Smith and Turner were "without doubt at the time of their deaths the two most efficient officers in the Battalion. The first to go into a fight, they were always the last to leave." Mosby, in his report, described them as "two of the noblest and bravest officers of this army."[33]

The Rangers arrived at Woodgrove about sunrise on the tenth. The belief was already festering within some of them that Stringfellow's hasty action caused the disaster. "If Stringfellow had not blundered," John Munson argued later, "Cole's Command would have been wiped from the face of the earth." The raiders believed that of the eight killed and mortally wounded, three were shot by their comrades during the fight. Loudoun Heights, Munson noted, was "always looked upon as our Waterloo, for the men lost seemed to us worth more than all Cole's Battalion." Ranger Crawford alleged that after the defeat Mosby developed a reluctance for night assaults because of the fear of his men shooting each other again.[34]

Back on Loudoun Heights a different view of the morning's combat was taking shape. Cole's men believed that they had whipped "Mosby's notorious rogues" in a stand-up fight. While the 34th Massachusetts Infantry ran to the cavalrymen's support from Harper's Ferry when they learned of the assault, Cole's troopers had stood alone. They lost six killed, fourteen wounded and six captured, but they had in their hands seven dead or dying Rebels and, as they soon learned, an eighth in the house of Levi Waters. The Marylanders and Pennsylvanians were proud of their achievement, and a joke raced through the campsite that the next time they met Mosby's men they wanted to be dressed properly. Brigadier General Jeremiah Sullivan, commander at Harper's Ferry, issued twenty gallons of whiskey to the battalion in celebration of the victory.[35]

Cole directed that the remains of the fallen Rangers be buried together "in one deep hole." Those interred, according to a source, included Smith, Colston, and Robinson. The bodies of Owens, William H. Turner and Yates probably shared the common grave with their comrades, but that is uncertain. Charlie Paxson, moments before he died among his foes, asked if Samuel McNair was still a member of the Union battalion. About a year earlier, McNair had fallen wounded near Leesburg, and his brother, H. S. McNair, found a local resident who agreed to haul the wounded soldier to Maryland. The civilian was Charlie Paxson's father, and he secured from H. S. McNair a promise that if his son, one of Mosby's men, should need help in the future, the McNairs would reciprocate. Samuel McNair came when told that a Rebel asked for him by name. Paxson identified himself, and McNair assured him that he would send word to his father. Paxson died shortly after being carried into a tent. A few days later his father arrived, taking his son home for a final time. A debt had been repaid.[36]

Mosby, in the weeks following the defeat at Loudoun Heights, temporarily suspended raids by the command. His scouts still prowled along Union lines and picket posts, and the guard details watched the roads into the Confederacy, but the Rangers took the time to heal. Some members of the Black Horse Troop of the 4th Virginia Cavalry, home on furlough in Fauquier County, rode with the partisans during these days. Mosby granted furloughs to a number of individuals, and he visited his family's home during the final days of

January and the first week of February. William Chapman served as commander in Mosby's absence.[37]

While en route back to the command, Mosby again detoured to Richmond, where he conferred with Secretary of War James Seddon about operations in the spring. He arrived in Upper Fauquier on February 6, the same day he was promoted to lieutenant colonel, to rank from January 21. Both Stuart and Lee had recommended the promotion, with the latter stating in a letter to Jefferson Davis that Mosby "is zealous, bold, and skillful, and with very small resources has accomplished a great deal." Lee concluded: "I do this in order to show him that his services have been appreciated, and to encourage him to still greater activity and zeal."[38]

Stuart, writing to Lee three days after the appointment, commended the partisan officer. "His sleepless vigilance and unceasing activity have done the enemy great damage," declared Stuart about Mosby. "He keeps a large force of the enemy's cavalry continually employed in Fairfax in the vain effort to suppress his inroads. His exploits are not surpassed in daring and enterprise by those of *petite guerre* in any age. Unswerving devotion to duty, self-abnegation, and unflinching courage, with a quick perception and appreciation of the opportunity, are the characteristics of this officer." If Mosby had not earned higher rank, Stuart believed, "no more can daring deeds essay to do it." The debacle at Loudoun Heights had not affected Lee and Stuart's estimation of Mosby's prowess.[39]

The official praise of and promotion for Mosby coincided with a debate in the Confederate Congress over the status of partisan commands. Ever since authorities in Richmond had approved the formation of partisan units in April 1862, the discussion over the value of these units continued. A few months earlier, on November 26, 1863, Secretary of War Seddon filed a report on partisan operations during the preceding year. "The advantages anticipated from the allowance of corps of partisan rangers, with peculiar privileges of prize to stimulate their zeal and activity," argued Seddon, "have been very partially realized from their independent organization and the facilities and temptations thereby afforded to license and depredations, grave mischiefs have resulted." The cabinet officer recommended that partisan commands should be "merged in with the troops of the line or disbanded and conscribed." If any units were to be retained, it should be at the discretion of the Secretary of War.[40]

A cavalry brigadier entered the discussion roughly seven weeks after Seddon prepared his report. Thomas Rosser, who was serving in the Shenandoah Valley at the time and saw firsthand the failures of partisan units stationed there, penned a scathing indictment of irregular commands to Lee on January 11, 1864. Rosser described the partisans as "a nuisance and an evil to the service," "without discipline, order, or organization," and "a band of thieves." "They are a terror to the citizens," he asserted, "and an injury to the cause. They never fight; can't be made to fight." The current system, Rosser believed, kept men out of the regular service who were needed, caused dissatisfaction among the regular troops and fostered desertion.[41]

Rosser then directed his argument toward Mosby's command. "It is almost impossible for one to manage the different companies of my brigade that are from Loudoun, Fauquier, Fairfax, etc., the region occupied by Mosby," he stated. "They see these men living at their ease and enjoying the comforts of home, allowed to possess all that they capture, and their duties mere pastime pleasures compared with their own arduous ones; and it is a natural consequence in the nature of man that he should become dissatisfied under these circumstance." While Rosser admitted that Mosby was "a gallant officer" and that the Rangers were "of inestimable service to the Yankee army in keeping their men from straggling," he finished by proposing that the "bad" partisan system "be corrected."[42]

Stuart and Lee read Rosser's letter. Stuart responded on the eighteenth, writing: "Major Mosby's command is the only efficient band of rangers I know of, and he usually operates with only one-fourth of his nominal strength. Such organizations, as a rule, are detrimental to the best interest of the army at large."[43]

The commanding general offered his evaluation of the proposal four days after Stuart. "As far as my knowledge and experience extends," Lee wrote, "there is much truth in the statement of General Rosser. I recommend that the law authorizing these partisan corps be abolished. The evils resulting from their organization more than counterbalance the good they accomplish." Lee then forwarded the correspondence to Seddon.[44]

Whether or not Rosser's letter and the endorsements by Stuart and Lee gave Seddon and legislators the final ammunition they needed, remains uncertain. Complaints from civilians and military authorities had been deluging the Confederate Congress and the administration for months. The Secretary of War, at the request of William Porcher Miles, chairman of the House Military Committee, drafted a bill which repealed the authority for the formation of partisan units. Congress enacted the bill into law on February 17. The legislation directed that all partisan commands organized under the April 1862 law were to be united with other organizations into battalions or regiments. The legislators granted Seddon the authority to permit certain units to operate within Federal lines. Two months later, when the repeal act went into effect, Seddon requested retention of only Mosby and John McNeill's commands in partisan service. McNeill also fought in Virginia, engaging Union forces in northwestern Virginia and the Shenandoah Valley. Seddon's exemption of the two units testified to the discipline of the units and the quality of their leaders. It also testified to the failure of irregular warfare in most of the Confederacy.[45]

In Mosby's Confederacy, meanwhile, the return of Lieutenant Colonel Mosby brought a resumption of raids. While the Rangers had been relatively inactive since Loudoun Heights, the Federals crisscrossed the region in more searches for the guerrillas. Cole's battalion came from Harper's Ferry with a new boldness; regiments from Charles Lowell's brigade came from the Washington defenses; and detachments from John Taylor's came from Warrenton. The efforts by the Yankees netted eight Ranger prisoners between January 13 and February 6. The Confederates dogged the heels of the columns but did not engage. Chapman sent parties to harass Federal pickets, which resulted in a handful of captives. A line in a February 2 letter of Major Caspar Crowninshield, 2nd Massachusetts Cavalry, indicated the quiet which had prevailed during the days before Mosby's return—"no alarms & no Moseby," the Union officer wrote.[46]

But Mosby's men soon faced a new threat. On February 16 or 17, Ranger John Cornwall had become embroiled in a dispute with Mosby and Walter Frankland, who acted as the battalion's quartermaster. Cornwall had hauled a wagonload of ammunition from Charlottesville to Fauquier and, when he submitted his expenses, Mosby and Frankland disallowed some of the items. Enraged by the decision, Cornwall swore vengeance against the command, fleeing to the Federals.[47]

Union officers interrogated the deserter and were convinced that Cornwall could lead them to Ranger hiding places. Brigadier General David Gregg issued the orders, stating: "The officer in charge of the party will take with him the prisoner, and if he should lead your party into a trap he will be shot. It is believed the prisoner's statement is reliable." Cavalry commander Alfred Pleasonton approved the operation.[48]

The raiding force rode out of Warrenton between 9:00 and 10:00 P.M. on February 17. The cavalrymen numbered 350, with troopers from the 1st Massachusetts, 1st New Jersey, 1st Pennsylvania and 3rd Pennsylvania. Lieutenant Colonel John W. Kester, 1st New Jersey, was the senior officer in command.[49]

The march went slowly. It was "one of the bitterest days of the year" with "a cutting wind," remembered a New Jersey trooper. A Pennsylvanian described it as "exceedingly cold." The chill penetrated through their overcoats to the bone, numbing arms, legs, hands and feet.[50]

But the frigid temperatures and icy winds abetted the Federal mission. The Ranger guard details had been pulled in for the night as no warning raced through the Confederacy until the bluecoats arrived. Upon reaching Piedmont, Lieutenant Colonel Kester divided the command into parties to cover the countryside from Markham to Paris. The Federals were ordered to search every house in their paths. Cornwall, riding with one group, pointed out the "safe houses."

Cornwall rode directly to the residence of Jamieson Ashby, where Mosby's quartermaster, Frankland, often lodged. The deserter personally conducted the search, but missed his nemesis. Frankland and two others were in the Ashby home, but were concealed in a secret closet. Not far from Ashby's, at the Ben Triplett house, Albert and Jim Wrenn avoided capture by jumping out of a window and hiding in a straw rick. The brothers, dressed in nightclothes, stayed under cover for three hours and nearly froze.[51]

Five Rangers were spending the night at Redmond F. Brawner's house outside of Paris when they saw Union horsemen ride past. They fled to safety in the mountains. Betsey and her daughter, "Tee," concealed three more partisans in the "secret hidding [sic] place" at "Belle Grove."[52]

A Pennsylvania cavalryman, writing in the regimental journal, described the encounters between the Northerners and the local populace as the troopers entered the premises. "The scout abounds with an unusual quantity of rich stories," he scribbled, "and the excuses . . . of young couples asleep in the next room, of invalids who could not bear disturbance, and that nobody was home. The laughable tales of routing out these poor folks."[53]

The Federal sweep reaped a harvest. At the residence of a Mr.
Gibson, five Rangers surrendered when their captors threatened to
burn the house. At other homes, the Yankees found one partisan
under the bed of a black servant, another crouched beneath a "pyr-
amid" of hoop skirts and a third sprawled flat under the mattress of
a couch. The raid netted twenty-eight prisoners and approximately
200 horses. Kester's men also destroyed a cache of medical supplies
and barrels of whiskey.[54]

The Union raiders went through homes in Piedmont, Markham,
Paris, Upperville, Middleburg, Salem and Rectortown and the farmhouses between the villages. William Chapman, with thirty Rangers,
skirmished with the detachment of the 1st Pennsylvania Cavalry at
"Belle Grove," but the Union veterans, deploying behind a stone
wall, swatted aside the partisans. The cavalrymen returned to Warrenton on the night of the eighteenth, having traveled by one member's estimate sixty-five miles in twenty-four hours. "Such is cavalry
service in winter," he concluded.[55]

Cornwall had exacted a tremendous retribution. The seizure of
twenty-eight Rangers was the largest loss of men Mosby experienced
at one time during the war. After the February 18 raid, the Confederates built huts in the mountains or selected caves for sleeping at
night. If some chose to remain in houses, they burrowed tunnels
beneath the floors or through cellar walls. It had been an ill-wind
which brought the winter of 1864 to Mosby's Confederacy.[56]

Chapter 9

THE COST OF WAR

 As he had on many previous mornings, Henry Cabell "Cab" Maddux, went to school in his hometown of Upperville, Virginia, on February 20, 1864. He was barely fifteen years old, if that, a short, very fat boy. "Cab" cared little for school; martial dreams filled his head. He and his schoolmates had seen much of war during the past year. Just two nights ago Yankee horsemen rode into Upperville in the dark of early morning, searched the houses and hauled away a number of Mosby's men.[1]

On this morning while "Cab" prepared for school, another column of "bluebelly" cavalry entered the village, once again hunting for guerrillas. The troopers in Upperville belonged to Cole's Cavalry,

200 strong. The victors of the nighttime battle of Loudoun Heights had marched from Harper's Ferry during the night on a scout through Loudoun and Fauquier to Front Royal. Major Cole halted them in Upperville about daylight, sending squads into the houses. The hunt flushed out nine Rangers, including John and Bartlett Bolling, who were at their parents' home in the village. The Federals at first believed that John Bolling, a thirty-year-old attorney from Petersburg, Virginia, who had been a classmate of Mosby at the University of Virginia, was Mosby. As the Federals prepared to leave, Rangers J. W. Coiner and William A. Brawner rode into the town and were captured.[2]

Cole had his men and eleven prisoners on the move before eight o'clock, leading them southward toward Piedmont. A short distance out of Upperville they surprised another partisan, a man named McCobb from Baltimore, at a "safe house." McCobb ran to his horse, swung into the saddle and spurred away. But as the mount jumped a fence, McCobb was thrown off, breaking his neck in the fall. The Yankees left the dead Confederate on the ground.[3]

The presence of 200 blue-jacketed horsemen in the heart of Upper Fauquier did not pass unnoticed. John Mosby, Johnny Edmonds, Jake Lavender and John Munson were enjoying breakfast at Joseph Blackwell's "Heartland" residence when Jimmy Edmonds, Johnny's younger brother, burst into the house, shouting that Yankees were marching on the road to Piedmont. The four Rebels hurriedly mounted; Lavender grabbed two carbines; and they speeded toward the railroad stop. When the four arrived at a point which overlooked the few houses, Cole's men were watering their mounts. Mosby and Munson opened fire with the carbines, killing a trooper and a horse. Several of the Federals responded with carbines until Cole ordered them to remount and move back toward Upperville.[4]

The gunfire had stirred up a small hornets' nest of Rangers. Between fifty and sixty of the Southerners joined Mosby outside of Piedmont as the tail of Cole's column disappeared toward Upperville. The Rangers pursued, stinging the rear guard of the Union troopers. By the time the Northerners reached Upperville, it was a horse race, both sides whipping their horses into a gallop. When the horsemen thundered past the school, the students were outside at recess. "Cab" Maddux's time had come. Mounting a horse, he followed the partisans. School ended for the teenager; he was on a road filled with the dreams of warriors.[5]

Three miles northeast of Upperville at Blakeley's Grove School, Cole halted his men, fanning some of them out behind a stone wall as skirmishers. The Rangers bridled up and fashioned a line of battle across the fields. The opponents exchanged carbine and pistol fire. Then a Federal officer, Captain W. L. Morgan, 1st New York Cavalry, who had accompanied Cole on the expedition, rode beyond his line and began shooting. Ranger Richard Montjoy, accepting the challenge, went forward, aimed his revolver and killed the New Yorker. Mosby allegedly exclaimed that Montjoy had earned an officer's commission.[6]

The Yankees then drove forward in a charge, but the Rebels beat them back. Cole's troopers attacked a second time, and then a third. The combat swirled around the school house until Mosby, dividing his force, outflanked Cole's dismounted men behind the stone wall. Cole ordered a withdrawal and, by deploying squads of men behind a succession of stone walls, repulsed Mosby's pursuit. The Union major extricated his command and retained the eleven prisoners. He reported his losses at two killed, three wounded and one missing, while Mosby claimed the enemy lost six killed and seven captured.[7]

Mosby's losses, exclusive of the eleven captured Rangers and McCobb, amounted to three wounded. In his report of the engagement, he praised eleven of his men, including Edmonds, Lavender, Munson, Montjoy and two of the wounded, Lieutenant Frank Fox of Company C and a Ranger named Starke. He described the encounter at the Blakeley's Grove School as a "sharp skirmish."[8]

Approximately 160 rangers gathered the next morning, February 21, in Piedmont for the burial of McCobb. During the funeral a scout rode in, reporting that another body of Union cavalry had entered Middleburg. The service concluded abruptly, and Mosby had his men on the road within minutes. Arriving at Middleburg, Mosby learned that the Federals had turned northward toward Mountsville. He directed William Chapman to take the majority of the men and follow Goose Creek to Ball's Mill, six miles south of Leesburg on the Old Carolina Road, while he trailed the enemy horsemen with a small squad. Mosby believed that the Yankees were marching toward Leesburg and then on to their camps outside of Washington.[9]

The Northern cavalry belonged to Charles Russell Lowell's brigade from Vienna, Virginia, consisting of three companies of the 2nd Massachusetts and one company of the 16th New York, 127 officers and men, under Captain J. Sewell Reed. They had left Vienna on the twentieth on what one of them called a "roving commission." Their guide was Charley Binns, a deserter from Mosby's command. Binns had joined the command in July 1863, but during the autumn he "committed some acts of rascality," in the words of a Ranger, and Mosby had ordered his arrest. Before he could be apprehended, Binns fled, entering Lowell's lines on November 3. "His name," wrote John Munson of the traitor, "became a by-word in Mosby's command."[10]

Reed's detachment, as Mosby anticipated, rode to Leesburg, where it proceeded eastward on the Leesburg-Alexandria Pike. By moving through Loudoun County and not into Upper Fauquier, the Federals seemed to have wanted to avoid contact with the Rangers. Reed halted his men at 2:00 A.M. on the twenty-second, six miles beyond Leesburg at the farmhouse of a Kephart family. There they met a scouting party from the 13th New York Cavalry, which had encamped for the night.[11]

Mosby followed the Yankees to their campsite. When the Northerners bivouacked, he hurried across country to the main party, leaving Sam Underwood and Walter Whaley behind to watch the Federals and to report their route of march that morning. Mosby had kept Chapman posted of the day's march by sending couriers to him. When the Union horsemen reached Leesburg, he ordered Chapman to ride to Guilford Station on the Loudoun & Hampshire Railroad, three miles southwest of Dranesville and two miles south of the Leesburg-Alexandria Pike. Mosby found Chapman and the Rangers near the depot before daylight. The Confederate commander had been in the saddle most of the day and all of the night, but he possessed a stamina few in the command could match. He stirred his sleeping men and had them on the march toward the Pike by sunrise.[12]

The Rangers halted, in Mosby's words, "at a point offering fine natural advantages for surprising an enemy." The location was on the south side of the Pike in a stand of pines and a thicket two miles west of Dranesville. Across the roadbed sat a blacksmith shop owned by a man named Anker. Mosby divided his force into three wings. In the center Mosby dismounted fifteen men armed with carbines under Richard Montjoy; on the right, deployed in a column of fours, were Company A and part of Company B, Lieutenant Frank Williams commanding; and, on the left, Captain William Chapman led the remainder of Company B and Company C mounted in a formation similar to Williams's. Montjoy's carbineers would open the attack and, when Mosby blew a whistle, the two mounted wings would charge. Finally, to lure the Federals into the ambush, Mosby stationed three men on the roadway with orders to engage the leading elements of the enemy and then ride past their concealed comrades.[13]

Reed's cavalrymen started late that morning, probably not much before ten o'clock. The contingent from the 13th New York Cavalry, instead of accompanying the larger force, followed country roads south of the Pike. The route of the New Yorkers' march, however, took them beyond supporting distance of Reed's men as the latter moved on the Pike. Mosby learned of the separation of the Union forces from Walter Whatley well before Reed approached the ambush point. At such times Mosby was at his best, plotting every detail, covering all the contingencies.[14]

The Federals came into view of the waiting Rangers minutes before eleven o'clock. Reed had advanced cautiously—"he was marching his men as we always march," Major Caspar Crownin-shield, commander of the 2nd Massachusetts Cavalry, wrote afterwards. Four troopers roamed in front, a hundred paces ahead of the column's van, which consisted of a sergeant and fourteen men. The main body trailed another 300 paces to the rear. Reed acted as if he expected trouble.[15]

When the four-man detail saw Mosby's decoy, the Yankees galloped after the Rebels. Behind them came the sergeant and his party. Montjoy's dismounted men took aim, and flames flashed from the pine trees. The blast blew several Yankees off their horses. Before the others could turn and flee, Mosby signaled the charge by blowing on the whistle. He had told his men to "go right through them . . . let every shot tell."[16]

The mounted Rangers rushed from their concealed position with "a terrific yell." Mosby asserted in his report that when his men attacked, the Federals were "surprised and confounded, with no time to form, they made but feeble resistance, and were perfectly over-whelmed by the shock of the charge." Other participants, both Northerner and Southerner, paint a different scene at the time of contact, however. Montjoy, not waiting for the main contingent of the enemy to reach the ambush site, opened fire on the van, and Mosby ordered the attack at the sound of the carbine fire. Consequently, when Williams and Chapman dashed forward to seal the trap, Reed and over one hundred of his men were beyond Chapman's left flank and immediately counterattacked.[17]

As Ranger John Munson remembered it, there was "confusion

everywhere." Horses and riders jammed the roadbed, with the combat overflowing into the nearby fields. The Rangers endeavored to "go right through" their opponents, but for several minutes the Yankees gave as good as they took. Some of Reed's men were from the California Battalion and, in Munson's words, they "were standing up to the rack like men, dealing out to us the best they had."[18]

In the midst of the violence rode Mosby. "I saw him weaving in and out of the fighting mass like a ferret," stated Munson, "fighting hand-to-hand with every man who would stand before him." Mosby's mare took a bullet in a leg but managed to carry her rider through it all on three legs.[19]

The struggle was often personal, face-to-face. John Munson was near Mosby, riding his horse "Champ." Munson had purchased it from Captain Billy Smith's widow upon the death of her husband at Loudoun Heights. "Champ," asserted Munson, was "absolutely controllable in the hottest sort of action," and the Ranger needed the animal's calm bearing.[20]

Munson seized a Yankee but, instead of disarming the captive, he spurred "Champ" after another foe. As Munson rode away, the Federal fired his pistol, the bullet striking Munson in the back less than an inch from his spinal cord. Ludwell Lake killed the assailant. Another comrade, holding Munson on "Champ," led him away from the fighting to a nearby farmhouse, where he was soon joined by his good friend Johnny Edmonds, who had been shot in the thigh. The day before Edmonds's mother had given him a small Bible which he had carried in a pocket of his pants and which deflected the bullet away from his leg bone.[21]

Union Captain Reed, like Mosby, rode in the forefront until Ranger Baron Robert von Massow made him a prisoner. Von Massow, a former officer in the Prussian army, had crossed the Atlantic to serve the Confederacy. A former comrade-in-arms of Heros von Borcke of Jeb Stuart's staff, von Massow secured a letter of introduction from Stuart to Mosby. He was a darkly complexioned warrior with black, piercing eyes. Von Massow wore a gray uniform, with green trimmings, a slouch hat with two plumes and carried a saber. He had not been in the command a long time and, after his first raid, exclaimed: "This beats the fox hunt of England."[22]

When the Prussian forced Reed to surrender, he, like Munson, let the prisoner keep his sidearm. Then, as von Massow went after more Yankees, Reed shot him in the back. Captain William Chapman killed Reed seconds later. Reed was the first officer of the 2nd Massachusetts Cavalry to be slain in combat. Von Massow eventually recovered from the serious wound at "Glen Welby," but his Ranger career was finished.[23]

The Federals, however, "had no chance," as Crowninshield informed his mother five days later. Outnumbered and nearly trapped, they finally broke and scattered across the fields. The Rebels drove a few of them into the Potomac River, where a number drowned in the current. Deserter Charley Binns disappeared early in the fight— "when Binn went the Lord only knows," stated a Northerner—and escaped. Mosby's men killed a dozen or more, wounded approximately twenty-five and captured seventy Yankees, along with roughly one hundred horses.[24]

The engagement, which the Rangers called "Second Dranesville," cost Mosby five wounded and one man killed. The dead man was J. Pendleton Chappalear of Upper Fauquier. Chappalear had served in the 6th Virginia Cavalry but, when his family needed him to manage the farm, he secured permission to transfer to the 43rd Battalion. He joined Mosby early in January 1864, and this operation was the first one in which he participated. A sister hauled Chappalear's body home, and the family buried him in a local cemetery.[25]

When news of the rout arrived at the camp of the 2nd Massachusetts Cavalry at Vienna, Crowninshield pursued with his remaining companies. The trail was cold, however, by the time the contingent reached the battle site. Crowninshield noted in a letter that they found Reed's body, stripped to shirt and drawers, in the road. "He was honest & brave & a great friend of mine," Crowninshield wrote of the fallen captain. Reed's wife was in the regiment's camp at the time of his death, and a designated officer informed her of the tragedy.[26]

When Jeb Stuart received Mosby's report of the victory, he endorsed it: "This is another of the brilliant exploits of this gallant leader," before sending it on to Robert E. Lee. President Jefferson Davis, after reading it, wrote to Stuart to "make complimentary acknowledgement to Colonel Mosby." Second Dranesville and the defeat of Cole's Cavalry at Blakeley's Grove School two days earlier helped to erase the stain of Loudoun Heights and the Yankee roundup of Rangers on February 17–18.[27]

Two days after Second Dranesville, on February 24, Lowell's brigade of three regiments, commanded by Crowninshield, marched through Loudoun County. The Union cavalrymen stayed in the area for two days, turned up no Rangers and returned to Vienna. The operation's conclusion inaugurated a lull in fighting between the Yankees and their guerrilla opponents which stretched through March. Mosby summarized his inactivity during these weeks by stating that "few opportunities" arose for strikes against the Federals, who "exert great vigilance." Mosby kept his scouts busy in southern Maryland, outside the Washington defenses and across the Blue Ridge Mountains in the Shenandoah Valley. He also assigned details to forage supplies from Union sympathizers along the Potomac River in Loudoun and Fairfax.[28]

On a handful of occasions Federal detachments crossed the path of Ranger parties and clashes flared. On March 9, Mosby and forty men attacked and routed a Union force near Greenwich, capturing nine of the enemy and ten horses. A day later, Lieutenant Dolly Richards led between fifty and sixty Rangers into the Shenandoah Valley, where they attacked a picket post of the 1st New York Cavalry. Major Jerry A. Sullivan and approximately twenty-five members of the New York regiment pursued the Confederates. Near Kabletown, the Rebels turned around and lashed the oncoming New Yorkers. Sullivan was killed, and his men fled in retreat. Richards secured an officer's sword and subsequently had it inscribed and presented to Mosby.[29]

Dolly Richards's performance on March 10 must have finally convinced Mosby to make a decision he had contemplated for weeks. Since Billy Smith's death at Loudoun Heights, Company B had been without a commander. Mosby did not regard Frank Williams, Albert Wrenn or Robert Gray capable enough to handle the responsibility, stating to Stuart that "all three Lieutenants of Co. B are deemed incompetent for the position" of captain. Instead, Mosby selected Richards of Company C, citing the lieutenant in his letter of recommendation "for both skill & gallantry shown on many occasions." Richards, wrote Mosby, "is besides a Gentleman of the highest tone of morality." Richards officially received his captaincy on April 6. Mosby waited another six months to fill Richards's vacancy in Company C.[30]

Other matters of personnel and organization received Mosby's attention during the final days of March. An enlistment officer in Richmond had been enrolling recruits for Mosby's 43rd Battalion and sending them to Mosby. This practice rankled Mosby, who wrote

Stuart on the twenty-sixth to say, "Please grant no papers to any man coming to join my command, unless he can furnish evidence of having been recruited by an agent of mine. . . . You can very readily understand how necessary it is for success in my operations to have none but first-rate men."[31]

The reminiscences and memoirs of Rangers indicate that the overwhelming majority of volunteers entered "Mosby's Confederacy" and personally asked Mosby if they could join the command. Those of conscription age, eighteen to forty-five years old, needed proof of a discharge or that they had not been drafted. The battalion could have become a haven for those who were trying to avoid conscript officers if Mosby had not screened recruits. As noted previously, a man might join, but whether he stayed or was sent back to the regular army depended upon his conduct in battle and among the local populace.

Recruiting never seemed to be a problem for the 43rd Battalion. Recruits kept finding their way into Upper Fauquier and enrolling. By the end of March, for instance, Mosby had enough men to warrant the organization of a fourth company. He called a meeting of the command for Paris on March 28.[32]

The names of the members of the new Company D were read, and then, as he had done in the past, Mosby presented his nominees for officers. He had heard the grumblings about his democratic methods, so he stepped forward and informed the men if anyone objected to his selections, he had the option of leaving the battalion and of being sent to Lee's army. The Rangers had dubbed the regular service "Mosby's Botany Bay" after the infamous penal colony in Australia. All candidates were confirmed without opposition.[33]

Mosby's choice for captain probably surprised no one present. Since May 1863 when Richard P. Montjoy joined Mosby, he had fought with a fearlessness few others matched. Montjoy was, in the words of John Munson, "conspicuously gallant: a sort of meteor that we could all see as he moved across the horizon of war." Even his enemies knew of Montjoy. A Michigan cavalry officer, writing in 1863, described the partisan as a "spy, scout, desperado, and all-around bad man." When Montjoy killed Union Captain W. L. Morgan in their duel between the lines at Blakeley's Grove School on February 20, it confirmed the mettle of the man.[34]

Montjoy was twenty-four years old, a Mississippian who had enlisted as a private in an infantry regiment in 1861. He was either discharged or transferred from the regiment and became a Ranger. Darkly handsome, with black eyes and hair, he stood slightly over five feet, seven inches, in height, and was regarded as one of the unit's "dandies." Montjoy rode the "finest horses that money could buy" and favored neat uniforms, claimed a Ranger. He had won the heart of Annie Lucas of Warrenton, and the couple were engaged to be married.[35]

The company's first lieutenant was Alfred Glascock, a native of Upper Fauquier. Glascock had been a lieutenant in the 7th Virginia Cavalry before transferring to Mosby's command in the spring of 1863. In one of his first raids, he suffered a severe wound at Seneca Mills, Maryland, on June 11. Upon his recovery, Glascock demonstrated the leadership qualities which had brought his earlier commission in the 7th Virginia.[36]

Mosby picked Charles E. Grogan for the second lieutenancy of Company D. Grogan, born in Clarke County, Virginia, resided in Baltimore when the war began. He served in the 1st Maryland at First Bull Run and by the summer of 1863 was a member of General Isaac Trimble's staff. Captured at Gettysburg, Grogan escaped from Johnson's Island prison in Ohio and enlisted in the 43rd Battalion.[37]

For the position of third lieutenant Mosby nominated another Marylander, William H. Trundle. A private in Company A, Trundle was a member when Mosby organized the command in June 1863. Twice captured and exchanged, he was on a scout in the Shenandoah Valley when the Rangers gathered at Paris for Company D's formation. But neither Mosby nor the men knew when they met that Trundle would never serve as one of their officers. The day before, on March 27, he and the other members of the scouting detail encountered a group of Federals and Trundle was killed in the action. A week or two later Mosby filled the slot with David Briscoe, a twenty-three-year-old from Baltimore.[38]

The selection of Marylanders for half of the company's officers reflected the composition of the unit. Company D, according to Ranger John Scott, was manned "almost entirely" by natives of that border state. They were also dandies, like their captain. In John Munson's description, the members were "the flower of the battalion" and "game fighters." Members of the other companies called them "Company Darling" and, when they rode past, their comrades whistled the tune "Dandy Jim from Caroline." Montjoy's men, however, came to earn their reputation for gallantry in battle as well as with young women. They regarded themselves as the best of the battalion, the "aristocratic company." Montjoy kept them in line and at their posts, exercising "extraordinary authority" over them.[39]

The addition of a fourth company extended the reach of Mosby's activities. During the last week of March and through the month of April, Mosby increased the number of scouting details. With the coming of spring weather and the resumption of active campaigning, Stuart and Lee wanted as much current intelligence as possible. They directed Mosby to watch closely the Orange and Alexandria and the Baltimore & Ohio railroads. The Rangers, consequently, covered a huge swath of northern Virginia from the Warrenton area northward into Fairfax, then westward along the Potomac River through Loudoun and beyond the Blue Ridge into the lower or northern end of the Shenandoah Valley.[40]

Mosby tracked the flow of trains on the railroads, listed the movements of specific Union infantry corps, knew which units manned the defenses of Washington, interrogated captives and read Northern newspapers for current information. During this time period he proposed an interesting scheme to Stuart. "I would be glad if you would furnish me with $2,000 secret-service money," Mosby asked Stuart, "as with my present opportunities I could use greatly to the public advantage." Mosby intended to buy a tobacco crop with cash, sell it and convert the profit into Federal greenbacks or paper money. What his "present opportunities" were and what "public advantage" he planned on securing he did not specify. The proceeds most likely were to be paid to informants. The records, however, do not indicate whether Stuart forwarded the money or whether Mosby's plan succeeded.[41]

The Rangers continued their attacks on Union picket posts and wagon trains. On April 9, Company A raided a group of wagons at Catlett's Station on the Orange and Alexandria Railroad, southeast of Warrenton. In the assault Ranger M. W. Flannery was shot in the chest. Stuffing a handkerchief in the wound, Flannery charged another Federal but soon toppled dead from the saddle. Flannery "was a determined man and a brave soldier," wrote James Williamson.[42]

While the scouting and raiding parties operated throughout the region, Mosby sent details into northern and western Loudoun County to seize livestock, horses and corn. That section of the county had a large number of Quaker and Union-sympathizing farmers. After the winter Mosby's men needed fodder for their mounts and

Lee's army could use the additional horseflesh and cattle. So Mosby targeted these inhabitants, extracting a tithe or 10 percent of their supplies.[43]

The impressment details centered their confiscations around the villages of Waterford, Hamilton and Hillsborough. "Major" William Hibbs oversaw the operations. The Rangers herded the animals and borrowed the victims' wagons to haul the grain. They were thorough at the farmsteads as evidenced by Charles Russell Lowell's statement on April 20 that only a little corn remained in the Waterford area. The Rebels apparently exceeded Mosby's figure of 10 percent.[44]

The farmers protested the seizures, but the Rangers ignored the complaints. Most of the confiscations occurred at the farms of Union sympathizers, but occasionally supporters of the Confederate cause lost either livestock or crops. Twenty-one citizens in the Hillsborough area, for instance, petitioned Mosby on April 9, for the return of two horses owned by James Janney, a miller and grain dealer in that locale. The petitioners stated that although Janney sold grain in Baltimore, he aided Southerners by loaning the team of horses to local farmers. Mosby, however, did not return the animals, which were valued at three thousand dollars.[45]

During the collection of supplies, Mosby, responding to an inquiry of Lee's on the reports of United States marshals enforcing the law in Loudoun County, boasted to Stuart: "No Federal foot presses the soil of Loudoun." If Mosby meant that no Union force occupied the county, he was correct; if he meant that the Yankees were not a constant presence in the area, he was wrong. As his operations accelerated in April, so did Union countermeasures against the partisans. By the end of the month, the Federal harvest of Ranger captives nearly equalled that of February, when the Yankees, according to the records, collected forty-one of the guerrillas.[46]

Mosby was himself embarrassed and victimized even before the Federals increased their counterraids. On March 25, he and several of his men, returning from a scout in the Shenandoah Valley, stopped at a farmhouse. With them were a handful of Yankee prisoners. When Mosby and some of his companions went inside the house, one of the Northerners, identified as a Sergeant Weatherbee, freed himself, leaped on a horse and galloped away. The animal he grabbed was Mosby's gray. Upon Weatherbee's arrival within Union lines, Mosby's saddlebags were opened and the contents examined. They found his commission as a captain, a copy of one of Stuart's orders

with the pencilled notation, "To Miss Laura with lasting regards of
J. E. B. Stuart," official documents which identified the Rangers as
regular soldiers and the enlistment papers of Ranger Charles Fenton
Beavers.[47]

The frequency and strength of the Federal incursions into
the "Confederacy" began four days after Mosby lost his horse. On
March 29, a 255-man contingent of the 13th Pennsylvania Cavalry
searched thoroughly every house in Aldie but uncovered only one
Ranger. The Pennsylvanians skirmished briefly with a group of partisans before returning to their lines.[48]

Eleven days later, on April 9, Federals targeted Aldie for a second
time. Troopers from the 2nd Massachusetts Cavalry entered the village after nightfall and once again went through the residences. This
time the hunt garnered five Rangers. One of those captured was
William E. Moore of Fairfax County. Moore, according to his captors, was "one of Col. Mosby's personal favorites and most noted
men." Moore and the three Underwood brothers acted as Mosby's
main scouts in that section of Virginia, so the New Englanders were
pleased with the seizure of a Ranger whom they regarded as a leader
of the attacks on their pickets around Vienna.[49]

During the next ten days detachments from Lowell's brigade,
including the 2nd Massachusetts Cavalry, 13th and 16th New York
Cavalry, scoured Loudoun County and parts of Fauquier, bringing
in another nine guerrillas. Members of the 13th New York, to believe
one of them, itched for months for a fight with the Rangers. They
had been issued Sharps carbines in December and now regarded themselves as "ugly customers." But Mosby's men did not offer battle,
and the operations proceeded without incident. On April 23, members
of the Massachusetts regiment, pursuing some Rangers who had attacked their vedettes, overtook First Lieutenant William L. Hunter
at Aldie Mill, at the east end of the town on the Little River Turnpike.
Hunter had no chance of escape and surrendered. Three weeks earlier
Mosby had promoted him to the new rank left vacant by William
Thomas Turner's mortal wounding at Loudoun Heights.[50]

Despite the mounting pressure applied by the Federals, eleven
Rangers rode into Leesburg on April 28. They halted at William
Pickett's public house, located on the northeast corner of the town
square, tied their horses to a low iron fence along the street and walked
inside for food and drink. No one stayed outside to act as a sentry.
It was a brazen, even foolish act.[51]

Major General Christopher C. Augur, commander of the Department of Washington, had ordered Lowell to conduct another raid into Mosby's Confederacy, searching designated houses which Augur had been informed harbored Rangers. Lowell started on the morning of the twenty-eighth with the 2nd Massachusetts and 16th New York. The cavalrymen were directed to march through Leesburg and then on to Upperville, Paris and Rectortown. They approached Leesburg that afternoon.[52]

Inside Pickett's hotel, meanwhile, the Rangers enjoyed themselves until someone burst through the door to exclaim that Yankees were on the Pike, only 200 yards from the square. A scramble ensued but, before most of the partisans could unhitch their horses, the head of the Union column saw them and charged. Rangers Elwell Atwell and Thomas Flack managed to swing into their saddles and race away. Atwell quickly abandoned his horse as pursuers closed in and, fleeing on foot, escaped. Flack did not make it, gunned down at the edge of town and killed. Near the square, Ranger John DeButts ran toward a blacksmith shop and was shot in the chest and captured. Two other Rebels eluded the Yankees by leaving through the rear of the hotel. But a half a dozen of their comrades stood in the square as prisoners.[53]

From Leesburg, Lowell's troopers rode into Upper Fauquier. During the next day, they captured twelve more Rangers and killed Edward Smith of Company B. The Federals marched eastward toward their camp late in the day, arriving that night or early on the morning of the thirtieth. The expedition cost them three killed, two wounded and four missing. One of the wounded was an officer who accidentally shot himself in the foot while holstering his pistol.[54]

The end of April 1864 marked the conclusion of four months of costly campaigning for Mosby and the 43rd Battalion. For the first time in the unit's existence, they had suffered the worst of it. From January 1 to May 1, the Rangers incurred significant casualties— seventeen killed or mortally wounded, including a captain and two lieutenants; fifteen wounded; and at least ninety captured, including a lieutenant. They inflicted their share of casualties on their opponents but, in relative terms, the toll incurred by the Confederate partisans was significantly greater than that of the Federals. The victories at Blakeley's Grove School and Second Dranesville did not compensate for the deadly morning on Loudoun Heights. And, with the coming of May and fine spring weather, Mosby's Rangers faced a newer type of war, a harder struggle, brought by an opponent led by warriors who heralded the future.[55]

The achievements or worth of a command could be measured beyond the cold numbers of casualties suffered and inflicted. For Robert E. Lee the 43rd Battalion and its leader were a singular command, unmatched by similar units. During the final weeks of discussion on which partisan commands should be retained under the law of February 17, 1864, Lee offered his judgment to Samuel Cooper, Adjutant and Inspector General of the Confederacy. Lee wrote on April 1: "I am making an effort to have Col Mosby's battalion mustered into the regular service. If this cannot be done I recommend that this battalion be retained as partisans for the present. Lt Col Mosby has done excellent service, & from the reports of citizens & others I am inclined to believe that he is strict in discipline & a protection to the county in which he operates."[56]

Lee continued, declaring: "Experience has convinced me that it is impossible, under the best of officers even, to have discipline in these bands of Partisan Rangers, or to prevent them from becoming an injury instead of a benefit to the service." Lee viewed such units as a haven for marauders and deserters and an enticement for regular army troops "to leave their commands." In his opinion, only Mosby's battalion should be retained and the other partisan commands in Virginia be disbanded.[57]

Shortly after Lee penned his letter to Cooper, a drama entitled *The Guerrilla; or, Mosby in Five Hundred Sutler-wagons* opened to Northern audiences in Alexandria, Virginia. The measure of prowess and fame could take various forms.[58]

Chapter 10

SPRINGTIME OF CHANGE

The American Civil War crossed a divide in the spring of 1864. Three years of carnage had brought no resolution of the struggle. The embattled Confederacy still stood, but with its borders reduced, its ports blockaded. Its armies, its capital and some citadels remained unconquered. With the warmth of a new spring, a hard war became even harder.

Architect of a new type of warfare was Lieutenant General Ulysses S. Grant, general-in-chief of the armed forces of the United States. Grant was an Illinoisan, forty-one years old, a West Pointer and Mexican War veteran. From the outbreak of the war, he had served in the West, that is, in the Mississippi River Valley, patching together a string of battlefield victories at Forts Henry and Donelson, Shiloh and Chattanooga in Tennessee. His brilliant campaign at Vicksburg, Mississippi, in 1863 resulted in the surrender of the river bastion and Union control of the great river.

By the winter of 1864 Abraham Lincoln believed he had found the man he had been searching for for three years—a general who could bring final victory. The president asked the Senate to revive the rank of lieutenant general—previously held only by George Washington—and confirm Grant. The Senate complied, and Grant came to Washington in March.

Grant was, in the words of Assistant Secretary of War Charles A. Dana, "an uncommon fellow—the most modest, the most disinterested and the most honest man I ever knew, with a temper that nothing could disturb and a judgment that was judicial in its comprehensiveness and wisdom." Grant's close friend and fellow general, William T. Sherman, however, admitted once that "to me he [Grant] is a mystery, and I believe he is a mystery to himself." He had been accused of drunkenness and incompetence, but he responded with hard fought victories. There was a core of iron to the man, and that is what Lincoln, contrary to many others, saw. "He was a man who always knew just exactly what he wanted to do," concluded a clerk in Grant's headquarters.[1]

What Grant wanted to do when he assumed overall control of the Union war effort in March 1864 was to unsheath a terrible swift sword against the Confederacy and its people. He possessed no romantic illusions about the art of warmaking. War, as he understood it, meant killing and maiming, the destruction of an enemy's armed forces and the sinews which sustained them in the field. Grant had behind him the agricultural, industrial, financial and human might of the North, a reservoir of resources his opponents could not match. He planned an unrelenting pounding of the rebellious South from Virginia to the Gulf Coast. Both the Confederate armies and the fabric of the country—the farms, factories, railroads and cities—were his targets. The nature of warfare would never be the same.

The concerted offensive formulated and ordered by Grant focused on Richmond, the Confederacy's political center, and Atlanta, Georgia, its railroad center. Against the latter city, Grant directed three armies under the command of Sherman. In Virginia, the general-in-chief fashioned a three-prong offensive. The main thrust against Robert E. Lee's Army of Northern Virginia Grant assigned to George G. Meade's Army of the Potomac, under

Grant's personal direction. A second force, Major General Benjamin F. Butler's Army of the James, was hurled against Petersburg, where five railroads intersected twenty miles south of Richmond. The third arm of the offensive was a small army, led by Major General Franz Sigel, whose task was to advance southward up the Shenandoah Valley and sever the rail links that connected Lee's troops to the harvests of the rich valley. Grant designated the first week of May for the start of the grand movement.

Before this onslaught across the breadth of the Confederacy, the Rebels were tested as never before. In Georgia, General Joseph Johnston's gray-clad soldiers slowed Sherman's advance by withdrawing from one defensive line to another. In Virginia, Butler quickly bogged down on a neck of land called Bermuda Hundred, between Petersburg and Richmond. Beyond the Blue Ridge, Sigel marched toward a battle fought at New Market on May 15 against troops led by Major General John C. Breckinridge, a former vice president of the United States. Finally, Meade's veterans collided with Lee's men on old killing ground west of Fredericksburg. The two foes ravaged each other in a string of bloody fights at the Wilderness and Spotsylvania Court House before moving southward toward Richmond. They bled themselves to the marrow.

For Mosby and the Rangers, Grant's offensive in Virginia meant months of unceasing activity. Ranger operations assumed an importance they had not had previously as the summer and fall campaigning in the Old Dominion determined the outcome of the war in the East. The demands of the struggle extended the 43rd Battalion's battleground and required a significant influx of recruits. Mosby's men, like their comrades in the regular forces, now confronted a newer, more formidable enemy. How the Confederates met that test would determine whether their nation could stay the darkness of final defeat.

The Union movements beyond the Rappahannock River and up the Shenandoah Valley, wrote Ranger James Williamson, "gave us plenty of work." Mosby extended the resources of the battalion the best he could, using mainly Companies A and D against the rear of Meade's army and Companies B and C against Sigel across the Blue Ridge. It was work the men knew well—attacks on supply trains, scouting and cutting communication lines. When scouts located weak points along Federal lines, the Rebels hit the points. It was the original mission—drain enemy troops away from the invading forces—only magnified.[2]

The raids began on May 8, four days after Grant sent Meade's army forward to give battle to Lee's veterans. Mosby led approximately fifty men from companies A and D toward the Rapidan River and Grant's supply arteries. The Federals had abandoned Warrenton in late April, so the Rangers encountered no enemy outposts until they reached the Orange and Alexandria Railroad. Squads burned bridges at Bealeton Station and Culpeper Court House as Mosby and two dozen men swung toward Belle Plain, Grant's supply base, located east of Fredericksburg on the Potomac River.[3]

Near Belle Plain Mosby discovered a wagon train en route to the depot. Belle Plain offered Grant a secure place for stockpiling goods with the Potomac River as the conduit. The Federals' reliance upon the Orange and Alexandria Railroad thus decreased, and extended by miles Mosby's effort to interdict the flow. If Mosby were to strike the strings of white-canvased wagons, it had to be in the eight-mile stretch of road between Fredericksburg and Belle Plain. The Rangers could not tarry in the region so far from the security of the "Confederacy" and had to contend with heavy guard details. At best, Mosby could only deliver swift, glancing blows.

On the night of May 8 a drizzle of rain was falling when Mosby came upon the twenty-wagon caravan. The Rangers worked swiftly, cutting the train into two by directing the rear section into a side road. Just as they completed the separation a Union officer of the escort reined up, demanding: "Who in the hell has stopped these wagons and turned them off the road?"

"Colonel Mosby," replied Sergeant W. Ben Palmer, drawing his revolver on the Yankee.

Palmer then led ten men to the front of the train, stopping the lead wagon. The Rangers unhitched the teams and, with the prisoners, horses and mules, disappeared into the darkness. A few shots were fired when several of the teamsters realized the situation.[4]

Detachments from companies B and C, under captains Dolly Richards and William Chapman, respectively, were meanwhile prowling through the Winchester-Berryville-Middletown section of the Shenandoah Valley. The two details separated as each searched for wagons laden with supplies for Sigel's command, which was marching southward toward New Market. Near Berryville, on May 9, Chapman, who had recently returned to duty after a thirty-day furlough granted to him upon his marriage, attacked a train and its cavalry guards. The Federal troopers belonged to the 1st New

York Cavalry. The New Yorkers despised the Rangers, with one of them calling the partisans "the most detestable characters that the war produced," likening them to "human hyenas."[5]

The Southerners' charge scattered the New Yorkers. Chapman's men gathered what they could manage and moved toward the mountains. A second detachment from the Union regiment overtook the Rebels outside of Millwood, but the Rangers repulsed the Yankees, moving on without further incident.[6]

Dolly Richards's party of roughly twenty Rangers tangled with a company of the 21st New York Cavalry south of Winchester on the same day Chapman struck near Berryville. Richards had captured the advance guard of Federals when someone fired a shot. The remaining New Yorkers charged, and a brisk gunfight ensued until the outnumbered Rangers withdrew. Richards lost two men wounded in the action.[7]

Then on May 12, Jeb Stuart died in Richmond. The previous day his cavalrymen had battled with Union horsemen at Yellow Tavern, north of the capital. In the swirling action a Michigan trooper shot Stuart in his right side below the ribs. The dashing cavalier lingered slightly more than twenty-four hours, dying on the twelfth at 7:38 P.M. Mosby probably learned of the tragedy within a day or two and was surely devastated by the news. Stuart had been his mentor and, as Mosby said, "his best friend in the army." After Stuart's death, Mosby began reporting directly to Lee, the only commander of a unit beneath corps level to do so.[8]

Duty, however, permitted little time for mourning, and Mosby undertook a second raid on Belle Plain within days of Stuart's fall. Fifty Rangers rendezvoused at Joseph Blackwell's, each man carrying five days of feed for the horses. They rode forth at noon, camping for the night near Catlett's Station. Another day's ride brought them to a point on the Potomac three miles from Belle Plain. A Union infantry brigade passed them as they hid in a woodlot. In the river a Federal flotilla lay at anchor and, as nightfall deepened, the ships "had the appearance of a large city lighted by gas," recalled one of the Confederate raiders.[9]

Mosby, with Charlie Hall and Johnny Edmonds, had spent much of the time reconnoitering. The trio located a park of wagons the following morning, but Mosby decided to wait until darkness before attacking. Giving command to Lieutenant Alfred Glascock, Mosby departed on a scouting mission into Fairfax County. Later in the day, however, someone warned the Confederates that the Yankees had discovered their trail and had dispatched a regiment of cavalry and of infantry to locate the party of horsemen. Glascock had the men in the saddle and on the move at once. As they approached a railroad spur which connected Fredericksburg to Aquia on the Potomac, the bluecoated infantrymen barred their escape route. Acting quickly, Glascock waved his men forward at a gallop, shouting: "Mosby is after us! get out of the way!" The Yankees mistook the Confederates for Union cavalrymen and spilled off the tracks, scurrying for cover as the Rangers raced through the opening.[10]

Upon his return from Fairfax County, Mosby assembled ninety-nine men at Paris on May 20, and led them westward across the Blue Ridge. They reached the Shenandoah River at dusk, only to find high water from recent rains. While the men bedded down in Ashby's Gap, Mosby secured a skiff, crossed the river and scouted ahead. The next morning when the Rangers arrived at the riverbank, six boats waited for them. Where Mosby located the boats and whose they were remain a mystery. But the command floated across as the horses swam the current. A message from Mosby soon arrived, directing the men to ride toward Guard Hill, a wooded knoll four miles from Front Royal on the road to Winchester. He cautioned them to use the backroads as Union mounted patrols were on the main highways. It was well past sundown when the Rangers reunited with Mosby several hundred yards north of Guard Hill.[11]

During the evening and night the garrison on Guard Hill, 200 members of the 15th New York Cavalry, held a party, which ended in a brawl and riot. Officers from the reserve post, half a mile away, had to ride in and settle the dispute. While the Yankees were thus engaged, Mosby and a handful of men captured the Federal picket post. From the prisoners he learned that the enemy totaled 200, instead of the one hundred he had expected.[12]

At daybreak on the twenty-second, Sam Chapman and half a dozen or so Rangers opened the attack with carbine fire. They fired one volley, and Mosby and the others thundered into the campsite on horseback. The Yankees melted into the brush and woods. The Rebels collared only sixteen, but seized about seventy-five horses. Near the end of the brief action a Union officer, Captain Michael Auer, galloped into the campsite, shouting, cursing and demanding an explanation for "all this fuss," as he put it.

"It means," said Chapman, "Mosby's got you."

Stunned by the words and the pistol pointed at him, Auer exclaimed: "Well, this beats hell, don't it?"[13]

The Rangers returned to their base that day, but another detachment, numbering 144 with Mosby in command, reentered the Valley
of Virginia within a week. From May 28 until June 1, this contingent
watched for wagon trains on the Valley Pike between Middletown
and Winchester. The Valley Pike, a broad, macadamized thoroughfare, ran the length of the region through its heart, and both sides
had utilized its stone bed for three years. For any Union army advancing southward through the Shenandoah, the Valley Pike was its
lifeline to supply depots at Martinsburg and Harper's Ferry.[14]

It was not until the thirty-first when a wagon train came creaking
southward toward the Rangers. The escort consisted of cavalry and
infantry, but the Rebels charged, routing the Federal horsemen. The
foot soldiers, however, stood firm and unleashed a volley which killed
Ranger William E. Embrey of Company B. Mosby disengaged, and
the wagons proceeded. The next day, as the Southerners rode homeward, they captured a Federal soldier who was trying to burn down
a house in Newtown. Mosby, wrote a civilian, "hung him instanter.
He also notified [Union Major General David] Hunter if any more
houses were burnt he would kill every prisoner he took."[15]

If Mosby sent such a message to Hunter, the records do not
indicate it nor did Mosby write of it after the war. Hunter, who had
succeeded Sigel following the latter's defeat at New Market, was
sixty-one years old, a professional soldier for over forty years, and a
man of passion. Ordered by Grant to resume Sigel's ill-fated advance
southward, up the Valley, Hunter planned to wage war not only
against enemy forces but also against civilians. He came as an avenging
warrior. The soldier who burned the house in Newtown was most
likely a straggler, but his handiwork was a precursor of darker days
ahead for the people of the beautiful Valley of Virginia.

Mosby was untiring in his movements during these weeks. Upon
his return from the Shenandoah Valley, he led roughly a hundred
men into Loudoun County. Traveling by night the Rebels reached
the Potomac River, where they tried to lure Federal units stationed
along the Maryland bank across the stream. When the Yankees stayed
put, Mosby pulled back from the river. Company B, under Dolly
Richards, rode to Hillsborough, remaining until June 5, enjoying
music, dancing and cards for three days. By the fifth, the entire body
of Rangers were back in the Confederacy.[16]

Another purpose of the four-day expedition into Loudoun was
the impressment of forage from the farmers in the county. Mosby
had continued sending what the men dubbed "Corn Details" into
Loudoun throughout May. On occasions an entire company performed the duty; at other times, "Major" William Hibbs and a few
men hauled the grain. Hibbs, stated John Alexander, possessed an
"unerring instinct" for locating a Union sympathizer's barn in the
dark of the night. Hibbs was equally adept at finding a local distil-
lery.[17]

Duty with the "Corn Detail" proved hazardous, however. From
the beginning of May through the first two weeks of June, Union
troops captured roughly forty Rangers. Of that number, some were
taken on scouting missions in the Shenandoah Valley, in Fairfax and
Prince William counties, and three were even nabbed in southern
Pennsylvania. At least a dozen Rangers fell into Federal hands in
Loudoun, while Ranger Benjamin Barton of Company A was killed
by Yankee cavalrymen as he loaded corn at a farmstead. On June 3,
Northern troopers grabbed James and George Gunnell and Charles
Fenton Beavers. The captors charged Beavers with violating the am-
nesty oath he had taken in February and with spying in Vienna and
Alexandria. The Federals, by order of Charles Russell Lowell, hanged
Beavers.[18]

The Rangers' old nemesis, Lowell's three regiments of cavalry,
probably was responsible for a majority of the captures. Patrols from
the brigade rode forth daily against what one of their officers termed
"the infernal and formidable guerrillas." Mosby's men, burdened
with their numerous raids, scouts and forage trips, avoided contact
with the Union horsemen. The captures of the partisans usually resulted more from good fortune, information from civilians or lack
of vigilance on the part of the Rangers than from the skill of the
Federals. The blue-jacketed troopers still followed the main roads,
avoiding the bypaths utilized by Mosby's men. Their accomplishments should not be dismissed, however, for the toll from the 43rd
Battalion mounted—approximately a Ranger per day after April 1.
Nevertheless, after nearly a year of service against the Rangers, the
Federals remained more the victims than the victimizers. For the most
part, it was Mosby who dictated when and where clashes between
the foes occurred.[19]

On June 22 Mosby held a rendezvous at Rectortown. He conducted the first roll call the battalion ever had, with 260 men an-

swering to their names. He also displayed for them a twelve-pound howitzer he had secured from Richmond. Once again, Lieutenant Sam Chapman, who served as the battalion's adjutant, was assigned to command of the gun crew. Finally, Mosby prescribed the limits of the Confederacy—which were outlined earlier—requiring all of the men to live within those boundaries. Roll calls, he cautioned, would be held at each rendezvous and, if a member missed two successive meetings without permission or an acceptable reason, he would be sent to Lee's army. At noon, approximately 200 of the Rangers, with Mosby commanding, started for Fairfax.[20]

The Confederates spent the twenty-third concealed as Mosby and/or others scouted for a target. The next morning some of them overran a four-man picket post of the 16th New York Cavalry. The gunfire brought a forty-man pursuit force from the regiment, led by Lieutenant Matthew Tuck. Mosby stayed ahead of the pursuers until Tuck halted his troopers to feed their mounts in a pasture. Turning back, Mosby's men charged. The Yankees never had a chance as every one of them, except for Tuck, were killed, wounded or captured, along with their horses. One of the prisoners was Boston Corbett, the soldier who in April 1865 would allegedly kill John Wilkes Booth as Lincoln's assassin fled through Virginia. On this day, Corbett emptied his pistol at the Rangers until surrounded.[21]

Four days later, on June 28, Mosby summoned the entire command to Upperville. About 250 men reported, and Mosby, taking Company A with him, rode toward the Shenandoah Valley. He ordered Captain William Chapman to follow with Companies B, C and D and the artillery piece. Crossing at Ashby's Gap, Company A passed through Kabletown before encamping for the night outside of Charlestown. Mosby planned to seize one of the trains of the Baltimore & Ohio Railroad somewhere along the tracks between Martinsburg and Harper's Ferry.[22]

While the members of Company A slept, Ranger John S. Russell reported to Mosby. Twenty-one years old, Russell was a native of the region, born and raised outside of nearby Berryville. He knew every backroad, deer path and hiding place in this section of the Valley, and Mosby trusted him implicitly. As Mosby's operations increased in the Valley, Russell's knowledge and skill became more important.[23]

Russell detailed the Federal dispositions—infantry, cavalry and artillery at Smithfield, four miles to the southwest; cavalry at Bunker

Hill, three miles beyond Smithfield; and the main garrison in Harper's Ferry, four miles northeast of Charlestown. No Yankees were in Charlestown, and, if Mosby avoided detection from the signal station on Maryland Heights, an eminence which towered above Harper's Ferry on the north bank of the Potomac, the Confederate raiders could reach the railroad tracks at a point Mosby selected.[24]

Mosby then fashioned the final plan. With the morning's light and while he waited for the arrival of Chapman and the three companies, he sent an unidentified local woman to Duffield's Station, a railroad depot three miles from Harper's Ferry, for a train schedule, and detached Lieutenant Joseph Nelson, acting commander of Company A, and twenty-two men to cover the Charlestown–Harper's Ferry road. Mosby instructed Nelson to fight any force that did not exceed twice his strength and to warn Mosby of any Federal advance toward Charlestown and the Rangers' escape route.[25]

Nelson's men rode directly through Charlestown, where the residents warmly greeted them. The lieutenant established his picket post just north of the town, with vedettes farther out on the road to Harper's Ferry. Soon after they settled in, the women of Charlestown brought them meat, bread, pies and milk, and "for a time we had quite a picnic," recalled one of them. It had the look of a pleasant day for Nelson's men.[26]

Chapman, with Companies B, C and D and the howitzer, meanwhile, joined Mosby. The woman arrived afterwards, and the Rangers spurred for the train station minutes before noon. A local boy, fifteen-year-old Willie Gibson, guided the Confederates on a route even John Russell apparently did not know. Gibson's mother, when she learned what her son was doing, sent a messenger after him, ordering him home. Gibson refused, telling the messenger that the success of Mosby's raid depended upon him. The teenager led the raiders to a point one mile from the depot.[27]

The Rebels cut the telegraph wires and captured four pickets from whom they learned that about sixty-five infantrymen garrisoned the depot and that the eastbound train was due in fifteen minutes. Sam Chapman's crew rolled the howitzer onto a knoll about a quarter-mile from the stockade and prepared to fire. Mosby then sent Dolly Richards, under a truce flag, to the depot, where he explained the situation to the lieutenant in command. The Federal officer returned with Richards to Mosby and, seeing the cannon and over 200 Rangers, surrendered.[28]

While Company D, Montjoy's "dandies," watched for the expected train, companies B and C ransacked the place. They found bolts of calico cloth and an artillery limber chest filled with coffee. (The Rangers subsequently dubbed the operation the "First Calico Raid.") With the goods removed, Mosby paroled the garrison and ordered the station and camp burned because the train had not appeared. (It had been delayed behind schedule, a fact Mosby could not have known.) The smoke would surely stir up some Federals, so the Southerners hurried southward. They had not heard from Nelson and expected their escape route to be open.[29]

Joe Nelson was a reliable officer; he had been with Mosby since the early days, had been wounded once, captured and exchanged twice. He had taken all the precautions while letting his men enjoy their "picnic." When Ranger James Williamson, an advanced picket, bridled up with the news of an approaching Union cavalry column, Nelson ordered his twenty-two Rangers into line and galloped off to count the oncoming horsemen. His orders from Mosby specified that if the enemy outnumbered him by more than two-to-one he should withdraw. But Nelson was more concerned with fighting than arithmetic and, when he calculated the Yankees at sixty, he decided to give battle. Using the old Ranger trick of placing two men as decoys in the road, Nelson attacked the Federals as they raced after the two Rebels. The enemy halted, fired a volley which missed its marks and then scattered as the Southerners poured down a hillside into their ranks. The Rangers killed three, wounded several and captured twenty-five. Nelson had no casualties.[30]

Nelson's detachment, with their prisoners, reunited with the main body beyond Charlestown. Mosby, keeping several men with him as a rear guard, ordered the rest back to the Confederacy. Mosby's party later skirmished briefly with a pursuit force and, during the exchange of gunfire, Mosby's horse balked. Ranger David "Graft" Carlisle killed a Federal as the latter closed in on Mosby. The entire command reached Upper Fauquier on June 30, a welcome sight, especially to the womenfolk when they saw the calico cloth.[31]

Brigadier General Max Weber, commander at Harper's Ferry, reported the destruction of Duffield's Station and the escape of the Rangers on the day Mosby and his men returned to the Confederacy. Weber promised that "the matter will be carefully investigated" and requested "a permanent force of good cavalry" for Harper's Ferry. Weber, however, would learn three days later that he needed far more than "good cavalry." On July 3, a wave of graycoated infantry, artillery and cavalry streamed into the lower Shenandoah Valley, coursing toward the Potomac River and Maryland. As it had in the past, the natural warpath of the Shenandoah Valley once again had become a strategically important battleground. For the next four months, the struggle for Virginia was interwoven with events in the great valley beyond the Blue Ridge.[32]

The presence of a substantial number of Confederate troops in the region resulted from Union Major General David Hunter's fiery march into the upper Shenandoah Valley. When Hunter replaced Sigel after New Market, Grant ordered the new commander to advance on Staunton, a Confederate supply base, destroy the facilities and, from there, penetrate deeper into the upper Valley, moving either toward Lynchburg or Gordonsville and Charlottesville east of the Blue Ridge. Grant's preference was Lynchburg, writing to Hunter: "It would be of great value to us to get possession of Lynchburg for a single day." Railroads connected in the city, and the James River and Kanawha Canal passed through. The Confederates could not afford the fall of the vital city.[33]

Hunter performed skillfully during the early phases of the operation. Sweeping aside a small Confederate force at the Battle of Piedmont on June 5, Hunter's 8,500-man army entered Staunton the next day. The work of destruction began immediately and, when 10,000 additional troops under Brigadier General George Crook joined Hunter on the eighth, the Federals marched southward. On June 11, the Yankees occupied Lexington, where Hunter ordered the burning of the Virginia Military Institute buildings. For two days Hunter's troops carried out his instructions, sacking the beautiful community. Hunter departed from Lexington on the fourteenth, marching toward Lynchburg.[34]

While Hunter applied the torch in Lexington, miles to the east Robert E. Lee had reached a crucial decision. His army presently manned miles of fieldworks near Cold Harbor, east of Richmond. Across the intervening ground, Meade's units filled their own series of entrenchments. The two behemoths had fought each other for forty days, from the stunted brush and trees of the Wilderness to the sweltering bottomlands of the Virginia Peninsula, where Cold Harbor lay. For the previous week, the campaign was quiet, but Grant still retained the strategic initiative. In order to stop Hunter before he took Lynchburg and to retake the initiative, Lee fashioned an audacious

plan, a gamble which might give him control of the campaign in
Virginia.[35]

On June 12, Lee conferred in private at his headquarters with
Lieutenant General Jubal A. Early, commander of the army's Second
Corps. Lee instructed Early to take the entire corps and two artillery
battalions, race westward to the Shenandoah Valley and assail Hunter.
If successful and circumstances permitted, Lee then wanted Early to
turn northward, advance down the broad valley, cross into Maryland,
confiscating supplies, and threaten Washington, DC, and Baltimore.
It was a bold undertaking, for Lee was detaching one fourth of his
infantry. If Early accomplished the goals, Lee believed that Grant
would have to forward troops from Meade's army to the Union
capital and thus give Lee an opportunity to strike on the Peninsula.
Lee had utilized a similar strategy two years earlier when Stonewall
Jackson rampaged through the Shenandoah Valley, disrupting Union
plans in that spring.[36]

Early's veterans, numbering about 9,000, filed out of the trenches
before daylight on June 13. They covered a hundred miles by foot
and by rail in four days, repulsed Hunter's advance on the outskirts
of Lynchburg and chased the Yankees into the Allegheny Mountains.
Early then combined his three infantry divisions and batteries with
John Breckinridge's troops and knifed down the Shenandoah Valley.
Before the gray onslaught, the Federals, commanded by the discred-
ited Franz Sigel, fled into the confines of Harper's Ferry. Early had
a clear path into Maryland and, beginning on July 5, his veterans—
Stonewall Jackson's famous "foot cavalry"—forded the Potomac
River, entering Northern soil.[37]

John Mosby learned of Early's large-scale raid on July 2 in Rectortown. There, he talked with Hugh Swartz, a member of Early's
quartermaster department, who was passing through Fauquier on the
way to the Shenandoah Valley. Mosby ordered a rendezvous for the
next morning. Approximately 250 partisans converged on Upperville
on the third; each man had attached a large sack to his saddle for
plunder.[38]

The Rangers started at midday, angling northeastward through
Loudoun County. Mosby kept the column closed up, allowing no
straggling. The pace was deliberate, as an afternoon sun blistered the
ground; temperatures approached one hundred degrees and the region
was suffering a drought. The heat and dust combined for an uncom-

fortable march. They halted outside of Purcellville, a town west of Leesburg, and encamped for the night.[39]

Mosby believed that he could assist Early by striking at Union communications lines—telegraph, railroad and canal boats—between Harper's Ferry and Washington. When his men remounted at daylight on the fourth, Mosby led them toward the Potomac River. Scouts fanned out from the main body, riding miles in advance. By eleven o'clock the Rangers arrived opposite Berlin, Maryland. Mosby waited an hour before some of the scouts returned from downriver and reported that a small detachment of Yankees held Point of Rocks, Maryland. The small village of Point of Rocks, located twelve miles east of Harper's Ferry, was a station of the Baltimore & Ohio Railroad and a stop for the traffic on the Chesapeake & Ohio Canal. Mosby, riding ahead to reconnoiter, ordered the men to follow.[40]

The Potomac River was a quarter of a mile wide opposite Point of Rocks. A small island lying in midstream divided the current. Because of the lack of rainfall the river was only chest-deep, fordable at almost any point. The troops holding the village consisted of two companies of infantry and two companies of cavalry. An infantry picket post manned the island while the other foot soldiers covered the river and canal from a small earthwork on a hill which overlooked the waters. A wooden bridge, lying at the foot of the knoll, spanned the canal.[41]

The Union horsemen were encamped in the village. They numbered about a hundred and were members of the Loudoun Rangers. An independent command organized in June 1862 in the northwestern section of Loudoun County by Samuel Means, a Waterford miller, the Loudoun Rangers were anathema to Mosby's men. The Confederates regarded them as "a band of renegade Loudouners." On occasion the two foes crossed paths, but the encounters had never amounted to much. "We ever bore a regard," John Alexander wrote disdainfully of the Loudoun Rangers, "ardent but misplaced in the sense that we could never get close enough to them to levy our attachment."[42]

Mosby tested the Federal dispositions by wading into the river and drawing gunfire from the island by the time the Rangers arrived. He positioned Sam Chapman's howitzer on high ground above the river and assigned about two dozen men armed with carbines to Lieutenant Albert Wrenn with orders to wade the stream and attack the island. The remaining men Mosby kept on horseback—they were to charge once Wrenn's detachment had eliminated the nest of Yankees on the island.[43]

Wrenn's sharpshooters stepped into the water; from the island, the flashes and smoke of musketry darted forth. The Rangers responded in kind and kept going through the chest-deep stream. Behind them, the bellow of Chapman's howitzer punctuated the cracks of carbine and rifle fire. The Northerners fought for a handful of minutes and then tumbled off the spit of land into the river. Reaching the island, Wrenn's carbineers started shooting at the Federals in the earthwork and along the opposite bank. At this point in the action, the mounted Rangers, looking like a giant gray arrow, with Captain Dolly Richards in the lead, splashed through the water.[44]

The Rangers on horseback scrambled up the riverbank to the canal. By the time they reached the waterway, however, a detail of the Loudoun Rangers had removed the planking. Caught on the bank, the Confederates milled about, exchanging gunfire with the Yankees in the earthwork. Richards dismounted a number of men, who ripped boards from a dilapidated building and began laying them across the bridge. Harry Hatcher, meanwhile, sprinted across the timber under a hail of fire and hauled down the Union flag in the camp. When the bridge was repaired, the Southerners bolted across and into the earthwork and village. By now, the Yankee infantrymen were fleeing on foot, and all the Rebels saw of the Loudoun Rangers was a cloud of dust in the direction of Frederick.[45]

Within minutes Mosby's men were off their horses, plundering the five stores in Point of Rocks. They were experts at such work and went through the establishments like a prairie cyclone. The Rangers grabbed shoes, bonnets, hats and rolls of crinoline cloth. A packet boat in the canal was emptied of liquor, cigars and food in one rush. A store owner, Lewis Meems, told Mosby that he was a Southern sympathizer, and Mosby ordered the men to return his wares. A train from Harper's Ferry clanged toward the village until Chapman's crew whistled a shell over the tracks. Screeching to a halt, the engine hissed and steamed back, westward. The raiders cut the telegraph wires and burned the Federal camp and canal boats before Mosby started them back across the Potomac. Not a man had been hit during the action.[46]

During the ride southward, many of the Rangers replaced their hats with the bonnets and draped the cloth across their shoulders. They "looked for all the world like a parade of Fantastics," recalled

John Alexander. They bivouacked for the night in a woodlot along the road to Leesburg. Some indulged themselves with the whiskey; others shared a large pound cake, shaped like a spread eagle, which had been confiscated from a Federal officer's quarters. The Rangers slept well that night.[47]

The next morning, July 5, Mosby had the men load three wagons with the booty and assigned a detail to take them back to Fauquier. He also gave Walter Bowie and Joe Nelson detachments, directing each of them to recross the river, move deeper into Maryland and sever telegraph lines. Finally, Mosby scribbled a note for Jubal Early and, giving it to Fount Beattie and Harry Heaton, told them to find the Confederate general.[48]

After the details had departed, Mosby led the others—now numbering about 150—back to Point of Rocks. Mosby planned to reenter Maryland but, when he arrived at the site of the previous day's fight, he saw Union cavalrymen in the town. Sam Chapman's gunners again unlimbered their artillery piece, and sharpshooters hid behind trees along the southern bank. The Yankees, the 8th Illinois Cavalry, shook out their skirmish line. For the next hour and a half, the opponents duelled across the river. Ranger John Scott asserted in his memoirs that a Miss Ellen Fisher of the village was accidentally killed in the exchange of gunfire. Mosby pulled out first, moving downstream. The Federals trailed the Rangers on the northern bank until the Confederates turned southward. Circling around Leesburg, the Rangers stopped five miles from the county seat. When a scout reported that Leesburg was full of Yankees, Mosby, concerned about the command's safety, relocated their camp farther west. The Confederates slept with their horses' reins in their hands.[49]

The Yankees in Leesburg—150 troopers of the 13th New York and 2nd Massachusetts Cavalry, Major William H. Forbes of the latter regiment, commanding—had been in the area for the past two days. Ordered by their brigade commander, Charles Russell Lowell, to reconnoiter toward the gaps of the Blue Ridge, the cavalrymen spent much of July 5 between Leesburg and Aldie. Forbes planned to stay in this section for another day before returning to their camps at Falls Church.[50]

The Federals clattered out of Leesburg on the morning of the sixth. Their precise route is uncertain, but they apparently rode due south on the Old Carolina Road. The pace was unhurried because it was not until late afternoon when they reached the Little River Turnpike at Mount Zion Baptist Church and turned eastward, halting at the farm of Samuel Skinner. The Yankees scattered in a field around the stone farmhouse, dismounted, fed their mounts and relaxed. Forbes placed sentinels toward Aldie, a mile and a half to the west, and farther east on the turnpike. The major allowed an hour for the break.[51]

Mosby and his Rangers, meanwhile, shadowed the trail of the Federals throughout the day. The Confederates entered Leesburg after the enemy horsemen had departed. Learning that the Yankees had marched southward, Mosby angled southeastward, moving via Ball's Mills and then across country on an "obscure road." The Rangers struck the Little River Turnpike east of Arcola Post Office, beyond the Skinner farm. Mosby scouted westward, located the Federals and brought his command forward to the base of a ridge less than a mile from the campsite. The gun crew rolled the howitzer onto the crest, loaded a charge and awaited the signal. The bulk of the Ranger force jammed the Pike in a column of fours while Lieutenant Harry Hatcher of Company A advanced on horseback with a dozen skirmishers, armed with carbines.[52]

Forbes's lookouts, who were stationed just west of the ridge, opened fire when they saw Hatcher's men and then bolted to the rear. The gunshots alerted the Federals, who were preparing to leave when the Rangers appeared. Forbes aligned his men into two ranks, the line extending through the field to the Pike. The Yankees, said a Ranger, looked as if they were on dress parade, their Spencer carbines at the ready.[53]

Forbes had barely aligned his troopers when the Rangers came on. It was, wrote John Alexander, "a straight charge over an open road upon an enemy who was fully prepared for us." Sam Chapman's gunners initiated the attack, shrieking a shell over the Federal ranks. It was a poor shot, admitted a Rebel, but when it exploded, horses of the front rank bolted with fright, the entire battle line splintering as each rider tried to control his unruly mount. It was all the edge the Southerners needed as they charged up the Pike. Harry Hatcher's twelve men spearheaded the assault "in a sweeping gallop," according to one of them. They reached the fence between the Pike and field and swiftly removed the rails, creating a gap for the main body.[54]

The Rangers poured through the hole in the fence before Forbes could realign. "Mosby and his rangers were upon us," stated a Union officer, "swooping down like Indians, yelling like fiends, discharging their pistols with fearful rapidity, and threatening to completely envelop our little band." Ranger John Munson remembered it similarly: "we swept into their line like a hurricane, each man with a drawn six-shooter."[56]

Forbes had a reputation for courage—he was known as "Lowell's fighting major" to the Northern public—and he demonstrated it on this day. As the "hurricane" of Confederates blew into the field, he rode along his disorganized line, rallying his men. Many of them, however, galloped away from the oncoming storm. Finally, Forbes shouted: "Form in the woods! Form in the woods!" The Yankees responded, peeling back toward the trees, a few hundred yards to the right and rear near the brick two-story Mount Zion Church.[56]

The Rangers were directly behind the retiring enemy and, when the Federals turned to give battle, the lines crashed together. "It was a mass of struggling, cursing maniacs, each striving to slay his antagonist," recalled John Munson. It was sabers against pistols, and the Southerners had the better of it. "No words can picture the confusion and horror of that scene," asserted a Federal.[57]

For several minutes, however, Forbes's men stood. They "fought as gallantly as any men could fight," stated Munson. Many of the Northerners with Forbes were from the California Battalion. The Rangers respected them above all their foes. After the war one of the Californians claimed that "when a fair, square fight could be obtained, the Californians were never beaten." He must have forgotten this day at Mount Zion Church.[58]

Outnumbered, surrounded and shoved rearward into a fencerow, the island of Union cavalrymen finally cracked when Forbes went down. The major, bobbing in and out between the combatants, yelling, "Now rally around your leader," thrust his saber toward Mosby, but Ranger Thomas W. T. Richards, Dolly's brother, wedged between the two warriors and was hit in the shoulder by the blade. At that moment someone shot Forbes's horse, and the beast collapsed, pinning its rider to the ground. Lieutenant C. W. Amory rode to assist Forbes and he was unsaddled by a bullet. That settled the issue, and the Yankees broke through the fence.[59]

Those of the Federals who escaped from the field raced around the Mount Zion Church and into the Old Carolina Road. The Rangers pursued and, during the chase, which covered miles, a Confederate mortally wounded Union Captain Goodwin Stone. John Munson remembered that as he cleared the fencerow he saw a Northerner on his knees, his left hand thrust into a wound in his side. Munson stopped, looked and saw that the enemy trooper was dead.[60]

Union losses at Mount Zion were reported as twelve killed, thirty-seven wounded, and approximately forty-five captured, or nearly two-thirds of the command. Forbes was among the captured. When Caspar Crowninshield learned of the fight, he wrote his mother the next day that he feared for Forbes's life. "I pray God he is safe," Crowninshield stated, "he is a man who would fight to the last & I fear he is killed." Mosby talked with Forbes, and a mutual respect and friendship developed between the pair, which lasted until their deaths.[61]

Mosby counted six wounded and one mortally wounded. William E. "Willie" Martin was clubbed insensible during the action by a carbine-wielding Federal. The dying Ranger was Henry Smallwood of Company A. John Alexander described Smallwood as "a quiet, unostentatious little fellow, and absolutely reliable."[62]

Surgeons William Dunn and J. Richard Sowers converted Samuel Skinner's house into a hospital, tending to both their men and the Federals. Alexander "Yankee" Davis and his daughter, who lived one half mile west of the church, also came and hauled the injured to their home. Davis, a Northerner by birth, was a known Union sympathizer and "a perfectly fearless man," who eventually was forced to leave his home and enter Federal lines. The Skinners and the Davises nursed some of the men for weeks.[63]

The Washington *Evening Star* editorialized on the Mount Zion fight on July 9, praising Mosby even as they misspelled his name. "This has been Moseby's bravest and largest capture," the newspaper stated, "and there is something about it almost unaccountable, when we know how efficient this cavalry force [Lowell's command] has been heretofore, the numerous times they have fought Moseby the past year, and the number of captures we have made."[64]

The Confederates departed the evening of the engagement, bivouacking for the night in a field near Middleburg. On the following day, July 7, according to Caspar Crowninshield, a "strong party" from Lowell's brigade visited the battlefield, gathered up the wounded who could travel and "scoured" the countryside around Aldie and Middleburg. But the Rangers had disbanded earlier in the day to rest and refit.[65]

During the seventh or eighth, the two details sent into Maryland returned. Walter "Wat" Bowie's party of ten men had crossed the

Potomac River at Edwards's Ferry and followed the towpath of the Chesapeake & Ohio canal upstream, cutting telegraph wires en route. At an aqueduct at the mouth of the Monocacy River, they met a small force from the 8th Illinois Cavalry. The opponents skirmished across the waterway until the Illinoisans disengaged. The Rangers then looted four canal boats before burning them. By this time more troopers from the Federal regiment appeared and Bowie, seeing a cloud of dust to the rear, ordered his men out. The Rebels moved rapidly along the river, seeking a crossing point. They collared a black man who agreed to show them an obscure shallows in return for a horse, money and goods. With the two Union detachments closing in, Bowie agreed, and the guide led them to the Virginia shore.[66]

The detachment under Joe Nelson had a more adventurous raid and a narrower escape than Bowie's. Nelson's men entered Adamstown, a stop on the Baltimore & Ohio Railroad six miles south of Frederick, before noon on July 6. The Confederates expected to find Union soldiers and discovered instead a sutler's store. Numbers of them dismounted and, within minutes, emptied the shelves. When Nelson bridled up, the owner convinced him that he was a Confederate loyalist. Nelson ordered the Rangers to either purchase the goods or return them. "I cannot do justice," John Alexander wrote years later, "to the feelings of disappointment and disgust with which we relinquished our booty." John Munson, however, handed the storekeeper a five-dollar Confederate note and toted away several hundred dollars' worth of merchandise. When Mosby subsequently learned of the incident, he told Nelson that the businessman was a Yankee and his store should have been cleaned out.[67]

Before the raiders left Adamstown, they leveled the telegraph poles. Riding eastward, they skirted a mountain before heading toward the river. They secured bottles of whiskey at another store and, when they encamped for the night, the Rangers began to drink. Some drank too much and became "reckless." A Private Moon, either Jacob L. or James M., and Nelson exchanged words with each other, finally drawing their pistols. Others interceded before either one fired.[68]

Some of the men were still feeling the effects of the liquor the next morning as they continued toward Noland's Ferry on the Potomac. Union pursuers were trailing them when William Elzey and another Ranger became so angry that they stopped, hitched their horses and began slugging each other. Their comrades, ignoring the pair, proceeded on. By the time the two finished the fistfight, the Yankees overtook them, and both were soon en route to a Northern prison.[69]

When the Rangers reached the river, more Federals, deployed on a bluff, barred the passage. Dividing his men, Nelson sent one group around the enemy's flank and led the other in a headlong charge. The Yankees opened fire. John Alexander was grazed in the head by a bullet and knocked unconscious. One or two others kept him in the saddle, leading his mount. But when the other wing stormed into the Federals' flank and rear, the enemy scattered, and the Southerners forded the river, in the words of one of them, under a "hail of bullets," delivered by the Union cavalrymen who had been trailing them. They made it by the slimmest of margins.[70]

While Bowie and Nelson accomplished their missions, more importantly for Mosby, Fount Beattie and Henry Heaton came in on July 7 from their meeting with Jubal Early. Mosby had selected the two men because Beattie was his trusted confidant and Heaton had served on Early's staff in 1862. They located Early at Sharpsburg, Maryland, on the sixth, delivering Mosby's message to the general. In the note, Mosby stated: "I will obey any order you will send me."[71]

Jubal Anderson Early was, by most human measures, a difficult man to like. He had a host of enemies within the officer ranks of Lee's army because he was cynical, opinionated and caustic. A faultfinder by nature, he criticized fellow officers freely, but was almost blind to his own mistakes. He resented, probably even hated, his critics and, like Mosby, seldom forgave. He preferred his own counsel, not that of subordinates. But Early was a brave soldier, a fighter, whom Lee had chosen for corps command in May 1864 because there was no one better in the army at that time. By the time Beattie and Heaton talked with him at Sharpsburg, Early had performed almost flawlessly since Lee sent him to the Shenandoah Valley.

In a postwar letter Mosby described the meeting between Early, Beattie and Heaton. The letter was written thirty years after the war and, by that time, Mosby loathed Early. In two other letters of the period, Mosby described Early as "that old fraud" and "a most malignant enemy of mine." Early had alleged in his own public writings that Mosby had not cooperated with him while the former was in Maryland. It was untrue, as Early knew, and the lie earned Mosby's wrath.[72]

Mosby accused Early of drunkenness in his letter. Early had a reputation for enjoying various spirits, but no one else who saw the general or worked closely with him during this campaign asserted that he was inebriated on July 6. Beattie and Heaton claimed to Mosby that the general "could scarcely stand" and took "several drinks" in Beattie's presence. Mosby made the charge in a private letter to a friend and because of Mosby's intense dislike for Early, his allegation might be dismissed.[73]

Early told Beattie and Heaton that his targets were Frederick and then Washington, DC. When Beattie and Heaton relayed Early's verbal message to Mosby on the seventh, the partisan commander made preparations for another sortie into Maryland. The Rangers started on the ninth, penetrating into the state as far as Seneca Mills, twelve miles west of Rockville, a town on Early's route of march. They destroyed an abandoned camp of the 8th Illinois Cavalry on Muddy Branch, but never made contact with Early's troops, who arrived at the defenses of the capital on July 11. Mosby recrossed the Potomac on the twelfth, returning to Fauquier the next day. He relieved the men, who needed a rest, and awaited developments. For a few days, Mosby's men took a brief respite from war.[74]

Chapter 11

INTO
THE
VALLEY

 A long column of Jubal Early's infantry and artillery snaked up the eastern face of the Blue Ridge Mountains through Snicker's Gap on Saturday, July 16, 1864. Early's troops were marching back to the Shenandoah Valley after a remarkable raid. Since Rangers Fount Beattie and Henry Heaton had visited Early's headquarters at Sharpsburg, Maryland, on the sixth, Early's men had defeated a Union force in the Battle of Monocacy on the ninth and then carried the war to the gates of Washington. On the eleventh and twelfth, they tested the huge fortifications which encased the Union capital, before withdrawing. They never had much chance of penetrating the fortress but, in their commander's words, "we haven't taken Washington, but we've scared Abe Lincoln like h——!"[1]

This Saturday marked their fourth day out from Washington. Union pursuers tracked their retreat route, but Early's men had encountered only minor interference with their withdrawal. As the Confederates approached the mountain defile, they entered the northwest quadrant of "Mosby's Confederacy." Here, in the gap, probably in the afternoon or evening, John Mosby found Jubal Early, and the two officers talked.[2]

Outwardly, the contrast between the two men was stark. Mosby was thirty years old, thin, clean shaven, well dressed; Early was forty-seven years old, with dark eyes, a gray beard and a frame bent by arthritis. One of his men thought that Early's eyes and whiskers reminded him of "a very malignant and very hairy spider." Another believed that "Old Jube" or "Old Jubilee," as the soldiers called him, looked "as preternaturally solemn as a country coroner going to his first inquest." The men in the ranks, however, respected his bravery and chuckled at his eccentricities. "Old Jube" was, in the estimation of one, simply "a queer fish."[3]

Despite the physical and personality differences between the two Virginians, Mosby and Early shared common attributes. Both had practiced law before the war; both had opposed the secession of the Southern states before Fort Sumter. Both were ambitious, with a deep-grained pride and a sharp edge to their personalities. Neither much sought the counsel of subordinates but, while Mosby praised his officers and men, Early did so with jealous reluctance. In the end, and most importantly, both possessed the tempered metal of warriors, fighters committed to common cause.

Mosby had Dolly Richards with him when he conferred with Early. The meeting could not have lasted long. Mosby stated in an unpublished postwar letter that he told Early "of my desire to cooperate with him." Early probably accepted the offer, but gave Mosby no specific orders. Mosby and Richards then left, riding eastward through the ranks of Early's marching troops.[4]

Early, however, ignored Mosby's offer. During the next four months as Early's outnumbered army defended the Shenandoah Valley, Mosby's Rangers operated without direction or cooperation from Early's headquarters. Mosby tried a second time, meeting Early at Bunker Hill, north of Winchester, on August 2. The results were much the same—Mosby reiterated his willingness to comply with Early's orders, but it ended at that. Early, as Mosby wrote in another letter, "never requested me to do anything," and never sent the partisan commander an oral or written message throughout the struggle for the Shenandoah Valley. Mosby, to his credit, did all that he could to assist Early, guided by his own judgment.[5]

Mosby's campaign in support of Early began the day after the meeting in Snicker's Gap. While Early rested his weary veterans on the seventeenth, Union cavalry, leading the pursuit force, stalked toward the gap. Rangers watched them from a distance and, after nightfall, attacked the camp of the 22nd Pennsylvania Cavalry. The Rebels inflicted between twelve and fifteen casualties, without the loss of a man. The historian of the Union regiment, writing years later of the action, vowed that if the Pennsylvanians "had caught John S. Mosby any time after the Snicker's gap affair (July 17, 1864) all he would have been worth to his country or his people would have been his insurance policy. Then and there his doom was for once sealed, the only man by them thus doomed during the Civil War."[6]

The next day, July 18, the Yankees, chasing Early, came in force to the "Confederacy." The roads to Ashby's and Snicker's Gap filled with ribbons of blue. Mosby gathered his four companies at Upperville and moved across the fields and woodlots to Middleburg, where the Rangers bedded down for the night. The next morning Mosby split the command—Dolly Richards and Company B were sent to Fairfax County on a scout; Richard Montjoy, with companies A and D, were ordered to the country between Leesburg and Snicker's Gap; and William Chapman and Company C drew the assignment of harassing Yankee cavalrymen in Ashby's Gap. Mosby accompanied Montjoy.[7]

Richards's scout into Fairfax harvested a few Union troops, but little else. Mosby and Montjoy, nipping at the rear of the enemy column, bagged 102 infantrymen, who had straggled from the ranks on the eighteenth. Chapman, meanwhile, charged the rear guard of Brigadier General Alfred Napoleon Alexander Duffié's mounted division near Ashby's Gap, capturing about thirty troopers and forty horses. In the assault, Ranger Benjamin Keene was killed, and First Sergeant C. Bohrer of the company was thrown from his horse, and died days later from the injuries. The Federals also nabbed Rangers Matthew Magner and Milton McVeigh. McVeigh, according to diarist "Tee" Edmonds, a cousin of the Ranger, was "a victim of King Whiskey and rushed right up" to the enemy's line. Duffié, a hot-tempered Frenchman, allegedly had instructed his men to shoot all prisoners who belonged to Mosby's command. Magner was spared, according to Ranger John Scott, when a civilian interceded and claimed the captive was a member of the 6th Virginia Cavalry. Magner showed papers which supported the assertion and the Yankees accepted it. McVeigh was not executed for unexplained reasons.[8]

While the Rangers dogged the Union force, beyond the mountains Early halted the retreat, turned and lashed the pursuers. On July 18, Northern units crossed the Shenandoah River and were bloodied when the Confederates counterattacked. The foes skirmished across the stream throughout much of the nineteenth, until Early resumed the march toward Winchester. The Yankees followed the next morning for several miles until their commander, Major General Horatio Wright, called off the pursuit. Leaving behind Brigadier General George Crook's 8,000-man Army of West Virginia to protect the lower Shenandoah Valley, Wright started his own troops, the Sixth Corps, toward Washington. Wright raced back to the capital, covering sixty miles in two days.[9]

A week of relative inactivity ensued for the Rangers in the wake of this so-called "Snicker's Gap War." Mosby took the opportunity to organize two additional companies. On July 28, the battalion met at Upperville, where Mosby formally created Company E.[10]

According to the Compiled Service Records at the National Archives, ninety-six men officially enrolled in the new company on that date. This influx of recruits marked the beginning of a six-month expansion of the battalion. The records also contain the enlistment forms for an additional 196 men, who joined the command between August 1 and December 31. Since the records are incomplete, this total of 292 volunteers is certainly low. The new personnel reflected the enlarged importance and territorial breadth of Ranger operations. At no other time during the war did Mosby require more new blood, and he filled his needs with an average of at least fifty recruits per month.[11]

The members of Company E unanimously endorsed Mosby's slate of officers. Undoubtedly they had heard of Mosby's ultimatum when Company D was organized that any man who protested his method of selecting officers would be sent to the regular army.

Mosby's choice for captain was First Lieutenant Samuel Chapman. Brother of the commander of Company C, Sam Chapman had been serving as the battalion's adjutant since January and as commander of the gun crew. Chapman was a month shy of his twenty-sixth birthday, a man of imposing stature, standing nearly six feet tall. He had deep-set hazel eyes, black hair and wore a mustache which curled around the corners of his mouth.[12]

A student of the ministry before the war, Chapman embraced combat as if it were an article of faith. Ranger Ludwell Lake once told his sister that Chapman was the bravest man he ever knew. He had been desperately wounded at Grapewood Farm on May 31, 1863, when he refused to abandon the cannon. Mosby described him "as the only man he ever saw who really enjoyed fighting, and who generally went into the fray with his hat in one hand and banging away with his revolver with the other." John Alexander called Chapman a "relentless pursuer," noting that on one occasion he chased four Yankee cavalrymen and returned with four horses.[13]

Mosby rewarded Fount Beattie with the first lieutenancy of Company E. Beattie was twenty-three years old, from Washington County, Virginia, one of the original fifteen Rangers. Beattie and Mosby had been messmates in the 1st Virginia Cavalry and, as Ranger John Munson wrote, Beattie "was Mosby's most intimate companion and friend, for they were enlisted together when the war broke out and were never separated."[14]

The Company's second lieutenant was William "Willie" Martin. He was, said Munson, "one of our shining marks." Captured and exchanged in 1863, Martin had been knocked senseless in the Mount Zion Church fight earlier in July.[15]

Sergeant William Ben Palmer of Company A was promoted to third lieutenant of Company E. Ben Palmer was nineteen years old— "only a boy," according to a Ranger—a native of Richmond. He was as tall as Sam Chapman, darkly complexioned, also with hazel eyes. Palmer rode a "little grey thoroughbred" and, in battle, he maintained an icy composure, even a gentlemanly politeness. "I believe," averred Ranger John Alexander, "Ben Palmer was the only man of whom I ever heard who could preserve the amenities to the point of killing a foe with apologies for his rudeness."[16]

Mosby named twenty-year-old Boyd M. Smith as first sergeant of Company E. A resident of Fairfax County, Smith had served in the battalion for nearly a year, falling wounded in the fight at Loudoun Heights on January 10. Smith had three sergeants and four corporals under his direction.[17]

The second company organized at this time was an artillery company. The accounts are imprecise as to the exact date of its formation, but it had to be during the last two weeks of July. On July 1, Mosby had sent Peter Franklin to Richmond with a letter to Secretary of War James Seddon in which Mosby asked for authorization to create such a company and for three more mountain howitzers. Seddon approved Mosby's request on the fourth, instructing the ordnance department to supply the artillery pieces. By month's end, Mosby had the cannon and had assigned officers to the four-gun battery.[18]

The Artillery Company had the fewest members of any company in the battalion, but Mosby staffed it with a full complement of officers and with a first sergeant. Peter Franklin was promoted to captain. He had served in the battalion since the previous autumn. Franklin's three lieutenants by rank were John J. Fray, John P. Page and Frank H. Rahm. Fray, like Franklin a Ranger for nearly a year, had commanded a battery during 1862 in the regular army. Page and Rahm had no previous service in an artillery unit but most likely had been members of the battalion's earlier one-gun crew. For the company's first sergeant, Mosby named A. G. Babcock. A tall, strapping man, Babcock was in his late twenties and had ridden with the Rangers for months.[19]

In a final organizational detail, Mosby appointed his brother, William H., as the battalion's adjutant to replace Sam Chapman. Three inches taller than his brother, thin, awkward and hatchet-faced, William Mosby was nineteen years old at the time of his promotion, which was dated from August 8. One of the men thought that the younger brother was "uncouth" and "obstreperous." He served as adjutant for the remainder of the war.[20]

Upon the completion of Company E's organization on the twenty-eighth, as was his custom, Mosby started the battalion from Upperville on a raid. Crossing the Potomac River into Maryland, the Rangers entered Adamstown the next day. With no Federal units in the area, Mosby left Company E behind to scout deeper into the state while he returned with the other companies to Virginia. By the thirtieth, Mosby and the main body were in the Shenandoah Valley but stirred nothing up. Walter Frankland, acting battalion quartermaster, and twenty men stayed in the fertile region, threshing wheat for the command.[21]

Sam Chapman and Company E, still in Maryland, had collided with a detachment of the 8th Illinois Cavalry along the Monocacy River, south of Frederick. The Confederates seized twelve prisoners, but the Northerners counterattacked. When Chapman's rear guard, under Fount Beattie, broke before the onslaught, the entire company fled. Chapman did not lose a man, but it had not been an auspicious beginning for the new command.[22]

On July 30, the day Company E clashed with the Illinoisans, not many miles to the north in southern Pennsylvania, Confederate cavalrymen led by Brigadier General John McCausland burned the town of Chambersburg. Sent by Jubal Early in retaliation for David Hunter's incendiarism in the Shenandoah Valley, McCausland demanded a tribute of $500,000 in cash or $100,000 in gold from town officials. When the community leaders refused the ultimatum, the Southerners looted businesses and private homes and applied the torch. The firestorm engulfed eleven squares of Chambersburg, consuming over 200 buildings. Jubal Early had his revenge.[23]

The burning of Chambersburg became the final act of a drama which had brought embarrassment to the Lincoln administration. Engaged in a reelection campaign, the president appeared helpless. Wherever Northerners looked, the outcome seemed no closer and the costs had reached staggering proportions. Grant had locked Lee into a siege at Petersburg, Virginia, but it might last for months, while William Sherman's three armies were still miles from Atlanta. Finally, Jubal Early's raiders had marched to the outskirts of Washington, escaped, routed George Crook's command in the Second Battle of Kernstown on July 24 and, now six days later, nearly destroyed an entire Northern community. When Early's troops were outside of the Union capital, the New York *Times* stated editorially that the Southern thrust across the Potomac River was "the old story over again. The back door, by way of the Shenandoah Valley, has been left invitingly open." If Lincoln expected an electoral victory in the fall, he needed battlefield victories. He had to shut forever "the back door."[24]

The Union command system, with its layers of bureaucracy and separate departments, had malfunctioned badly as Early's army penetrated into Maryland; it required unification and one overall commander. With that as the agenda, Lincoln and Grant conferred in person on July 31. They arrived at no resolution but, the next morning, Grant appointed George Meade's cavalry commander, Major General Philip H. Sheridan, to command of what would become the Middle Military Division and the Army of the Shenandoah. Grant additionally supplied Sheridan with a powerful weapon—an army of approximately 45,000 men, comprised of two cavalry divisions and the Sixth Corps from the Army of the Potomac, two infantry divisions of the Nineteenth Corps and Crook's Army of West Virginia.[25]

Lincoln, Secretary of War Edwin Stanton and Chief of Staff Henry W. Halleck voiced concern about Grant's choice of Sheridan, who was only thirty-three years old. Lincoln, however, deferred to Grant's judgment, and Sheridan formally assumed command on August 7. To counter Lee's daring strategy, Grant knew what he wanted to achieve in the Shenandoah Valley and knew the man he had sent there.[26]

Philip Sheridan had come from the West with Grant in the spring of 1864. He had commanded at regimental, brigade and divisional levels before Grant gave him Meade's cavalry corps. There was not much to Sheridan physically; he stood about five feet, three inches, tall and weighed roughly 120 pounds. But "Little Phil," as he was nicknamed, possessed an aggressiveness, an inner flame of combativeness. Sheridan, like Grant, understood that an army was an instrument to be used. As Grant viewed it, Sheridan's orders were simple: he should "put himself south of the enemy and follow him to the death. Wherever the enemy goes let our troops go also."[27]

Three days after his appointment, on August 10, Sheridan marched his army southward from the Harper's Ferry area into the beautiful Shenandoah Valley. Lying between the Blue Ridge to the east and the Allegheny Mountains to the west, generally thirty miles in width, the Shenandoah Valley ran from the Potomac River southwestward for 165 miles to Lexington. The Indians had given it its name, which meant "Daughter of the Stars." For centuries the native Americans had lived amid its beauty and lushness, fought over the fields and woodlots and then lost their home to the white man, who prospered from the land's richness.

When the Civil War began in 1861, the Valley, as it was commonly called, had a military significance second only to the Mississippi River Valley. Its farms and mills fed Confederate armies; its location made it three times an avenue of invasion into the North for the Rebels. With the arrival of Sheridan and the Army of the Shenandoah, however, the region and its defenders, Jubal Early's Army of the Valley, confronted an unparalleled threat. The stakes for both sides rose and, with Early outnumbered roughly three-to-one, the Southerners sought every musket and cannon. John Mosby, despite Early's indifference to him, embraced the struggle for the Valley. The

"Daughter of the Stars" beckoned the Rangers as never before.[28]

"Hardly a day passed from the first of August, 1864, til mid-winter," remembered Ranger John Munson, "that some of our men were not troubling Sheridan." The main objective of the Ranger campaign into the Valley, as Mosby put it, "was to vex and embarrass Sheridan and, if possible, to prevent his advance into the interior of the State." To achieve that objective, Mosby planned to guard Early's flank along the Blue Ridge, attack Sheridan's outposts on a daily basis and disrupt the flow of supplies to the Federals. A secondary phase of his operations was to prevent reinforcements from the defenses of Washington being sent to Sheridan by keeping "Augur in remembrance of his duty to guard the Capital." As a consequence, as Ranger detachments passed through the gaps of the Blue Ridge, other details cantered toward Fairfax County and the ring of Union outposts.[29]

In order to "keep the enemy so busy," Mosby strained the resources of the 43rd Battalion. The burdens of the operations Mosby began sharing with Dolly Richards, Richard Montjoy and the Chapman brothers. Mosby, wrote Munson, "had such confidence in the ability of his officers that he permitted them frequently to lay out their own work, or rather details of it." Mosby assigned them to a section of the Valley or to a sector in Fairfax County and then left the accomplishment of the raid to their judgment and planning. The major operations, which utilized a number of companies, Mosby personally led.[30]

When the Rangers rode toward the Shenandoah Valley, they usually crossed at one of four gaps—Chester and Manassas, toward Front Royal; Ashby's, on the road through Millwood to Winchester; and Snicker's, toward Berryville. The Rebels favored the Snicker's Gap route more and more as the campaign unfolded because at Berryville, they could canter westward to Winchester or northward to Charlestown, Harper's Ferry and the Baltimore & Ohio Railroad.[31]

Once across the Blue Ridge, which a Federal said "looked as though a race of titans had been at war, and had thrown up these long ridges as breastworks for opposing forces," Mosby's men encountered the barrier of the Shenandoah River. Numerous shallows and ferries, however, laced the waters. The Rangers frequently used the crossings west of Snicker's Gap—Rock Ford, Castleman's Ferry and Berry's Ferry. At the latter point, John Thomas Lindsey operated the boat and a tavern, continuing a business which was begun as early as 1757 by Joseph Berry.[32]

As was the case east of the mountains, "safe houses" dotted the region, offering the Rangers food, shelter, information and guides. Berryville served as the hub of this network in the lower Valley. A Dr. Neill in the town provided important intelligence, and Mosby stopped as often as he could for coffee at the home of David McGuire. Three miles east of Berryville, the partisans camped in Champ Shepherd's woods. About ten miles to the north, outside of Charlestown, lived Miss Amy Shepherd, who acted as a guide in that vicinity. Perhaps she was the woman who had assisted Mosby in his attack on Duffield's Station the previous April.[33]

The Berryville native John S. Russell now emerged as Mosby's most valuable scout. As noted previously, he had a matchless knowledge of the terrain and of reliable citizens. Russell's family had lived in the Valley for over half a century, and his home, called "Rock Hill," was situated roughly three miles west of the town. An uneducated man, Russell possessed "great shrewdness and nerve, and an instinctive knowledge of men." In a command filled with able scouts, he and Bushrod Underwood "were without rivals," said Ranger John Alexander. By the time Ranger operations ensued against Sheridan, Russell had established daily contact with the Union general's headquarters. On almost any night, Russell and three or four other Rangers could be found prowling along or within Federal lines.[34]

Mosby's initial foray against Sheridan resulted from information brought by Russell. Sheridan's headquarters, reported Russell, was in the home of Haight Willis in the Charlestown area, and Russell proposed that they endeavor to kidnap "Little Phil." On August 8, two days after Sheridan arrived in the region, Mosby, Russell and a small contingent of Rangers entered the Valley. The next day they hung on the fringes of the Union army, capturing several enemy soldiers. After nightfall, they sneaked to a point within 300 yards of the Willis residence. Campfires encircled the house; Mosby sent John W. Hearn forward to count the number of troops around the headquarters. But Hearn, jumping a fence, landed among some sleeping Yankees. A sentry challenged him and, when Hearn grabbed for the musket, the guard shouted the alarm. Hearn disappeared into the darkness and rejoined his comrades, who abandoned the incredible scheme.[35]

The following morning Sheridan's Army of the Shenandoah lumbered southward toward Early's Army of the Valley. The Confederates withdrew before the advance, halting on the twelfth at Fisher's Hill, a bluff south of Strasburg. The Federals trailed behind, encamping along Cedar Creek, four miles to the north. Here the opponents stayed, skirmishing with each other, until the fifteenth, when Sheridan began a retrograde movement, having learned of the approach of Confederate reinforcements, sent by Lee, on his left flank and rear.[36]

John Russell informed Mosby of Sheridan's advance on the eleventh, a day after it began. Russell stated that hundreds of wagons were preparing to leave Charlestown for Sheridan's army. Mosby ordered a rendezvous for noon of the twelfth at Rectortown. Rangers from Companies A, B, C and D, numbering between 250 and 300, and the artillery crews with a pair of howitzers reported to the meeting. They started at once through Snicker's Gap and across the Shenandoah River at Castleman's Ferry. Mosby marched deliberately, not passing the river until after nightfall. They stopped at the farm of a James Ware, three miles east of Berryville, bedding down for a few hours rest in the barn.[37]

While the men slept, Russell scouted ahead. He was gone probably an hour or two before he returned and awakened Mosby. Dozens of wagons were parked on the Berryville-Charlestown Pike at Berryville, Russell reported. Mosby, with Russell and three other men, hurried forward to select a site for an attack. The five Rebels halted on a hill on the farm of a man named Barnett east of the roadway, opposite the brick Buck Marsh Baptist Church, a mile outside of Berryville. The darkness and a morning fog limited their vision, but Mosby could discern that Russell had located a prize. He ordered Russell to gallop back to the Ware house and have Captain William Chapman bring the men.[38]

When Chapman arrived, Mosby deployed into a battle line. On the left, he placed Dolly Richards and a squadron, with orders to charge the caravan where it entered Berryville. On the right, Chapman and another squadron filed into position, aligned to strike toward the center and rear of the string of wagons. On Barnett's hill, where Mosby stationed himself, Lieutenant Alfred Glascock, leading Company D, acted as a reserve and as support for the cannon. Beside Mosby, seventeen-year-old Robert Stockton Terry unfurled the battalion's new flag. The wagons, with their teamsters and infantry guards, lay less than a hundred yards away.[39]

Lieutenant Frank Rahm of the Artillery Company unlimbered a

howitzer on the brow of the hill. The artillerists had only one cannon with them because during the ride across rugged terrain the second howitzer had broken a wheel and had to be left behind. Mosby told his officers that two rapid shots from the cannon would be the signal to charge. But as the gunners wrestled the piece into position, they placed it on a nest of yellow jackets. The bees did not welcome the intruders and, swarming up, scattered the crew. Mosby's horse became "frantic" and reared. Sergeant A. G. Babcock, braving the onslaught, rushed to the howitzer and, with the help of others, wheeled it to another spot on the knoll. The gunners rammed in a shell, cut the fuse and waited the order to fire. Mists still clung to the ground; the morning sun creased the peaks of the Blue Ridge to their rear.[40]

In the roadbed the teamsters and their infantry escorts were stirring when the Rangers came up. This park of wagons comprised the rear section of the supply train, numbering between 500 and 600 vehicles, for the entire Army of the Shenandoah. Beginning in the late afternoon of the twelfth, the caravan had creaked into Berryville, where it had turned westward at the town square into the road to Winchester. Hour after hour the current of four-team, canvas-topped wagons had flowed through the village. Brigadier General John R. Kenly in overall command allowed two breaks for feeding and watering the horses and mules, but kept the train rolling because he wanted to reach Winchester by daylight of the thirteenth. A cavalry escort rimmed the front, while infantrymen trudged among the wagons, spaced at points along the entire column.[41]

The wagons parked on the Berryville-Winchester road at Buck Marsh Church had stopped there about two o'clock on the morning of the thirteenth. This section was the supply train of Sheridan's cavalry corps, and Captain E. P. McKinney, commissary officer of the Reserve Brigade of the First Cavalry Division, had ordered the halt. McKinney allowed the drivers to unhitch the teams and sleep for a few hours. The guards, companies of the 144th and 149th Ohio National Guard, also enjoyed the rest. Thus, as the sun rose, the teamsters were busy rehitching the animals while the Ohioans were boiling water for coffee.[42]

The initial shot from the howitzer screeched above the wagons and exploded, beheading a mule. The second round followed seconds later, and then the Rangers charged. Along the Pike bedlam ensued at once. The drivers in the direct path of the attack around the Buck Marsh Church ran away, as several of their harnessed teams, frightened by the cannon fire, careened down the road. The teamsters in Berryville, however, managed to get their wagons underway, lashing the teams forward on the Winchester road.[43]

Richards's men struck the train at the church. The Ohio infantrymen, preparing breakfast in the churchyard, grabbed their rifles and scrambled to a stone wall at the edge of the yard. They were "100-days' troops," men who enlisted during times of emergency for the designated period. The Ohioans had no combat experience and less than a month left in the service. One quick look at Mosby's men was enough for many of them, who joined the drivers in flight. "Our guard behaved rascally," groused a quartermaster officer who lost his horse and had to escape on foot.[44]

The Ohioans who remained behind the stone wall unloosed a volley. The blast wounded two Rangers, killed Lewis Adie and mortally wounded Welby Rector. A former cadet at V.M.I., Adie, "a fine boy" in Mosby's words, died instantly with a bullet in the forehead. Guy Broadwater, who saw Adie fall, galloped back to Mosby on the hill and reported the Ranger's death. "I can't help it," replied Mosby.[45]

The single volley ended Federal resistance. An Ohio captain shouted to his men to scatter and save themselves. "Well, we ran," admitted one of them. The Rangers dashed into the church grounds, corralling as many Yankees as they could. Part of Richards's detachment, slicing into the train between the church and the town, spurred westward through the fields and intersected the Winchester road a mile beyond Berryville. They seized approximately twenty wagons at this point and repulsed a brief counterattack by a handful of Union cavalrymen.[46]

Farther down the Charlestown Pike from the church, Chapman's Company C barreled into the train. A few guards shot at the Confederates, wounding Charles Walker, and then took flight. Chapman's men rounded up over 200 beef cattle. In all, the Rangers seized about a hundred wagons, between 500 and 600 horses and mules and roughly 200 prisoners.[47]

The Confederates rifled through the wagons, which were loaded with "forage, subsistence, and regimental property" of the cavalry corps. They grabbed feed for their mounts and rations for themselves. Somebody overlooked the paymaster's chest of the 6th New York Cavalry, stuffed with $112,000 in Federal currency. Several Rangers discovered a number of fiddles in a wagon and confiscated them.

★
*Brig. Gen. Edwin H.
Stoughton, USA, captured
by Mosby's men at his
headquarters, Fairfax Court
House, Virginia, the night of
March 8–9, 1863.* (United
States Army Military History
Institute, Carlisle Barracks,
Pennsylvania)

★
*President Abraham Lincoln.
Concern that Lincoln might
be kidnapped by Mosby's
Rangers led Union officials to
remove the planks from the
Chain Bridge over the
Potomac River every night for
several weeks in 1863.*
(USAMHI)

★ *John S. Mosby, CSA, in the uniform of a lieutenant colonel, photo probably taken in fall of 1864.* (USAMHI)

★
*Maj. Gen. James Ewell
Brown "Jeb" Stuart, CSA,
commander of the Cavalry
Corps, Army of Northern
Virginia, Mosby's superior
officer and "best friend" in
the army, who died from
wounds, May 12, 1864.*
(USAMHI)

★
*Gen. Robert E. Lee, CSA,
commander of the Army of
Northern Virginia, who
approved and praised Mosby's
operations.* (USAMHI)

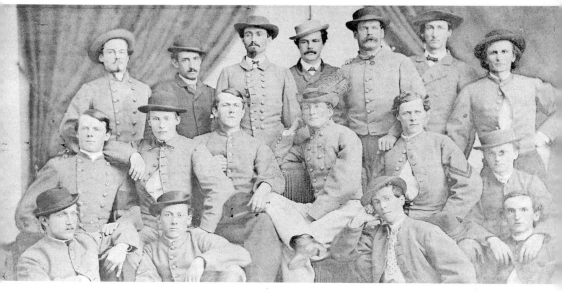

★ *Group of Mosby's Rangers: front row, left to right: Walter Gosden, Harry T. Sinnott, Otho L. Butler, Isaac A. Gentry; middle row, left to right: Robert B. Parrott, Thomas Throop, John W. Munson, John S. Mosby, ——— Newell, Charles H. Quarles; back row, left to right: Lee Howison, W. Ben Palmer, John W. Puryear, Thomas Booker, A. G. Babcock, Norman V. Randolph, Frank H. Rahm.* (Maryland Historical Society)

★ *Group of Mosby's Rangers: seated, left to right: J. Monroe Heiskell, Henry Slater, Daniel Murray Mason, Lt. Charles E. Grogan, Joshua Riggs, Gresham Hough; standing, left to right: Claiborne Robinson, John S. Mosby, Harris C. Blanchard, D. Giraud Wright, J. Henley Smith, Alexander G. Carey.* (Maryland Historical Society)

★ *Four of Mosby's most reliable officers: clockwise from upper left: Lt. Franklin Williams, Co. B.; Lt. Geo. H. Whitescarver, Co. A.; Lt. Joseph H. Nelson, Co. A.; Capt. Walter E. Frankland, Co. F.* (Williamson, *Mosby's Rangers*, p. 29)

★ *"Billy" Smith, an officer of much promise until slain at Loudoun Heights, January 10, 1864.* (Williamson, *Mosby's Rangers*, p. 95)

★ *Capt. Adolphus ("Dolly") E. Richards, CSA, one of the finest officers in the 43rd Battalion, who rose to the rank of major, second only to William H. Chapman in rank after Mosby.* (Williamson, *Mosby's Rangers*, p. 158)

★

Capt. Samuel F. Chapman, CSA, commander of Company E, 43rd Battalion, brother of William H. Chapman and a former divinity student who waged war with the fury of an Old Testament warrior. (Williamson, *Mosby's Rangers*, p. 232)

★ *Lt. John S. Russell, CSA, Mosby's most trusted scout in the Shenandoah Valley.* (Williamson, *Mosby's Rangers*, p. 232)

★ *Capt. Richard P. Montjoy, CSA, commander of "Company Darling," a fearless officer, who was killed on November 27, 1864.* (Williamson, *Mosby's Rangers*, p. 312)

★
*Photo of William H.
Chapman as an artillery
officer prior to his service in
the 43rd Battalion. Chapman
rose to the rank of lieutenant
colonel and was second-in-
command to Mosby.*
(Collection of Robert Moore III)

★
*Lt. Gen. Ulysses S. Grant,
USA, general-in-chief of
Union forces in 1864–65,
who directed that if one of
Mosby's men was captured,
he should be hanged.*
(USAMHI)

★
*Col. Caspar Crowninshield,
USA, commander 2nd
Massachusetts Cavalry,
which opposed Mosby's
command for over a year.*
(USAMHI)

★ *Union cavalry officers who operated against the 43rd Battalion in the Shenandoah
Valley in the summer and fall of 1864: seated left to right: Bvt. Maj. Gen.
Wesley Merritt, Bvt. Maj. Gen. George A. Custer; standing left to right: Maj.
Gen. Philip H. Sheridan, Bvt. Brig. Gen. James W. Forsyth, Bvt. Brig. Gen.
Thomas C. Devin.* (USAMHI)

★ *A favorite target of Mosby's Rangers—a Union sutler's tent, photographed at Brandy Station, Virginia, February 1864.* (USAMHI)

★ *"Glen Welby," home of Richard Carter, located north of Salem, Virginia, and used by John Mosby as one of his "headquarters." Photograph probably taken in the 1930s.* (Virginia State Library and Archives)

★ *"Clover Hill," home of W. Morgan, located south of Salem, Virginia, and a "safe house" for Mosby's Rangers. Photograph probably taken in the 1930s.* (Virginia State Library and Archives)

★ *Outbuilding used by Mosby's Rangers on "Heartland," home of Joseph Blackwell, located north of Piedmont, Virginia. Photograph taken in 1931.* (Virginia State Library and Archives)

★
*Lt. Gen. Jubal Early, CSA,
commander of the Army
of the Valley during the
Shenandoah Valley Campaign
of the summer and fall of
1864. He and Mosby
shared a mutual dislike for
each other.* (USAMHI)

★
*Capt. Richard Blazer, USA,
commander of "Blazer's
Scouts," who proved to be
worthy foes of the Rangers in
the Shenandoah Valley in the
fall of 1864.* (Williamson,
Mosby's Rangers, p. 300)

★ *Eyewitness sketch by artist James E. Taylor of Blazer's Scouts riding forth on a mission against Mosby's Rangers, October 11, 1864. Blazer's Scouts were routed by the Rangers in the Shenandoah Valley on November 18.* (Western Reserve Historical Society)

★ *Taylor's sketch of an attack of Mosby's Rangers on a Union ambulance in the Shenandoah Valley on October 12, 1864. Two of General Philip Sheridan's staff officers were mortally wounded in the action.* (Western Reserve Historical Society)

★
Bvt. Maj. Gen. George Armstrong Custer, USA, the dashing cavalry commander whom Mosby blamed for the executions of six Rangers at Fort Royal, Virginia, September 23, 1864. (USAMHI)

★ *The drawing of lots by Union troops for execution by the Rangers at Rectortown, Virginia, on November 6, 1864. Most of the Federals belonged to the command of George Custer. Drawing by Taylor.* (Western Reserve Historical Society)

★ *Col. John S. Mosby, CSA, photo taken in Richmond early in 1865.* (USAMHI)

★
*John S. Mosby, CSA, in the
uniform of a colonel, photo
probably taken in 1865.*
(USAMHI)

★
*Postwar photo of Fountain
Beattie, one of the original
fifteen members of the
partisan command and
Mosby's closest confidant.*
(Maryland Historical Society)

★ *A group of former Rangers at a reunion at Marshall (formerly Salem), Virginia, in 1895. Identification by number: 1, Thomas Lake; 2, James E. Pickett; 3, J. M. Miller; 4, Vincent Kerns; 5, Joseph Bryan; 6, Robert M. Harrover; 7, J. Y. Yates; 8, Frank Johnson; 9, Charles H. Dear; 10, Philip B. Eastham; 11, James W. Bell; 12, Cornelius J. Coiner; 13, G. W. Anderson; 14, J. N. Hoffleblower; 15, Charles Biedler; 16, George Slater; 17, Robert W. Eastham; 18, Brock Dear; 19, Henry Brock; 20, W. G. Pearson; 21, Robert F. Heflin; 22, James E. Legg; 23, James A. Silman; 24, Enoch Kirkpatrick; 25, John W. Hammond; 26, P. H. Reardon.* (Warren Rifles Confederate Museum, Front Royal, Virginia)

Mosby reported the haul as "many valuable stores."[48]

With much of the material removed, Mosby ordered his men to burn the wagons. Sam Moore, a young boy from Berryville, wrote many years later that he and others of his age assisted the Rangers. Moore remembered their fascination with the elusive partisans. "It seemed to us boys," Moore stated, "that they sprang up in almost every field where their presence was needed; that they grew almost as the weeds grow in a neglected field, and that wherever one of Mosby's men was needed, there he and some of his companions were sure to be found. They had for us all the glamour of Robin Hood and his merry men, all the courage and bravery of the ancient crusaders, the unexpectedness of benevolent pirates and the stealth of Indians."[49]

The Southerners finished the work by 6:30 A.M. and marched eastward. They carried the body of Lewis Adie with them but left Welby Rector with the townsfolk. Upon his death, the citizens buried the Loudoun County native in the Episcopal Church cemetery. When the partisans reached the disabled howitzer, Mosby asked Artillery Lieutenant Frank Rahm what he intended to do with the cannon. "I'm going to take it back home on the other gun, if I have to hold it there," Rahm replied. His artillerists lifted the disabled howitzer on top of the other one, and Rahm sat on both. The Rangers were in high spirits during the ride, with several of them entertaining the column with old plantation melodies played on the fiddles. John Munson thought the music was "hideous." Upon their arrival at Rectortown, Mosby promoted John Russell to lieutenant. "*You,*" Mosby told him years later, "are entitled to more credit for our success that day than any one else." Mosby also praised William Chapman and Dolly Richards in his official report of the action, which the Rangers dubbed the "Berryville Wagon Train Raid." The men divided the horses among themselves, and Mosby assigned a detail to drive the mules and cattle to Richmond.[50]

Within a half hour of the Rangers' departure, the 1st Rhode Island Cavalry arrived at the scene. The regiment had been bivouacked a few miles from Berryville when a quartermaster officer reported the attack. "Away we flew at double-quick even for cavalry," asserted a member. By the time they bridled up at Buck Marsh Church, the flames and smoke had enveloped the wagons. The Rhode Islanders extinguished eighteen fires and saved the cash box of the 6th New York Cavalry. They learned that a number of townsfolk had confiscated barrels of sugar and other foodstuffs before the wagons were destroyed. The Yankees threatened to burn every house in which they found the stolen goods if the citizens did not return the items. The search, however, never transpired, and the Berryville folk enjoyed sweeter meals for weeks to come.[51]

The Federal government convened a board of inquiry into the disaster on September 8. The presiding officers listened to testimony from participants for the next several weeks when military duties did not interfere. Finally, on November 13, after the campaign's conclusion, the board rendered a decision, concluding that Captain E. P. McKinney halted the section of the train without authorization, that the guard escort "was insufficient for the number of wagons" and that "no sufficient picket [was] established" which might have prevented the surprise attack. But the board did not cite McKinney or anyone else for negligence.[52]

The Army of the Shenandoah learned of the loss of the wagons and the contents as it withdrew from Cedar Creek to the Harper's Ferry area, a movement which lasted a week, from August fifteenth until the twenty-second. No command in the Union army was more infuriated by the news than the cavalry corps, particularly Brigadier General Wesley Merritt's First Division, which was the victim of the raid. The records, the camp equipment, the rations and the forage of Colonel Thomas Devin's brigade were partially destroyed, while the Reserve Brigade, ironically commanded by Colonel Charles Russell Lowell, the Rangers' old antagonist from the Washington defenses, lost its entire train. When the 6th Pennsylvania of Lowell's brigade found out that their rations had been lost, the hungry troopers butchered a farmer's flock of sheep, dining on mutton. The Yankee horsemen festered with hatred of Mosby's men.[53]

The brutal nature of the struggle between the Union cavalrymen and the Rangers manifested itself within days after the wagon train raid. As Sheridan's army marched back toward Harper's Ferry, the commanding general implemented, to a limited degree, one of his orders from Grant. When Sheridan assumed command, Grant told him: "In pushing up the Shenandoah Valley, as it is expected you will have to go, first or last, it is desirable that nothing should be left to invite the enemy to return. Take all provisions, forage, and stock wanted for the use of your command; such as cannot be consumed, destroy."[54]

Sheridan's horsemen, screening the withdrawal of the infantry and artillery units, ranged through the countryside, burning barns, crops and grist mills, and confiscating livestock or, as the 6th Pennsylvania did, consuming the animals. The operation was neither thorough nor systematic. The Yankees bypassed numerous farms, but the pillars of smoke were precursors of the future.

The Rangers returned to the Valley in the midst of the burning. Rainstorms blew into the region on the seventeenth and eighteenth, abating the destruction. On those two days, detachments from the 43rd Battalion clashed with parties of Union cavalry. Dolly Richards's Company B routed a squad from Lowell's Reserve Brigade, killing or capturing every trooper except one. When Richards described the fight to Mosby, the latter exclaimed that he was pleased that one escaped "so he could tell Sheridan what happened to the rest of them." Lieutenant Alfred Glascock with fifteen men from Company D likewise met a column of Yankee cavalry. The Rangers were wearing rubber ponchos over their uniforms because of the rain, and the Union officer in charge believed them to be fellow Northerners. Glascock allowed the enemy to pass between his men, then gave a signal, and the Rangers drew their revolvers, disarming and bagging thirty Federals without firing a shot.[55]

During the skirmishes one Confederate, allegedly Lieutenant Joseph Nelson of Company A, rode upon a Yankee who was skinning a sheep. Angered by all that he had seen, Nelson killed the man on the spot. He then cut the hoof off the carcass and rammed it in the dead soldier's mouth. Before he remounted, Nelson attached a note to the body: "I reckon you got enough sheep now."[56]

On August 19, William Chapman and companies C, D and E were east of Berryville. (Some of the Ranger narratives date the incident on the twentieth, but contemporary and other sources place it on the nineteenth.) Sometime after midday, a Ranger scout reported to Chapman that Union troopers were burning houses. The Federals belonged to the 5th Michigan Cavalry in Brigadier General George Armstrong Custer's brigade. The night before, according to one account, a picket of the brigade had been killed. In retaliation, Custer ordered that the torch should be applied to nearby residences.[57]

The Michiganders, numbering thirty, had destroyed the homes of Province McCormick and William Sowers when Chapman's men caught them at the brick home of Benjamin Morgan, southeast of Berryville. The Yankees were preparing to set fire to the house as the Rangers charged; Chapman rode in the forefront, screaming:

"Wipe them from the face of the earth! No quarter! No quarter! Take no prisoners!" A Union survivor said later he heard an officer exclaim: "Shoot the d———n Yankee son of a b———."[58]

"It was a sharp, quick, and clean little fight," wrote a Southerner. The Rangers overwhelmed the entire Union force. The Confederates subsequently asserted that they killed every trooper in the attack and took no prisoners. But a newspaper account published days later offered a different version. One of the Michiganders, Trooper Samuel K. Davis, survived, after being shot in the face and feigning death. Davis testified that ten of his comrades were executed in a ditch along the Morgan farm lane after they surrendered. The newspaper added that the detail which recovered the bodies found most of these men had been shot in the head. Two other cavalrymen had their throats cut. The evidence is not conclusive, but twenty-nine of the thirty Federals did die in the shadow of Benjamin Morgan's home. A small, stone marker today denotes the site. It states that Mosby's men "Took No Prisoners."[59]

Mosby in his report to Richmond wrote of the incident: "Such was the indignation of our men at witnessing some of the finest residences in that portion of the State enveloped in flames that no quarter was shown, and about twenty-five of them were shot to death for their villainy." He stated in an unpublished postwar memoir that he issued an order for his men to kill all Federals engaged in burning barns and houses, adding: "The order was superfluous." A diarist living near Mosby's base jotted in his journal under the date of August 22: "heard Mosby raised the black flag on the Yankees Saturday [20th]."[60]

The romantic notions of warfare that both sides believed in 1861 were meaningless three years later. The plumed hats and scarlet-lined capes worn by some of the Rangers were as outdated as the attitudes they symbolized. Northerners and Southerners had unleashed hellish furies which forever altered the nature of warfare. The furnace of the Civil War seared the nation's soul. When the past collided with the future, as it did in Benjamin Morgan's farm lane, more than just men died. That terrible swift sword was swifter, and far more terrible, than Americans could have known in the springtime of 1861.

To the comrades of those slain at Morgan's, the meaning was evident. A Northern trooper asserted that Mosby "had given us to understand he would continue" to kill barn burners. Another cavalryman wrote: "Naturally and justly, these things warmed our blood with indignation. . . . for cowards, sneaks, and cut-throats, men who would murder the wounded, and defenseless . . . we had no tender sentiments or gentle philosophy." Neither the Rangers nor the Union cavalrymen could expect mercy from their opponent.[61]

The Federals soon implemented countermeasures against the 43rd Battalion. Guard details on wagon trains were augmented. Wesley Merritt, commanding the First Cavalry Division, instructed his brigade commanders on August 20 to "give strict orders that no men go more than half a mile from camp, save in organized parties, under officers." These were, however, only half-measures; a concerted countercampaign was required if the Federals were to cripple Mosby's operations.[62]

Proposals for such a drive came from General-in-Chief Ulysses S. Grant. Three days after the Berryville Wagon Train Raid, Grant sent Sheridan two telegrams. "The families of most of Mosby's men are known and can be collected," the commanding general wired. "I think they should be taken and kept at Fort McHenry, or some secure place, as hostages for the good conduct of Mosby and his men. Where any of Mosby's men are caught hang them without trial."[63]

Two hours later, at 3:30 P.M., Grant telegraphed a second message. "If you can possibly spare a division of cavalry," suggested Grant from headquarters at City Point, outside of Petersburg, "send them through Loudoun County, to destroy and carry off the crops, animals, negroes, and all men under fifty years of age capable of bearing arms. In this way you will get many of Mosby's men."[64]

Sheridan received the first telegram the morning of the seventeenth; the second, the next night. In response, Sheridan wired: "Mosby has annoyed me and captured a few wagons. We hung one and shot six of his men yesterday." Sheridan had not learned yet of the Berryville attack when he wrote the reply. But his claim of killing seven Rangers is not supported by the records or other accounts. His men might have captured partisans from one of the smaller guerrilla units in the area and reported them as Mosby's Rangers.[65]

As to Grant's advice—"where any of Mosby's men are caught hang them without trial"—Sheridan evidently did not direct his subordinates to comply. At least, he did not publish an order to that effect. While Sheridan shared his troops' sentiments toward the Rangers, he might have believed that in a campaign of reprisals Mosby could execute more of his men than he could of the Confederates.

Sheridan did comply with the main point of Grant's instructions, issuing a circular to his army on the nineteenth: "All able-bodied male citizens under the age of fifty who may be suspected of aiding, assisting, or belonging to guerrilla bands now infesting the country will be immediately arrested by corps and independent commanders and forwarded to these headquarters as prisoners of war to be confined in Fort McHenry, Md. A written statement should be forwarded in every case."[66]

Perhaps Grant and Sheridan did not know that a similar strategy had been attempted on a smaller scale by troops from Washington's defenses since Mosby began operations in the winter of 1863. Male civilians were arrested and confined in prison for periods of time, but Ranger attacks continued. Mosby had given every indication that the incarceration of citizens would not deter him from his mission.

Grant's second proposal—the destruction of crops and live-stock—had merit. Sheridan, however, believed that he could not spare one of his three cavalry divisions for such a raid and demurred. Instead, Sheridan assigned the duty to Christopher Augur, commander of the Department of Washington. Sheridan wrote on the twenty-fifth: "All wheat, hay, and fodder in Loudoun County that can be burned up should be. General Grant directs that all the crops be carried off or destroyed." He added that he wanted Augur to maintain a picket force in Snicker's Gap.[67]

Augur had a message in Sheridan's hands that same day. It had been Augur's luckless task to formulate the major campaign against Mosby for nearly a year. He had tried various measures, but none had eradicated the partisans. Recently, his cavalry units had established listening posts of five or six men throughout Fairfax County with the objective of detecting the raiders before they attacked the outposts. This device had proved defective because just yesterday the Rangers shelled the garrison at Annandale, midway between Fairfax Court House and Alexandria. The post commander refused to surrender when Lieutenant Harry Hatcher rode in under a flag of truce. The officer responded to Hatcher's demand, saying: "Tell Colonel Mosby I will not surrender, and if he sends that rag up here again, I'll shoot it to hell."

"Don't do that," rebutted Hatcher, "it's the only handkerchief I've got."[68]

So when Sheridan recommended counterraids into Loudoun and a picket detail for Snicker's Gap, Augur offered little optimism. "To get information from Snicker's Gap," Augur contended, "would require a force able to manage Mosby, whose headquarters are on the route there." As to the destruction of foodstuff and animals in Loudoun, Augur did not have sufficient cavalry. "I will do all I can, however," he promised.[69]

Augur ordered the 8th Illinois Cavalry into Loudoun and Fauquier on August 28. The regiment had just returned from "a thorough scout" in the country. This time, Augur directed, the troopers should arrest all males between the ages of eighteen and fifty, except for Quakers, who had been exempted by Grant. "The special object of your scout," stated Augur, "is to destroy, as far as practicable, the sources from which Mosby draws men, horses, and support."[70]

The 8th Illinois, Lieutenant Colonel David R. Clendenin commanding, rode out two days later. They had tangled a few times with the Rangers in Maryland during June and July and, as one of them claimed, believed that they were "a thorn in Mosby's side." John Munson conceded that the Rangers had "a proper respect" for the Illinoisans. "These men," Munson noted, "would fight at the drop of a hat, and we knew it meant bloodshed whenever we came together." Ranger John Russell was less gracious or impressed with the Union troopers; he referred to them as "the hated minions of the Sucker State."[71]

Crossing the Potomac River from Maryland, the Illinoisans ranged through Loudoun County, arresting thirty-two alleged "guerrillas," confiscating over fifty horses and mules and two wagons full of cotton yarn, and burning four other wagons. They destroyed no crops and the "guerrillas" they seized were farmers. The regiment covered 120 miles in the circuitous search, returning to their camp on September 2.[72]

In a month of campaigning against Sheridan's army, Mosby and the Rangers had fared well. The gains far outweighed the price. Mosby had lost two killed or mortally wounded, six wounded and only three captured. A tragic accident, however, resulted in the death of Lieutenant "Willie" Martin of Company E. On August 20 as the company was scouting along a road, a Ranger riding beside Martin accidentally discharged his pistol, shooting Martin. One of the battalion's "shining marks" died within minutes and was buried the next day in Upperville. As September began, the ledger favored Mosby, but difficult days lay ahead.[73]

Chapter 12

BLOODY
SEPTEMBER

 "The feeling is becoming desperate there is no safety in leaving the command even short distances the bushwhackers fire on them on all occasions," William Thompson wrote to his wife around the beginning of September 1864. A quartermaster officer in Wesley Merritt's cavalry division, Thompson spoke for thousands of his comrades in the Army of the Shenandoah. Each day, it seemed, brought a new attack or incursion by Mosby's Rangers.[1]

Several days after Thompson penned the letter to home, a party of Union soldiers discovered the bodies of several members of the 5th Michigan Cavalry. The Michiganders had been foraging for food at farmhouses when Confederate guerrillas captured them. The Rebels shot or hanged every one of them and, on one of those hanged, tied a ham to each leg and pinned a card. On the card, according to a Northerner, a partisan scribbled "with oaths that that was the way every Michigan man would be served caught out foraging." The Federals blamed Mosby's men.[2]

About the same time a train of ambulances belonging to George Crook's command were moving on a road near Kabletown, a small village between Berryville and Charlestown. Suddenly, a group of horsemen galloped up, shouting that the ambulances were under attack by Mosby's men. "This spread through our train and before anything could be done the whole thing was in confusion," reported an officer. It was a frantic dash away from something unseen, but known. The Rangers were not attacking and, as the officer concluded: "The affair was disgraceful."[3]

The fear of a Ranger assault disquieted the camps of Sheridan's army. Mosby, a New Yorker avowed, was "a terror to all soldiers disposed to straggle." A Michigan cavalryman called the partisans, "Mosby and cutthroat band," a term also favored by William Thompson. A veteran member of the 3rd Pennsylvania Cavalry believed that "this is the most dangerous place to picket I ever saw." No small party of Union soldiers, or wagon train, or picket post or guard detail appeared safe.[4]

Indicative of the grip Mosby had achieved upon the Federals in a month was an incident which occurred about the first of September. A dozen or so members of Company B, 23rd Ohio Infantry ran into their brigade campsite, swinging their hats and yelling: "See the prisoners! Mosby a prisoner!" Soldiers scrambled to get a look at the famous partisan; others relayed the startling news from regiment to regiment. Then, as brigade commander Colonel Rutherford B. Hayes related, "the thing took and the whole camp clear to army headquarters a mile off or more, perhaps ten thousand men, followed their example. Officers of course ran, major-generals and all. Then the 'sell' was discovered, and such laughing and shouting I never heard before." At least some Yankees had retained their sense of humor.[5]

Several factors explain Mosby's fearsome reputation among Union troops. During much of August the Rangers enjoyed notable success with few casualties. Secondly, for Mosby, the campaign against Sheridan was the most vital in the battalion's history. Mosby correctly assessed the stakes involved for the Confederacy in the Val-

ley and threw all his men and resources into the operations. He now
had six companies, with more recruits pouring in, and his raids involved more men than he had previously utilized. Because of the skill
and experience of his officers, Mosby could divide the battalion si-
multaneously into two or three attack forces. This extended the command's range, enabling Mosby to apply pressure at more points along
Sheridan's line of communication and against his patrols. Finally, the
element of surprise employed by the Rangers—a hallmark of the unit
since its formation—often gave them the decisive edge in actions. It
was, for the Yankees, combat with specters, the shadow warfare
brought from Fairfax and Loudoun across the Blue Ridge on a larger
scale.

Phillip Sheridan believed, conversely, that he could not spare the
requisite number of cavalrymen for a conclusive campaign into Mosby's Confederacy. His foremost mission remained the defeat of Early's army and the reduction of the Shenandoah Valley as a granary
for Robert E. Lee's army at Petersburg. But Mosby, if not eliminated,
could not be ignored. Before the end of August, Sheridan approved
the creation of an independent command with the sole mission of
operating against the Rangers.

The idea for such a unit apparently was suggested by Major
General George Crook, one of Sheridan's corps commanders. Sheridan and Crook were longtime friends and former roommates at West
Point, and "Little Phil" trusted Crook and sought his advice. For the
better part of the war, Crook had served in the newly created state
of West Virginia amid the valleys of the Allegheny Mountains. Irregular troops infested the rugged terrain, so in early 1864 Crook
organized a hundred-man force, called the Legion of Honor, to gather
intelligence for him and to suppress the guerrillas. When Crook's
Army of West Virginia was assigned to Sheridan, the Legion of Honor
still functioned.[6]

Sometime around the middle of August, Crook proposed to Sheridan that the Legion of Honor be assigned exclusive duty against the
Rangers. Sheridan accepted and on the twentieth wrote to Major
General Christopher Augur, commander of the Department of Washington: "I have 100 men who will take the contract to clean out
Mosby's gang. I want 100 Spencer Rifles for them. Send them to me
if they can be found in Washington." The Spencer rifle was a seven-
shot repeater, which used metal cartridges and gave its users a volume
and range of firepower Confederate single-shot rifles and carbines and

six-shot Colt pistols could not match. Although many of Sheridan's cavalry regiments carried the shorter-barreled Spencer carbine, which had not proved to be very effective in the type of combat waged by the Rangers, Sheridan evidently thought the repeating rifle was necessary "to clean out Mosby's gang."[7]

Sheridan retained Crook's selection as commander of the unit, Captain Richard Blazer. A native of western Virginia, Blazer had piloted a steamboat on the Ohio River and allegedly fought Indians in the West before the war. When the conflict began, he enlisted in an Ohio infantry regiment, rising to his present rank. Blazer was a stern-looking man, a no-nonsense officer who had done well as leader of the Legion of Honor.[8]

Blazer planned to operate much like his antagonists. His men had to move swiftly, be in the saddle before daylight and camp late at night. Their raids generally lasted three days with scouts or outriders encircling the main body as they moved. He also believed that if he and his men treated the local folk with kindness the locals might not so readily inform the Rangers of their presence in the area. Officially organized as part of Company G, 23rd Ohio, the hundred volunteers soon became known as "Blazer's Scouts" in the Union army.[9]

The Scouts started hunting for Mosby's men before they received their Spencer rifles. During the final days of August, they watched the fords of the Shenandoah River, crossed the Blue Ridge into Loudoun County and tracked Ranger details. Blazer reported that the Scouts killed a half-dozen Rangers and captured four by the end of August. If his figures were accurate, the guerrillas killed and taken did not belong to Mosby's command. On September 1, Blazer informed Crook that he was preparing for a raid on Upperville.[10]

Two days later, while Sheridan's army abandoned their lines around Charlestown and marched for Berryville, Blazer's men rode toward the Blue Ridge. The Scouts moved slowly as heavy rains fell throughout much of the day. By nightfall they were still west of the mountains when they bivouacked. An informant or scout told Blazer that Mosby "with a considerable force" was at Snickersville, at the eastern opening of Snicker's Gap. Blazer planned to start at first light on the fourth.[11]

The report that Blazer received was reasonably accurate—Mosby and approximately ninety Rangers were encamped, not in Snickersville, but in the gap at the top of the mountain. During the third, companies A and B met Mosby at Rectortown. From there, they rode into southern Loudoun, passed through Bloomfield and Snickersville before halting for the night in Snicker's Gap. The inclement weather slowed Mosby as it had Blazer and, instead of reaching the Valley as Mosby planned, the Rangers slept beneath the trees, trying to keep dry.[12]

A second detachment of Rangers—Companies C and E, under Sam Chapman—had preceded Mosby's squadron, entering the Valley on the second. Ordered by Mosby "to harass" Sheridan's troops in the Berryville-Millwood area, Chapman led the two companies through Ashby's Gap, where they turned into the Mount Carmel Church Road and followed it to Shepherd's Ford on the Shenandoah River. Chapman encamped on the river's east bank. The next morning, September 3, the Rangers moved across country to a point west of Berryville and entered a section of Jubal Early's lines. Learning from some infantrymen that Federal troops, seen earlier in the day, had withdrawn, Chapman proceeded toward the town, approaching it from the southwest.[13]

One-half mile from Berryville, the two Ranger companies ran into a Union cavalry regiment deployed in a field of the Gold family farm. The Yankees were the 6th New York Cavalry, Major William E. Beardsley, commanding. The regiment, acting as an advance force for Sheridan's infantry, which was marching toward Berryville, had arrived at the Gold farmstead when scouts reported the presence of Confederate infantry to the west. Beardsley dismounted skirmishers to cover the front and both flanks and positioned the regiment in a field, enclosed by a fence, next to the road.[14]

When the Rangers came into view, the skirmishers along the front opened fire. For the Confederates, the field, the fence and the enemy dispositions had the look of the Mount Zion Church fight of July 6 all over again. Chapman split the companies into two attack wings, ordering Lieutenant W. Ben Palmer and Company E to charge through a gate in the fence while he and Company C attacked upon the road.[15]

Company E thundered forward, and the Union skirmish line exploded. The New Yorkers, armed with repeating carbines, delivered a withering fire. Ranger Robert Jarman, leaping from his horse, ran to open the gate and died. Palmer then sent Benjamin Iden forward, and he died too. Finally, Palmer unlatched the gate, and the Rangers burst through into the field. The New Yorkers scampered to the rear before the oncoming Rebels. Beardsley shouted the charge, and the Yankees galloped forward in a counterattack. Palmer's men reeled back, but it was only momentarily as Chapman and Company C, spilling in through a gap in the fence, hit the New Yorkers.[16]

Chapman's assault engulfed the Federals, who were "almost surrounded," said one of them. Beardsley yelled: "Fall back toward the woods and we will give them hell there!" Those of the New Yorkers not trapped streamed toward the trees at the opposite edge of the field. The Rangers, however, were relentless, shoving the Northerners into a corner of the fence where, wrote a Northerner, "the Johnnies were having a great harvest in killing, wounding and taking prisoners." Finally, a Federal opened another gate, and his comrades escaped annihilation. Some scattered through a cornfield; others raced down a cowpath toward Berryville. Beardsley's losses, according to the regimental historian, numbered forty-two killed, wounded and captured.[17]

In Gold's field, the Rangers disarmed the prisoners and searched them for money and valuables. Mosby's men commonly rifled the pockets of captives, hunting for greenbacks and watches. They were certainly not alone in this, as it had become a practice of both sides, including regular troops. If a Yankee responded slowly to the request to empty his pockets, the Rangers pointed a pistol at his head to expedite the proceeding.[18]

Besides Jarman and Iden, Chapman lost two men mortally wounded and one wounded. Lieutenant Frank Fox of Company C had an arm so badly mangled that he had to be left behind. Later that day, other Federal troops found him among their fallen comrades, placed him in an ambulance and hauled the native of Fairfax County to Harper's Ferry, where surgeons amputated the arm but could not save Fox's life. The second Ranger with a mortal wound was Henry Clay Adams. Adams had been shot through the body, the bullet severing his spinal cord, paralyzing his legs. His comrades carried him back to his family's home in Paris, where he lingered a few months until his death. A deaf man, Adams could have avoided military service.[19]

Chapman began the return march to the Confederacy after the engagement, arriving on the fourth. He must have traveled back through Ashby's Gap, as his command did not join Mosby, who with companies A and B descended Snicker's Gap at daylight. Mosby, intending to strike in the Charlestown area, brought his men to Myers's Ford on the Shenandoah River, approximately a half dozen miles southeast of Charlestown. Taking fifteen Rangers with him, Mosby scouted to the north across the river while Dolly Richards and several men forded the stream, searching for Union troops to the west. Lieutenant Joseph Nelson assumed command of the two companies, who hid in a stand of trees on the river's eastern side. Nelson placed pickets along the river, while most of the men relaxed in the woods.[20]

Richards's party returned shortly after hearing reports from civilians that a Union cavalry force was on patrol east of the river in the vicinity of Nelson's men. Mounting Company B, Richards followed the river northward, found no tracks and decided that the informants were mistaken. He led the company back to Nelson's campsite, before recrossing the river with his scouts. The seventy or so Rangers resumed their leisure activity. The pickets maintained their watch to the west across the waters.[21]

Mosby's constant campaign against Sheridan had offered the Rangers few times such as this—a warm late summer day, several hours for rest, camaraderie and the pleasure of a slow-burning pipe. Most lay or sat on the ground; the horses, tied to trees, waited. Suddenly, at two o'clock in the afternoon, the storm broke, a lightning bolt of blue, coming in from the east. Blazer's Scouts had located their resting ground after hours of tracking. Blazer had been to the crest of the Blue Ridge, learned that Mosby had gone toward Charlestown and, as he stated, "by a forced march" overtook the Rangers at Myers's Ford.[22]

The surprised Rangers scrambled for their arms and horses. Nelson and Sergeant Horace Johnson rallied a handful of men, who stalled the Federals. Most of the Rangers, however, "were completely demoralized and fleeing in all directions." Blazer dismounted numbers of the Scouts, and they began firing with the Spencer repeaters. The initial Union attack shoved the Southerners out of the woods, and now they stood exposed in an open field. The Confederates, wrote Blazer, "fought with a will, but the seven-shooters proved too much for them."[23]

Nelson's island of defenders held for thirty minutes in that field, firing their pistols and taking their losses. James H. Mallory fell mortally wounded, and a McQuinn or McKim broke his neck as he fled. Nelson took a bullet but still fought on. Three others were wounded, including Frank M. Woolf, who had recently recovered from a wound he had incurred at Mount Zion Church. Finally, the Scouts burst from the woods, routing the enemy. The Yankees overran five of the Rebels, and one Federal clubbed Ranger William R. Stone senseless with his rifle. Left for dead, Stone walked to the river after the Scouts departed, where he found Francis Marion Yates. Yates had also been hit but eluded the pursuers and was hiding when Stone came upon him. Both returned safely to the Confederacy.[24]

Blazer listed one killed and four wounded in the action. The Scouts, by moving swiftly, following the backroads, utilized Ranger methods to inflict a stunning defeat upon the Confederates. Mosby had lost more men in several engagements, but the partisans had almost invariably paid a cheaper price in blood than their opponents. Not so at Myers's Ford, and the rout stuck in the craws of the Rangers. Blazer and the Scouts had earned the respect of Mosby's command.[25]

For the next fortnight, from September 4 to 18, the campaign between Jubal Early and Phillip Sheridan stalled, and the Rangers savored Sam Chapman's victory at Gold's farm while they healed the wounds from Myers's Ford. A Michigan officer had described the previous weeks of movements as "backward and forward and forward and backward again. Up a hill and down again, has been the programme." But that period of maneuver and countermaneuver ended when Sheridan advanced toward Berryville on the third. By nightfall of the fourth, the Yankees had constructed eight miles of fieldworks east of Opequon Creek, from Berryville to Summit Point. Behind them Sheridan's army remained for the next two weeks. Early twice probed the entrenchments before retiring toward Winchester. The opponents, separated by the Opequon, remained in place until September 19 when Sheridan attacked Early at Winchester.[26]

During this two-week interlude in the campaign between Early and Sheridan, Mosby undertook no major raid into the Valley. Union cavalry watched closely the fords of the Shenandoah Valley in the army's rear, sealing the main Ranger entry points. Small detachments of Rangers penetrated the screen on occasion. Lieutenant Alfred Glascock and ten men rode through a Federal camp, were not halted or questioned and captured fifteen Yankees. East of the mountains, near Paris, Captain William H. Chapman's Company C attacked a contingent from the 8th Illinois Cavalry. In the gunfight, Ranger Joseph Johnson of Leesburg was mortally wounded. Chapman's men seized eighteen Federals and forty horses, but the Illinoisans withdrew with five Rangers as captives.[27]

With the brief lull in fighting, Mosby organized the battalion's seventh company on September 13, at Piedmont. Since Company E and the Artillery Company had been formed at the end of July, between sixty and seventy recruits enlisted in the command. From that pool of new manpower, Mosby officially created Company F.[28]

Mosby appointed Captain Walter Frankland, the battalion's acting quartermaster, as commander of Company F. Frankland was twenty-five years old, a native of Fauquier who had served in the 17th Virginia Infantry. He, George Whitescarver, Joseph Nelson and Frank Williams had joined Mosby in February 1863, each one rising to a command position in the battalion. When Whitescarver was killed at Seneca Mills, Maryland, on June 11, 1863, Frankland lost his best friend in the command.[29]

Frankland was a universal favorite among the Rangers. A small man, at five feet, seven inches, he always rode at the head of the column or in the front rank of battle, waving his plumed hat. "As an individual fighting man," John Munson believed, Frankland "had no superior in the command." He had been a captain since October 1863 because of his quartermaster assignment, but Mosby now selected him to lead men in combat.[30]

Frankland's first lieutenant was James F. "Big Yankee" Ames. The former deserter's loyalty to Mosby was unquestioned. Ames had proven on numerous raids and in combat that he was "one of the safest and best soldiers in our Command," according to Munson.[31]

Company F's second lieutenant was a former Maryland lawyer named Walter Bowie. Twenty-seven years old, "Wat" Bowie had enlisted in the battalion in the fall of 1863. Appointed a captain in the fall of 1861, after service in a Virginia battery, Bowie had engaged in clandestine operations in his native state until he joined the Rangers. Mosby had utilized Bowie as a scout on raids into Maryland. Bowie, said John Scott, possessed "a certain cool daring."[32]

Mosby chose James Frank Turner for the company's third lieutenant. A Ranger since the previous autumn, Frank Turner had been captured, exchanged and received a sixty-day furlough in May 1864 after spending nearly a week in Chimborazo Hospital in Richmond for abscesses on the legs. Rejoining his comrades in July, Turner served as a private until the promotion.[33]

A recent recruit, Hugh M. McIlhany, was appointed first sergeant of Company F. A native of Warrenton, McIlhany was twenty-three years old, a former member of the 17th Virginia Infantry. He had held the rank of quartermaster captain on the staff of General James

Longstreet. He must have been well known to a number of Rangers and, with his previous record, Mosby selected him for the noncommissioned officer's post.[34]

Unlike his usual practice, Mosby did not send the new company on a raid after the organization. Instead, Mosby, with Rangers Guy Broadwater and Tom Love, scouted into Fairfax County on the fourteenth. As the trio cleared Centreville, five troopers from the 13th New York Cavalry attacked the Confederates. The foes exchanged pistol shots until the Southerners spurred away. The Yankees gave chase for over a mile when Mosby wheeled his horse around and opened fire with both of his Colts. He killed the mounts of the two leading cavalrymen and stopped the other three. Corporal Henry Smith, pinned to the ground under his dead horse, fired the final round in his pistol. The bullet struck one of Mosby's revolvers, caroming into his groin. Smith knew that he had hit the Rebel as he saw his enemy reel in the saddle.[35]

Mosby remained on his horse as he, Broadwater and Love disengaged. They rode to The Plains, where Mosby had the wound dressed. One of his surgeons examined it, deciding that the bullet could not be removed. Mosby needed time to heal so he was transported to near Lynchburg in Amherst County, where his father had relocated. He carried the bullet in his body for the remainder of his life. The Federals confirmed a week later that the wounded Ranger was Mosby, and Colonel Henry Lazelle, commander of the Union cavalry brigade in Fairfax, sent a detachment into Fauquier on a hunt for the partisan commander, but Mosby had departed days earlier. Corporal Smith received a promotion to sergeant.[36]

Before his wounding, Mosby submitted a report to Robert E. Lee in which he summarized the battalion's operations during the previous six months. Lee replied a week later, on the nineteenth, stating: "I am much gratified by the activity and skill you have displayed, and desire to express my thanks to yourself and the brave officers and men of your command for the valuable services rendered to the country. The smallness of your loss, in comparison with the damage inflicted upon the enemy, is creditable to your own judgment and to the intelligence and courage of those who executed your orders."[37]

Lee endorsed Mosby's report and forwarded it to the War Department. In the endorsement, the Confederate commander noted the number of enemy troops, horses, wagons and equipment seized by the Rangers and the importance of the information gathered by Mosby and his men on Federal movements. "His operations," concluded Lee, "have been highly creditable to himself and his command. As for the present," Lee recommended in his letter to Mosby, "I hope you will continue to harass the enemy's troops as much as possible, and restrain his efforts to exercise civil authority in the counties in which you are operating."[38]

On the day Lee wrote to Mosby, Monday, September 19, Philip Sheridan's Union army attacked Jubal Early's Confederates at Winchester. For six weeks the opponents had marched back and forth in the lower Valley—Sheridan acting with caution; Early skirting danger with boldness before the numerically superior Federals. Sheridan had been cautioned by Edwin Stanton and/or Henry Halleck about the military and political consequences of another Union defeat in the Valley. He acted appropriately, hiding behind fieldworks, offering Early little opportunity for a strike. On September 2, however, Atlanta fell to William Sherman's troops, and Lincoln's presidential campaign received the battlefield victory it desperately needed. Two weeks later, Grant visited Sheridan at Charlestown. The general-in-chief wanted action, and Sheridan outlined an offensive against Early. Grant listened, questioned and finally told Sheridan, "Go in."

Sheridan struck at first light on the nineteenth. Early's divisions were separated, and the Confederates faced piecemeal destruction. But Sheridan funneled most of his infantry and artillery through a narrow canyon, giving Early the time he needed to regroup. When the foes finally locked into combat, they gripped it with a fervor. For several hours, until dusk, the Northerners and the Southerners slugged it out in a vicious stand-up fight. Sheridan's numbers prevailed in the end, and much of Early's army fled southward in a headlong flight.[39]

The Union army pursued the next morning, trailing the Confederates, who by midday filed into their old works on the crest of Fisher's Hill. The Federals arrived later in the day and deployed along the ground north of the formidable position. That night Sheridan convened a council of war which decided to assail Early's line on the twenty-second. As a secondary, but important, phase of the offensive, Sheridan ordered his cavalry commander, Brevet Major General Alfred T. A. Torbert, to take two mounted divisions and sweep up the Luray Valley, a small glen nestled between the Blue Ridge and the Massanutten Mountain to the east. The Massanutten began opposite Fisher's Hill and extended fifty miles southward, narrowing the main valley floor. Torbert was directed to cross the Massanutten at New Market Gap and bar Early's retreat path when Sheridan's army attacked at Fisher's Hill.

The Union assault came late on the afternoon of the twenty-second. Early had stretched his thinned ranks as far as he could, but it was not enough. The Yankees crushed the Rebel left flank, rolling up the entire line. The Confederates fled in a rout worse than at Winchester. The door to the upper Shenandoah Valley lay open as Early's army streamed southward. In the Luray Valley, Torbert, however, retired northward after attempting a feeble attack on a Confederate cavalry division. Sheridan had not achieved all that he had planned, but Fisher's Hill was a spectacular victory.[40]

At about the same time Sheridan's troops stampeded Early's men at Fisher's Hill, 120 Rangers, Captain Sam Chapman commanding, entered the Shenandoah Valley through Chester Gap, east of Front Royal. When the news of Early's defeat at Winchester reached Mosby's Confederacy, Captain William H. Chapman, who commanded the battalion in Mosby's absence, ordered his brother to take a detachment into the Valley and operate against Sheridan's lines of communication and supply as the Federals advanced southward. Sam Chapman bivouacked his men for the night between the gap and the town. Chapman learned from residents of Front Royal, which lay at the northern end of Luray Valley where the North and South Forks of the Shenandoah River merge to form the larger stream, that enemy cavalrymen—Torbert's two divisions—had passed through the day before, moving toward Luray, and that they had heard gunfire earlier on the twenty-second toward the village of Milford, several miles to the south.[41]

Chapman and several Rangers were on horse at daybreak on September 23, probing toward Milford. They followed the Gooney Manor road east of the main Front Royal–Luray Pike. A few miles north of Milford the Rebels saw an ambulance train, with a small mounted escort, en route toward Front Royal on the Pike. Turning back, Chapman and the men hurried ahead, meeting the main body outside of Front Royal.[42]

Believing that the ambulances were moving back toward Winchester while the Union cavalry continued southward, Chapman fashioned an attack plan. He separated his force, assigning forty-five men to Captain Walter E. Frankland with orders to strike the front of the train as it rolled between a wooded hill and a gorge near the edge of the town. Chapman, with seventy-five Rangers, would circle eastward, charging into the rear of the ambulances. With that settled, Frankland led his men to their attack point while Chapman trotted ahead of his detachment for a final look at the Federals before the Rangers struck.[43]

Chapman probably felt confident as he rode toward the inviting target—he had not had such an opportunity since his promotion to captain of Company E. Urging his horse forward, he halted on the crest of a bluff. Down below, the ambulances creaked toward Frankland's waiting men but, directly behind the train, as far as Chapman could see, came an unbroken column of Union cavalrymen. He had erred grievously—the ambulances were the van of a retrograde march of Torbert's entire two divisions.[44]

Prodding his mount, the Ranger captain rushed back to his men who had arrived at their assigned position. Chapman, explaining the situation, ordered Lieutenant Harry Hatcher to lead the seventy-five Rangers to Chester Gap while he rushed to warn Frankland. Chapman knew that it was a race against a possible disaster—if Frankland's men charged they could be overwhelmed. Finding Frankland on Prospect Hill, Chapman, bridling up, yelled: "Call off your men! You are attacking a brigade!"

Frankland, who did not understand what Chapman meant, replied: "Sam, we can't stop now. We've got them whipped!"[45]

Frankland had no sooner spoken when the Federal cavalrymen, wrote John Scott, "enveloped the devoted band like a cloud." Chapman had arrived too late; Frankland's men were already among the ambulances, shooting the drivers and chasing the escort. But when the Rangers hit the train, the Union troopers to the rear counterattacked. The Yankees, said a teenager who witnessed the action, "came up like a flock of birds when a stone is cast into it." The forty-five Confederates fought valiantly, but they "quickly scattered and fled in all directions," wrote a Federal officer.[46]

Chapman and Frankland, plunging into the "cloud" of blue-jacketed horsemen, rallied the men, guiding them across the fields toward Chester Gap. Harry Hatcher, meanwhile, disobeying Chapman's orders, stopped his men in the bottomlands of "Oak Hill," the farm of Perry Criser, near the Chester Gap road. Hatcher was a fighter, and he refused to abandon his comrades to an unknown fate. Here at "Oak Hill" the two Ranger detachments linked up.[47]

The Union cavalrymen trailing the ambulances belonged to Charles Russell Lowell's Reserve Brigade, the command whose wagons had been destroyed by the Rangers at Berryville. When Frankland's men attacked the ambulances, the leading regiment of the brigade, the 2nd United States Cavalry, divided—one section rode to the vehicles; a larger contingent, scaling the embankment along the Pike, sped across to the Gooney Manor Road. This group then galloped toward Chester Gap to cut off the retreat of the Southerners. By the time Chapman rejoined Hatcher, the Yankees had reached Criser's farm and faced the Rangers.[48]

The Confederates pitched forward, trying to punch a hole in the cordon of Union cavalrymen. The fighting had no form. Each Ranger was on his own as he endeavored to escape. Thomas Carter had his horse shot from under him, but Joe Millan, riding past, had Carter jump on his mount and both escaped into the woods. Thomas Moss saved the life of Lieutenant Fount Beattie, killing a Federal who had his revolver a foot from Beattie and ready to fire. Thornton Leach and several others were nearly trapped until Leach shot a Yankee's horse in the head. When the animal collapsed, Thornton and his comrades lanced through the narrow opening. Ranger Charley Dear took a bullet but eluded his pursuers, while Frank Robey escaped in the confusion after being captured.[49]

The vast majority of the Rangers fought their way through, plunging into the woods on the mountainside. Their casualties, although not precisely known, were slight; not a man was killed. The gunfire had been fierce, but not deadly. Six Rangers, however, were ridden down in the pursuit and were now being led into Front Royal.[50]

One of the Federal casualties was Lieutenant Charles McMaster, who was lying desperately wounded in the gap. McMaster had the bridle rein of his horse severed by a bullet in the action and, unable to control the animal, rode into the midst of Chapman's oncoming men. A Confederate shot him in the head. When his troopers found him, he was conscious. McMaster, an Irish immigrant who had joined the regular army before the war, had enough strength to tell the men that he had been gunned down after he surrendered.[51]

Had this been true, it would have been a grave breach of accepted rules of combat. Years later, after the details of this day were recalled and written about, the Rangers denied McMaster's assertion. Mosby was most emphatic in the denial, writing: "There was no time to parley or take prisoners. The momentum of Chapman's charge swept away all before it." McMaster, claimed Mosby, was shot as the Confederates galloped past him. "Lieutenant McMaster was never a prisoner—no prisoners were taken," Mosby concluded. In an unpublished account, Mosby stated that "even admitting that Mc-Masters [sic] offered to surrender when killed," his men might not have known it in the confusion or perhaps refused quarter.[52]

Ranger John Scott in his memoirs admitted that McMaster had dismounted, adding, "it is supposed, intending to surrender." But, argued Scott, the officer retained his pistol and sword and was fired upon as the Rangers, as Mosby alleged, rode by.[53]

Perhaps it was as Mosby and Scott reconstructed it—the Rebels, seeing an armed Union officer on foot in the roadbed, believed him to be a dangerous foe and opened fire. The evidence indicates that McMaster spoke the truth, however. The support for the Union allegations comes from two civilians who lived in Mosby's Confederacy. "Tee" Edmonds recorded in her diary under the date of September 25: "Our men had captured a Colonel [McMaster was a lieutenant and only officer taken] and were overtaken, surrounded by the enemy. Our men shot the Colonel, giving him several shots after his begging and pleading with them not to kill him. He lived long enough to tell the Yankees what they did." Also, Catherine Cochran wrote in her journal that the Rangers shot a number of Yankee prisoners. Both women could only have learned the details either directly or indirectly from the Ranger participants. Edmonds's words reveal that she heard the story firsthand from one or more of the boarders at "Belle Grove."[54]

The case presented by Mosby and Scott remains "unconvincing," as a historian of the Union cavalry has asserted. McMaster, who died from the wounds on October 15, had surrendered and, when his captors could not lead him out with them, shot him where he stood. Their deed unleashed a rampage of vengeance in the streets of Front Royal.[55]

McMaster's statement, recounted a Union captain, "incensed his fellow officers and volunteers." By the time the Yankees led their six Ranger captives into Front Royal, the shooting of McMaster had been relayed from unit to unit. When the 6th Michigan Cavalry entered the place, they "found the town in an uproar." The Federals clamored for revenge; the demands expressed most forcefully by men from McMaster's regiment. But they were not alone; too many of these regiments had suffered at the hands of the partisans. A New York

trooper, writing after the war with exaggeration, explained his comrades' sentiments: "Our soldiers in that territory at that time had
become desperate. To be caught by Mosby's men then was almost
certain death. We found bodies of our men hanging in trees with all
their clothes, except shirt and drawers gone; throats cut; pierced by
bullets, bayonets, sabers and knives; often with papers pinned to them
bearing abusive messages."[56]

Memories of the burned wagons at Berryville, the dead Michigan
troopers in the ditch at Benjamin Morgan's, the disappearance of
pickets and forage details kindled the flames ignited by McMaster's
fatal wounding. Rational thought was rare in Front Royal on this
morning; in fact, it had vanished weeks ago among the Federals when
it came to the Rangers. The cavalrymen wanted to settle accounts, a
reckoning tabulated only in blood.

All the units' ranking officers were present—Torbert, Wesley
Merritt, George Custer and Lowell. Whoever requested that the prisoners be executed is unknown. Although Lowell in a letter home
attributed the order for the executions to Merritt, his division commander, it was Torbert, the cavalry commander, who gave the troopers permission. Merritt undoubtedly approved Torbert's decision. As
for Custer, he probably concurred, but there is no evidence that he
was involved in the decision making. Some of Custer's men from
the Michigan Brigade had a role in what was about to transpire.[57]

Two of the prisoners—David L. Jones and Lucien Love—were
taken together to a town lot behind the Methodist Church. Jones was
from Fredericksburg, Virginia, a member of Company A, who had
been captured in May 1863 and was not exchanged until March 3,
1864. He had rejoined the 43rd Battalion after his release. Love, like
Jones, hailed from Fredericksburg. He was only seventeen years old
and belonged to Richard Montjoy's "Company Darling."[58]

The execution of the two fellow townsmen was swift. The Northerners stood the pair together in the shadow of the church and opened
fire. The squad of executioners then turned and walked away, leaving
the two dead men where they lay.[59]

Another squad escorted a third prisoner, Thomas E. Anderson,
to Perry Criser's farm. Anderson was thirty years old, a husband and
father of two children from Markham in Fauquier County. During
the fighting, Anderson, a stocky man with a well-groomed beard
and mustache and sad-looking eyes, had his horse killed from under
him and was captured as he ran on foot. He died under an elm tree.[60]

The fourth victim was not an enrolled member of the 43rd Battalion, but seventeen-year-old Henry Rhodes of Front Royal. Rhodes, like Cab Maddux and many other youths, dreamed of riding with Mosby's men, but he remained at home, supporting a widowed mother and a sister. When the Rangers rode through the town on their way to attack the ambulances, Rhodes could not resist and, borrowing a neighbor's horse, joined his heroes. His mount, however, collapsed during the race toward Chester Gap, and the teenager was overtaken by the Federals.[61]

Henry Rhodes came home that same morning, his arms lashed to the saddles of two Union cavalrymen, who dragged the youth up Chester Street. When Mrs. Rhodes saw her son, she ran screaming to him, hugged him and pleaded with the Yankees to spare his life. One of the captors, brandishing a saber, threatened to behead both mother and son. A young man's dream had become a family's nightmare.[62]

The troopers, men from Custer's Michigan brigade, led Rhodes to a field on the "Rose Hill" farm of a Richardson family. His mother followed; her cries had not ceased. The cavalrymen untied the ropes, and Rhodes stumbled into the pasture. A Michigander drew his revolver, and it was done.[63]

Two eyewitness accounts of Henry Rhodes's final seconds of life present a conflicting picture. A civilian stated that his executioner "ordered the helpless, dazed prisoner to stand up in front of him, while he emptied his pistol upon him." The other version, written by a Union officer, is unclear if the victim was Rhodes, but the description fits. The lieutenant, a member of Torbert's staff, "saw one of the prisoners running and throwing up his arms as if to ward off the bullets that were being fired at him. I did not see him fall but of course he did fall."[64]

From a window at "Rose Hill" Sue Richardson had watched. She knew Henry Rhodes, was probably close to him in age and never forgot his death. The scene haunted her, and she wrote in her diary: "Such excitement and cruelty as never was witnessed here before . . . poor Henry Rhodes should be shot in our field, nearly in front of our door. We could see the crowd assembled around him, then we had the pain of seeing the stock passing over him before his body could be removed. His poor mother is almost crazy."[65]

Two were left—William Thomas Overby and a Ranger named Carter. Overby was a twenty-seven-year-old, tall, darkly complexioned native Virginian, whose family had moved to Georgia when he was a child. He had fought in the 7th Georgia Infantry, falling with a wound at the Second Battle of Bull Run in August 1862. A member of Company D, Overby was in the battalion by the spring of 1864. As for Overby's fellow prisoner, Carter, few details of his life are known. His comrades in the command described him as a short, slightly built man from Virginia. A letter from a descendant, filed in an archive, claimed that Carter was born and raised in South Carolina, however. Overby regarded himself as a Georgian and, if Carter were a South Carolinian, these two soldiers from the Deep South found themselves now together in a Virginia town, sharing a common fate.[66]

Sergeants, corporals and privates from McMaster's regiment, the 2nd United States Cavalry, took Overby and Carter to a wagon yard owned by a man named Petty. Torbert was there and offered the Rangers their lives if they revealed the location of Mosby's headquarters. Neither man replied. Torbert then directed Captain Theodore W. Bean, provost marshal of Merritt's division, to interrogate the prisoners. Bean spoke to each Rebel individually, but he received only silence. With his patience spent, Torbert ordered Bean to hang the pair of Rangers.[67]

By now a sizable crowd of troopers, mainly from McMaster's regiment, had gathered in the wagon yard, and they led Overby and Carter away. The condemned soldiers walked the final three-quarters of a mile, across the forks of the river, which the local people called the "Laughing Waters," to the home of W. E. Carson. A woman, watching the procession pass, recalled: "Well do I remember the picture: Overby, with head erect, defiant, and Carter overcome and weeping." A regimental band accompanied the throng, playing again and again the dirge, "Love Not, The One You Love May Die."[68]

The Federals mounted Overby and Carter on two horses, threw ropes across the limb of a walnut tree and adjusted the nooses around the Rangers' necks. Bean came forward, offering them one final chance to spare themselves by betraying Mosby. Both again rejected the offer. The distraught Carter asked for a Bible, read a few passages and then prayed. Someone in the crowd told him to hurry. Overby "looked on with indifference," according to a Rhode Island trooper. A minister from the town spoke to both men, trying to comfort them before the passage. Overby assured the pastor that he was not afraid to die. Defiant to the end, the Georgian told his enemies: "Mosby'll hang ten of you for every one of us." Finally, two whips cracked and then silence. If anyone listened, however, they could hear the endless sound of the "Laughing Waters."[69]

A number of the onlookers admired the courage of their two foes. Some of the Northerners believed that the executions were a mistake, an invitation for reprisals by the Confederate partisans. Sergeant Samuel C. Willis of the 1st Rhode Island Cavalry, writing years later, avowed: "Those men should never have been hung *for not betraying their Commander.*" Continuing, he stated: "I think the order of Gen. Torbert was unwise, narrow and cruel in the extreme." Willis compared Overby to Nathan Hale of the American Revolution. Lieutenant Colonel Caspar Crowninshield, commander of the Rangers' old antagonist, the 2nd Massachusetts Cavalry, informed his mother of the incident a week later: "I am glad to say that my Regt. had nothing to do with this."[70]

Torbert, meanwhile, had learned of Sheridan's victory at Fisher's Hill on the previous day, so he ordered the cavalry divisions into marching formation. With Sheridan moving southward, Torbert turned his column around, retracing their route of the morning, up the Luray Valley toward Milford. Before the Yankees departed, one of them tied a placard around the body of Overby. On it, the Yankee had scribbled: "This will be the fate of Mosby and all his men."[71]

Behind them, Torbert's horse soldiers left six corpses and the shocked residents of Front Royal. The following day a detachment of Rangers entered the town. Frank Angelo cut down the bodies of Overby and Carter, while others gathered up the remains of Jones, Love, Anderson and Rhodes. Burial details interred three of them—Jones, Love and Rhodes—in Prospect Hill Cemetery, from where Frankland's men had attacked the ambulances. Anderson's body was returned to his widow and children in Markham, while Overby's and Carter's were probably carried back to Fauquier and buried.[72]

The interment of the dead, however, could not remove the memories of those few hours for the people of the community. "The sight," wrote a teenaged boy, "was the most ghastly incident our citizens had ever witnessed." A woman resident, a child at the time, still remembered the terror, the shouts, the gunfire many years later. "The 'dark day' of 1864 is indelibly photographed in my memory," she wrote. "I have often wished I could blot it out, for it clouded my childhood."[73]

Thirty-five years later, on September 23, 1899, approximately

150 of Mosby's Rangers returned to Front Royal. Elderly men now, sustained by the accepted glory of their youth, they formed into a column, marched to Prospect Hill Cemetery as a crowd estimated at 5,000 watched. Among the gravesites, speakers talked of the "dark day" of 1864, and then the veterans and the spectators dedicated a twenty-five-foot-high granite monument to their executed comrades. Proceeds for the purchase of the marker had been secured by the sale of pieces of the walnut tree used as the scaffold for Overby and Carter. The granite shaft stands today and, as a morning's sun clears the Blue Ridge, its shadow ascends the hillside, almost touching the graves of those it honors.[74]

But in 1864, what the deaths of the six Rangers meant, no one could be sure. Catherine Cochran, who lived in Fauquier, thought about the portent and to her journal she confided: "where it will end God only knows."[75]

Chapter 13

WAR
ON
RAILROADS

 John S. Mosby returned to the 43rd Battalion on Thursday, September 29. Although the groin wound had healed, to move around he needed crutches, which were made for him by a family slave. When he wanted to ride, one or two of his men lifted him into the saddle. He looked thinner, and a two-week stubble of a beard covered his face. Mosby was physically strong, in excellent condition, and that accelerated his recovery. More importantly, the command required his presence.[1]

During his journey back to the "Confederacy," Mosby met Dolly Richards, Alfred Glascock and Richard Montjoy at Gordonsville. The three officers were traveling to Richmond on a furlough. From them, he learned of the fight at Front Royal and the executions of the captured Rangers. When Mosby arrived in Fauquier, he surely questioned Sam Chapman, Walter Frankland and a number of the men. Mosby wanted to know which Union officer was responsible for the act. One or several of the partisans stated that according to some of the citizens of the town George Armstrong Custer ordered the shootings and hangings. Mosby accepted that and continued to believe it for the rest of his life.[2]

The townsfolk had no way of knowing whether Custer gave the order and, as noted previously, they were wrong. Custer's crime evidently was that he was conspicuous on the twenty-third. Anybody who dressed as he did stood out, even in a crowd of thousands. A male resident of Front Royal, seeing Custer ride through the streets, penned a graphic description of the young brigadier. "He was dressed in a splendid suit of silk velvet," wrote the man, "his saddle bow bound in silver or gold. In his hand he had a large branch of damsons [plums], which he picked and ate as he rode along. He was a distinguished looking man, with his yellow locks resting upon his shoulders."[3]

Mosby, because of subsequent actions on his part, took great pains after the war in both private correspondence and published writings to argue the case against Custer. "Custer had a grudge against us for the killing of his barn-burning men," Mosby argued in an unpublished memoir. To one of his men, Mosby wrote in a letter, dated December 12, 1899, that "a man who will burn houses *from revenge* over the heads of women and children as Custer did would commit murder—a murderer generally denies it."[4]

To Mosby, the crucial piece of evidence against Custer, Wesley Merritt, Alfred Torbert and Charles Russell Lowell was the absence of an account of the Front Royal action in any of the officers' official reports which were published after the war. In a journal article, published thirty-five years after the incident, Mosby asserted: "It was their duty to report the fact, and if justifiable, then the circumstances that justified it. No matter whether they were active or merely passive in the business, their silence gives it a dark complexion." Finally, in his published memoirs, Mosby put it bluntly: "I don't care a straw whether Custer was solely responsible for the hanging of our men, or jointly with others. If we believe the reports of the generals, none of them ever heard of the hanging of the men; they must have committed suicide. Contemporary evidence is against Custer."[5]

The charges and countercharges—many of the Rangers eventually accepted Custer's innocence—lay years ahead; for the present, Mosby blamed Custer and decided that when he had captured enough of the Union general's troopers, he would exact his own retribution for Front Royal. As he subsequently argued in his reminiscences, "Reprisals in war can only be justified as a deterrent."[6]

The Front Royal engagement, however, was only one item in a list of problems which Mosby faced when he arrived. Even before he rejoined the Rangers, he learned at Gordonsville when he spoke with Richards, Glascock and Montjoy that the battalion seethed with discord, particularly among the company officers. " 'My command,' I saw," he admitted later, "was going to pieces from the jealousy of the officers." Acting commander Captain William H. Chapman was the cause of the difficulties. Richards, Glascock and Montjoy—perhaps others—resented what they viewed as Chapman's desire to take credit for the Rangers' accomplishments during Mosby's absence. The antagonisms between the officers must have been festering for some time, because in less than two weeks they had exploded. Montjoy agreed to return with Mosby, but Richards and Glascock continued to Richmond. Both of them, however, resumed their posts within several days. Mosby's presence with the battalion smothered the rivalry for the immediate future.[7]

Just prior to Mosby's return, the Federals struck in southern Loudoun and Upper Fauquier. The incursions resulted from both Grant and Sheridan's ongoing demands for counteroperations in the region. Grant had told Sheridan earlier in September that "it is our interest that that county [Loudoun] should not be capable of subsisting a hostile army." Sheridan relayed the gist of Grant's message to Major General Christopher Augur in Washington, stating: "I think it best to clean out that section of country."[8]

Augur acted slowly, however. One of his cavalry units swept through the Snickersville-Paris-Upperville section during mid-month, the raid netting five Rangers. But on September 23, instructions were given to the department's cavalry commander, Colonel Henry Lazelle, to send a force into the heart of the region and, if circumstances permitted, burn the home and outbuildings of Joseph Blackwell, whose residence Mosby used as a headquarters, the Federals had learned.[9]

Colonel Henry Gansevoort, with his own 13th New York Cavalry and companies from the 16th New York Cavalry, started from Fairfax on the evening of the twenty-fourth. The troopers followed the abandoned tracks of the Manassas Gap Railroad through Thoroughfare Gap in the Bull Run Mountains to Rectortown and Piedmont. They arrived at Blackwell's place, northeast of Piedmont, on the twenty-sixth. Details searched the premises, finding "a large quantity" of pistols, carbines, ammunition and equipment, including the sword and scabbard which Dolly Richards had inscribed and presented to Mosby. The home, Gansevoort reported, "evidently was Colonel Mosby's arsenal and headquarters." The Yankees burned the house, the barn and outbuildings; when the flames reached the cache of arms and ammunition, the explosions "resembled a small fight."[10]

Mosby learned of his friend's losses and the destruction of the command's store of arms and equipment when he met his men at Piedmont. The news "very much enraged" him, in the words of diarist "Tee" Edmonds. As for Blackwell, according to a Ranger, he "had an honest dread of Yankees" afterwards. Today, the house's chimney still stands in a silent watch, marking the location of one of Mosby's headquarters.[11]

Gansevoort's raid served a second purpose besides the burning of Blackwell's residence. Accompanying him was an engineer officer whose mission was to examine the roadbed of the Manassas Gap Railroad for the feasibility of reconstruction. If the Federals could rebuild the tracks of the railroad to its terminus at Strasburg in the Shenandoah Valley, the line could be the major supply artery for Sheridan's army. The key barrier in a rebuilding operation was the presence of Mosby's Rangers—the tracks passed through the heart of the Confederacy.[12]

The impetus for the resupply plan came from Grant. Since the victory at Fisher's Hill, Sheridan's army had been occupying the Harrisonburg area in the Shenandoah Valley, roughly seventy miles south of Winchester. From that base, Sheridan's cavalry ranged south, east and west, burning crops, barns and mills, making this section of the lush Valley "a barren waste," as Sheridan informed Grant. Sheridan believed that for his army the best course of action "will be to let the burning of the crops of the Valley be the end of this campaign and let some of this army go somewhere else."[13]

Grant, however, looked at the strategic horizon with a broader vision than Sheridan. With Jubal Early's twice-defeated army camped along the Blue Ridge and Sheridan triumphant in the upper Valley, Grant saw an opportunity for a strike across the mountains by Sheridan. The general-in-chief wanted Sheridan to advance on Charlottesville and the railroads into the town. If Sheridan could take that railhead and then continue toward Richmond, Robert E. Lee would be caught between an anvil and a hammer of Union might. The Confederate capital might fall before winter.[14]

When Grant discussed his idea with Sheridan, Sheridan objected, citing supply problems for such a movement. Grant, Secretary of War Edwin Stanton and Chief of Staff Henry Halleck offered to reopen the Orange and Alexandria Railroad, which had been shut down since Grant's operations did not require its use. Again, Sheridan responded with objections. "I am ready and willing to cross the Blue Ridge," he telegraphed Halleck, but it was beyond "my present means." Finally, on October 2, Grant instructed Halleck to transfer the work gangs from the Orange and Alexandria to the Manassas Gap Railroad. Sheridan's argument prevailed, and his troops were soon withdrawing northward down the Valley.[15]

Constructed between 1851 and 1854, the Manassas Gap Railroad extended from Manassas Junction through the Bull Run Mountains to Fauquier County, crossing the Blue Ridge at Manassas Gap and on to Strasburg. The railroad served as a direct route from the Shenandoah Valley to eastern Virginia and Washington, DC, hauling the harvests of the lush region to the growing markets. Once the war began, the tracks carried troops and materiel through the strategically important section of the Old Dominion. In the face of Union advances, the Confederates abandoned the line in May 1862, removing the rolling stock and engines to other railroads. Neither side attempted to use the railbed until Grant ordered it.[16]

On the same day Grant instructed Halleck to begin the work on the railroad, October 2, the chief of staff assigned the task to Christopher Augur and his Department of Washington, whose troops protected the capital and manned defenses in northern Virginia. Augur acted immediately, forming construction crews and directing Brigadier General John R. Slough, military governor of Alexandria, Virginia, to furnish troops as guards. Slough pulled in troops from the Orange and Alexandria details—the 5th Pennsylvania Heavy Artillery and the 201st and 202nd Pennsylvania Infantry. Augur added a company from the 13th New York Cavalry and, by the third, the work gangs and the troops were steaming toward Upper Fauquier.[17]

The advance contingent of the Union operation rolled into Salem on the morning of the fourth. As the Federals had come in from the east, details were stationed at Thoroughfare Gap and at The Plains. At Salem, the laborers checked the bed, the ties and the rails while the infantrymen posted themselves along the tracks. The railroad ran along the northern and eastern edge of the town before bending sharply northward to Rectortown, where it turned westward again to Piedmont and Manassas Gap.[18]

In Washington, Halleck wired Grant on that day: "In order to keep up communication on this line to Manassas Gap and the Shenandoah Valley, it will be necessary to send South all rebel inhabitants between that line and the Potomac, and also to completely clean out Mosby's gang of robbers who have so long infested that district of country." Halleck had little faith in the ability of Augur's troops to accomplish the mission, describing them as "cowed and useless" when confronting the Rangers. He suggested that Grant order Sheridan to send the latter's cavalry into the region. Otherwise, although he did not state it directly, Halleck despaired of success.[19]

Grant might not even have read Halleck's telegram by the time the Union work crews arrived in Salem on the fourth. When the Yankees arrived at Salem, Mosby summoned the Rangers to a rendezvous. By that afternoon, he had 250 men and two howitzers poised south and east of the village. The artillery crews unlimbered the cannon on Stevenson's Hill, a half-mile from Salem; skirmishers dismounted and fanned out while the main body remained mounted to charge through the streets. The Northerners, meanwhile, continued their repair work, maintained a watch and were busy erecting a camp.[20]

The Ranger skirmishers advanced on foot as the gunners opened fire. But the artillery rounds fell short of the target—one ripped a hole in the house of John Frye; a second damaged a brick wall of the Episcopal Church and a third shattered the garden fence of Philip Klipstein, a former Ranger. The explosions stirred up the Yankees, who tried to rally. By then, the skirmishers were among the tents, and the mounted Rangers were pounding toward the railroad. The Union cavalry company offered token resistance as the infantrymen and workers piled onto the train or fled on foot toward Rectortown. A rear guard of the infantry deployed where the tracks passed through a ravine, but Richard Montjoy, leading the pursuit force, scattered the foot soldiers, capturing about fifty. But the Northerners mortally wounded two of the rebels—Edward Thompson and a man named Stinson.[21]

The Federals' commander, Colonel George S. Gallupe, heard about the attack at Salem that night or on the morning of the fifth. He relayed the news to Augur in Washington and brought forward the infantry at The Plains, where he had his headquarters, and at Thoroughfare Gap. By day's end, Gallupe had relocated headquarters to Rectortown and had over 2,000 troops stationed there and at Piedmont. The troops erected fortifications around their camps.[22]

The Rangers struck again on October 6. While a detachment wrecked the tracks at Salem, Mosby with most of the men shelled the Yankee camps and works at Rectortown. A repair crew and its guards rebuilding a bridge over Goose Creek outside of Piedmont stopped the work and fled into Rectortown. Another trainload of infantry approached Salem but, when the engineer saw that the rails were removed and the Rangers started shooting, he reversed the train.[23]

October 7 brought a renewal of the action. Once again, Mosby's battery engaged the Federals at Rectortown. At Salem another group of Rangers attacked Federal infantry. The Northerners regrouped on Stevenson's Hill and held firm. Mosby rejoined the men at Salem and disbanded them for the night. The war for the railroad clearly favored the Confederates.[24]

Augur, in Washington, had read the reports from the front and grasped the gravity of the situation. He concluded that without a sizable Union cavalry force stationed along the railroad, the reconstruction of the tracks would cease. Union infantry huddling behind fieldworks could not stop the attacks by Mosby's partisans. Consequently, on the sixth Augur ordered Colonel Henry Lazelle to collect his cavalry brigade and march to the front. Augur also plucked 600 troopers, mostly new volunteers and stragglers, from Camp Stoneman, the cavalry remount camp, and he pulled the 8th Illinois Cavalry from Maryland into the campaign. To the commander of the latter regiment, Augur advised that the regiment proceed through Middleburg to Rectortown, noting that "it is possible you may have to fight Mosby on the road about Middleburg. Be prepared for him. Be in haste." With the details completed, Augur boarded a train to take personal direction of the operation.[25]

The commander of the Department of Washington arrived at The Plains at 7:00 A.M., October 7. He listened to recent updates and then planned his counteroffensive. He ordered a repair crew with guards sent to Salem to replace the damaged rails; he ordered the construction of blockhouses in the towns and the formation of details to cut down trees along the tracks. When this last request reached Washington, officials gathered employees of various departments for the duty, but forty-seven workers of the quartermaster department refused to comply and ended up in a prison. Later in the day Augur learned of the Ranger attacks at Rectortown and Salem, but telegraphed Halleck: "As soon as the cavalry arrives, all will be well here."[26]

The van of the horsemen began filtering in that night. By the next morning, the Federals renewed their efforts. Two trains had derailed during the night because of decayed ties which shifted the rails under the weight. Crews replaced them while other laborers resealed the break in the line at Salem. Lazelle's troopers guarded the tracks, and the Rangers were quiet. By day's end, trains rolled into Rectortown, moving "Tee" Edmonds to write: "The old whistle and snort of the iron horse seems as natural as in days past."[27]

This lasted but one day, October 8. As the Yankees pushed westward from Rectortown toward Piedmont on the ninth, the Rangers reappeared. About a mile southeast of Piedmont at "Yew Hill," the 116-year-old home of a Shacklett family, Mosby and eighty men charged three companies of the 8th Illinois Cavalry, which had come in the day before. The Illinoisans, whom the Confederates fought before, were, in John Alexander's opinion, "no holiday soldiers, but by considerable odds the best fighters we ever tackled." The antagonists lashed each other in a hand-to-hand struggle in the yard in front of "Yew Hill." Lieutenant William "Big Yankee" Ames, proving his valor and loyalty once more, was in the thick of it and died there. Mosby was thrown to the ground, and his horse trampled one of Mosby's legs. The Northerners finally cracked, and the Confederates chased them toward the railroad. Neither side reported its casualties, except for Ames.[28]

The Rangers dispersed after the engagement at "Yew Hill." Mosby sent William H. Chapman and three companies to the area south of the railroad; Richard Montjoy and Company D went north of the tracks. With the presence of Federal cavalry, Mosby decided not to use the artillery battery so he ordered the gun crews to conceal the cannon on Big Cobbler Mountain, a spur of the Blue Ridge, southwest of Salem. That night Mosby and Montjoy's men slept in the stable loft of Richard Carter's "Glen Welby." Since Blackwell's place had been destroyed, Mosby used "Glen Welby" more frequently as headquarters.[29]

Not all the Rangers slept on the night of October 9–10. Lieutenant Alfred Glascock and a small detail removed a rail from the tracks one mile west of The Plains and waited in ambush. Near dawn a train carrying troops approached from Salem, hit the gap in the tracks and careened into a field. The Rangers started shooting at once, killing seven Northerners, including the railroad's assistant superintendent and the train's conductor, and wounding several more. Glascock disengaged and rode away long before Union troops arrived at the wreck.[30]

The derailment of the train and the deaths of the men infuriated Augur. He had reported to Halleck on the ninth that the repair crews should reach Front Royal beyond the Blue Ridge within eight days. But, now this new, more dangerous, attack by the guerrillas could disrupt that timetable. More forceful measures were required—he ordered the construction of more blockhouses and the arrest of prominent male residents who lived near the railroad. Augur planned to put those arrested on each train. If Mosby wrecked and fired upon another, he could be killing his own people.[31]

The implementation of Augur's countermeasures began on October 11. Infantrymen wielded axes, felling trees for the fortifications. Other details confiscated corn, meat, cattle, furniture and slaves from the local folk and, loading them on the trains, sent the cargo on to Alexandria. Catherine Cochran recorded in her journal that "the war in this section is assuming a very savage aspect." Within days of the Federals' sweep, the people living along the railroad "are almost destitute," she noted. "It has been a scourage [sic] to the country." Living conditions, with the lack of necessities for the families, had been bad; now they worsened.[32]

The Union roundup of male citizens netted fewer men than anticipated. When the Federals first arrived, Mosby warned the civilians of the possibility of incarceration, and many fled. "A few old and infirm men," as Augur described them, remained, and it was these elderly gentlemen the Northerners took from their homes. The group arrested included Jamieson, Albert and Samuel Ashby, Benjamin Triplett and J. W. Foster. "They should be confined as to render escape impossible," Halleck suggested to Augur of the captives, "and yet be exposed to the fire of the enemy." Jamieson Ashby, whose home had welcomed Rangers from the command's earliest days, was accidentally shot and killed by a guard.[33]

When informed of Augur's retaliatory actions, Secretary of War

Edwin Stanton said the situation demanded a harsher policy. On the twelfth, Stanton ordered the general to level every house within five miles of the railroad, arrest all sympathizers for imprisonment in Old Capitol Prison and escort the women and children into Maryland. If any men were found within the five-mile area, they should be treated as bushwhackers and robbers, added the secretary. Stanton, for reasons not clear, rescinded the directive later that same day but admonished that if the "depridations" [sic] continued, he would reinstate the order, extending the designated area to ten miles.[34]

Mosby offered but slight resistance while the Yankees gathered the civilians and seized the foodstuffs and property. When the enemy came in force to the region, the Rangers nipped at the fringes of the Federal units but could not stop the operations. Parties of Rangers skirmished with Union cavalrymen on the tenth and eleventh and grabbed a few stragglers. A brief, sharp fight occurred in Salem with the Confederates routing their opponents, but that was the extent of Ranger successes during these days.[35]

Despite Augur's war on the people, Mosby had no intention of ceasing his campaign against the railroad. In James Williamson's retelling, Mosby promised that "no matter what they do, I will not swerve one inch from my path of duty. They might as well place women and children in front of their lines of battle. My mode of warfare is just as legitimate as that of the army fighting in their front. I am placed here to annoy them and interrupt their communications as much as possible. This I intend doing, and should I again have an opportunity of throwing off a train I will do it, even if I knew my own family were upon it."[36]

"I have been engaged in a perpetual strife with the Yankees ever since my arrival," Mosby wrote his wife on October 12. While most of that "perpetual strife" involved the Manassas Gap Railroad, he had not forgotten about Philip Sheridan's army in the Shenandoah Valley or ceased other missions. He kept scouts in Fairfax County and along the Potomac River and assigned Dolly Richards and Company B to the duty of interdicting Sheridan's supply wagons beyond the Blue Ridge.[37]

One mission, which Mosby learned the results of at this time, had been undertaken at the end of September. During his convalescence from the wound or earlier, Mosby evidently concocted a scheme to kidnap Maryland Governor Augustus Bradford from his residence in Annapolis. The plan had little, if any, military value, and the headlines in newspapers of another dramatic capture could not justify the risks to the Rangers involved in the venture. Some historians in a book on the Confederate secret service and its involvement in the assassination of Abraham Lincoln conjecture that the genesis of Mosby's plan might lie either in a meeting with Robert E. Lee or in conjunction with a secret service team sent to Washington at roughly the same time. Mosby met with Lee before his return to his command, but neither man left an account of the details discussed. Furthermore, a member of the secret service party, according to the historians, visited Mosby in Fauquier within a time frame when he was still recuperating in Amherst County. The historians' argument is speculative at best.[38]

Mosby assigned the operation to Lieutenant "Wat" Bowie of Company F. A Marylander, Bowie had served as a Confederate secret agent, conducting a courier system from Maryland to Richmond. As Mosby knew, Bowie could be counted upon in the most difficult of spots and was familiar with the bypaths of his native state. If there were a connection to the Confederate secret service, it was through Bowie. More likely, though, the Marylander was simply the obvious choice for the kidnapping attempt.[39]

When Bowie and twenty-five men started on the mission is uncertain but, by October 2, they were in northeastern Virginia, across the Potomac River from Charles County, Maryland, approximately twenty to thirty miles east of Fredericksburg and, as the crow flies, seventy-five miles south of Annapolis. Bowie could not ferry the men and horses across the river, so he and two Rangers crossed in a boat. Learning from a Confederate sympathizer that a small party of troopers of the 8th Illinois Cavalry was stationed in Port Tobacco, Bowie returned to Virginia. He kept seven men, sending the other eighteen back to Mosby. With this number, he recrossed the Potomac and entered the town. The Rebels spent the evening of the second eating and drinking in a hotel until after midnight. They then walked to the courthouse, where the Federals slept, captured the Yankees and took their mounts, riding away into the darkness.[40]

The eight Rangers camped during the third until nightfall, when they journeyed to Bowie's family home, located fifteen or so miles west of Annapolis. Bowie's brother, Brune, a member of the 1st Virginia Cavalry who was home on leave with a wound, joined the group. They relocated to the village of Collington on the fifth and, during the next day, Wat Bowie entered Annapolis alone. He discovered that Governor Bradford was too well guarded to attempt a seizure, and he rejoined his men. Riding westward, the Rebels arrived before midnight at Sandy Spring, a Quaker village north of the District of Columbia. They confiscated the contents of a store belonging to two members of the Society of Friends, before heading southward toward Rockville and the Potomac River.[41]

At daylight on October 7, seventeen villagers formed a posse and followed in pursuit. The civilians spotted the Rangers encamped in a stand of pine trees three miles outside of Rockville. The townsfolk attacked, but the veteran fighters repulsed them, mounted and charged. One of the citizens, a carriage maker and blacksmith named William H. Ent, blasted an oncoming Rebel with his double-barreled shotgun. The buckshot riddled the face and head of Wat Bowie. The lieutenant died a few hours later at a nearby farmhouse, cared for in his final moments by his brother.[42]

The other prong of Mosby's secondary operations—minor raids into the Shenandoah Valley—achieved limited success. Dolly Richards and Company B had plenty of targets and were kept busy. Strings of Union wagons shuttled back and forth between Sheridan's army at Harrisonburg and the supply base at Martinsburg, a distance of one hundred miles. Following the victories at Winchester and Fisher's Hill, Sheridan relocated his stockpike of material from Harper's Ferry to Martinsburg, a strongly Unionist town on the Valley Pike and the Baltimore & Ohio Railroad. At Winchester, twenty-odd miles south of Martinsburg, Sheridan posted the infantry brigade of Colonel Oliver Edwards as escorts for supply trains and as protection for the hospitals located in the community.[43]

Duty along the dangerous route brought a chorus of complaints from the Federals. Although Mosby's men conducted raids in smaller groups during the three weeks after the affair at Front Royal, unauthorized guerrilla units stalked the Valley Pike. One such body of men, led by Captain John Q. Winfield, harassed wagon trains between Harrisonburg and New Market. These marauders, combined with the Rangers, moved one Yankee to grouse that guerrillas "are as thick as *Fiddlers down below.*" Oliver Edwards at Winchester averred that to "safely guard a train of 200 wagons, from here to the front, a guard of at least 1,500 men are necessary." A Connecticut veteran, assigned to escort duty, described it as "hard and very dangerous work for inexperienced men who were so near used up from hard service during the war."[44]

Dolly Richards's men roamed along the busy roadway, seeking weakly defended caravans. The Federals did their jobs well, and few attack opportunities arose. But on October 11, Richards and thirty-five Rangers discovered one ambulance and a fifty-man escort from the 17th Pennsylvania Cavalry near Newtown, just south of Winchester. The Confederates, sweeping in, charged the Yankees. The Pennsylvanians resisted briefly and then scattered but not before a dozen were captured. During the fighting two officers, riding in the ambulance, were mortally wounded. One was Colonel Cornelius Tolles, quartermaster of the Union Sixth Corps; the other, Doctor Emil Ohlenschlager, Sheridan's medical director. Tolles took a bullet in the brain, dying three days later, never regaining consciousness. Ohlenschlager lived but two hours after being struck in the abdomen. The deaths of the two officers enraged Sheridan and many of his troops.[45]

On the same day Richards attacked at Newtown, Ranger Jim Wiltshire, returning from a scout in Shenandoah Valley, reported to Mosby. Wiltshire, a native of Jefferson County, had been sneaking around his home area when he located a gap in the Union lines which protected the Baltimore & Ohio Railroad between Harper's Ferry and Martinsburg. He also secured a time-table of the trains. Mosby called Wiltshire "one of my best men," and he knew that the information was reliable. Mosby ordered a rendezvous for the next day.[46]

Eighty Rangers from various companies answered the call at noon at Bloomfield in southern Loudoun County, well beyond the range of Augur's troops. Before he left for the Valley, Mosby had ordered William Chapman to take another contingent and raid into Maryland. Mosby's band rode from Bloomfield after midday, crossed the Blue Ridge at Snicker's Gap, and forded the Shenandoah River after nightfall. They rode on through the night, halting before daybreak in a secluded place.[47]

The Confederates relaxed and slept until dusk of the thirteenth when they remounted. Wiltshire guided the way, bringing them to a "long, deep cut on the railroad." The night was star-bright, with a chill in the air. Mosby had decided to derail a westbound train because, as he wrote later, "I knew it would create a greater sensation to burn it than any other." With the schedule in hand, Mosby waited until an eastbound train hurtled past and then directed Lieutenant Harry Hatcher and a fifteen-man squad to remove a rail. The other men lay down on the bank of the cut and slept, with Mosby using the lap of Lycurgus Hutchinson as a pillow.[48]

The night express out of Baltimore departed the city on schedule at 9:15 P.M. German immigrants, following that westward star which had pulled so many others in that direction, filled one of the coaches, chattering in their native language. Two United States army paymasters, David C. Ruggles and Edwin L. Moore, shared seats with three other officers and civilians in another coach, while William Delaroche, an agent of the Adams Express Company, busied himself in the mail car. Down to Relay House, on through the dark Maryland countryside, to Monocacy Station, along the Potomac River, around a spur of Catoctin Mountains at Point of Rocks and over the bridge to Harper's Ferry. Conductor A. P. Shutt checked his watch; his train was on time and only a few miles remained until Martinsburg and safety from Confederate guerrillas.[49]

Suddenly, shortly after 2:00 A.M., on the fourteenth, a quarter of a mile beyond Duffield's Station, the locomotive veered off the track, slamming into an embankment. Inside the cars the passengers lurched in their seats; women and children screamed. Within seconds, the boiler of the engine exploded, after the baggage car rammed into it, spewing red-hot cinders into the air. The passengers had not recovered from the eruption when the doors at the ends of the coaches flew open. "It's Mosby's men!" yelled someone in a car, as the Confederates, pistols drawn, stepped through the passageways.[50]

The crash and explosion had awakened the Rangers, who scrambled down the bank of the cut. Jim Wiltshire and Charlie Dear were first on board, each into a coach. When Dear entered the coach, a Union officer drew a revolver, and Dear killed the foe before he could fire. Conductor Shutt, stepping off the train, said: "All right, gentlemen, the train is yours," as more Rangers piled on board. Several women fainted at the sight of the Rebels, who walked from seat to seat, demanding purses, wallets and jewelry. West Aldridge, lifting a blanket, uncovered Major Ruggles crouched on the floor. Aldridge led his prisoner outside and, returning, found a large metal box where Ruggles had been. Ranger Billings Steele, from Maryland, had a reunion with his brother, Harry, who was a passenger. In the coach filled with Germans, neither side understood each other as the Rangers searched for valuables.[51]

Mosby stood outside on the ground; he could only hobble on one foot because of the injury he had received in the "Yew Hill" fight, five days earlier. He assisted the women from a car and, when nearly all had been removed, issued orders to burn the train. One of the Rangers hurried to him, exclaiming that the Germans, not understanding English, refused to leave. "Set fire to the car and burn the Dutch, if they won't come out," rebutted Mosby. Gathering stacks of the New York *Herald*, the Rangers lit them and tossed them into the cars. When one bundle landed in the Germans' coach, they hustled each other through the doors.[52]

Cab Maddux, the ex-schoolboy from Upperville, galloped in at this time. He had picket duty along the tracks and announced that Yankee troops were approaching. Mosby, dubious about the news, ordered the men to mount as a precaution and sent one man to verify Maddux's sighting. When the scout reported that there were no Federals nearby, Mosby turned to Maddux. As he recounted it: "I was very mad with Cab for almost creating a stampede and told him that I had a good mind to have him shot." Maddux admitted to Mosby after the war that he spread the false alarm because he resented not being able to share in the spoils. The teenager, however, grabbed all he could carry before he and his comrades departed. [53]

As the flames spread through the cars, creeping out the windows and onto the roofs, the Confederates finished their work. They led the male passengers into nearby woods and stripped the men of their clothing, except for underwear. West Aldridge and Charlie Dear, meanwhile, carried the paymasters' box to Mosby. Mosby questioned Moore or Ruggles about the amount of money inside the box, and learned that it contained $168,000. Gathering together lieutenants Charles Grogan and David Briscoe, Jim Wiltshire, West Aldridge and Charlie Dear, Mosby instructed them to put the cash into saddlebags and ride ahead of the main body. The Rangers, Mosby added, would meet them at Bloomfield.[54]

Within an hour of the derailment, Mosby and his men were in the saddle, riding away in the darkness. The passengers huddled by the tracks, with the men trying to keep warm without their garments in the cold morning air. Some of the women tended to the engineer, William Collins, and his son, who had been scalded by the steam from the exploding boiler. Federal troops found them after daylight and took them to Martinsburg. When Ruggles and Moore reported the loss of the payroll, Jonathan Ladd, a paymaster in the town, locked himself and his money in a room of a hotel and placed an entire infantry regiment around the building as guards. What the German immigrants thought of the mystifying experience is unrecorded. In the land of opportunity, they had met as fine a group of opportunists as the divided nation offered.[55]

The Rangers rode until daylight, halting near Kabletown. A local sympathizer informed them that a camp of Blazer's Scouts was nearby, along the Shenandoah River. The men wanted to attack— they had not settled the account with the Scouts for Myers's Ford on September 4. Mosby agreed and, advancing toward the river, the Rebels charged into an abandoned site. Fording the river, they scaled the Blue Ridge at Snicker's Gap.[56]

The next morning, October 15, at Ebenezer Church in Bloomfield, the Rangers met for a division of the money. Grogan, Briscoe, Lieutenant Fount Beattie and Sergeant Charlie Hall, at Mosby's direction, counted the greenbacks. The cash amounted to $173,000, with each member of the raiding party receiving roughly $2,100. Mosby took none, but weeks later the "stockholders," as they called themselves, presented him with a thoroughbred named "Coquette." The splendid animal became Mosby's favorite horse. Lieutenant Grogan stated that following the "Greenback Raid" money "circulated so freely in Loudoun that never afterwards was there a pie or blooded horse sold in that section for Confederate money." Other members of the battalion envied, and probably resented, the good fortune of the "stockholders."[57]

The festive mood at Bloomfield ended for Mosby and his men when they learned that during their absence the Yankees had captured the battalion's artillery battery. On October 13, Ranger John Lunceford of Company B surrendered to Augur's troops along the railroad, telling the Federals that he no longer wanted to serve with Mosby. Upon interrogation, Lunceford agreed to lead the enemy to the hidden camp of Mosby's four cannon. Colonel Henry Gansevoort took the 13th New York Cavalry and two companies of infantry with him. Only eight members of Mosby's artillery company were in the camp on Big Cobbler Mountain when the Northerners charged in. The Rangers never fired a shot and, with the four artillery pieces, were hauled away. "This artillery," Gansevoort stated in a letter, "has been the secret of Mosby's success. In the valley, and in this county, it has been dreaded." The Federals forwarded the captives to a prison and eventually confined Lunceford in Fort Warren in Boston harbor, where other Rangers had been placed.[58]

Mosby reported the loss of the cannon to Robert E. Lee, explaining the circumstances which led to the capture. "After the enemy had accumulated such a force on the Manassas road that I could no longer oppose their progress in front," he wrote, "I withdrew my command inside their lines north of the road, in order to be in a position to assail both Sheridan's communications in the Valley and also to strike the road whenever opportunity offered." Continuing, Mosby related that the battery was withdrawn "to a place of concealment" and remained there until Lunceford betrayed his comrades. Mosby then inaccurately stated that the Federals "captured no men or horses with it." Since the Northerners began work on the tracks, he concluded, "we have killed and captured over 300 of them. My loss so far has been only four wounded and one captured." Again, he misstated the facts, ignoring the death of "Big Yankee" Ames on October 9. Why Mosby was less than truthful with Lee can only be guessed; perhaps, he was so embarrassed by the seizure of his cannon that he tried to lessen its impact and the cost in personnel.[59]

The conclusion of the "Greenback Raid" and the affair on Big Cobbler Mountain initiated a fortnight of relative quiet along the Manassas Gap Railroad. Teams of axemen continued to remove trees from the sides of the tracks; infantrymen manned the blockhouses; and the blue-jacketed cavalrymen patrolled. Only a few brushes between the Yankees and the Rangers occurred during these weeks. Augur's strength, as Mosby told Lee, precluded numerous attacks. Most importantly, Union authorities decided at this time to abandon the work on the railroad—the strategic situation in the Shenandoah Valley had changed.

Philip Sheridan's Army of the Shenandoah had begun its retrograde march northward from the Harrisonburg area on October 6. As the infantry and artillery units followed the Valley Pike, Sheridan's cavalry roamed across the Valley from the Blue Ridge to the Alleghenies, destroying barns, mills, crops and livestock in their path. The systematic destruction lasted three days and, when completed, left the region "a barren waste." Residents living in the swath of flames and smoke remembered it for years as "The Burning." By the tenth, the Union army halted on the north bank of Cedar Creek, on the outskirts of Middletown. The day before the horsemen routed a Confederate cavalry pursuit force at the Battle of Tom's Brook, chasing the Rebels nearly twenty miles.[60]

To Sheridan, the campaign against Jubal Early had ended with the withdrawal to Cedar Creek and the devastation of the granary of

the Confederacy. Once he reached Cedar Creek, Sheridan agreed to
a conference in Washington with Edwin Stanton and Henry Halleck
to discuss the future of his army. On the fifteenth he started for the
capital, meeting Augur at Rectortown the next day, and together they
arrived in Washington at eight o'clock on the morning of the seventeenth. Sheridan's argument prevailed—the bulk of his army would
be sent to Grant at Petersburg while the remaining units would man
a defensive position east of the Blue Ridge at Manassas Gap. Sheridan
boarded a train at midday for the return trip to the Shenandoah Valley.
He arrived in Winchester twenty hours later and decided to spend
the night in the town. The general slept well, assured that "Old Jube,"
as a Union soldier wrote, had been "thoroughly and permanently
broken, dispirited, and disposed of."[61]

The wily Confederate, however, was not finished. At first light
on October 19, after an all-night march, Early's troops poured into
the Union camps at Cedar Creek. The surprise assault, shielded by
a thick fog, routed most of the troops in Sheridan's three infantry
corps. By late morning, the Federals had been driven to a position a
mile north of Middletown. Early's veterans had achieved a remarkable
victory, its execution unparalleled in the annals of the war. But Sheridan rejoined his men about 10:30 A.M., after a storied ride from
Winchester. When one of his generals stated that his command was
prepared to protect the rear during a retreat to Winchester, Sheridan
fired back: "Retreat–Hell! we'll be back in our camps tonight." When
Early did little more than cautiously test the new Union line during
the afternoon, Sheridan hurled his units at the Rebels in a massive
counterattack at four o'clock. The Southerners broke under the onslaught, and Sheridan's army retrieved all that had been lost and more
during the morning.[62]

Six days after the Battle of Cedar Creek, on October 25, Halleck
telegraphed Augur: "The Manassas railroad will be taken up back to
Manassas Junction, and all iron and material of the road, as well as
the telegraph, will be brought in and disposed of as may be directed
by the chiefs of those departments. The troops will be drawn in as
fast as the road is taken up." Cedar Creek had finished the duel
between Sheridan and Early once and for all. Sheridan was planning
to remain in the lower Shenandoah Valley while his units were forwarded to Grant. He had no need for a rebuilt Manassas Gap Railroad,
so Halleck ceased the operation.[63]

Mosby, in the interim, undertook another raid into the Valley.

He learned of Cedar Creek after its disastrous conclusion for the Confederates. Years later he asked one of Early's staff officers why the commanding general never informed Mosby of the planned attack, because the Rangers could have attacked Sheridan's rear. A member of the staff evidently suggested such an idea to Early before the battle, and "Old Jube" shot back: "By G—d I was not going to do the fighting & Col. Mosby do the plundering," as Mosby stated it in a postwar letter.[64]

Approximately 400 Rangers—Mosby's largest force to date—rendezvoused at Bloomfield at sunrise on October 24. They filed through Snicker's Gap, crossed the Shenandoah River at Castleman's Ferry and bivouacked for the night near Summit Point. The next morning Mosby led them to a position beside the Valley Pike six miles north of Winchester. The Rebels waited but a brief time until a small spring wagon with an escort of twenty-five Union cavalrymen came into view. William Chapman and several dozen Rangers charged, scattering the troopers.[65]

Rangers Boyd Smith and John Dickson stopped the wagon and discovered inside Union general Alfred N. A. Duffié, the cavalry commander who had threatened to hang every Mosby man his horsemen captured when they pursued Early's army through Loudoun County in July. Smith and Dickson turned the prize over to Mosby. When Sheridan learned of Duffié's capture, he requested the Frenchman's dismissal from the service. "I think him a trifling man and a poor soldier," Sheridan wrote. "He was captured by his own stupidity." Confederate officials paroled Duffié in February 1865.[66]

An hour or so later, a train of 200 wagons, protected by infantrymen, cavalrymen and two cannon, rolled up the roadway toward the Confederates. Mosby's men formed a battle line. Minutes before they sprang forward, Ranger Joseph Bryan, a recruit from Richmond on his first raid, asked Charlie Dear how a new member could acquire a reputation among the Rangers. Dear replied that when Mosby gave the signal, Bryan should race ahead of the others at full speed. Lieutenant Harry Hatcher, overhearing the conversation, turned to John Puryear and said: "John, did you hear what Charlie Dear told that boy? He must be trying to get him killed in the first round, before the water gets hot."[67]

Mosby waved companies A and B forward, and the Rebels broke from concealment. When the Union horsemen saw the attackers, they disappeared down the Pike. The foot soldiers, numbering by one estimate 3,000, and the artillery crews stood firm, greeting the Rangers with rifle and shell fire. It was more than the Southerners could handle, so Mosby disengaged. As for Joseph Bryan, he rode in the forefront, "before the water gets hot." Captain Richard Montjoy, watching the youthful fighter, remarked afterwards that Bryan "has won his spurs in the first round."[68]

The Rangers turned southward after the engagement, seizing seven wagons just outside of Winchester. Mosby then divided the force into two squadrons. William Chapman, with over half the men, was ordered to return to Fauquier by Ashby's Gap and harass the Federals along the railroad between Piedmont and Rectortown. Captain Walter Frankland and companies A and B retraced the route through Snicker's Gap, patrolling the ground north of the tracks. Mosby accompanied Frankland's squadron.[69]

The removal of the rails from the Manassas Gap Railroad began on October 27, a day after the Rangers returned from the Valley. Beginning at Piedmont, the gangs of laborers made slow progress; by nightfall of the twenty-eighth, they had reached the midpoint between Piedmont and Rectortown. During the twenty-eighth, Augur ordered a detachment of the 8th Illinois Cavalry, between 200 and 300 troopers, to arrest "one of Mosby's boarding-house keepers" reported to be residing near Snickersville. The cavalrymen located the identified civilian, took him into custody and then searched the village and nearby farmhouses. The hunt snared fifteen partisans, and the Federals bedded down for the night in the vicinity.[70]

Word of the Union raid reached Mosby that night. He dispatched couriers, calling for a rendezvous where the Little River Pike bridged Goose Creek west of Middleburg for the morning of the twenty-ninth. Captain Walter Frankland and 107 Rangers met Mosby. Believing that the Illinoisans would most likely return via Upperville and Rectortown, Mosby directed Frankland to prepare an ambush for the Yankees along the road between the two towns. When the men rode forth, Mosby, with Captain J. Wright James, battalion quartermaster, and Lieutenant Harry Hatcher, scouted westward to Upperville, where, as he anticipated, the enemy was entering on the road from Snickersville. He spurred across the fields to Dolly Richards's home, a mile or so northeast of Upperville. Richards and thirty men had just returned from the Shenandoah Valley, and Mosby ordered them into the saddle as quickly as possible. Before Mosby went to find Richards, he sent James and Hatcher to Frankland to remind the captain of his instructions.[71]

Frankland had brought his command to a point a mile or so south and east of Upperville. The Confederates reined up behind a crest of a hill on Henry Dulany's "Oakley" farm. Frankland's scouts reported that the Federals were clearing Upperville, approaching the intersection of the Pike and the Upperville-Rectortown road. The Union horsemen, however, instead of following the road, turned into Dulany's property. Frankland saw them as they cleared a woodlot and entered the pasture fields of "Oakley," approximately 300 yards from the Rangers. The Illinoisans came on at a walk.[72]

Frankland was full of fight and ordered a charge. He told Lieutenant Charles Grogan to take thirty men and circle behind the hill and hit the Federal right and rear near Dulany's farmhouse while Lieutenant Albert Wrenn and the other Rangers would assail the front of the column. When J. Wright James and Harry Hatcher, who had joined Frankland, heard the attack scheme, they protested that it constituted a disobedience of Mosby's orders. A heated exchange ensued, with Grogan and Wrenn supporting Frankland. Hatcher, whom Mosby described as "the bravest man in the Southern Army," refused to join in the assault, telling Frankland that "it was murder in the first degree."[73]

Grogan mounted his wing and cantered westward behind the hill. Wrenn's detachment swung into the saddles, urging their mounts up the slope. The morale among the Rangers was high; they had been swapping jokes and laughing as they waited. When Wrenn's men cleared the brow of the hill, thundering down the opposite hillside, the front ranks of the Union column dismounted and ran for a stone wall and fence near the farmhouse. Some of the Rangers thought afterwards that the Illinoisans knew they were coming.[74]

The Yankees, armed with Spencer carbines, unleashed a volley. Ranger George Turberville clutched his thigh as a bullet ripped into it. Nearby, George Gulick tumbled from the saddle; he was dead when he hit the ground from a bullet in the forehead. A second time, the troopers scorched the oncoming Rebels. Luther Carrington was killed, and John Atkins and Edgar Davis lay on the ground, their lives draining away. Atkins was from County Cork, Ireland, and, when Mosby saw his body after the battle, he allegedly stated: "There lies a man I would not have given for a whole regiment of Yankees."[75]

The gunfire splintered Wrenn's ranks—some of the Rangers stayed on horseback and raced along the front of the Federal line, emptying their revolvers at close range; others dismounted, engaging the enemy across the fenced-in barnyard. Several Rebels drove toward the gate, where a hand-to-hand melee flared until the Yankees drove them back. Cab Maddux and Joseph Bryan fell wounded; five more Rangers, including John Munson, were overwhelmed and captured. In the midst of the combat, Rozier Dulany, seven-year-old son of the owner of "Oakley," sneaked out of the house and sat on a fence rail, watching the fighting.[76]

Wrenn's fighters had taken all they could endure, and the lieutenant pulled them back behind the hill. Grogan's wing, meanwhile, had floundered, caught in a maze of a ditch and a fence. By the time they cleared the obstacles, their comrades had retreated. Grogan swept forward in a mounted charge, glanced off the wall of fire from the Federals and turned away. He suffered one or two casualties before withdrawing.[77]

A member of the 8th Illinois Cavalry described the engagement at Dulany's as "the prettiest fight I ever saw." He and his fellow troopers had fought bravely, killing or mortally wounding four of the Confederates, wounding another five and capturing five. Ranger John Alexander put it well: "We were whipped in detail." Frankland, disobeying Mosby's orders, rushed into battle, dividing his numerically inferior command. He also did not reconnoiter Grogan's attack path, resulting in a delay which brought the two sections into action at different times. Frankland's assault was, as Harry Hatcher predicted, "murder in the first degree."[78]

Mosby was irate when he learned the details of the debacle. The next morning he summoned Frankland to a private meeting. Frankland must have given an explanation of his actions, but Mosby could not abide the captain's disobedience of a direct order. In an unpublished postwar letter, Mosby described his feelings: "Frankland did not go with either party. He wanted to get the glory of beating them before I could get up. It was a perfect massacre & I can never forgive him. Some of my best men were killed."[79]

Mosby took no action at the time but, several weeks later, he asked Frankland to submit his resignation as captain. Before Frankland complied, Mosby was seriously wounded again, and Frankland's company left for the winter for another section of Virginia. When the captain returned to Fauquier, Fount Beattie, at Mosby's direction, wrote to Frankland, stating that he "should never command" under Mosby again. Frankland met with Mosby at Salem and presented a petition from Company F which requested that their commander be retained. Mosby replied that if his men wanted him "they could have him, but that he could never serve as an officer under me again." The end of the war came a short time later, and the dispute no longer mattered. Mosby, as he stated in the letter, never reconciled with Frankland. No one in the 43rd Battalion disobeyed an order from its commander, causing the loss of men, and received forgiveness.[80]

The defeat at "Oakley" finished, in most respects, the Ranger campaign against Augur's troops and the railroad. The Northerners continued the dismemberment of the line into the first days of November. By the tenth of the month the entire track from Piedmont to Manassas Junction had been cleared of rails. When the Federals withdrew, they sent the citizens whom they had arrested to Alexandria, where authorities locked them in a room of a former slave prison. The jailers, however, permitted family and friends to visit and bring "such comforts" as the prisoners requested.[81]

John Mosby argued after the war that his command's operations against the Manassas Gap Railroad were, as he stated in his memoirs, "of greater military value than anything I did in the war, for it saved Richmond for several months." The campaign, he wrote in a letter, "vindicated the right of our command to all the reputation it had. Its operations in the Valley and on the Manassas road prevented Sheridan's cooperation with Grant and saved Richmond six months."[82]

Had the 43rd Battalion prevented Philip Sheridan from marching across the Blue Ridge, linking up with Ulysses Grant and saved the Confederate capital, prolonging the American Civil War by six months? Had the Rangers accomplished "the most important thing we ever did"? Mosby's men, not surprisingly, accepted that judgment. In fact, Ranger attacks along the Manassas Gap Railroad and against supply lines in the Shenandoah Valley ultimately mattered little in the decision of the Union high command to abandon the reconstruction of the railroad and not to send the Army of the Shenandoah across the mountains to Charlottesville and beyond.[83]

Philip Sheridan, not John Mosby, prolonged the conflict in the East several weeks or months. Sheridan opposed Grant's plan of marching Sheridan's army across the Blue Ridge from the time Grant suggested it on the day after the Battle of Fisher's Hill. Sheridan offered a string of reasons for the impracticality of the plan, stressing the vulnerability of his supply lines. His rationale was more of a smokescreen than an actuality. When Grant ordered work begun on the Manassas Gap Railroad on October 2, Sheridan objected to it, advising nine days later that the repairs "be stopped." The threat to the Confederate capital and to Robert E. Lee's army at Petersburg if Sheridan had advanced on Charlottesville and then toward Richmond is unquestioned. Jubal Early would have offered battle, but the outcome would probably have been no different than that of Winchester and Fisher's Hill. In the end, Richmond and Petersburg withstood the Union siege until April 1865 because Philip Sheridan lacked the strategic vision of his boss, Ulysses S. Grant.

The abandonment of work on the Manassas Gap Railroad brought a welcome reprieve to the residents of Upper Fauquier. For Mosby's Rangers, it brought a renewal, a time to settle an old grievance. Front Royal still cast a dark shadow across the collective memory of the 43rd Battalion.

Chapter 14

REPRISAL

 The brick storebuilding in Rectortown, Virginia, smelled of life
and of death. The odor of sweat,
tobacco, excrement and blood hung in the room. For the twenty-
seven Union soldiers jammed inside, the place was "a wretched hole,"
said one of them. Rank mattered for little as officers, privates and
drummer boys shared space on the oak plank floor or on the tops of
two empty counters along the walls. They were men in transit, prisoners of war en route southward.[1]

Before noon on November 6, 1864, their captors, Mosby's Rangers, herded them outside. At the direction of a guard, the Yankees
walked half a mile to the banks of Goose Creek. Despite the "wretched
hole," the Northerners had kept their morale. It was a crisp autumn

day; the sky sparkled in its blueness, and the prisoners joked with each other as they stood in a ragged line along the stream. It felt good to be outside—a fall day such as this in Virginia could remind a man, a soldier, of the worth of life.[2]

John Mosby was present, but distant from Goose Creek and the prisoners. Ever since he had returned to the battalion on September 29, he had known that this time would come. During the battalion's war on the Manassas Gap Railroad and its raids against Philip Sheridan's army in the Shenandoah Valley smoldered the memory of Front Royal. The partisans, claimed Ranger Landon Mason, were "wondering sorely what Col. Mosby was going to do about the treatment of his men who had been captured."[3]

When Mosby learned of the executions and concluded that George Custer was responsible, he instructed his men that whenever a member of Custer's command was captured, the prisoner should be separated from other captives and not forwarded to Richmond. Mosby told Robert E. Lee in a letter of October 29 precisely what he had decided: "It is my purpose to hang an equal number of Custer's men whenever I capture them." Lee gave approval to Mosby through William H. Mosby, who had carried his brother's letter to the Confederate commander. When Lee transmitted Mosby's letter to the War Department, Secretary James Seddon concurred.[4]

Willie Mosby returned from Petersburg with Lee's authorization by November 4, and John Mosby decided to act. By this date, a seventh Ranger had been executed by the Federals. On October 13, Ranger Absalom C. Willis, while on some unspecified mission, was captured and hanged by Union cavalrymen from the division of Colonel William Powell in Rappahannock County. Sent by Sheridan on a raid against Gordonsville, Powell's troopers discovered the body of a Union soldier in the area. When they seized Willis, Powell ordered the hanging, probably believing that the dead Northerner had been bushwhacked by guerrillas. Mosby claimed later that the Federal was a spy, shot down while trying to escape from a Confederate soldier who was home on furlough. Willis, a Baptist minister, "met his fate bravely," according to an eyewitness.[5]

On November 6, therefore, Mosby rode to Rectortown and ordered the twenty-seven Yankees confined in the store building to be brought outside and taken away from the village. Years later he offered justification for what was to transpire. "I determined," he wrote, "to demand and enforce every belligerent right to which the soldiers of a great military power were entitled by the laws of war. But I resolved to do it in the most humane manner, and in a calm, judicial spirit. . . . It was not an act of revenge, but a judicial sentence to save not only the lives of my own men, but the lives of the enemy. It had that effect. I regret that fate thrust such a duty upon me; I do not regret that I faced and performed it."[6]

As the Union prisoners stood beside Goose Creek, one of the Rangers, probably Sergeant Major Guy Broadwater, spoke. His words were probably terse—direct, sharp and stunning, like a well-aimed volley of musketry. A hat containing twenty-seven slips of paper, he told them, would be passed along the line, and each man would draw one slip. Seven of the pieces had a mark on them and, if a man pulled out one of those, he was to be executed.[7]

The jesting, the talking among the prisoners ended, smothered by the words of the Southerner. Most of the Yankees, not all, belonged to Custer's command, but no one protested—a silent acceptance seemed to have gripped those in line. A Ranger stepped forward and removed the cap of Union Captain Charles E. Brewster. A commissary officer in Custer's division, Brewster was one of only two officers among the prisoners, having been captured in the Valley just two days earlier. Brewster recalled afterwards that during the journey to Rectortown "we crossed fields of all kinds, forded streams, followed hidden paths and by-ways, through thickets of bushes and woods of heavy undergrowth, passing silently and in single file where one hand was required to keep brush and overhanging branches from our faces." He claimed that before they forded the Shenandoah River, a Ranger on the opposite bank signalled that it was safe to cross.[8]

The Ranger who took Brewster's cap placed the slips of paper inside it and, beginning at one end of the line, held it above the head of the first prisoner as the latter reached for a slip. The Rebel stepped to the second man in line, then to the third and the fourth. As the hat moved along—slowly, inexorably—some of the waiting Federals prayed aloud; one laid his head on the shoulder of a comrade and cried. A drummer boy, as the cap neared him, became hysterical, sobbing: "O God, spare me! Precious Jesus, pity me!" With a trembling hand and with a final plea of "Merciful God," the youngster picked a slip. When he saw that he had been spared, he leaped into the air, shouting, "Damn it, ain't I lucky."[9]

When the Ranger finished his walk along the line, seven prisoners had chosen the marked pieces of paper. The condemned included another drummer boy. Sergeant Broadwater, who with most of the Rangers disliked the duty, when he was told about the drummer boy, rode to Mosby. The latter had stayed in the village because "I could not witness the painful scene." Broadwater stated that a drummer boy had been condemned; the sergeant did not ask for a reprieve or for Mosby to intercede. "I didn't know before there was a drummer boy in the lot," as Mosby recounted the conversation with Broadwater. "I *immediately* ordered his release & lots again to be drawn."[10]

Broadwater had one of the men repeat the "painful scene." Only nineteen Federals drew again—the two drummer boys and the six condemned men stood to the side. One of the Northerners picked the fateful slip and was placed with the others. The final lot of seven included two corporals from the 2nd New York Cavalry, James Bennett and Charles E. Marvin; a private of the 5th Michigan Cavalry, George H. Soule; a Private Melchior H. Hoffnagle of the 153rd New York Infantry; and Lieutenant Israel C. Disosway, 5th New York Heavy Artillery.[11]

The identities of the other Federals cannot be ascertained with certainty. As the condemned were being led to the place of execution in the Shenandoah Valley, the Ranger guard detail met Captain Richard Montjoy and Company D in Ashby's Gap. As was his custom, Montjoy was dressed fastidiously with a Masonic pin on the lapel of his coat. Lieutenant Disosway, a member of the order, flashed the Masonic distress signal to Montjoy. The Ranger captain convinced Edward Thompson, the Ranger in charge of the detail, to swap Disosway for a Custer trooper Montjoy had with him. Thompson agreed, and Disosway was released to Montjoy for a cavalryman. When Montjoy later told Mosby of the trade, the latter reminded the commander of Company D that the 43rd Battalion "was no Masonic lodge."[12]

The replacement for Disosway was one of three men—a Sergeant Dodge of the 1st Vermont Cavalry or one of two members of the 5th Michigan Cavalry, privates Frank Hooker or a George or Wallace Prouty. The sources conflict, but a contemporary newspaper account listed Dodge and Hooker as two of the seven. One or both of them drew a marked slip at Rectortown. If Prouty were one of the condemned, he was the man exchanged for Disosway. Finally, the evidence indicates that the seventh man was not Prouty but an infantryman from either the 4th West Virginia or 23rd Ohio.

Five, perhaps six, served under Custer and, of that total, all could have been in Front Royal when the Rangers were executed.[13]

With the drawing completed, Mosby assigned the mission to Thompson and an unknown number of Rangers, probably about a dozen. Thompson, a member of the battalion for a few months, was from Fairfax County and had performed scouting duties for Jeb Stuart in 1862 before enlisting in the 5th Virginia Cavalry. Mosby had probably ridden with Thompson in that year and knew the man's reliability. Thompson was a bearded, strapping man, standing six feet tall, aged either twenty-five or twenty-seven years.[14]

Thompson's detail mounted the Federals and tied their left wrists together with bed cord. A Southerner rode in front of and behind each prisoner as they started for the Valley. After the trade in Ashby's Gap, the horsemen descended the Blue Ridge, crossing the Shenandoah River at Berry's Ferry. A cold rain began falling as they moved past Millwood and on toward Berryville. Thompson halted about four o'clock on the morning of November 7 in Beemer's Woods on Grindstone Hill, less than a mile west of Berryville beside the road to Winchester. The riders dismounted, and Thompson prepared to carry out Mosby's instructions.[15]

Mosby had specified that four of the prisoners should be shot— for Jones, Love, Anderson and Rhodes—and three hanged—for Overby, Carter and Willis. The Rangers acted deliberately, like men who preferred not to do what they had been ordered to do. Private George Soule requested some time for prayer, and it was granted. Soule had been trying to loosen the cord and, as he knelt, he freed his hands. Soule leaped to his feet, punched Thompson in the face and escaped into the woods and darkness.[16]

Soule's escape apparently spurred the Rangers into action. One of the Confederates grabbed Corporal Bennett and shot him in the head and left arm; another shot private Hoffnagle in the head and right arm. A third Ranger, placing his revolver to the head of Corporal Marvin, squeezed the trigger. But the pistol misfired, and Marvin, knocking the executioner to the ground, ran away. That left three—Sergeant Dodge, Private Hooker and Private Prouty or an infantryman. The Rangers remounted them, adjusted the nooses and, as it had been at Front Royal, whipped the horses. On the body of one of the three, the Rebels hung a note: "These men have been hung in retaliation for an equal number of Colonel Mosby's men hung by order of General Custer, at Front Royal. Measure for measure."[17]

Later that morning a local resident discovered the grisly scene. He examined Bennett and Hoffnagle, both of whom were still alive. Indicative of the Rangers' lack of ardor for the duty, they never checked to see if the two Yankees were killed. The two men recovered; Bennett lost much of his eyesight and the use of his arm, while Hoffnagle had his right arm amputated. The civilian then cut down the three dead men, buried them and, getting a wagon, hauled Bennett and Hoffnagle into Winchester, turning them over to the Federals. He also delivered the note to Colonel Oliver Edwards.[18]

Back in Fauquier several days later, Mosby heard the specifics of the incident. The escape of two of the prisoners did not bother Mosby. As he explained it later, "If my motive had been *revenge* I would have ordered others to be executed in their place & I did not. I was really glad they got away as they carried the story to Sheridan's army." His object, he said, "was to prevent the war from degenerating into a massacre . . . It was really an act of mercy."[19]

Mosby believed that his "act of mercy" in Beemer's Woods had settled the issue. To insure that, he wrote a letter to Sheridan on November 11. He asked Lieutenant Charles Grogan to carry it to Sheridan in Winchester, but Grogan refused. Lieutenant John S. Russell then volunteered. Mosby wrote:

General: Some time in the month of September, during my absence from my command, six of my men who had been captured by your forces were hung and shot in the streets of Front Royal, by the order and in the immediate presence of Brigadier-General Custer. Since then another, captured by a Colonel Powell on a plundering expedition into Rappahannock, was also hung. A label affixed to the coat of one of the murdered men declared that "this would be the fate of Mosby and all his men." Since the murder of my men not less than 700 prisoners, including many officers of high rank, captured from your army by this command, have been forwarded to Richmond, but the execution of my purpose of retaliation was deferred in order, as far as possible, to confine its operation to the men of Custer and Powell. Accordingly on the 6th instant seven of your men were, by my order, executed on the Valley Pike, your highway

*of travel. Hereafter any prisoners falling into my hands will be
treated with the kindness due to their condition, unless some new act
of barbarity shall compel me reluctantly to adopt a course of policy
repulsive to humanity.*

MOSBY LT. COL.[20]

John Russell, carrying a flag of truce, entered Sheridan's lines near
Millwood. Union cavalrymen blindfolded him and brought him to
army headquarters, the Lloyd Logan home in Winchester. After he
had read the contents, Sheridan talked privately with Russell and then
wrote a response to Mosby. Neither man revealed the contents of
this second letter, but the "measure for measure" ended the matter—
no replications of Front Royal and Beemer's Woods occurred. All
that was left was the war itself, and it went on.[21]

The same day Mosby wrote to Sheridan, November 11, he held
a rendezvous of the battalion at Rectortown. As the fortunes of the
Confederacy waned, more and more soldiers deserted from the regular armies. A number had attached themselves to the Ranger command, and Mosby ordered the meeting to weed the deserters and
shirkers out of the battalion; such men were unwanted. "They were
a set of men," stated J. Marshall Crawford, "who very seldom went
on a raid; and when they did go, and there was any fighting or horses
captured, would lag behind, and when it was all over, would lead
the horses out, take the greenbacks from the prisoners, and when
near their homes would *flank out* with a horse, and never come up
to a division of the property. In that way they lived."[22]

Approximately 500 Rangers reported to Rectortown. Mosby's
strength in the autumn of 1864 probably approached 800 men. A staff
officer of Jubal Early conducted the inspection and roll call with
Mosby. They disarmed and removed from the rolls all "unruly and
negligent" members and sent them under guard to a provost marshal
in Gordonsville. The records do not contain the name of any Ranger
dismissed on this date. When Mosby held a similar inspection on
October 19, at least thirty-three men were removed from the battalion
for "inefficiency." If Mosby even doubled that number on November
11, he still had, allowing for casualties, between 600 and 700 men in
the command at this time.[23]

Although the campaign between Sheridan and Early ended with
the Union victory at Cedar Creek, the Federals had remained in the
lower Shenandoah Valley. Sheridan had not forgotten about Mosby

nor Mosby about Sheridan. Raids and counterraids still characterized the duel that had never really ceased. On November 7, for instance, Colonel William Powell's cavalry division, entering Fauquier through Manassas Gap, rode through Markham, Piedmont, Rectortown, Upperville and Paris, collecting cattle and horses and burning crops and a few barns.[24]

Mosby countered several days later, dispatching Richard Montjoy and Company D to the Valley. Montjoy raided along the Valley Pike between Winchester and Newtown on the fifteenth. His men bagged about twenty prisoners and their mounts. Starting back for Fauquier the next day, Montjoy's men dispersed en route, with the Rangers who boarded in Loudoun County turning northeastward to cross the Shenandoah River at Castleman's Ferry. Montjoy, with thirty men, proceeded toward Berry's Ferry and Ashby's Gap. About two miles west of the crossing, a detachment of Blazer's Scouts attacked the Rebels. The Yankees' gunfire killed Ranger Edward Bredell and scattered the others. Montjoy and Lieutenant Charles Grogan rallied the men a mile or so to the east at "Vineyard," the home of John Esten Cooke, one of Jeb Stuart's staff officers. But the Scouts came on with a relentlessness, gunning down William A. Braxton, wounding five other Rangers and capturing two. The remaining Confederates splashed across the river and escaped.[25]

The Scouts' modest victory at "Vineyard" continued their string of successes over the Rangers. Since the command's formation in late August, Blazer's Scouts had not eliminated the Rangers—they lacked the numerical strength—but they had shadowed Ranger detachments, inflicted casualties and incurred few losses. Blazer boasted on October 24 that his men had killed forty-four guerrillas, wounded twelve and captured another dozen, while losing only five killed, seven wounded and eight captured. His figures included more than Mosby's command; in fact, of the forty-four killed, only two were Rangers who fell at Myers's Ford on September 4. Except for Myers's Ford and now "Vineyard," the two antagonists had not locked in combat.[26]

A key factor in the success of the Scouts, besides their tactical methods, was their treatment of Valley citizens. "Capt. Blazer was not only a brave man and a hard fighter," declared Ranger James Williamson, "but by his humane and kindly treatment, in striking contrast with the usual conduct of our enemies, he had so disarmed our citizens that instead of fleeing on his approach and notifying all soldiers, thus giving them a chance to escape, but little notice was taken of him. Consequently many of our men were 'gobbled up' before they were aware of his presence."[27]

As for Mosby, he had in most respects ignored the Scouts. With the battalion strained to limits in its dual campaign against Sheridan in the Valley and against the Manassas Gap Railroad, he had been unwilling to commit a company or two to a specific operation against Blazer's unit. If an opportunity beckoned for a strike upon the Scouts, Mosby took it as he had on the return march from the "Greenback Raid." Otherwise, he focused on his two primary targets. But the fight at "Vineyard" changed Mosby's mind. He now could spare the men, and he wanted the Scouts finished once and for all.

On the night of the sixteenth, after Montjoy reported in, Mosby summoned Captain Dolly Richards to headquarters, which were probably located at "Brookside," the home of John R. Holland, a woolen manufacturer, outside of Rectortown. Infuriated by Montjoy's defeat, Mosby told Richards to take companies A and B, find the Scouts and "wipe Blazer out! go through him." Mosby then directed Rangers Robert Walker and J. Richard Sowers, a physician, to ride to the Valley and locate the Federals.[28]

Roughly one hundred members of the two companies joined Richards at Bloomfield on the morning of November 17. When Walker and Sowers arrived, they reported that the Scouts were on a raid toward the Allegheny Mountains. Richards doubted the accuracy of the information and, taking five men with him, rode toward Snicker's Gap. At Snickersville, a citizen stated that Blazer had passed through the village earlier in the morning, moving toward Hillsborough. This intelligence conflicted directly with that of Walker and Sowers, so Richards sent two men toward the latter town as he and the others returned to Bloomfield. Deciding not to wait for the two scouts, Richards led the Rangers through Snicker's Gap and into the Valley. Blazer had generally operated out of the Kabletown area, between Berryville and Charlestown, and toward there the Rebels cantered. As they forded the Shenandoah River, "a terrible rain" blew in and, when Richards finally halted them for the night in Castleman's woods, northeast of Berryville, he allowed no campfires. The Rangers slept as best they could without shelter and warmth from the downpour.[29]

During the night, a scout came in with the news that he had located a Scouts' camp near Kabletown. Richards moved out before first light, bringing the Rangers to the campsite before sunrise. When the sun edged above the Blue Ridge, the Southerners stormed into a deserted bivouac. Fires still burned; a "huge pile" of corn and an unopened bundle of newspapers lay upon the ground. Blazer's men had to be close at hand, but where?[30]

Richards called for Charles McDonough and John Puryear. If any of the Rangers could find the Scouts, these two could. Charley McDonough and his pals, Nick Carter and Charley Hall, had an unsavory reputation in the battalion. They were "brevet-outlaws who accompanied us only by the tolerance of the Colonel," stated John Munson. Often the three men disappeared, riding off on "wild adventures." But Mosby, when they were with the command, forbade them from indulging "in reprehensible actions." They knew no fear, and McDonough, in particular, had incurred the wrath of Union troops stationed in Fairfax County. The Federals had offered a reward for his apprehension.[31]

John Puryear, a Richmonder in his mid-twenties, possessed a honed edge to his personality. His comrades admired his courage but, as Munson argued, he "lacked judgment and the prospect of his acquiring it was extremely remote." Puryear disdained caution and ignored danger. "All that he knew about war," continued Munson, "was what he gathered in each mad dash through the ranks of the enemy, with his long black hair flying in the wind and his revolver hot with action."[32]

Such men Richards needed if he were to flush out the Scouts, and the pair of Rangers started for Kabletown at once. As McDonough and Puryear entered the village, a small party of horsemen, dressed in gray uniforms, approached. The Rangers should have acted with caution, but that trait was foreign to them. Before they could react, the riders, a number of Blazer's men, drew their pistols and fired. McDonough wheeled his horse around and galloped away under a curtain of lead. But Puryear did not make it as the Yankees cut him off and captured him.[33]

McDonough found Richards and the Rangers a few miles south of Kabletown. It seemed as if two blind giants were stumbling across the countryside, waiting for a collision. Richards, wanting to trap or ambush the Yankees, pulled his men back to the river. They filed beneath a cliff above the stream, near the home of Albert Davis. Sometime later, perhaps within an hour, Captain Blazer and several

Scouts halted at the Davis residence. They moved deliberately around the house toward the river. One of them caught sight of the Confederates, and the entire party raced away.[34]

Blazer rejoined his main body, numbering in all about sixty-two men, between Kabletown and Myerstown. One of his officers, a Lieutenant Cole, had been interrogating Puryear about the whereabouts of his comrades. When Puryear refused, Cole clubbed him with a rifle and threatened to hang him. Cole had the wrong man and learned nothing from Puryear.[35]

The shadow dance between the two antagonists neared a resolution. Blazer had the Scouts on the move toward Myerstown soon after he rejoined them. Richards, meanwhile, circled south of the village, reining up in a pasture on the farm of a George Harris, less than a mile from the town along the road to Myers's Ford. The Rangers deployed en masse in a hollow of the field on the south side of the road. A stand of timber edged the road approximately 200 yards to the Southerners' front. Between their position and the woods a stone fence divided the field into sections. Behind them, on the hillside a rail fence marked the pasture's southern limits. Richards warned the men that when they attacked not to "fire a shot or raise a yell until you hear shooting in the front. Don't shoot until you get close to them, among them."[36]

With the trap coiled, Dolly Richards and his brother, Thomas, crossed the field into the trees. But when they saw the van of Blazer's column approaching, Ranger David "Graft" Carlisle bridled up beside them. Carlisle had been drinking whiskey and, feeling the effects, drew his revolver and fired a shot at the oncoming Yankees. He then turned his mount around and galloped back to his waiting comrades. Lieutenant Harry Hatcher pulled Carlisle in, asking furiously: "Carlisle, what do you mean by shooting about here?"

"Harry, if you will go with me we can whip them," Carlisle rebutted.[37]

When Dolly Richards came up, he must have been even more irate than Hatcher. He probably thought that he should shoot Carlisle on the spot—all his careful plotting had been ruined by a drunken fool, who believed John Puryear had shouted to him to charge. Richards had no choice now but to react to Blazer.

The Scouts had begun filing off the road into the woods by the time Richards rejoined his men in the swale. Once inside the woodlot, the Yankees dismounted, and a squad of skirmishers advanced to the stone wall. Richards could not launch a mounted assault across the pasture into the teeth of the Union fire, so he decided to draw them out from the trees. He ordered Hatcher, with Company A, to open the fence in the rear and act as if the Rangers were preparing to withdraw. If Blazer took the ruse and entered the field, Hatcher should turn and charge when he saw Company B attack. If not, Hatcher should retreat and Richards would follow.[38]

Richard Blazer was an experienced, capable officer—the three-month campaign against the Rangers had demonstrated that. But when he saw company A ascending the hill out of the hollow, he signaled his men to horse. Blazer did not know with reasonable certainty the numerical strength of his enemy, but he must have concluded that the retiring Confederates comprised the entire force. Dolly Richards had chosen his battlefield well—the depression in the field had shielded his men from the Northerners. His decision was about to pay rich dividends.[39]

When the Scouts cleared the treeline, Company B surged out of concealment, emerging like specters from the bowels of the earth. "Richards's attack was very much like a dynamite explosion at close range," Munson declared, "inasmuch as it was entirely unexpected." The Scouts answered with rifle fire from their Spencers, but Company B hit their front like a hammer. Hatcher and Company A, wheeling about, knifed into the enemy's flank. At this close range, the Southerners' pistols had the advantage. Blazer's men "fought desperately," remarked James Williamson, "but our men pressed on, broke them and finally drove them from the field."[40]

The Federal ranks disintegrated in a flight toward Myerstown. Blazer rallied a number of Scouts in the town, where they fought from behind houses. But the Rangers overwhelmed the Scouts, killing more of them and capturing others. Most of the Yankees had ignored Blazer's order and had raced toward Rippon, a small village to the west, with the Southerners in pursuit. Blazer fought his way out of Myerstown and, as he followed his men, Ranger Sydnor Ferguson, mounted on a thoroughbred named "Fashion," overtook the Union commander near the home of a Daniel Heflebower outside of Rippon. Ferguson, rising in the stirrups, hit Blazer in the head with his pistol, knocking the officer to the ground. Syd Ferguson, the son of a wealthy landowner in Fauquier County, was only eighteen years old.[41]

Among the Confederate pursuers was John Puryear. When Richards had charged, the captured Puryear slugged his guard and rejoined his comrades. During the horse race toward Myerstown he borrowed a revolver from John Foster. He wanted Lieutenant Cole, and his "rage was something terrible to look upon." Like a hunter on the trail of a wounded prey, Puryear found Cole near the village's blacksmith shop as the officer surrendered to John Alexander. Puryear leveled his pistol at Cole, but Alexander interceded, saying: "Don't shoot this man; he has surrendered!"

"The rascal tried to hang me this morning," protested Puryear.

Alexander asked Cole if it were true. Cole turned to him, pleading, "Oh save me!"

"Yes, I will save you," Puryear responded and squeezed the trigger.

Cole reeled into the side of Alexander's horse and crumpled to the ground. He lived less than a minute with the bullet in his chest. Puryear, leaping from the saddle, "burst out crying like a child, and collapsed, sob after sob shaking his body," said Alexander.[42]

The Rangers regrouped in Myerstown, bringing in the captured Yankees and horses. The number of prisoners has been listed as anywhere from eleven to over thirty. Various Ranger accounts placed the number killed at twenty, twenty-one or twenty-two, but Sheridan reported the total at sixteen. A Confederate cavalryman declared in his memoirs that he saw the bodies of twenty-two of Blazer's men laid out in front of the blacksmith shop in Myerstown the next day, but his account seems doubtful.[43]

When Syd Ferguson brought in Blazer, the Union captain attracted attention. He had earned the respect of the Rebels, and he asked that his men be treated well. Mosby sent him on to Richmond, where authorities confined him to Libby Prison. In early 1865, Blazer was among a group of officers exchanged, and he rejoined his former regiment in the Shenandoah Valley. Near the war's conclusion, he attended the negotiations between Union officers and Mosby. Syd Ferguson accompanied Mosby and, when the two foes recognized each other, they "hugged each other like long lost brothers." Blazer died from yellow fever in Gallipolis, Ohio, in 1878. Few Union officers had earned the admiration of the Rangers as did Richard Blazer. Years later, someone found his sword in the wall of a carriage house on a farm in Fauquier. Syd Ferguson must have hidden it there.[44]

Ranger casualties amounted to one killed—T. Hudgins of Company B—and five wounded—including Lieutenant Joseph Nelson and

Charley McDonough. The cost had been minimal when weighed against the results. Dolly Richards and companies A and B, as ordered by Mosby, had wiped out Blazer's Scouts. The Union command was finished as a fighting force, although the Federals did not disband the Scouts until July 17, 1865.[45]

During the next several days, from November 20 to 27, Mosby undertook a series of raids into the Shenandoah Valley and Loudoun County. One or two companies comprised the raiding forces, each detachment operating separately and at various points along the Valley Pike east of Winchester or toward the Potomac River through Loudoun. The sorties netted approximately one hundred prisoners and nearly 250 horses and mules. The battalion lost six men captured. A seventh, Ranger Frank Angelo, called the "Mocking-bird" by his comrades, was seized by Federal troops in the Valley but, during his first night in the Martinsburg jail, broke out and escaped.[46]

The 43rd Battalion, however, suffered an irreparable loss on the twenty-seventh. In a skirmish between "Company Darling" and roughly three dozen Loudoun Rangers outside of Leesburg, Captain Richard Montjoy was fatally wounded. The Confederates had dispersed the despised Loudoun Rangers when Montjoy gave chase. As he pursued an enemy, the Federal, without aiming, fired his pistol over his shoulder. The bullet struck Montjoy in the head, and he tumbled into the roadbed. When he fell, in the words of one of the Rangers, "every man of his company who witnessed the tragedy reined in his horse voluntarily and groaned."[47]

His men carried the dying captain—"one of the most brilliant officers" in the command, believed J. Marshall Crawford—to Leesburg. Montjoy lingered a few hours and was gone. A poor boy from Mississippi, he had risen up through the battalion, his combat record the equal of that of the Chapmans and Dolly Richards. He had controlled the "dandies" of Company D, whipping them into an excellent unit. The "dandies" hauled his body to Warrenton, where his fiancée, Annie Lucas, lived, and buried him in the town's cemetery. They later erected a tombstone which bore the inscription: "His death was a costly sacrifice to victory. He died too early for liberty and his country's cause, but not too early for his own fame." Company D had lost its soul.[48]

The demands of war offered but a few moments for mourning, even for a warrior such as Richard Montjoy. The next day in Fauquier, Mosby organized Company G. New volunteers and former members

★

of the Artillery Company, which had been disbanded on November 2, comprised the seventh company in the battalion.⁴⁹

Mosby picked Dolly's brother, Thomas W. R. Richards, for the captaincy of Company G. A former member of the 8th Virginia Infantry and 7th Virginia Cavalry, Thomas Richards joined the Rangers in the spring of 1863. Wounded twice—at Warrenton on May 3, 1863 and at Mount Zion Church on July 6, 1864—he had earned the promotion on a number of fields.⁵⁰

The company's three lieutenants—John N. Murphy, W. Garland Smith and John Puryear, respectively by rank—were elected at a later date. First Lieutenant Murphy, a former captain in the 9th Virginia Cavalry, had ridden with the Rangers for less than six weeks prior to the promotion. A Richmonder, Second Lieutenant Smith was twenty-four years old, enlisting in the battalion after a stint of duty in the 55th Virginia Infantry. Third Lieutenant Puryear had also served in the regular army before he volunteered for duty with Mosby in the spring of 1863. When Mosby informed Puryear of the appointment, he told him: "Puryear, I am going to make you a Lieutenant for gallantry. But, I don't want you to ever command any of my men." As John Munson understood it, "Mosby wanted Puryear to fight for him, but not to think for him."⁵¹

On that same day, November 28, Ashby's Gap filled with a solid column of Union cavalrymen. As the troopers descended the mountainside, they carried with them the wrath of this fearful war. Philip Sheridan had unsheathed Ulysses Grant's terrible sword against Mosby's Confederacy.

Chapter 15

DAYS
OF FLAMES,
DAYS OF
DARKNESS

 "I will soon commence work on Mosby," Philip Sheridan informed Union Chief of Staff Henry Halleck on November 26, 1864. "Heretofore I have made no attempt to break him up," wrote Sheridan from Winchester, "as I would have employed ten men to his one, and for the reason that I have made a scape-goat of him for the destruction of private rights. Now there is going to be an intense hatred of him in that portion of this Valley which is nearly a desert. I will soon commence on Loudoun County, and let them know there is a God in Israel."[1]

Although Sheridan admitted that "Mosby has annoyed me considerably," he believed that "the people are beginning to see that he does not injure me a great deal, but causes a loss to them of all that they have spent their lives in accumulating." If the Federals can make the residents of Loudoun and Fauquier "poor" by destroying their property and "comforts," the residents of that region "will cry for peace," concluded Sheridan.[2]

Such a course of action, as described previously, had been proposed by General-in-Chief Ulysses S. Grant since August. Sheridan deferred a decision while he battled with Jubal Early for control of the Shenandoah Valley, but Grant, a relentless foe, continued to urge an operation into Mosby's base throughout September and October. Grant's most recent message on the subject he wrote on November 9: "There is no doubt about the necessity of clearing out that country so that it will not support Mosby's gang. . . . So long as the war lasts they must be prevented from raising another crop." With his decisive victories in the Shenandoah Valley, Sheridan could no longer refuse to comply. He issued orders for the large-scale raid on the twenty-seventh, one day after he wrote to Halleck.[3]

Sheridan assigned the duty to Brevet Major General Wesley Merritt's First Cavalry Division. No command in the Army of the Shenandoah had suffered more at the hands of the Rangers than Merritt's three brigades. They had done the work at Front Royal; some of them had died in Benjamin Morgan's lane and in Beemer's Woods. Sheridan could not have picked better men for the task.

The instructions Sheridan gave to Merritt were detailed and lengthy. The division should leave at 7:00 A.M., on the twenty-eighth, march via Ashby's Gap into Fauquier. The area of destruction should extend from the Manassas Gap Railroad on the south to the Potomac River on the north, and from Bull Run Mountains on the east to the Shenandoah River on the west. Sheridan designated Snickersville as Merritt's "point of concentration." "This section," the orders stated, "has been the hot-bed of lawless bands. . . . To clear the country of these parties that are bringing destruction upon the innocent, as well as their guilty supporters, by their acts, you will consume and destroy all forage and subsistence, burn all barns and mills and their contents, and drive off all stock in the region the boundaries of which are described above. This order must be literally executed, bearing in mind, however, that no dwellings are to be burned, and that no personal violence be offered the citizens." Sheridan gave Merritt four days for the completion of the work.[4]

The destruction began on the afternoon of the twenty-eighth as the Union cavalrymen cleared Ashby's Gap. Merritt had two brigades with him—a third joined the expedition the next day. At Paris, at the eastern foot of the gap, Colonel Peter Stagg's First Brigade turned southeastward toward Piedmont and Markham. In their paths stood the homes of Ashbys, Tripletts, Shackletts and Edmondses. Stagg's regiments fanned out, stopping at each farm, gathering the livestock, setting fire to barns and outbuildings. At "Belle Grove," diarist "Tee" Edmonds watched as the flames consumed the family's barn. Nightfall brought no end to the Federal efforts. The fires glowed red against the blackness of the night.[5]

To the north of Stagg's men, Brevet Brigadier General Thomas Devin's Second Brigade covered the ground from Paris to Upperville. The New Yorkers and Pennsylvanians in the brigade gutted a stone mill near Upperville, applied the torch to barns, corncribs, smokehouses and mounds of harvested crops and gathered cattle, sheep and horses. Late at night the two brigades regrouped at Upperville.[6]

The swath of fire and smoke widened on the twenty-ninth. Stagg's regiments pushed toward Rectortown, Salem, The Plains, Middleburg and Aldie, while Devin's horsemen concentrated their work in the region from Upperville to Snickersville, along the eastern base of the Blue Ridge. John Holland's woolen factory, located a mile north of the ruins of Joseph Blackwell's "Heartland," was a smoldering ruin by day's end. Holland had manufactured uniforms for both Northern and Southern troops, but that did not exempt him. His family moved to the North within weeks.[7]

Outside of Middleburg, Catherine Broun watched closely as the flames and pillars of smoke advanced toward her farm. She, her husband and children packed trunks with valuables and clothing. "We have had a terrible day today expecting every moment to be burned up all around us are on fire," she recorded in her journal during the anxious hours. At eight o'clock at night she turned again to her journal, entering: "the whole heavens are illuminated by the fires."[8]

The Brouns were spared—Stagg's horsemen turned back toward the mountains before they reached the Broun farm. Lieutenant Colonel Caspar Crowninshield's Reserve Brigade came in that afternoon. Merritt had with him now his entire division, approximately 3,000 troopers, all encamped around Snickersville. With the arrival of another morning's sun, the Federals marched northward into the heart of Loudoun Valley. Here they stayed through November 30 and December 1. When they departed, the region, as Sheridan expected, was a "desert."[9]

The destruction embraced this section of Loudoun from the boundary of Fauquier to the Potomac River, between the Blue Ridge and Catoctin Mountains. The fires encircled the villages of Philomont, Hillsborough, Lincoln, Hamilton, Waterford, Lovettsville, Purcellville and Union. A Massachusetts officer with Crowninshield described what he saw during these two days. "It was a terrible retribution on the country that had for three years supported and lodged the guerrilla bands and sent them out to plunder and murder," he declared. Women and children shrieked; men begged for mercy. "This was the most unpleasant task we were compelled to undertake," he wrote. By his estimation two regiments in the Reserve Brigade burned 150 barns, 1,000 haystacks, six flour mills and seized 50 horses and 300 head of cattle in one day.[10]

As Sheridan predicted to Halleck, the accumulations of lifetimes disappeared in the flames. Between Lincoln and Purcellville, Bernard Taylor, Yardley Taylor, John Brown, Samuel Brown, William Smith, Ruth Smith and Lott Tavenner lost their barns; James Hoge, his barn and corncrib; Thomas Smith, the barn and outbuildings; Israel Young, his house; and Asa Janney, "one of the most thoroughly loyal citizens we have," his flour and saw mills and 3,000 bushels of wheat. All that remained at Janney's was the stone house Janney had built himself. At the Jonathon Taylor farmstead, Taylor's young son pleaded with officers to spare the family's barn. The officers relented, but their men took with them a blind horse, four cows, three calves and twenty-five sheep. Near Lovettsville, Christian Nicewarner lost all his livestock and his entire crop when the barn collapsed into a huge rubble of ashes and burnt wood. The smoke from the devastation could be seen by people across the Potomac in Maryland.[11]

Many, if not most, of the victims in Loudoun were Quakers or Union sympathizers. Their pacifist beliefs or allegiances did not exempt them, however. At Waterford, for example, two young women, sitting on a fence, watched their family's hay burn and, waving United States flags, shouted: "Burn away, burn away, if it will prevent Mosby from coming here." One Quaker estimated that his fellow Friends incurred $103,000 in losses, and the damages to the property of Union men amounted to $256,000.[12]

On December 1, as Devin and Crowninshield's commands finished their incendiarism in Loudoun, four regiments from Stagg's brigade returned to the Middleburg-Aldie area. Edwin and Catherine Broun again prepared to evacuate their home as the fires ringed their land. For some reason, the family escaped the destruction, but they were one of the few isolated cases in the paths of the Federals. By nightfall of the first, the Yankees had regrouped at Snickersville, before recrossing the Blue Ridge on the second. Even to disbelievers in Fauquier and Loudoun, the bluecoated cavalrymen had proven that "there is a God in Israel."[13]

The devastation staggered those left in its wake. "If old Satan himself had thrown open the gates of hell and turned loose all the devils in there," asserted Ranger J. Marshall Crawford, "they could not have inflicted greater misery and woe than Custar's [sic], Torbert's, and Merritt's inflicted on these people in this raid." Official estimates of damages exceeded a million dollars. After the war, at least 208 Union-sympathizing families in Loudoun filed claims against the government for payment. The people of Loudoun and Upper Fauquier "paid dearly for being a part of Mosby's Confederacy."[14]

The days of flames reduced uncounted numbers of families to poverty, as Sheridan planned. All Mrs. Isham Keith of Fauquier could say about conditions in the region was "our bare acres." A young girl in the county described her family's plight as existing, not living. With another winter close at hand, days of darkness could not be far away.[15]

Throughout the "Burning Raid," as it became known, the Rangers roamed along the fringes of the Union squadrons. Merritt posted strong details along the flanks, denying the Confederates openings for attacks. The Yankees swept approximately a dozen of Mosby's men into their net during the four days. One Ranger alleged in his memoirs that they caught about fifty of the barn burners and shot all of them. Regardless, the Rangers were nearly helpless in preventing the Federals from executing Sheridan's orders.[16]

The Rangers countered Merritt's handiwork with a series of raids into the Shenandoah Valley. The minor operations lasted from December 3 until the eleventh, achieving minimal results. Before they were initiated, Mosby held an inspection of the entire battalion. An officer from Richmond came to Fauquier to oversee the inspection. He and Mosby's officers prepared three lists of the membership— one, with the names of men who enlisted before October 8, 1864; a second which covered those recruits who joined after that date; and, a third which contained the muster rolls of all the companies. The purpose of the inspection and scrutiny of the rolls was to ferret out all deserters from the regular service and those avoiding conscription. Desertion and the avoidance of the draft had become a plague upon the Confederacy.[17]

Shortly after the inspection, probably on the third or fourth, Mosby departed for Richmond and Petersburg. Accompanied by Sergeant Boyd M. Smith of Company E, Mosby traveled to the cities to confer with Robert E. Lee and to propose a reorganization of the 43rd Battalion. He met with Lee at army headquarters in Petersburg on the sixth. Lee invited Mosby to join him for dinner. The two Virginians dined on a leg of mutton, which Lee "intimated that some of the staff must have stolen." Following the meal, Mosby borrowed Lee's desk, penning his proposal for Secretary of War James Seddon.[18]

Mosby presented his recommendation to Seddon in the capital the next morning. "I beg leave to recommend, in order to secure greater efficiency in my command," Mosby wrote, "that it be divided into two battalions, each to be commanded by a major. The scope of duties devolving upon me being of a much wider extent than on officers of the same rank in the regular service, but small time is allowed me to attend to the details of organization, discipline, &c. I am confident that the arrangement I propose would give me much more time both for planning and executing enterprises against the enemy." He then proposed that William H. Chapman and Dolly Richards be assigned to command of the battalions. "They have both on many occasions been distinguished for valor and skill," Mosby stated of the two company commanders.[19]

Seddon approved the request, and Mosby personally delivered his letter, with the Secretary's endorsement, to General Samuel Cooper, Adjutant and Inspector General of the Confederacy. A clerk in Cooper's office mislaid the document, delaying action on it for a month. Cooper finally asked Seddon for a copy and, on January 9, 1865, Mosby was promoted to colonel, to rank from December 7, and the 43rd Battalion was reorganized into a regiment. Mosby had to resubmit his recommendation for the promotions of Chapman and Richards, which were authorized three weeks later, on January 30, with the ranks of lieutenant colonel and major, respectively.[20]

Upon his return to Fauquier, Mosby, anticipating official approval, implemented the reorganization. He assigned companies C, E, F and G to Chapman, and companies A, B and D to Richards.

For the time being, however, the effectiveness of the restructuring remained uncertain. Ranger operations all but ceased from the conclusion of the Valley raids on December 11 through year's end. The records and memoirs of Rangers indicate that from the eleventh until the twenty-first, only one member of the command, Lieutenant Charles Grogan of Company D, was either killed, wounded or captured. Grogan, while visiting "Kinloch," the home of Edward Turner near The Plains, on the seventeenth, was trapped inside by some Federal cavalrymen and decided to fight his way out. A Yankee shot him in the thigh and, when a surgeon with the squad declared that the wound would make Grogan unfit for service, they left him with the Turner family. Grogan eventually recovered and resumed his duties.[21]

A highlight for the Rangers during this period was the forthcoming marriage of Jake Lavender to Judith Edmonds, scheduled for December 21. Lavender, the command's ordnance sergeant and a favorite of Mosby, probably met the bride-to-be at Joseph Blackwell's home. Lavender stayed there frequently and Miss Edmonds was the sister of Blackwell's wife and Ranger Johnny Edmonds. During the days prior to the wedding, several Rangers assisted with the preparations and ran errands for the bride's family.[22]

The guests, family members and wedding party gathered at "Rosenix," the home of the bride's aunt, located a mile or so from the ruins of Blackwell's "Heartland." How many Rangers attended is uncertain, but Mosby was present. He posted scouts throughout the area, and during the reception one of the outriders came in, reporting that a force of Union cavalry had entered Salem. Taking Tom Love with him, Mosby rode toward the village, where he learned that the Yankees had marched toward Rectortown. Mosby followed, found them bivouacked for the night and sent a Ranger, who had joined him and Love, to Chapman and Richards with orders for a daylight attack.[23]

It had become a miserable night with a mixture of rain and sleet falling as Mosby and Love rode northward. Icicles hung from trees, and the sleet coated the road. Before nine o'clock the pair stopped at "Lakeland," the home of Ludwell Lake, who, said Mosby, "was famous for always setting a good table." "Lakeland," a beautiful, two-story ashlar stone house built about 1787, sat beside the road from Rectortown to Rector's Cross Roads, about a mile south of the latter.[24]

When Mosby knocked at the door, one of Lake's daughters, either Sarah or Mrs. Ladonia Skinner, probably answered. Ludwell weighed 450 pounds and seldom moved. Mosby was warmly greeted, for Ludwell's son and namesake served in the partisan command. Love offered to remain outside as a sentry, but Mosby insisted that he come inside, warm himself and have something to eat.[25]

While the daughters prepared a meal in the summer kitchen behind the house, Mosby and Love took the chill from their bodies and dried their clothing before the fireplace in the living room on the right half of the downstairs. Mosby recalled later that "I was better dressed that evening than I ever was during the war." He had on a black beaver-cloth overcoat and a cape lined with English scarlet cloth. A gray cloth, also lined in red, covered the overcoat because of the weather. His hat was adorned with an ostrich plume, a gold cord and a star. His uniform consisted of a coat, made of gray sack cloth, with two stars on the collar for a lieutenant colonel, and gray trousers, with yellow cords down the legs. A pair of long cavalry boots finished his attire. The material for the entire outfit and the boots he had secured from the North.[26]

When the meal neared completion, the host, Mosby and Love walked across the hallway to the dining room in the back left rear of the first floor. Next to the dining room was the parlor which had been converted into Ludwell's bedroom. Because of his girth—Mosby said he "was as broad as he was long"—he could not ascend the narrow stairway. The men and Ladonia sat at the table as Sarah brought in spareribs, rolls and coffee. Sleet still rattled against the windows, and Sarah wore a cloth bonnet on her head.[27]

Sarah had just carried in the last item when they heard the sounds of hoofbeats and shouts outside the house. Mosby and Love stood up, starting to move away from the table, when a shot was fired through the dining room window. Mosby clutched his abdomen, exclaiming, "Oh, my God, I'm shot. Give me something." Sarah quickly untied her bonnet and handed it to Mosby, who applied it into the wound, the bullet striking him two inches to the left of his navel and lodging in his right side. Blood gushed from the hole, soaking his blue flannel shirt. Ladonia, still seated, screamed.[28]

Mosby crawled or staggered into Ludwell's bedroom, where he had laid his overcoat and uniform coat. Sarah assisted him in concealing both items under the bed. He then collapsed on the floor—

"In those few minutes it seemed to me I lived my whole life over again," he wrote in his memoirs.[29]

Seconds later, Major Douglas Frazar and several officers and troopers of the 13th New York Cavalry burst through the door. A member of the regiment's advanced guard, identified as a Corporal Kane, fired the shot through the window. When the Yankees entered "Lakeland," Tom Love surrendered. What he had been doing during "those few minutes" after Mosby was hit is vague. Love apparently offered no resistance because of the Lake family and handed his fire-arms to his captors.[30]

Frazar walked to the Confederate on the floor of the bedroom, whom he described as "in great agony." Kneeling down, the Union major asked Mosby to identify himself. "Lieutenant Johnston, Sixth Virginia Cavalry," responded Mosby, who could smell whiskey on the breath of the Federal. Frazar opened Mosby's trousers, examined the wound and declared it to be mortal. Some of the other officers checked it, agreeing with Frazar. An orderly in the group picked up Mosby's hat, but no one found his uniform coat. The Yankees, with Love as a prisoner, soon departed, remounting their horses and dis-appearing into the sleet and night. They left Mosby's horse, with a pair of pistols in saddle holsters, where he had tied it.[31]

Ludwell, Ladonia and Sarah acted quickly as soon as the Federals rode away. One of them, probably Sarah, went for one of their slaves, Daniel Strother, a boy of five or six years, ordering him to hitch two calves to an ox-cart and bring it to the house. The Lakes helped Mosby outside, laying him in the crude vehicle. It was a scene which beggared disbelief—a young black boy hauling one of the most renowned and hunted Confederates in a cart, pulled by calves, down a farm lane through a sleet storm.[32]

Strother brought the desperately wounded man to "Rockburn," the farm of Mrs. Quilly Glascock, located a mile or two southwest of "Lakeland" along Goose Creek. The stone farmhouse had acci-dentally burned and was being restored. Mrs. Glascock, a widow, lived in her tenant house, and there Strother carried Mosby. The mistress of "Rockburn" tended the wound and sent a servant or family member into Rectortown for a doctor. Fearing a search of farmhouses in the area, Mrs. Glascock had Mosby removed to a hiding place in nearby woods that night or the next morning. There, Dr. Samuel H. Halley of Rectortown attended to the wound and internal bleed-ing.[33]

In Rectortown, meanwhile, Frazar interrogated eight Ranger prisoners captured earlier in the day. The ride from "Lakeland" to the village must have sobered Frazar and, when he examined the hat taken from the Lakes', realized that it belonged to a field grade officer—major and up—not a cavalry lieutenant. Each of the captives denied that the hat was Mosby's. On the following morning, Frazar showed it to Lieutenant Colonel David R. Clendenin of the 8th Illinois Cavalry and commander of the Union force. Clendenin ordered a detail to "Lakeland," but it was too late. By December 27, either through an informant or from rumors, the Northerners knew that the wounded officer had been Mosby. Colonel William Gamble, commander of the cavalry brigade, issued instructions that all wounded Confederates should henceforth be brought into Union lines.[34]

Accounts of the shooting at "Lakeland" raced through Upper Fauquier and southern Loudoun. Many of the people heard that the wound had proven fatal to the Ranger commander. On December 26, one resident jotted in a diary that "Col. Mosby is dead." Two days later, Federal troops confirmed his death and, on New Year's Day, the New York *Times*, claiming that the information had come from captured partisans, announced Mosby's death.[35]

Although Mosby had survived, he was grievously wounded. Ranger surgeons William Dunn and Aristides Monteiro extracted the bullet and stanched the internal hemorrhaging. The loss of blood and a fever gravely weakened Mosby, and he could be moved only short distances at a time during the initial week after the shooting. Fearful of his capture, the Rangers relocated him one house to another, posting strong details on the roads into Upper Fauquier. By the end of the month he was fit enough to travel, so, with Monteiro in attendance, Mosby started for the family home in Amherst County. He knew it would be weeks before he resumed command of the Rangers.[36]

About the same time Mosby departed, William H. Chapman traveled to Petersburg for a conference with Robert E. Lee. Since the "Burning Raid," the shortages of food for the people and fodder for animals had become dire. Catherine Broun described the situation among the residents in the Middleburg area as "a pitiable condition." Compounding the difficulties, the 35th Battalion of Virginia Cavalry, the famous "Comanches," had come into the region for the winter, scattering throughout Loudoun and Fairfax counties, the home area for most of its members. Secondly, Thomas Devin's brigade of Union cavalry, sent by Sheridan from the Shenandoah Valley, occupied northern Loudoun, quartered around Lovettsville. "Mosby's Confederacy" could not sustain the entire complement of Rangers during the next three months.[37]

Chapman described conditions in the "Confederacy" to Lee. "I saw plainly that General Lee did not know how we had subsisted as soldiers in Fauquier and Loudoun counties," Chapman wrote afterwards. Lee recommended that one of the two battalions relocate for the winter in eastern Virginia, where the supplies were more plentiful. The commanding general cautioned Chapman that the area could be subjected to Federal incursions and he should move the men frequently. With that settled, Chapman left for Upper Fauquier.[38]

Companies C, E, F and G, Chapman's battalion, met at Salem on January 3, 1865, the day Mosby arrived at his father's home. One estimate placed the number of Rangers present at 600. A number of young women, who surely regretted their leaving, cooked a farewell meal for the men. They soon mounted, with saddlebags packed, and marched eastward. When they reached the so-called Northern Neck region, the land between the Rappahannock and Potomac rivers, east of Fredericksburg, Chapman dispersed the battalion. Members of Company C found refuge with the residents of Westmoreland County; Company E stayed in Richmond County; companies F and G in Northumberland and Lancaster counties.[39]

The Rangers lived with the people of the Northern Neck until the second week in April. Each company held regular meetings for cavalry drills—"there was little else for us to do," admitted Chapman. Details watched Union gunboats pass on the Potomac River; other squads picketed roads, scouting for Yankee raiders. Sometime in March Company E clashed with enemy horsemen in a skirmish, and Captain Samuel Chapman was severely wounded in the thigh. But the presence of the Rangers caused difficulties. Authorities in Richmond received a number of complaints from the local folk. The citizens groused about alleged robberies and vague "unprincipled acts." The guilty parties had identified themselves as Mosby's Rangers but, in all likelihood, the thieves were deserters and marauders who infected nearly every region of the dying Confederacy. For two years Mosby's men had conducted themselves well among friends and supporters, but Chapman's lack of control over the widely dispersed companies might have resulted in some incidents.[40]

Back in Mosby's Confederacy, Dolly Richards's battalion—companies A, B and D, between 300 and 400 men—had settled in for the winter. Richards assigned daily guard mounts on the roads and kept scouts in the saddle. At Mosby's direction from Amherst County, Richards and the Rangers assisted conscription officers in their enrollment efforts. Mosby impressed upon Richards the importance of the latter duty, because Major General Fitzhugh Lee, Mosby's old antagonist and commander of Jeb Stuart's Cavalry Corps, was again stirring up trouble for the Rangers. Lee requested Mosby's muster rolls, claiming that conscripts had been enrolled in the partisan command. Major General James Kemper, commander of the Reserve Forces of Virginia, interceded on Mosby's behalf, writing to Lee: "Col. Mosby has manifested so much interest in enforcing conscription, his cooperation in this respect is of such value and the importance of his command in all respects so great, that I respy. suggest he be allowed to retain such of the men on Lists 'A' and 'B' as he may deem needful to the efficiency of his command." Lee dropped the matter.[41]

On January 30, Richards and nearly thirty Rangers set out one more time from Bloomfield on a raid into the Shenandoah Valley. Philip Sheridan, with two cavalry divisions and some infantry units, was spending the winter in the lower Valley around Winchester, but Richards planned to avoid that area and attack a train of the Baltimore & Ohio Railroad between Harper's Ferry and Martinsburg. Arriving in the familiar stretch of roadbed about midnight, the Confederates found heavy infantry details and mounted patrols which passed along the tracks every half-hour. Richards abandoned his scheme but learned that a small cavalry camp was close at hand.[42]

After capturing two pickets and securing the countersign from them at gunpoint, Richards led nine men into the bivouac site. Cabins lined one side of the street, with the stables across the snowy roadway. While some of the Rangers disarmed a handful of sentries, others untied the horses. But when Bartlett Bolling ordered a guard to surrender, the Yankee fired a shot. With the alarm sounded, the Rebels turned and galloped back along the street, yelling and firing their pistols into the canvas-roofed cabins. Ranger Hern lost control of his mount when its bit broke, and he shouted at Richards: "For God's sake catch my mare, or I'll go to hell."

"I have been expecting you to travel that road for some time," shot back Richards as he spurred to Hern's assistance.

They escaped with no casualties and eight Union horses. As they passed through Charlestown, they exchanged gunfire with Northern troops, again emerging unscathed. The Rangers arrived back in Fauquier later in the day.[43]

During the following week a half dozen of the Rangers concluded that they and their comrades needed relief from the tedium of the winter's duty. Couriers spurred through the Confederacy, summoning the partisans to a fox hunt on February 8. Approximately one hundred men showed up at the designated location, accompanied by an equal number of hounds. For an entire day the thoughts of war were replaced with the invigoration of the chase through snow a foot and a half deep. The yells of riders mingled with the bays of the hounds. The sounds harkened to earlier days, echoes of the past, before there was a "Confederacy," which must have seemed to both the participants and the onlookers a millennium ago. The hunt garnered five animals.[44]

The day was a pleasant interlude among weeks of routine duty. Except for the abortive strike against the railroad, Richards kept his men in Fauquier and southern Loudoun. He had the Rangers watch the roads, but the Yankees were a scarce commodity in the region throughout the cold, snowy weather. Enemy patrols captured approximately a dozen partisans during January and early February, but no large-scale Union force raided into the Confederacy until late in February. On the eighteenth—one year earlier to the day a similar Federal operation netted twenty-eight Rangers—two contingents of enemy cavalrymen crossed the Blue Ridge into Fauquier.[45]

The Yankees—225 officers and men from the 14th Pennsylvania and 21st New York Cavalry, Major Thomas Gibson commanding—came through Ashby's Gap under the cover of night. Guided by two unidentified Ranger deserters, the horsemen separated at Paris—Gibson and his Pennsylvanians turned toward Markham; the New Yorkers, under Captain Henry E. Snow, marched due east toward Upperville. The raiders searched every "safe house" in their paths and caught eighteen of Richards's men. One of the deserters led a squad of New Yorkers to "Green Garden," the Richards family home. As had been true on a number of previous occasions, the enemy troopers went through every room in their hunt for the Ranger officer and left empty-handed. He was there, standing behind a wall panel.[46]

After their fruitless hunt through Upperville—it netted two Rangers—Snow and his troopers returned to Paris, where the men uncovered two barrels of whiskey. While they waited for Gibson's detachment to rejoin them, the New Yorkers drained the barrels. Snow estimated that a third of his men were drunk by the time they had finished. In disobedience to orders, Snow decided to recross the mountains without the Pennsylvanians. He left behind six of his men who could not mount a horse in their drunken stupor.[47]

The Pennsylvanians arrived in Paris after seven o'clock on the morning of the nineteenth. They had with them sixteen Ranger prisoners, including Jeremiah Wilson, whose wedding was scheduled for the next day in the village. When his fiancée saw her betrothed among the prisoners, she ran to Gibson, pleading with the major for Wilson's release. Gibson ignored her.[48]

Snow had been gone for nearly two hours, so Gibson started his men up the road into Ashby's Gap. By now, Dolly Richards had gathered about forty men, and they closed on the Federals. At Mount Carmel Church in the gap, the Rangers splintered Gibson's rear guard, knifing into the main column. The Colt revolvers gave the edge to the Confederates in the hand-to-hand combat. Within minutes over two-thirds of Gibson's command, approximately ninety, were killed, wounded and captured, including the major himself. The Southerners freed all of their captured comrades, while losing one man killed, John Iden, and one wounded, J. Richard Sowers. Jeremiah Wilson made his wedding the following day. Mosby, years later, described the fight as "the most brilliant thing our men ever did."[49]

The Rangers rode into Paris in triumph later that day. Such moments as these had been uncommon in Fauquier during the winter. But the cheering could only have had a hollowness to it. The Rangers and the local folk must have known that the capture of less than a hundred Yankees mattered little. Together, they could only wait— wait for the inevitable which was striding across the ashen ruin of the Confederacy. Nearly two months earlier, on the last day of 1864, Catharine Broun recorded in her journal: "During the last year I have been more unhappy than I have ever been in my life." She was not alone.[50]

Chapter 16

TOWARD
SALEM

There he stood before the House
of Delegates in Richmond, Virginia, accepting the praise and ad-
miration accorded a genuine military hero. He had met with Governor
William Smith, conferred with Robert E. Lee and visited a prisoner-
exchange boat in the James River. He sat for a portrait, dressed in
the uniform of a Confederate colonel with a scarlet-lined cape across
his shoulders, and discussed his command's exploits with a French
artist for a series of paintings. "I have had every mark of respect &
attention shown me," Mosby informed his wife on February 3, 1865.[1]

It was as it should have been. By birth and by upbringing, he
was one of them, a Virginian who had fought for his native state
during the past four years with a prowess and success few could

equal. In this winter of blighted dreams and impending defeat, he and his men stood unconquered, unlike much of the Confederacy. Atlanta lay in ruin; Savannah and Mobile were occupied by the enemy; Lee's army starved in the trenches of Petersburg; and South Carolina, the den of fire-eating secessionists, prepared for the terrible onslaught of William T. Sherman's Union armies. Within this darkening landscape, there John Singleton Mosby stood, a warrior feted by the governor and the legislature, a soldier worthy of history's remembrance as interpreted by artists.

John Mosby had detoured to Richmond en route back to Fauquier from Amherst County. He tarried in the capital, surely enjoying the attention and recognition, although he had been away from the Rangers for several weeks. His wound had healed, but it left him thinner, even gaunt-looking. A physically weaker man might have succumbed to the grievous wound but Mosby's natural strength and the past two years of endless labor on horse and on foot stood him well during the recovery. He now wore a full, sandy-colored beard and mustache.

He left Richmond during the middle of the month, resuming command of the Rangers about February 20 or 21. Only Dolly Richards's battalion of three companies welcomed him—it would be nearly another two months before William Chapman's battalion returned from Northern Neck. Richards and his men had done well during Mosby's absence, highlighted by the Mount Carmel Church action of a few days earlier. They had struck when opportunities beckoned, but they were few and far between. The war in Virginia had now bypassed the Shenandoah Valley and the counties along the line of the Orange and Alexandria Railroad. It had become a matter of enduring, waiting for a resolution at Petersburg and in the Carolinas.[2]

Mosby focused his early activities upon the collection of forage and food from the Quakers in Loudoun and the enforcement of conscription in that region. He separated companies into ten to twelve-man detachments, sending them to collect the tithe and to live with the pacifist farmers. But the cupboards in Loudoun were as bare as those in Fauquier, and loyal Confederates no longer wished to serve a forlorn hope. As a perceptive Union officer stated regarding the sentiments of Loudouners, "The desire is to have peace—with coffee, sugar, etc."[3]

When the Rangers appeared in the burned-over area, they were met with animosity. Sentiments had shifted, and the locals adjusted to the new order of things, which meant Federal control. A number of the residents now assisted their occupiers, supplying them with information. Consequently, forage duty for the Rangers in Loudoun became increasingly more dangerous. On March 12, Francis Marion Yates of Company D was accidentally shot and killed by a comrade in a skirmish with the 13th New York Cavalry. Three days later John T. Waller of Company A died instantly from a bullet in the head in a firefight with the 8th Illinois Cavalry. The Yankees also captured at least eleven Rangers during these weeks, including Lieutenant Harry Hatcher of Company A, whom Mosby regarded as the bravest man in the command.[4]

Several days later, on the twentieth, a scout informed Mosby that a Union force of infantry and cavalry from Harper's Ferry had reached Hillsborough in western Loudoun. Mosby ordered a rendezvous for the following morning, and 128 Rangers met him in Upper Fauquier. Riding northward, with outriders posted, the Confederates arrived at Hamilton, five or six miles southeast of Hillsborough and two miles east of Purcellville, after midday when scouts reported the approach of the enemy detachment from Purcellville. The Federals, under Colonel Marcus A. Reno, consisted of the 12th Pennsylvania Cavalry, the 1st Veteran Volunteer Infantry and the Loudoun Rangers, numbering over 1,000 strong. The Northerners had spent the morning searching the area for caches of food, grain and livestock.[5]

Mosby initially aligned his men into a battle rank near the Quaker meetinghouse at the edge of town but, uncertain of the Federal strength, retired a mile to a strip of woods east of Hamilton. Lieutenant Alfred Glascock with Company D and part of Company A concealed themselves in the woods, while Jim Wiltshire and about two dozen members of Company A stayed on the road, baiting the Yankees into the trap. When Reno's cavalrymen saw the small party of Rangers, they charged. Wiltshire fled as directed until the enemy reached the point on the road opposite Glascock's men when his detachment wheeled around and counterattacked. Glascock ripped into the left of the Union column; Wiltshire hammered the front.[6]

The Southerners caught the "astonished" Yankees in the roadbed, causing a jam of horses and men. The Pennsylvanians held briefly before the Rangers broke through the mass, splintering the Federal ranks. As the chase neared Hamilton, Union infantrymen behind a hedgerow raked the pursuers. Rangers James Keith and seventeen-year-old Wirt Binford tumbled from their saddles, killed by the blast. The infantry fire broke the impetus of the Confederate charge, and the Rangers pulled back.[7]

Several of the Rangers followed the Northerners into Hamilton. One of the Sinclairs gunned down a Yankee on the porch of a house. When Sinclair saw that his victim had a "brilliant diamond ring" on a finger, he halted and leaped from his horse. Gunfire and shouts were around him, but Sinclair pulled on the ring. When he could not remove it, he severed the finger.[8]

Mosby finally called off his men, retiring southward. Besides the two killed, he lost five wounded and four captured. Ranger John Chew suffered a crippling wound in the hip or back. His brother Robert tried to carry him with them, but he refused. The Federals tended to the injury, but John Chew never walked again. Reno reported his casualties at twenty.[9]

A rainstorm with heavy downpours swept in that night. The Rangers bivouacked in southern Loudoun; the Yankees, in Hamilton. Reno stayed in the area for four more days, searching villages and farmhouses for guerrillas, grain and provisions. The Rangers skirmished with Union parties on a few occasions. When the 8th Illinois Cavalry joined Reno at Middleburg on the twenty-third, Mosby withdrew into Fauquier, dispersing the two companies.[10]

A week later, on March 30, Charley Wiltshire, George Gill, Bartlett Bolling, John Orrick and Robert Eastham scouted toward Berryville in the Shenandoah Valley. As the five Rangers trotted up the lane of Colonel Daniel Bonham's farm, east of the town, they saw two Union soldiers run into Bonham's barn. Wiltshire spurred forward, followed closely by Gill. When they reached the door, Wiltshire shouted for the trapped Yankees to surrender. One of them replied, "Never," and Wiltshire grabbed for his pistol. Before he could unholster the revolver, Lieutenant Eugene Ferris, 30th Massachusetts Infantry, fired. Wiltshire reeled in the saddle, tumbling to the ground with a bullet in the neck. Bursting the door open, Ferris and his orderly stepped into the barnyard. Ferris shot Gill before the Ranger could discharge his weapon.[11]

The Northerners had mounted—Ferris on Wiltshire's horse, the orderly on his own—when Bolling, Orrick and Eastham entered the barnyard. Ferris was a match for all three of them, wounding both Bolling and Orrick in an exchange of gunfire. The Federals escaped through the gate, but the three Rangers pursued. Bolling, with a bullet in his chest, overtook the orderly, dragging him to the ground. Eastham, called "Bob Ridley" by his comrades, ran Ferris down, but the lieutenant ducked when Eastham swung at him with a pistol and outdistanced the Ranger. Ferris won the Congressional Medal of Honor for his day's work.[12]

Back in Bonham's barnyard, Eastham, Bolling and Orrick placed their fallen comrades on horses and rode toward the Confederacy. George Gill made it as far as the mountains, where he was taken into a house. Gill died the next day, saying at the end: "I die at least in a good cause." Gill was a twenty-four-year-old Marylander, a graduate of Princeton University, trained in the legal profession. His cousin, Ranger John Gill, buried him in a small cemetery on the mountain.[13]

Eastham, Bolling and Orrick carried Charley Wiltshire to the home of a Gilbert family in Fauquier. The Gilberts and a Ranger surgeon cared for him, but Wiltshire expired on April 6. A Virginian, he had fought in the regular army in both an infantry and a cavalry regiment before a disabling wound ended his service. When he joined his brother Jim as a Ranger, he still needed crutches and, in his first action, unhorsed a Federal with one of them. Mosby regarded him highly, and "Tee" Edmonds described him as "the chivalrous, the brave, the daring."[14]

Around this time, Mosby received a letter from Robert E. Lee, dated March 27. Lee directed Mosby to guard the Piedmont region from Gordonsville northward to Fauquier and the gaps of the Blue Ridge toward the Shenandoah Valley. "Your command," wrote Walter Taylor, an aide of Lee's, "is all now in that section, and the general will rely on you to watch and protect the country. If any of your command is in Northern Neck call it to you."[15]

Lee's instructions revealed the straits to which his army had been reduced during the past year. He could spare no one from the Petersburg trenches, so he assigned Mosby the task of guarding a huge swath of the Old Dominion which at one time was a strategically vital section in the defenses of Virginia. But not now, and both Lee and Mosby probably recognized that fact. Mosby obeyed in part, dispatching couriers to William Chapman in Northern Neck, but he ignored the territory around Gordonsville. He did not possess enough men until Chapman's battalion returned to operate that far south of Fauquier. As a final measure, Mosby organized an eighth company.[16]

Mosby gathered together the new members of Company H at North Fork Church in Loudoun County, on April 5, 1865. Many of the approximately fifty volunteers had served in the Prince William Partisan Rangers, which had been disbanded on December 4, 1864. The others were men either seeking to avoid conscription or willing to serve in a lost cause at the end.[17]

When the recruits were in line near the church, Mosby stood before them and said: "Men, I nominate George Baylor, of Jefferson county, captain of this company. All in favor of Baylor as captain, say aye." In Baylor's retelling, "there was a feeble response along the line."

Then Mosby announced: "George Baylor is unanimously chosen captain."[18]

Twenty-four-year-old George Baylor had fought in the Stonewall Brigade and with Turner Ashby, rising to the rank of lieutenant in the 12th Virginia Cavalry. Mosby knew Baylor and, when the latter resigned from his regiment, Mosby wanted him in his command. Ranger J. Marshall Crawford asserted in his memoirs that the company was formed just to reward Baylor with a captaincy.[19]

Mosby selected Edward Thompson, Jim Wiltshire and B. Franklin Carter, Jr., for the company's lieutenants. Thompson, a native of Fairfax, had led the detail which executed the Federals in Beemer's Woods in November 1864. Wiltshire, from Jefferson County, was close to Thompson in age and had distinguished himself in a number of engagements. His information resulted in the "Greenback Raid." For Wiltshire, however, no promotion could assuage the pain of his brother's mortal wounding. Nineteen-year-old Frank Carter was from Loudoun, a Ranger for less than a year with no prior military service.[20]

When Mosby completed the organization of Company H, he ordered Baylor "to go out and see what he could do." The next morning, about two o'clock, Company H stormed into the campsite of the Loudoun Rangers along the Shenandoah River. The Federals, who were only a shadow of their former selves, were "annihilated" by the Rangers. The Confederates captured forty-seven of the Loudoun Rangers, effectively ending the unit's existence. Brigadier General John Stevenson reported from Harper's Ferry that Baylor's men had "cleaned them out."[21]

Three days later, on April 9, Baylor and Company H, along with some members of Company D, entered Fairfax County to attack a wagon train. When the detachment learned that the target had already arrived within Union lines, Baylor bivouacked for the night at a farm near Burk's Station on the Orange and Alexandria Railroad, northeast of Manassas Junction. Baylor must not have posted sentries because, at daylight on the tenth, the 8th Illinois Cavalry charged into the campsite. Surprised by the assault, most of the new recruits fled at the first gunshot. Baylor, the three lieutenants and a handful of veteran Rangers fought, acting as a rear guard.[22]

The tough Yankees pursued. Their brigade commander, Colonel William Gamble, had remarked two months earlier that "The Eighth wants one more chance at" Mosby's men. This was it, and they took to it with a vengeance. The Illinoisans captured five Rebels, including Thomas F. Harney, an officer from the Torpedo Bureau on special assignment to Mosby. Ranger Charley Dear was unhorsed in the flight, tumbling into a ravine. Before he bedded down the night before, Dear had written his last will and had given Joseph Bryan a new pair of socks. But the Federals missed Dear, and he made it back to Fauquier, arriving the next day. The Union troopers halted the chase near the Bull Run battlefields. Jim Wiltshire and Frank Carter each fired one more shot—the final rounds fired by the 43rd Battalion in the war.[23]

Not only on the bloodied ground of the conflict's first major battle but across the entire Confederacy, the guns were silencing. The day before, Palm Sunday, April 9, 1865, at Appomattox Court House, Virginia, Robert E. Lee surrendered to Ulysses S. Grant. For a week after the fall of Petersburg and Richmond, Lee's army had tried to elude the Army of the Potomac. But the Federals closed the escape route at Appomattox, and Lee submitted to the inevitable. President Jefferson Davis and the cabinet were in flight southward. The only army the Confederacy had left was General Joseph Johnston's in North Carolina. Confronting the might of William Sherman's three armies, Johnston's men awaited their fate.

John Mosby learned of Lee's surrender when he read an account of it in the Baltimore *American* newspaper. He still had with him only Richards's battalion; Chapman's battalion would not arrive until the thirteenth. But Mosby could see among his men what John Munson stated: "We had begun to feel some of the weariness, the exhaustion and the satiety that invariably come to an army, with bloodshed." Still, Mosby balked, as long as Johnston's army remained in the field, he would not abandon the struggle.[24]

The disposition of Mosby's command had not gone unnoticed by either Union authorities or Confederate officials during these turbulent days. On April 10, Major General Godfrey Weitzel, commander of the occupation troops in Richmond, telegraphed Grant that "the people here are anxious that Mosby should be included in Lee's surrender. They say he belongs to that army." Grant responded that day, wiring Secretary of War Edwin Stanton that negotiations with Mosby should be handled by Major General Winfield S. Hancock, commander of the Middle Military Division, with headquarters in Winchester.[25]

Winfield Scott Hancock, a Pennsylvanian, was one of the finest combat officers the Civil War produced. A West Pointer and veteran of the Mexican War, Hancock received a brigadiership a few months after the war began. During the first three years of the struggle, he rose to command of the Second Corps, Army of the Potomac, distinguishing himself on all the major battlefields in the East. Nicknamed "Hancock the Superb," he and his troops repulsed the final Confederate charge at Gettysburg on July 3, 1863. Wounded in the action; he relinquished command of the corps until year's end, but returned to lead it through the vicious fighting of the spring and summer of 1864. When his wound reopened, he reported to Washington and, on February 27, 1865, he replaced Philip Sheridan as commander of the Middle Military Division. An honorable man and a soldier's soldier, Hancock could be expected to deal fairly and honestly with Mosby.[26]

Before Hancock had received Grant's instructions, he had proposed to Washington an expedition of infantry and artillery into "Mosby's Confederacy." He speculated that such an operation would require several days, and he hesitated to dispatch the necessary troops for that length of time. He left it at that, concluding: "I think everything should be kept ready for the march until we learn General Grant's wishes."[27]

The War Department forwarded "Grant's wishes" to Hancock on the tenth or eleventh. Stanton included a message of his own: "All detachments and stragglers from that [Lee's] army will, upon complying with the conditions agreed upon, be paroled & permitted to return to their homes. Those who do not so surrender will be brought in as prisoners of war. The guerrilla chief Mosby will not be paroled." Stanton also directed Hancock to publish and circulate the correspondence of Grant and Lee at Appomattox. Grant had offered Lee generous terms as long as the Confederates laid down their arms and returned home. Stanton believed that if unsurrendered Confederate troops read the articles of surrender, they would come in for parole.[28]

Hancock had his chief of staff, Brevet Brigadier General Charles H. Morgan, compose a letter to Mosby on April 11. Morgan wrote:

> *Colonel: I am directed by Major-General Hancock to inclose to you copies of letters which passed between General Grant and Lee on the occasion of the surrender of the Army of Northern Virginia. Major-General Hancock is authorized to receive the surrender of the forces under your command on the same conditions offered to General Lee, and will send an officer of equal rank with yourself to meet you at any point and time you may designate convenient to the lines for the purpose of arranging details should you conclude to be governed by the example of General Lee.*[29]

The Federals knew that J. H. Clarke, a hotelkeeper in Millwood, was a trusted informant for the Rangers, so Hancock asked Clarke to act as an intermediary and deliver the letter to Mosby. Clarke located Mosby at "Glen Welby" on the twelfth or thirteenth. The letter could not have been unexpected because Union Colonel William Gamble, the cavalry commander in Fairfax, had previously contacted Mosby, informing him of Lee's surrender. A Washington newspaper reported in its edition of the thirteenth that Mosby responded to Gamble that "he does not care a d——n about the surrender of Lee, and that he is determined to fight as long as he has a man left. He may fight his way to the gallows."[30]

Hancock, while he waited for a reply, speculated to Henry Halleck that Mosby would probably disband his command, instead of surrendering. "All his men have fine animals, and are generally armed with two pistols only," stated Hancock. "They will not give up these things, I presume, as long as they can escape. I will employ the cavalry force here in hunting them down." Two days later, on the fourteenth, Hancock followed with another telegraph, reiterating his earlier plan to send infantry and cavalry into Fauquier and Loudoun and "break up Mosby's command entirely."[31]

Hancock received Mosby's reply on the morning of the sixteenth when his aides escorted Lieutenant Colonel William H. Chapman and Dr. Aristides Monteiro into his headquarters. Mosby had sent the two Rangers, along with Lieutenant William H. Mosby and Captain Walter Frankland, to Winchester. Adjutant Mosby and Frankland had remained with Colonel Marcus Reno, whose pickets had met the four

Confederates with a flag of truce. Hancock offered Chapman and Monteiro a glass of wine and cigars while he read Mosby's letter and prepared a response.[32]

Dated April 15, and written in Warrenton at the home of a family named Washington, Mosby's letter read in full:

> *General: I am in receipt of a letter from your chief of staff, Brigadier-General Morgan, inclosing copies of correspondence between Generals Grant and Lee, and informing me that you would appoint an officer of equal rank with myself to arrange details for the surrender of the forces under my command. As yet I have no notice through any other source of the facts concerning the surrender of the Army of Northern Virginia, nor, in my opinion, has the emergency yet arisen which would justify the surrender of my command. With no disposition, however, to cause the useless effusion of blood or to inflict on a war-worn populace any unnecessary distress, I am ready to agree to a suspension of hostilities for a short time in order to enable me to communicate with my own authorities or until I can obtain sufficient intelligence to determine my future action. Should you accede to this proposition, I am ready to meet any person you may designate to arrange terms of an armistice.[33]*

When Hancock finished reading, he conferred with Chapman. The Ranger officer, as Hancock recounted later that day, inferred that, although he had not stated as such in the letter, Mosby would agree to a surrender of the partisan command. They agreed to a meeting at Millwood, on Tuesday, the eighteenth, at noon, and to an immediate ceasefire. With this concluded, a staff officer of Hancock put the terms on paper and handed the message to Chapman for delivery to Mosby. Chapman and Monteiro departed, reuniting with William Mosby and Frankland, and together dined with their old antagonist at Front Royal, Alfred Torbert, before starting back across the Blue Ridge.[34]

That evening Union Chief of Staff Halleck wired from the capital that Grant had authorized Hancock to accept the surrender of Mosby's command. Halleck added that any Ranger from a Northern state or the District of Columbia must obtain "special permits" from the War Department before he could return to his home.[35]

Secretary of War Stanton also sent a telegram to Winchester. "In holding an interview with Mosby," Stanton suggested, "it may be needless to caution an old soldier like you to guard against surprise or danger to yourself; but the recent murders show such astounding wickedness that too much precaution cannot be taken. If Mosby is sincere he might do much toward detecting and apprehending the murderers of the President."[36]

Stanton's last sentence addressed the final tragic act of this far-too-tragic war. Abraham Lincoln had died at 7:22 A.M. on the morning of April 15, after being shot in the back of the head by John Wilkes Booth at Ford's Theater in Washington the night before. The president never regained consciousness and, when he died in a boarding house across the street from the theater, Stanton said: "Now he belongs to the ages." The authorities knew the identity of the assassin and had begun a massive manhunt for Booth and his fellow conspirators. A mass of rumor and conflicting information deluged Washington, and officials started believing that Mosby was involved in the plot.[37]

A connection between Mosby and Booth is an intriguing subject. Three historians in a recent book have endeavored to make such a connection, presenting a conspiratorial cloth from "some dangling threads," in the authors' words. It is a case built upon assumptions and convoluted reckoning. A former Ranger, Lewis Powell, alias Lewis Paine, was one of the conspirators. He botched an attempted assassination of Secretary of State William Seward, was captured, tried and hanged. Powell had deserted from the command in January 1865, took an oath of allegiance and joined Booth's fellow conspirators in Baltimore. The historians allege that he was recruited and possibly sent by Mosby, although there is no proof of the latter point.[38]

Furthermore, the authors argue that when the 8th Illinois Cavalry captured Thomas Harney of the Torpedo Bureau on April 10 at Burke's Station, the troopers foiled a plot to blow up the White House. Harney had been sent to Mosby for passage through Union lines. It was a secret mission, but it could be reasonably argued that Mosby knew its purpose. If so, it is out of character for the man and the officer. Neither he nor any of his men, who wrote rather voluminously about their exploits, ever hinted of any link to the Booth plots. Until solid proof is forthcoming, the case is unproven. In the immediate wake of Lincoln's death, Union officials grasped for any leads, and Mosby was assuredly an important and perhaps likely target because of his skill, renown and geographic location.[39]

Between the time Mosby wrote to Hancock and the agreed upon meeting, Lieutenant Channing M. Smith of Company E returned from Richmond. Smith had transferred to the Rangers from the 4th Virginia Cavalry upon the request of Mosby in November 1864. Mosby asked for him because of his ability as a scout and his "valor & skill." Smith had traveled to the occupied capital to contact any Confederate officials not incarcerated. On the fifteenth, he talked with Robert E. Lee, who had just arrived from Appomattox, and the defeated general advised that Mosby should cease hostilities and disband the Rangers. "Channing," Lee counseled, "go home, all you boys who fought along with me, and help build up the shattered fortunes of our old state."[40]

Mosby, all his commissioned officers and some of his "most trustworthy scouts" arrived at Millwood about 11:30 A.M. on the morning of the eighteenth. Mosby, said a watching Union officer, Colonel James Kidd, rode in "like a highland chief coming to a lowland council." Kidd thought the partisan commander was "restless and full of fire," adding that "there was nothing ferocious in his appearance but when in the saddle he was not a man whom one would care to meet singlehanded." The Northerner also noticed Dolly Richards, "a swarthy-looking soldier."[41]

The Rangers met Hancock's delegation at "Carter Hall," a magnificent brick mansion owned by a Burwell family, on the eastern edge of Millwood. Mosby dismounted and shook hands with the assembled Union officers, beginning with Brigadier General George H. Chapman, a cavalry officer and Hancock's representative. When Mosby reached Colonel Kidd, the Federal asked him how much he weighed—128 pounds, replied Mosby. Chapman told him that the owner of "Carter Hall" had agreed to serve a meal, and the old enemies went inside, where Northerner alternated with Southerner around the dining table.[42]

The conference between George Chapman and Mosby went as smoothly as the meal, but resolved very little. Hancock had honored Mosby by appointing a brigadier to negotiate with a colonel. Chapman reiterated that Hancock offered Mosby and his men the same terms granted Lee's troops at Appomattox—relinquish arms and horses, sign a parole and go home. But Mosby demurred, stating that he awaited instructions from Richmond and the outcome of the campaign between Joseph Johnston and William Sherman in North Carolina. Mosby had already advised the Rangers that any of them could surrender and accept a parole. Then, as Chapman reported it, Mosby "said he had no favors to ask, being quite willing to stand by his acts, all of which he believed to be justifiable, and in the course of my conversation with him he remarked that he did not expect to remain in the country."[43]

Mosby requested a forty-eight-hour extension of the ceasefire, and Chapman agreed, until noon of April 20. The Union brigadier also granted a conditional truce for another ten days, but implied strongly that such a long suspension of hostilities would not be accepted by his superiors. Both men consented to a second meeting for noon on the twentieth. "The interview throughout was characterized by good feeling," Chapman declared. Before the Confederates departed, they expressed their regrets about Lincoln's assassination.[44]

Hancock reported the details of the meeting the next day to Henry Halleck. He asked if the truce should be extended for ten days and then stated: "The people are all anxious for Mosby to surrender." Halleck disapproved the extension of the ceasefire and that evening Grant wired: "If Mosby does not avail himself of the present truce end it and hunt him and his men down. Guerrillas, after beating the armies of the enemy, will not be entitled to quarter." Hancock replied within hours, telling Grant that he had already informed Mosby that the truce ended at noon on the twentieth.[45]

Lieutenant Channing Smith, meanwhile, had returned from his meeting with Lee. Mosby respected Lee above all others and, if the magnificent fighter advised disbandment, Mosby could hardly ignore it. With the end inevitable, Mosby met his officers in Paris at 10:30 A.M., April 20, and they cantered toward Millwood. In North Carolina, Johnston was preparing to surrender to Sherman.[46]

The second meeting took place in the brick house and tavern owned by J. H. Clarke. About fifteen Federals and twenty Confederates crowded into the parlor. Mosby sat at a small mahogany table next to George Chapman. The cordiality of the first meeting was gone. Mosby, wrote Hancock afterwards, became "very much agitated" when Chapman refused new terms or an extension of the truce. At that point, Ranger Hern, who came along without permission, burst into the room, exclaiming that he had seen Union cavalry in nearby woods.[47]

"Colonel," piped Hern, who had some vague notions of Federal duplicity, "the d——d Yankees have got you in a trap: there is a thousand of them hid in the woods right here."

Mosby turned toward the dirty, "uncouth" Ranger, and Hern said: "Let's fight 'em Colonel. We can whip 'em."

Mosby stood up slowly, placing his hand on his revolver, and in that low voice of his, stated: "If the truce no longer protects us, we are at your mercy; but we shall protect ourselves."[48]

Nobody moved or spoke. "It was a scene difficult to describe but never to be forgotten," wrote Surgeon Monteiro years later. "Every partisan was well prepared for instant death and more than ready for a desperate fight. Had a single pistol been discharged by accident, or had Mosby given the word, not one Yankee officer in the room would have lived a minute."[49]

But Mosby turned and walked through the door, trailed by his men. When they reached their horses, he said: "Mount and follow me." He prodded his mare, and the Rangers galloped eastward. Before them towered the Blue Ridge, their guardians for over two years. Behind them stood their enemies, watching, unknowing witnesses to a historic ride. They were the last group of Union soldiers to see an organized contingent of Mosby's Rangers.[50]

EPILOGUE

It was an unlikely day for warriors. An early morning rain had
ceased, but "thick fog hung like
a pall over the face of the country," remembered Ranger James J.
Williamson. Still the horsemen came, summoned by orders. A few
rode alone, silent with their thoughts; others arrived with comrades,
but no one had spoken much. It was before midday, Friday, April
21, 1865, by the time the Rangers converged on Salem, Virginia.
"All looked sad," recalled one of them. It was a day for silence and
sadness.[1]

John Mosby arrived late, but he was there, clean-shaven now,
pacing up and down Salem's main street, occasionally speaking in

low tones to the incoming riders. He and they knew the reasons
for the meeting—rumors of such a gathering had abounded. Since
yesterday's meeting in Millwood, time had quickened. With the
truce ended, the Federals threatened the desolation of Fauquier and
Loudoun. Mosby could not subject the people to more days of
flame for a hopeless cause, and so he and the Rangers came to
Salem. "It was done to save the country from destruction," he
wrote afterwards.[2]

Minutes before noon the Rangers formed into ranks, by companies, in a field just west of the village and south of the Rectortown
road. Company officers checked the alignment—eight companies,
scarcely 200 men, posted according to their date of organization: on
the left, Company A, formed at Rector's Cross Roads, the original
unit born in a spring of expectant hopes; Company B, forged in
combat by Billy Smith and Dolly Richards; Company C, William
Chapman's, steady and reliable; Company D, the "Darlings," dressed
for a ball but without their original leader, Richard Montjoy; Company E, inspired by Samuel Chapman, a Joshua in Confederate gray;
Company F, created in the midst of the bloody campaign beyond the
Blue Ridge; Company G, a hybrid, an amalgam of artillerymen without cannon and wide-eyed recruits; and Company H, the last to be
formed and the last to be bloodied.[3]

Mosby urged his mount forward to the end of the line, opposite
Company A. Slowly, glancing at the various faces, he passed along
the front in a final review and inspection, warrior honoring warrior.
From one end to the other, and back again. If he thought of those
not there, of those slain for the mission, he never said. An unsenti-
mental man, he was nevertheless touched by the moment. He spoke
not a word but, wheeling his horse back to the center of the formation,
he halted between William Chapman and Dolly Richards. At their
sides Lieutenant William H. Mosby, holding a sheet of paper in his
hands, read aloud:

Fauquier Co.

*Soldiers! I have summoned you together for the last time. The vision
we have cherished of a free and independent country, has vanished,
and that country, is now the spoil of a conqueror. I disband your
organization in preference to surrendering it to our enemies. I am
now no longer your commander. After association of more than two*

*eventful years, I part from you with a just pride, in the fame of
your achievements, and grateful recollections of your generous kindness to myself.*

*And now at this moment of bidding you a final adieu accept the
assurance of my unchanging confidence and regard.*

Farewell.

Jno S Mosby Colonel[4]

A "profound silence," in Williamson's words, enveloped the
ranks as the younger brother read the address but, at its conclusion,
the Rangers emitted three "hearty" cheers for their commander. But
few moved, reluctant perhaps to accept the finality. "Tears flowed
profusely," as it was later described to diarist "Tee" Edmonds, as
each bid farewell to his comrades. Slowly, at last, the trickle began.
Mosby, who had penned the address at "Glen Welby" the night before
or earlier in the morning, stood at the edge of the Rectortown road,
shaking the hand of each passing man. That iron composure of his
had cracked and, according to one, he "cried like a child." "It was,"
remembered James Williamson, "the most trying ordeal through
which we have ever passed."[5]

Decades later Mosby, thinking of the day, described it as "the
sad, sorrowful and pathetic scene at Salem." Today, a century and a
quarter later, a housing development covers the field and, on a street
corner in Marshall (Salem's modern name), carved words on a stone
marker remind later generations of the final rendezvous of Mosby's
Rangers.[6]

The disbandment, however, was not the final act—the Rangers
were required to sign paroles, officially accepting the defeat of the
Confederacy. Thus, on the following day, William Chapman and
most of the officers led about 200 men one last time together across
the Blue Ridge into the Shenandoah River. Many of them rode lame
or blind horses, expecting to have their mounts confiscated. At Winchester, they signed the papers, and the Federals allowed them to
keep their horses. Winfield Hancock talked with Chapman, whom
Hancock described "as important as Mosby." Others soon followed
Chapman and the men's example, reporting in at Winchester, Harper's Ferry, Charlestown or Berryville. Within three weeks Hancock's
troops accepted the paroles of 332 Rangers. Hundreds more signed
the documents in their hometowns, in Washington or at Union army

posts. At least 779 members of the 43rd Battalion were paroled out by the end of June 1865.[7]

But not John Mosby. When he rode away from Salem, he had decided to travel southward and learn the fate of Joseph Johnston's army. With roughly a half dozen or so companions, Mosby headed for Richmond. They moved cautiously—Hancock had offered a reward of $2,000 (subsequently raised to $5,000) for Mosby's capture. Newspapers even reported that some of his men, induced by the money, had joined the hunt. When they arrived on the outskirts of the former Confederate capital, now blackened by fires, Mosby sent John Munson and Henry Coley Jordan into the city for information.[8]

While Mosby and the others waited, Ben Palmer secured a newspaper which announced the surrender of Johnston. Munson and Jordan soon reported back, proposing a plan for the capture of Union officers quartered in the former White House of the Confederacy. Mosby dismissed the idea, saying: "Too late! It would be murder and highway robbery now. We are soldiers, not highwaymen."[9]

That settled it, and they all knew it. Turning westward, they rode to the home of Ranger Robert Walker outside of Orange Court House, where Mosby told them to return to their homes. He and his brother spent the next several weeks hiding near their father's home outside Lynchburg and at their uncle John Mosby's place in Nelson County. Twice during the early days of June, William Mosby visited the provost marshal's office in Lynchburg. On the second trip, a Major Swank assured him that his brother would be paroled if he surrendered. John Mosby reported the next day, June 13, only to learn that Swank's promise had been countermanded by superiors in Richmond. Still a hunted man, Mosby eluded the patrols. Finally, upon the direct intervention of Ulysses S. Grant, Mosby had his parole by month's end. By September he was back in Fauquier, practicing law and joined by Pauline and the children, whom he had seen rarely during the past two years. Now, it was history's turn.[10]

John Mosby and the Rangers emerged from the Civil War as the most famous colonel and battalion of men that war produced. A month before he began his legal practice in Warrenton, the New York *Times* declared that his wartime career "will show a succession of startling personal adventures unsurpassed by those of any partisan chief on record."[11]

During the next several decades this opening note sounded by the newspaper grew into a chorus. Friend and foe alike, as they came to write of the greatest experience of their lives, praised Mosby and the 43rd Battalion. Former Rangers John Scott, J. Marshall Crawford, John Munson, John Alexander, Aristides Monteiro and James Williamson penned graphic reminiscences which enhanced the prowess and the exploits of their commander and comrades. Alexander, typifying the memoirists, stated: "The truth is that Mosby conceived a plan of warfare, sought and found a favorable theater, attracted and made the most of suitable men, and with them worked out his conception to glorious results."[12]

No other Confederate unit of the size of a battalion or regiment received such remembrance by former members. Four decades separated the publication of Scott's book in 1867 and Alexander's in 1907. Mosby's memoirs were released in 1917, one year after his death. Numerous magazine articles, written by Mosby and his men, added to the storied saga of the Rangers.

Former antagonists, privates and generals, were not immune, echoing the views of Rangers for a man the Yankees had called the "Scarlet Cloak." An undertone of animosity toward the guerrillas remained in Union memoirs and regimental histories, but former Northern veterans extolled the partisans' record. An infantry captain with Philip Sheridan in the Shenandoah Valley argued that "a more harassing enemy could not well be imagined" than Mosby's Rangers. Another officer in that army thought: "They were a most dangerous element, and caused perhaps more loss than any single body of men in the enemy's service." In the words of a New York cavalryman, Mosby's command "was truly *unique* in its leader, its composition, and its *modus operandi*." Finally, Ulysses S. Grant in his superb, best-selling memoirs wrote of Mosby: "There were probably but few men in the South who could have commanded successfully a separate detachment in the rear of an opposing army, and so near the border of hostilities, as long as he did without losing his entire command."[13]

Grant's work was published in 1886 at a time when Southerners were creating a new image of their struggle of the 1860's, the "Lost Cause." The effort to perpetuate the memory of the Confederacy served social and cultural needs of the era, but it also wrapped the war years in an aura of romanticism. From these immediate decades before the twentieth century a Confederate tradition emerged. Southerners, a historian of the movement has written, "remembered the battle but had forgotten its pain, its cost, and its issues."[14]

Mosby's Rangers fit snugly within the confines of the "Lost

Cause" interpretation. For over two years they had waged war, given battle and defeated their opponents at the very doorstep of the Union capital. Emerging from the mists of early morning or from the depths of darkness, these knights, dressed in plumed hats and red-lined capes, captured a Union general in his bed, seized thousands of enemy soldiers, horses and arms, derailed trains and rode away barely scathed by the encounters. In the end, they accepted defeat but did not surrender.

It was a popular image, woven from strands of fact and fiction, which has endured with a persistence. But the reality of their warfare and its impact on the war are much different. The veneer of fascination and romanticism should not hide the harsh nature of the struggle in which they were engaged. Mosby did not adhere to such sentimentality, asserting in a postwar letter that he viewed war not as "a tournament or pastime, but as one of the most practical of human undertakings; I learned the maxims on which I conducted it from Napoleon and not from Walter Scott."[14]

The Ranger saga was more than the victories—the capture of Edwin Stoughton, Miskel's Farm, Second Dranesville, Mount Zion Church, the calico raids, "Berryville Wagon Raid," the "Greenback Raid," Gold's farm, Kabletown and Mount Carmel Church. Places like Warrenton Junction, Grapewood Farm, Loudoun Heights, Myers's Ford, Benjamin Morgan's lane, Front Royal, Dulany's, the "Burning Raid," Fort Warren and Old Capitol Prison counterbalanced the ledger. Service in the 43rd Battalion carried a price.

Ranger casualties amounted to between 35 and 40 percent of the command. While precise figures are probably an impossibility, eighty-five identified members of the command were either killed, mortally wounded or executed. An additional sixteen known Rangers died in prison or from disease. The number of men who fell in combat with a wound exceeded one hundred. The Federals also captured at least 477 Rangers during the command's existence. While many of these captives were exchanged and returned to the battalion, the danger of capture was a constant reality in a Ranger's life. Finally, approximately twenty-five members of the battalion deserted.[16]

It was a bloody business in which the Rangers engaged. But one salient fact emerges—John Mosby and the 43rd Battalion had no equal as guerrillas during the Civil War. Primary credit for that belongs to the commander. With a keen intellect, an uncompromising discipline and a sure grasp of the potential of guerrilla warfare, Mosby welded the Rangers into a matchless partisan command and hampered Union campaigns in a strategic region of Virginia. The casualties the Rangers inflicted, the horseflesh, supplies and armament they seized far outweighed the losses incurred. Mosby supplied Jeb Stuart and Robert E. Lee with invaluable intelligence and severed Union lines of communication and supply. If he had achieved nothing else, the information he secured for his superiors and the troops he drained from invading hosts were important accomplishments in themselves.[17]

Union countermeasures against the Rangers never achieved the goal of eliminating or neutralizing the partisan command. Bluejacketed horsemen rode forth on numerous counterraids and patrols, arrested civilians and eventually burned sections of Fauquier and Loudoun. But their superiors neither developed a plan of operations nor committed the resources and manpower to them. The administration in Washington and commanders in the field seemingly placed little importance on the struggle with the Rangers. "From first to last," Civil War historian Bruce Catton has written, "the Northerners never really found an effective answer, not even when they had ruthless operators like Grant and Sheridan on the scene." But their reluctance, even indisposition, to search diligently for "an effective answer" insured that it was never found.[18]

In the end, Mosby and the Rangers prevailed in their "war of wits" against Union cavalrymen and earned a place among some of the finest guerrilla warriors in history. With ingenuity, skill, valor and tirelessness they maintained an island of resistance to Federal efforts in northern Virginia for nearly twenty-eight months. But as they rendezvoused one final time at Salem, the 43rd Battalion had neither prolonged the war in the Old Dominion for several months— as discussed in Chapter 13—nor had they kept thousands of Union troops away from the front. The conclusion seems inescapable that, as a historian of Union cavalry has argued, Mosby's Rangers and fellow partisans "accomplished anything more than to increase the cost and bitterness of the war." The monument in Prospect Hill Cemetery in Front Royal reminds us of that price exacted from a divided nation.[19]

The memory and pride of their service in the 43rd Battalion sustained the Rangers as they followed a myriad of roads from Salem. They were farmers, carpenters, livestock breeders, teachers, merchants and businessmen. Some, like their commander, practiced law—Dolly Richards, Fred Bowen, David Briscoe and Daniel

Wright. Boswell Anderson, C. A. Fox, Joseph Wayman, J. J. Williams and Jim Wiltshire practiced medicine. Charles Grogan was a court bailiff in Baltimore; A. R. Brady, a Washington, DC, policeman; and Sam Chapman combined a career in the ministry with that of a United States marshal in Staunton, Virginia. William Mosby became a postmaster in his native state. William H. Chapman, Fount Beattie, Charles Dear, John Ballard, Frank Angelo and George R. L. Turberville found employment with the United States government. Joseph Bryan became a noted publisher in Richmond; Edward Thompson, a justice of the peace; and Walter Gosden fathered a son, Freeman, who entered show business as Amos of "Amos and Andy."[20]

Charley McDonough, one of the command's "brevet-outlaws," rendezvoused with a different fate. Refusing a parole, McDonough hid in northern Virginia, evading Union patrols and swearing he would never be captured. Finally, in June 1865, several Federals, hunting for the Ranger, surrounded McDonough. He emptied his pistol, except for one round, and placing the muzzle in his mouth, squeezed the trigger. The conflict had taken its last Ranger.[21]

John Mosby had a varied postwar career, but he still lowered his shoulders into the prevailing winds. He practiced law, watched his family grow to four sons and four daughters and struggled with grief when a son, George, died in 1873, and Pauline and an infant son, Alfred, died in 1876. He had, however, reconciled himself to the outcome of the war and eventually became friends with President Ulysses S. Grant, switching to the Republican Party. To Southerners, it was an act of apostasy, but Mosby ignored the firestorm of condemnation which resulted. Grant and future Republican presidents rewarded him with a consulship in Hong Kong, a post in the General Land Office and an assistant attorneyship in the Department of Justice. He wrote extensively on the war during these years as he continued in the legal profession. On May 30, 1916, at the age of eighty-two, John Mosby died in Washington, DC, in the capital of his former enemies. A train hauled his remains to Warrenton, where he was buried beside Pauline and the deceased children. Not far away, down a slope, was the grave of Richard Montjoy.[22]

As the decades lengthened after the war, the surviving Rangers, dwindling in numbers, gathered for annual reunions. They passed resolutions, held parades, answered to roll calls, planned fund-raisers for memorials and shared memories. Surely, in those times of remembrance, they thought of those who were not with them, of those who had fallen in the defense of the cause and for the mission. It would have been a different roll call, a name and a place—George Whitescarver, Seneca Mills; Billy Smith and "Fighting Tom" Turner, Loudoun Heights; Thomas Anderson, David Jones, Lucien Love, William Overby, Henry Rhodes and Carter, Front Royal; "Big Yankee" Ames, "Yew Hill"; the deaf Clay Adams, Gold's farm; Welby Rector and Lewis Adie, Berryville; Charles Wiltshire and George Gill, Berryville; and, Richard Montjoy, Loudoun. The roll was not complete—it did not have to be, for no one answered the call.[23]

Mosby avoided most of these reunions, making excuses. But in 1895 he came to one and, during the course of his talk to his veterans, he said: "Life cannot afford a more bitter cup than the one I drained at Salem, nor any higher reward of ambition than that I received as Commander of the Forty-third Virginia Battalion of Cavalry." The listeners understood.[24]

APPENDIX

 The following list of members of the 43rd Battalion of Virginia Cavalry contains the names of 1,902 individuals. While my compilation does not purport to be a complete and final roster of Mosby's Rangers, it is the fullest accounting of the command's membership yet published. The total number of men who served with Mosby, as noted in Chapter 4, far exceeded previous estimations. But a definitive and full compilation of every man in the unit would probably be impossible to tabulate because of the fluid nature of the battalion's organization.

Three primary sources were utilized in the preparation of this list. The most important source was the Compiled Service Records of Mosby's Regiment, Record Group 109, National Archives. The CSR contains enlistment forms, clothing receipts, promotion records and/or Union records of captives for hundreds of the Rangers. Unfortunately, the file is not complete as the documentary material for hundreds of other Rangers was either lost, misfiled or never received by the government. The CSR remains the basic source for a compilation, but not a full accounting.

As supplements to the CSR, the membership rolls published in James J. Williamson's *Mosby's Rangers* and a ledgerbook compiled by Virgil Carrington "Pat" Jones, author of *Ranger Mosby*, were utilized. Williamson developed his roster through the assistance of comrades in the battalion. Pat Jones prepared his list over a period of fifty years and it is a trove of names and information on the Rangers. He donated his ledgerbook to the collections of the General Stuart–Colonel Mosby Museum, American Historical Foundation in Richmond, Virginia. Finally, additional names of Rangers were extracted from various published and unpublished sources.

Each man who officially enrolled in the battalion, participated in a raid, or attached himself temporarily to the unit and with documentary proof has been included in the list. Some Rangers signed papers and never rode on an operation; some never officially enlisted but fought with Mosby on several occasions; and, some enlisted but were captured before they had an opportunity to fight. As a final note, rank and company are not included because such information for hundreds of the Rangers cannot be confirmed.

Jacob — ABRAHAM
David — ACRES
Clay — ADAMS
Henry Clay ADAMS
John — ADAMS
Joseph A ADAMS
Thomas W ADAMS
Lewis B ADIE/ALDIE
John M ADRIAN
Joseph West ALDRICH
B R ALEXANDER
David — ALEXANDER
John — ALEXANDER
John H ALEXANDER
Lawrence — ALEXANDER
Samuel — ALEXANDER
Tiphen W ALLEN
William — ALLISON
James W ALMOND
James F AMES
John F AMISS
A M ANDERSON
Boswell P ANDERSON
Ed — ANDERSON
G W ANDERSON
Isaac B ANDERSON
Peyton — ANDERSON
Samuel — ANDERSON
Thomas E ANDERSON
William A ANDERSON
William C ANDERSON
Frank — ANGELO
Arthur David ARCHER
John A ARMSTRONG
Joseph A ARMSTRONG
Samuel R ARMSTRONG
John — ARNETT
James W ASH
Joseph A ASH
Henry S ASHBY
John R ASHBY
Nimrod T ASHBY
Lawrence — ASHTON
John — ATKINS
Ewell — ATWELL
William H ATWILL
Fenton — AUD

George B AUSTIN
Thomas E AYLOR
Thomas F AYLOR
John L AYLOR
John M AYLOR
George H AYRE
J F AYRES
A G BABCOCK
J — BAGGASBY
John T BAILEY
Samuel J BAILEY
Absalom R BAINBRIDGE
B F BAKER
O L BAKER
Thomas R BAKER
J A BALDWIN
Albin P BALL
Benjamin F BALL
John N BALLARD
G R BALTHROPE
Charles L BANKHEAD
James M BARBEE
Samuel A BARBEE
Slice H BARBER
William T BARBER
Henry S BARBOUR
L A BARKER
John E BARKER
John (Jack) H BARNES
Charles N BARR
H — BARR
Phillip — BARRETT
Walter — BARRITT
Andrew R BARTENSTEIN
Benjamin — BARTON
Roslin — BATES
J P BAYLEY
George — BAYLOR
R W BAYLOR
Henry T BAYNE
John C BAYNE
Richard B BAYNE
Washington — BAYNE
Charles A BEA
John T BEAL
Joseph R BEAL
Brooke — BEALL

Charles A BEAR
Fountain — BEATTIE
W G BEAUCHAMP
Abram — BEAVERS
Charles Fenton BEAVERS
George G BECKHAM
John G BECKHAM
William L BECKHAM
— — BELL
James W BELL
John W BELL
Thomas — BELT
John A BELVIN
W D BELVIN
G T BENCHLER
John H BENCKE
Lewis — BENEDICT
Franklin — BENJAMIN
Theodore S BENTON
Edmund — BERKELEY
C N BERN
Frank C BERRYMAN
Marcellus — BERRYMAN
Richard A BEST
Edward R BETTS
J — BEVERLEY
Richard H BIBBS
James M BICKERS
William — BICKHAM
Andrew J BIEDLER
Charles E or S BIEDLER
William T BIEDLER
Ballard W BINFORD
Wirt M BINFORD
Charley — BINNS
— — BIRNEY
S — BIRTHAM
John H BISHOP
Stephen G R BISHOP
Stacey B BISPHAM
John T BIVINS
Thomas — BLACKMAN
Joseph H BLACKWELL
Harris C BLANCHARD
Richard T BOARMAN
C — BOHRER
Bartlett — BOLLING

John M BOLLING
Samuel M BOLLING
William A BOLLING
James M BOLTON
Dallas — BONNELL
Thomas — BOOKER
John T BOTTS
A J BOWEN
Charles O BOWEN
Frederick F BOWEN
Henry Clay BOWEN
James — BOWEN
James W BOWEN
John W BOWEN
J P BOWEN
William B BOWEN
Brune — BOWIE
John — BOWIE
John W BOWIE
Walter — BOWIE
Walter — BOWIE
D R BOWLIN
E S BOXLEY
Henry C BOYD
Henry P BOYD
— — BOYLE
Gabe V BRADDEN
John M BRADLEY
— — BRADSHAW
— — BRADSHAW
Adam R BRADY
William B BRADY
Charles — BRAGG
William M BRAGG
N — BRAMHAM
John P BRANCH
William H BRANDER
Abram — BRAUN
C W BRAWNER
Henry N BRAWNER
Richard — BRAWNER
William A BRAWNER
William G BRAWNER
William Armstead BRAXTON
Isaac — BREATHED
Edward — BREDELL
James R BRENT

Charles W BREWER
C F BRICKHOUSE
G W BRIDGES
James — BRIEN
David S BRISCOE
William S BROADUS
Guy — BROADWATER
Richard F BROADWATER
George W BROCK
Henry/Harry — BROCK
Jacob H BROCK
William T BROCKE
H A BRONNER
Beal — BROOK
William T BROOKE
Charles — BROOKS
Thomas R BROUN
A J BROWN
Daniel F BROWN
Eugene — BROWN
F S BROWN
Joseph D BROWN
J P BROWN
L B BROWN
Leonard B BROWN
R H BROWN
Robert T BROWN
Thomas R BROWN
T S BROWN
William D BROWN
Lafayette — BROWNING
Thomas E BROWNING
E T BRUMBACK
E S BRUMBUCK
Joseph — BRYAN
C — BUCHANAN
John Charles BUCHANAN
John T BUCHANAN
Richard P BUCKNER
Joseph — BUDD
Alex — BUMERS
T L BUNDLE
D — BUNELL
Alex — BURGESS
M M BURGESS
Moses T BURGESS
J C BURK

Arthur — BURKE
Edward A BURKE
John C BURKE
Thomas T BURKE
John — BURLES
James N BURNLEY
John M BURNS
Charles N BURR
Tobe — BURR
Harrison — BURTON
Henry Clay BURTON
Charles E BUTLER
D — BUTLER
J F BUTLER
Otho L BUTLER
Samuel — BUTLER
William B BUTLER
John E CAHILL
C E CALDWELL
Joseph C CALVERT
C B CAMPBELL
Joel H CAMPBELL
John W CAMPBELL
Joseph — CAMPBELL
W S CAMPBELL
Ciras — CANNON
George W CANNON
Alexander G CAREY
H E CAREY
James — CAREY
David Grafton CARLISLE
T A CARPENTER
Lawrence — CARR
Richard F S CARR
Upshur — CARR
Luther — CARRINGTON
— — CARROLL
— — CARTER
B Franklin CARTER
Charles P CARTER
Eli — CARTER
Isaiah — CARTER
Joseph M CARTER
Nick — CARTER
Thomas A CARTER
Thomas W CARTER
James — CARUTH

James K CARUTH
Joseph M CARVER
Alex — CARY
John R CASTLEMAN
Jefferson — CELLS
H H CHAMBERLAIN
Henry Clay CHAMBLIN
J M CHAMBLIN
Thomas — CHAMBLIN
George W CHANCELLOR
James M CHANCELLOR
Henry H CHANDLER
Hugh — CHANDLER
P K CHANDLER
Samuel — CHAPMAN
William George CHAPMAN
William H CHAPMAN
J Pendleton CHAPPELEAR
Irvine K CHASE
— — CHEATWOOD
Charles F CHELF
John A CHEW
Robert — CHEW
B F CHEWNING
Walter Scott CHEWNING
William D CHICHESTER
F M CHILDS
G P CHILTON
James V CHILTON
Benton — CHINN
John P CHINN
Edmond W CHRISTIAN
John Hunt CHRISTIAN
J — CHURCH
Johnson — CLAGGETT
John J CLARK
Joseph B CLARK
William — CLARK
J — CLARKSON
F W CLAYBROOK
— — CLOYD
James — COAKLEY
J Frank COCHRAN
Thomas Benton COCHRAN
William F COCKE
George H COCKRELL
John — COCKRELL

John H COCKRELL
William — COCKRELL
E M COFFMAN
Edwin M COFFROTH
J C COGHILL
Cornelius Jerome COINER
John N COINER
Edward D COLE
Clarence — COLEMAN
Nathaniel R COLEMAN
W A COLEMAN
William E COLSTON
J B COLVIN
Lawson — COMPTON
Z T COMPTON
F — CONE
Elisha — CONNELL
F M CONNER
Charles E CONRAD
George W CONRAD
M O CONRAD
Demetrius — COODE
Enoch — COOK
William T COOK
William — COOKE
Morgan — COOKSEY
Frank A COONS
Henry C COONS
John William COONS
W C COONS
Robert — COOPER
James — COPELEY
George W COPENHAVER
John W COPENHAVER
John E COPPAGE
John W CORBIN
Lemuel A CORBIN
George E CORDELL
Butler — CORDER
John H CORE
John — CORNICK
John — CORNWALL
Elilsha — CORNWELL
George — CORNWELL
J L CORNWELL
R H CORNWELL
Benjamin R COWHERD

Charles — COWLING
Richard — COWLING
J E COX
George — CRABBE
Milton O CRABLE
Francis T CRAIG
D H CRAMM
James K CRAUTH
George William CRAWFORD
JAMES — CRAWFORD
J Marshall CRAWFORD
John T CRAWFORD
Magrus S CRAWFORD
Robert — CRAWFORD
Robert J CRAWFORD
Eppa H CREEL
BEVERLY S CREWS
William G CRIGLER
William — CROMWELL
Oliver T CROOK/CREEK
Robert N CROOK
John E CROPP
T A CROPPER
Charles — CROSS
Samuel E CROSWEN
Elias — CROUCH
Joseph — CROUCH
T W CROW
Barney — CROWLEY
Samuel E CROWSIN
C A CRUM
Edgar M CRUTCHFIELD
John — CULBRETH
G W CUMMINGS
James H CUMMINGS
Martin S CUMMINGS
G — CUNNINGHAM
John W DAME
J H DANIEL
John — DANIEL
Peter M DANIEL
Charles — DANNE
Dennis — DARDEN
Francis M DARDEN
Philip A DARNEILLE
— — DAVIS
Alexander — DAVIS

Americus — DAVIS
Charles — DAVIS
Edgar — DAVIS
Francis C DAVIS
George C DAVIS
Gipson — DAVIS
G W DAVIS
Henry — DAVIS
Henry C DAVIS
J C DAVIS
John B DAVIS
John W DAVIS
J P DAVIS
Littleton Morgan DAVIS
Peter J DAVIS
Philip A DAVIS
Thomas F DAVIS
W Daniel DAVIS
William D DAVIS
Reuben — DAWSON
Alexander — DAY
Brock — DEAR
Charles H DEAR
Henry Clay DEAR
J William DEAR
T W DEAR
Washington E DEARMONT
Robert — DEATHERAGE
John P DEBUTTS
Richard E DEBUTTS
— — DEEMS
C W DEHAVEN
A A DEILMAN
Jacob H DELAPLANE
J — DENNING
C H DENNIS
William F DENNIS
George — DENT
S L DEROSANE
William — DEWITT
Charles — DICKELL
E S DICKEY
Thaddeus C DICKINSON
John T/G DICKSON
Ludwell — DIGGS
Edgar — DISHMAN
S — DISHMAN

William W DIVINE
George Y DODD
George Z DODD
B F DONOHOE
Charles — DONOHOE
J W DORRITY
Charles — DORSEY
Harry — DORSEY
Pugh — DORSEY
Reuben — DORSEY
S P DOUGLAS
Peter G DOWELL
Thaddeus — DOWELL
John "Jack" A DOWNING
William H DOWNING
Albert — DRAIN
C O DRUMMOND
Sam — DUCHEANE
French — DULANEY
Daniel F DULANY
John — DULIN
Robert — DULY
John W DUME
W D DUNCAN
William L DUNN
Roger W DUNNAWAY
John — DUNNING
Charles A DUNNINGTON
King Agrippa DUNTON
R A DUNTON
Arthur — DUTRETRE
Wiley — EARLY
W W EASLY
Philip Byrd EASTHAM
Robert W EASTHAM
Wellingham — EASTHAM
William Bird EASTHAM
William Braxton EASTHAM
Woodford — EASTHAM
Sidney — EASTON
Benjamin S EDMONDS
Clement W EDMONDS
Henry — EDMONDS
John C EDMONDS
Philip M EDMONDS
John T EDWARDS
Joseph — EDWARDS

William H EDWARDS
W M EDWARDS
Falcott — ELIASON
Thomas — ELIASON
John S ELKINS
James W ELLIS
J R ELMORE
Robert T ELZEY
William — ELZEY
William A EMBREY
Frederick D EUBANK
John — EVANS
Arthur W FAIRFAX
Thomas — FAIRFAX
Wellington — FAIRFAX
Rezin S FARR
Richard R FARR
John — FARRAR
Charles — FARRELL
James F FAULKNER
Walter W FAULKNER
Alfred — FEAGANS
Champ — FERGUSON
Sydnor G FERGUSON
Charles — FERRIS
James R FINKS
William — FINKS
George — FINLEY
Charles W FISH
A N FISHER
Champe S FITZHUGH
Thomas — FLACK
M W FLANNERY
M N FLEMING
O J FLEMING
Benjamin L FLETCHER
Benton — FLETCHER
Robert W FLETCHER
R V W FLETCHER
William H FLETCHER
William — FLEURY
P R FLINN
James A FLINT
A C FLIPPO
Mark — FLORENCE
Samuel C FLOWEREE
A E FLYNN

James — FLYNN
John F FLYNN
John N FLYNN/FLINN
Robert N FLYNN
William — FLYNN
Joseph R FOGG
Ira — FOLLIN
John M FORD, JR
John M FORD, SR
P G FOREMAN
E F FORRER
Judah — FORRER
James I FORREST
John T FORTNEY
James William FOSTER
John H FOSTER
Robert O FOWLES
A J/P FOX
Albert — FOX
Charles A FOX
Frank — FOX
Joseph — FOY
Walter E FRANKLAND
Benjamin — FRANKLIN
Benjamin — FRANKLIN
Isaac N FRANKLIN
Peter A FRANKLIN
John J FRAY
Burr F FRED
Frank L FRED
William R FREE
John L FRENCH
George — FRERE
— — FRIENDS
T W FRINK
French — FRISTOE
Gus — FUGITT
John W FULLER
Rich A FURLEY
John — FURLING
Dallas — FURR
Thompson — FURR
David — GAINES
William Henry GAINES
T B GALE
Christian — GALL
Herbert T GALT

George W GAMMON
Thomas P GANTT
L M GARDNER
— — GARNETT
Henry W GARRETT
Washington H GARRISON
James H GARTH
John W GARTH
Hezekiah — GASKINS
— — GAULT
Isaiah P GAYLE
Mordecai J GAYLE
Thomas B GAYLE
B F GENTRY
Isaac A GENTRY
B — GEORGE
Frank — GESCHKY
Adolphus — GESSELL
Willie A GIBBS
A L GIBSON
Edwin — GIBSON
Henry C GIBSON
Howard — GIBSON
John E GIBSON
John T GIBSON
Moses M GIBSON
Ned — GIBSON
S — GIBSON
Willie — GIBSON
George M GILL
John — GILL
John — GILLESPIE
John W GILLILAND
George W GILMER
Edwin — GIPSON
William — GLADDING
Alfred — GLASCOCK
Aquilla — GLASCOCK
S O GLASS
I/H H/T GODDIN
James H GODDIN
J H GOFF
J L GOFF
Adolphus A GOG
T R GOLDING
William N GOLDING
Charles — GOLDSBOROUGH

James J GOOCH
Abner — GOODALL
George W GOODING
Lewis E GOODING
Joseph B GOODWIN
Manley — GORDON
Jesse P GORE
Walter W GOSDEN
James K GOUGH
J A GOURA
Charles Henry GRAY
James Albert GRAY
John — GRAY
Robert — GRAY
Thaddeus — GRAY
Thomas — GRAY
William — GRAY
Ed — GRAYSON
James T GRAYSON
John Tyler GRAYSON
Robert O GRAYSON
T F GRAYSON
W E GRAYSON
John W GREEN
Matthew — GREEN
Thomas Nelson GREEN
Henry H GREGG
Henry W GREGG
James R GRESHAM
Alfred — GREY
William — GREY
G C GRIFFIN
Joseph — GRIFFIN
John B GRIFFITH
John — GRIFFITH
T M GRIGSBY
Charles E GROGAN
— — GROGEN
Benjamin — GROVE
Philip E GROVE
John — GROVES
George M GULICK
James F GULICK
John T GULICK
James D GUNNEL
George West GUNNELL
Samuel — GUTHRIE

George — HACKLEY
Lewis A HACKLEY
Samuel — HACKLEY
Thomas B HACKLEY
A — HAISLIP
Charlie Landon HALL
J C HALL
J P HALL
J W HALL
Richard N HALL
S — HALL
J C HAMELL
Alex C HAMILTON
James W HAMMOND
John W HAMMOND
Thomas — HAMMOND
John A HAMNER
Gilbert — HAMRICK
John H HANCOCK
J H HANER
George W HANES
Walter T HANES
James E HANEY
W James HANEY
James F HANSEN
Samuel P HANSEN
C C HANSFORD
George — HANSON
F M HARDEN
Thomas W HARDING
G B HARDWICK
C Tyler D HARN
Gus B HARNER
Thomas F HARNEY
John C HAROLD
John C HARRELL
Middleton D HARRELL
Charles W HARRIS
D S HARRIS
Henry G HARRIS
John W HARRIS
Henry H HARRISON
James — HARRISON
W H HARRISON
Robert M HARROVER
R A HART
William — HARVEY

John — HASSETT
Dan — HATCHER
Harry — HATCHER
Richard Welt HATCHER
James — HATTON
Charles T HAWLING
T M HAYS
M — HAZLETT
John W HEARN
Henry — HEATON
Townsend — HEATON
Edward — HEFFLEBOWER
John N HEFFLEBOWER
H W HEFLIN
John W HEFLIN
J/T A HEFLIN
L R HEFLIN
Robert F HEFLIN
William H HEFLIN
James Monroe HEISKELL
Frank M HELM
John — HENDERSON
U B HENDERSON
G B HENDRICK
C M HENNING
G W HENNINGTON
W T HENRY
— — HERN
C M HERNING
George W HERRINGTON
Peter M HERTER
James J HEWSON
Henry C HIBBS
William — HIBBS
William — HIBBS, JR.
Samuel B HICKES
George W HICKSON
Clarendon — HILL
Francis L HILL
Wyatt T HILL
— — HINES
Frederick S HIPKINS
John — HIPKINS
P M HITER
Burgess W HITT
E Wallace HITT
David — HIXON

Levi — HIXSON
R W HIXSON
A J HOBSON
H A HOBSON
J R HOBSON
Noah — HOCKMAN
James M HODGES
H H HOFFMAN
John M HOFFMAN
Charles E HOGE
Byron M HOGG
Franklin B HOLLINGSWORTH
John W HOLMES
Gustavus B HOMER
Robert C HOMER
Robert M HOOE
H H HOPKINS
John E HOPKINS
Richard — HOPKINS
R C HORNER
Thomas — HORNES
C C HORSEFORD
John D HORSLEY
Bradford Smith HOSKINS
Rufus A HOUDERSHELL
Gresham — HOUGH
Robert M HOVE
James H HOWARD
Reuben T HOWARD
Thomas W HOWARD
William B HOWARD
Rufus A HOWDERSPELL
Rodney — HOWELL
William P HOWERTON
H Lee HOWISON
George — HOYLE
John W HUDGINS
T — HUDGINS
Thomas H HUFF
G W HUFFMAN
J M HUFFMAN
W H HUFFMAN
John — HUGHES
Richard A HUGHES
George W HUGHLETT
H M HULL
P G HUME

★

E P HUMPHREYS
Charles B HUNDLEY
E M HUNT
George W HUNT
Lewis — HUNT
Rinaldo — HUNT
Silas G/W HUNT
William L HUNTER
Ernest C HUNTON
Isaiah — HUNTON
John W HUNTON
Ned (Edward) S HURST
James Thomas HURT
Thomas W HUTCHERSON
John R HUTCHINSON
Lewis — HUTCHINSON
S F HUTCHINSON
Joshua M HUTCHISON
Lycurgus E HUTCHISON
Philip — HUTCHISON
H M HUTT
Benjamin — IDEN
John — IDEN
Jacob P IMBODEN
A — INLOES
Edgar M JACKSON
N H JACKSON
Robert A JACKSON
William E JACKSON
J H JAMER
B Russell JAMES
Henry — JAMES
J Wright JAMES
Meredith Clay JAMES
William A JARBOE
Henry — JARMAN
R H JARMAN
Robert — JARMAN
B F JARVIS
Nimrod J JENKINS
Matthew W JENNINGS
Lucius L JETT
William — JETT
William P JOHNS
Ballard P JOHNSON
Charles W JOHNSON
Edward — JOHNSON

Frank — JOHNSON
G W JOHNSON
Horace — JOHNSON
James D JOHNSON
James M JOHNSON
James W JOHNSON
Joseph — JOHNSON
L D JOHNSON
Smith — JOHNSON
Thaddeus H JOHNSON
William — JOHNSON
Charles J JOHNSTON
G A JOHNSTON
John — JOHNSTON
Thomas — JOHNSTON
William A JOHNSTON
A H JONES
Charles S JONES
Christopher — JONES
David L JONES
D — JONES
D — JONES
E M JONES
F J JONES
H C JONES
Jasper N JONES
J W JONES
L T JONES
Montgomery A JONES
Philip — JONES
Robert — JONES
Thomas B JONES
Thomas T JONES
W H JONES
William — JONES
William D JONES
Zach T JONES
Henry Coley JORDAN
James H JUDD
James C KANE
John C KANE
W S KAUFMAN
C M KEBLINGER
Wilber — KEBLINGER
Samuel W KEEN
Benjamin — KEENE
Isham — KEITH

James — KEITH
James W KEITH
John C KELLEY
J S KELLEY
James F KEMPER
Joseph H KEMPER
John — KENDELL
John — KENIN
Joseph — KENNALLY
F J KENNEDY
Thomas — KENNEDY
William H KENNEDY
J Frank KENNERLY
George S KENNON
William M KENNON
William Dison KENNY
Clinton — KEPHART
J R KEPHART
F Howard KERFOOT
John N KERNER
Jacob V KERNS
Vincent — KERNS
John S KERR
John Randolph KERRICK
Phillip — KEY
William — KEYES
William A KEYS
Hugh P KEYSEAR
L T KEYSEAR
Thomas — KIDD
E — KILPATRICK
J C KINCHELOE
Redmond S KINCHELOE
William S KINCHELOE
W W KINCHELOE
James W KINES
Edwin D KING
John T KING
Thomas — KING
Gabriel — KINSEY
James R KIRBY
Joseph H KIRBY
T R KIRBY
Enoch — KIRKPATRICK
M — KIRKPATRICK
W S KIRKPATRICK
John — KIRWIN

Charles E KITE
James P KITE
Martin — KITE
Thomas O KITE
— — KITT
— — KITT
Philip A KLIPSTEIN
Edward — KLOMAN
Ludwell — KNAPP
Richard — KNOTT
Otto — KUPFERSCHMIDT
Jerome — KUTH
M P LACY
Frank — LAKE
James R LAKE
Ludwell — LAKE
Thomas W LAKE
Charles P LAMBERT
Maurice W LAMBERT
J A LANALLEN
Thomas W LANDING
Willis J LANDRUM
W J LANDRUM
David D LANE
David Frank LANE
Francis — LANE
Mortimore — LANE
Thomas — LANSDALL
J R LANSFORD
Harrison C LARRABEE
— — LARRY
F — LATHAM
Thomas R LATHAM
Jake — LAVENDER
David — LAW
Jimmie M LAWRENCE
John Mason LAWRENCE
John — LAWS
Theodore F LEACH
Thornton — LEACH
Ninian W LEACHE
William A LEAVAE
Edmund G LEAVELL
Clifton — LEE
Philip — LEE
Thomas — LEE
James E LEGG

James L LEGG
David E LEONARD
John B LEWIS
Richard C LEWIS
James T LILLISTON
J W LIMBRICK
Joseph B LINDSEY
D — LINKINS
John W LINTHICUM
William F LINTZ
James T LITTLETON
John A LLEWELLYN
W Frank LOBBINS
John W LOCKE
Robert N LOCKE
George S LOFLAND
James A LOUNDS
Lucien — LOVE
Thomas R LOVE
William O LOVELACE
Josiah — LOW
Daniel — LOWE
Charles D LOWNDES
James — LOWNDES
Fielding — LUCAS
William J/B LUCAS
Robert C LUCIUS
Robert W LUCK
S T LUCKETT
E C LUNCEFORD
John H LUNCEFORD
J W LUNSFORD
Thomas R LUNSFORD
Alexander — LYLE
Michael — LYNCH
Albert — LYNN
Albert W LYNN
G E LYNN
James Shirley LYNN
John F LYNN
John T LYNN
William Benjamin LYNN
William T LYON
James — LYONS
Robert — MACKALL
Thomas — MACLAY
Beatty C MACOY

Lafayette — MADDOX
James H MADDOX
Martin — MADDOX
Henry Cabell MADDUX
George — MADISON
Thomas H MAGILL
Matthew F MAGNER
Philip — MAJOR
Augustine L/C MAJORS
J B MAJORS
James H MALLORY
Thomas F MALLORY
William L MANLY
Anthony E MANNEYETTE
"Captain" — MANNING
Ed — MANYOTT
J H MARCELLUS
John A MARCHANT
Meredith W MARMADUKE
Milton M MARMADUKE
J H MARSELAS
G R MARSHALL
James Edward MARSHALL
J P MARSHALL
J R MARSHALL
P H MARSHALL
C S MARTIN
Thomas — MARTIN
William — MARTIN
Charles — MASON
Daniel Murray MASON
John S MASON
John T MASON
Landon R MASON
S D MASON
George W MASSIE
Henry L MASSIE
John R MASSIE
George W MATTHEWS
L F MATTOCK
Robert W MATTOCKS
Joseph — MAYHUGH
Richard — MAYHUGH
William — MAYO
W·L MC ALLISTER
William Armstead MC ATEE
Charles — MC BLAIR

James W MC BROOM
Joseph W MC CARTY
Ranger — MC COBB
C A MC COURT
— — MC COY
John — MC CUE
Mahlon T MC DANIEL
Charles — MC DONOUGH
James — MC DONALD
John F MC DONALD
Samuel M MC DONALD
William L MC DONALD
Frank — MC GINNIS
Hugh M MC ILHANY
John W MC ILHANY
Charles H MC INTOSH
C R MC INTOSH
James L MC INTOSH
James L MC INTOSH
Jesse P MC INTOSH
Thomas B MC KAY
Charles L MC KEM
John — MC KENNEY
Allan — MC KIM
F M MC LANE
Thomas — MC LANE
William — MC QUEEN
— — MC QUINN
Milton — MC VEIGH
Newton — MC VEIGH
Richard — MC VEIGH
E S MEADE
John — MEEKS
John T MEGGINSON
James M MELTON
John W MELTON
Henry S MENEFEE
Corbin W MERCER
Lewis E MEREDITH
S G METCALFE
Arthur V MILHOLLAND
Jospeh C MILLAN
Alexander — MILLER
George R MILLER
James N MILLER
J M MILLER
John — MILLER

Oscar D MILLER
T A MILLER
Thomas I MILLER
William M MILLS
J — MILTON
John W MILTON
Theodore D MILTON
Albert G MINOR
A B MITCHELL
B P MITCHELL
James Jackson MITCHELL
Thomas — MOCLEIR
Daniel J MOFFET
David G MOHLER
Lee H MOHLER
Theodore — MOHLER
Charles W MONROE
L S MONROE
Aristides — MONTEIRO
Richard P MONTJOY
Jacob L MOON
James M MOON
Henry R MOORE
James B MOORE
James H MOORE
William E MOORE
Richard — MORAN
William H/E MORECOCK
Benjamin — MORGAN
Thomas — MORGAN
J L MORRIS
W T MORTON
John S MOSBY
Junius B MOSBY
William H MOSBY
Thomas — MOSS
J W MOZINGO
John W MUNSON
A W MURKLAND
John — MURPHY
R W MURPHY
Thomas L MURPHY
John — MUSE
William H MUSSER
Alamander — MYERS
Elemander — MYERS
Stephen — MYERS

Benoni F NALLS
Enoch — NALLS
James K/Polk NALLS
S P NALLS
Ludwell — NAPP
Cincinatus A NASH
G W NAYLOR
D — NEAL
John — NELSON
Joseph H NELSON
Lucian M NELSON
Robert E NELSON
William J NEWBILL
L W NEWBY
D S NEWCOMB
John — NEWCOMB
— — NEWELL
Bushrod — NEWLAND
Sylvester — NEWMAN
Charles E NICHOLAS
Joel R NIXON
— — NOEL
George — NORFOLK
Williamson — NORRIS
— — NORTHCRAFT
Andrew H NOTT
Roger — NOTT
John J NOTTINGHAM
Tobe — NOTTINGHAM
William S NUCKELLS
John W NUNN
George M O'BANNON
Persley Henry O'BANNON
Edward H O'BRIEN
John — O'BRIEN
Thomas — O'MEARA
John — O'NEIL
Archibald — ODEN
Thomas J OGG
Alexander Washington OMEAR
William E ORMSBY
John C ORRICK
Robert H ORRISON
Robert, Jr — OULD
William Thomas OVERBY
Marshall — OVERFIELD
James G OWEN

John/Joseph W OWENS
Morris/Mauri B OWENS
William M OWENS
John P PAGE
Mortimer W PAGE
Undrel M PAGE
J R PAIGE
William Ben PALMER
William H PALMER
James H PARKER
Joseph — PARKER
Thomas — PARR
Robert B PARROTT
— — PARROW
Charles E PARSON
Alexander Lee PATTERSON
Warden — PATTERSON
William W PATTERSON
H W PATTIE
O H PATTIE
Thomas — PAVOE
Charlie — PAXSON
G W PAYNE
John A PAYNE
John R PAYNE
William W PAYNE
Craven — PEARSON
H Clay PEARSON
John W PEARSON
Luther E PEARSON
Taylor — PEARSON
W G PEARSON
James — PEEBLES
C H PENDLETON
C Mason PENDLETON
Palmer — PENDLETON
Rupert R PERCIVAL
— — PERRON
S — PERRON
John Taylor PERRY
P M PERRY
J M PETERS
W O PETTY
Jeff — PHELPS
John W PHILLIPS
Walter S PHILLIPS
William — PHILLIPS

George — PICKETT
James E PICKETT
John Emery PITTS
Thomas E PIXLEY
George William POLLARD
Johnson — POMEROY
Nathaniel — PONTIER
Joshua — POOL
Edward — PORTER
John A PORTER
John J PORTER
Lack — PORTER
H A POSTON
B — POWELL
Homer F POWELL
John James/Audubon POWELL
Lewis — POWELL
Rupert R POWELL
S T POWELL
Richard — PRESGRAVES
C D PRICE
Joseph — PRICE
George H PRIEST
John H PRIEST
John W PRINCE
A F PRINTZ
Isateus — PRINTZ
John David PRINTZ
John T PRITCHARD
L H PROSSER
Ralph Hylton PROSSER
John B PROUT
John W PURYEAR
S W PUTNAM
Charles H QUARLES
Henry W QUARLES
Frank H RAHM
Addison T RALLS
John C RALLY
Ashton — RAMEY
D W RAMEY
J M RAMEY
L W RAMEY
Matthew — RAMEY
— — RAMSEY
Joseph — RANCK
Haney — RANDOLPH

John — RANDOLPH
Norman V RANDOLPH
William — RANEY
B B RANSOM
Charles — RATCLIFFE
George E RATCLIFFE
John — RATCLIFFE
George E RAUM
W T RAYMOND
John W READ
Ashton — REAMY
Robert — REAMY
Louis — REARDON
Patrick J REARDON
P H REARDON
Edward W RECTOR
Thomas B RECTOR
Welby H RECTOR
J O REDD
Polk D REDD
J D REDMOND
John — REDWIN
James — REED
John R REED
John W REED
Joseph — REED/REID
S W REEN
David — REEVES
Thomas H REILEY
J S RENNER
J W RENNER
J — RENWICK
George L REVERCOMB
P N REVERCOMB
S H REYNOLDS
William L REYNOLDS
Henry C RHODES
Lafayette — RHODES
Nathaniel — RHODES
James W RICE
Thomas B RICE
Adolphus Edward RICHARDS
Adolphus J RICHARDS
Dulany — RICHARDS
Henry — RICHARDS
J M RICHARDS
Thomas W/T RICHARDS

Andrew — RICHARDSON

G H RICHARDSON

John A RICHARDSON

Montague L RICHARDSON

W A RICHARDSON

John E RICKETTS

Charles — RIDDICK

T R RIDGELEY

Samuel — RIDGELY

J T RIDGEWAY

Joshua — RIGGS

P O RILEY

Noble B RINKER

G W RINSEY

David H RITTER

James M RIXEY

R — RIXEY

Thomas E RIXEY

W — ROBBINS

Franklin — ROBERTS

Ed — ROBERTS

George A ROBERTSON

W G ROBERTSON

William H ROBERTSON

Francis E ROBEY

John W ROBEY

Clairborne — ROBINSON

D F ROBINSON

Henry H ROBINSON

John D ROBINSON

John — ROBINSON

Julien/Jului C ROBINSON

Monroe — ROBINSON

William H ROBINSON

D — ROBSON

Fayette — RODES

James — ROGERS

Samuel E ROGERS

Samuel S ROGERS

S E ROGERS

Addison — ROLLA

M H ROLLER

L R ROLLINS

Sanders B ROLLINS

Stephen Brooks ROLLINS

— — ROSAN

Alex Fontaine ROSE

S T ROSERN

John A ROSSER

John A ROSSON

Edwin — ROWZEE

George A ROWZEE

John E ROWZEE

J W ROWZEE

Lawrence — ROYSTER

James W ROYSTON

John W ROYSTON

Matthew — ROYSTON

A C RUCKER

Washington Irving RUCKER

W J RUCKER

Frank M RUDASILL

J A RUDASILL

Royal S RUDD

Noble — RUNKLE

B W RUSSELL

H C RUSSELL

Henry — RUSSELL

James B RUSSELL

John S RUSSELL

John W RUSSELL

Thomas A RUSSELL

Thomas — RUST

W H RUTLEDGE

H — RUTTER

James W RUTTER

Albert — RYAN

G W RYAN

Lawrence — RYAN

Frank — SANDERS

John H SANDERS

J W S SANDERS

E L SANFORD

John A SAUNDERS

John — SAUNDERS

Thomas — SAUNDERS

William E SAUNDERS

James W SCOTT

John — SCOTT

Robert — SCOTT

W — SCOTT

Matthew V SCURRY

John Thomas SEALOCK

J C SEATON

James J SEATON
James — SEATON
Thomas R SEAY
Frank — SEDGWICK
George — SEIBERT
John — SEIBERT
Albert — SETTLE
Henry C SETTLE
C/G W SHACKLEFORD
Durand — SHACKLEFORD
Elzey D SHACKELFORD
John L SHACKLEFORD
Edward — SHACKLETT
J M SHAMBLIN
Christopher C SHAW
Henry/Harry — SHAW
Jackson — SHAW
George — SHEAFER
George — SHEARER/SHEAR
John W SHEARER
J B SHEPHERD
John M SHEPPARD
J Will SHEPPARD
R S SHERMAN
William — SHERRY/SHERRE
— — SHIELDS
— — SHIELDS
James J SHIELDS
W Ben SHIPLEY
Tom Benton SHIPLEY
J D SHOWALTER
Charles E SHRIVER
B J SHUMATE
Zack — SHUMATE
J M SHYECK
G — SIDNOR
Braden T SILCOTT
James A SILMAN
John A SILMAN
John W SIMONS
Henry — SIMPERS
Benjamin T SIMPSON
James Polk SIMPSON
John T SIMPSON
N V SIMPSON
Matthew A SIMS
Charles — SINCLAIR

George A SINCLAIR
James W SINCLAIR
John A SINCLAIR
John C SINCLAIR
John M SINCLAIR
Joseph — SINCLAIR
Harry T SINNOTT
Henry — SINNOTT
W B SINNOTT
Andrew J SISK
James H SISK
Nicholas B SKELTON
Lemuel — SKILLMAN
George — SKINNER
H W SKINNER
J M SKINNER
Williamson — SKINNER
John — SLACK
George M SLATER
Henry B SLATER
Daniel F SLAUGHTER
Henry — SMALLWOOD
John L SMALLWOOD
John M SMALLWOOD
W — SMALLWOOD
Boyd M SMITH
Channing M SMITH
Charles Edward SMITH
David L SMITH
Edward — SMITH
Edward T SMITH
Fred — SMITH
George A SMITH
George W SMITH
Henry E/C SMITH
Henry — SMITH
H H SMITH
James M SMITH
James P SMITH
J B SMITH
J Henley SMITH
John — SMITH
Norment — SMITH
Philip — SMITH
Randolph C SMITH
R F SMITH
Samuel H SMITH

W Garland SMITH

William R SMITH

W J SMITH

J G SMOOT

Joseph K SMOOT

William F SMOOT

Edwin B SNEAD

William J SNEAD

Alonzo B SNYDER

W E SOMERS

W S SOURS

John F SOWERS

J Richard SOWERS

J W SOWERS

William D SOWERS

Z T SOWERS

Christopher C SPAIN

John C SPALDING

J H SPENCE

J M SPENCER

John M SPENCER

Charles H SPICER

James A SPICER

Benjamin — SPINDLE

Robert — SPINDLE

Alexander — SPINKS

Lewis — SPITTLE

William R SPITTLE

Charles H SPITZER

P A SPOTTSWOOD

Charles — ST CLAIR

William Howard STANLEY

James P STARK

J T STARK

William — STATON

Billings — STEELE

David — STEPHENSON

Charles — STETTLER

John C STEWART

— — STINSON

James E STONE

Thomas — STONE

William R STONE

J M STONESIFFER

Joanis E STORKE

J E STOWE

Thomas Emmett STRATTON

B Frank STRINGFELLOW

Alfred M STROTHER

Francis A STROTHER

James M STROTHER

James W STROTHER

George W SUMMERS

Jerome — SUMMERS

William — SUMMERS

William — SUTTON

Baynard — SWANN

Hugh L SWART

James — SWEENEY

B Harry SWEETING

John A SWITZER

George R SYDNOR

John W SYMONS

Henry H TABER

John — TALIAFERO

L — TALIAFERO

S C TALLEY

William H TALLEY

Gustave R TANEY

Wallace N TANSILL

John, Jr — TAYLOE

Alfred — TAYLOR

George W TAYLOR

William C TAYLOR

William H TAYLOR

William P TAYLOR

— — TEMPLETON

Robert Stockton TERRY

Daniel L THOMAS

John H THOMAS

Robert — THOMAS

Thurp — THOMAS

William P THOMAS

Alfred — THOMPSON

Edward — THOMPSON

Edward — THOMPSON

E F THOMPSON

F D THOMPSON

George W THOMPSON

Gilbert — THOMPSON

John D THOMPSON

John — THOMPSON

Minor — THOMPSON

Thomas J THOMPSON

D — THORNE
Arthur — THORP
Benjamin — THRIFT
Thomas — THROOP
James — TILLETT
John R TILLETT
William B TOMPSON
Thomas William TONGUE
Lalley P TOOMEY
Gustave — TOUNEY
E M TOWLES
Robert O TOWLES
James T TRABORO
James Philip TRAMMELL
L B TRAMMELL
WIlliam — TRAMMELL
Michael — TRAPP
Alonzo — TRAVERS
James T TRAYHON
J S TRENARY
B F TRICE
S — TRIMNELL
B Addison TRIPLETT
F D TRIPLETT
George W TRIPLETT
James P TRIPLETT
L B TRIPLETT
Reuben — TRIPLETT
Richard C TRIPLETT
S B TRIPLETT
Samuel H TRUNDLE
William H TRUNDLE
Berkeley M/B TUCKER
R B TUCKER
George R/L TURBERVILLE
Richard A TURLEY
James Frank TURNER
John W TURNER
W B TURNER
Thomas B TURNER
William H TURNER
William Thomas TURNER
William W TURNER
Charles E TYLER
Bushrod — UNDERWOOD
John — UNDERWOOD
Samuel — UNDERWOOD

U — UNDERWOOD
B D UTTERBACK
A S UTZ
John C UTZ
Charles — VANDEVANTER
D H VANDEVANTER
Joseph H VANDEVANTER
L C VANDEVANTER
Townsend H VANDEVANTER
William — VANDEVANTER
Edward C VANHORN
Franklin D VAUGHN
James — VAUGHN
P D VAUGHN
W H VERNON
Charles B VEST
Thomas A VEST
Charles O VIERS
Robert — VON MASSOW
Jacob W VORHEES
James — WADDLE
W — WADDY
W E WADE
Samuel M WAGGAMAN
Denis C WAITS
Willaim O WALDEN
Arthur S WALKER
Charles H WALKER
Charles P WALKER
C S WALKER
George C WALKER
George R WALKER
J M WALKER
John E WALKER
John P WALKER
Lewis F WALKER
Robert S WALKER
John T WALLER
William A WALLS
William B WALSTON
— — WALTERS
Henry S WALTERS
Jerry — WARD
Felix H WARE
Richard Dorsey WARFIELD
Thomas R WARING
Grandison — WARRING

George — WASHINGTON
Lloyd — WASHINGTON
Hugh T WATERS
John C WATKINS
John R WATKINS
John — WATT
Cornelius C WATTS
John W WATTS
Edward F WAYMAN
Joseph — WAYMAN
Newton B WAYMAN
James W WEAVER
Robert L WEAVER
Thomas J WEAVER
Z Taylor WEAVER
G W WEEMS
F H WEIR
William B WEIR
William — WELCH
W R WELCH
Zero W WELLS
Frank A WENTZELL
William P WEST
Walter S WHALEY
Alex J WHARTON
Henry — WHARTON
John W WHEATLEY
W L WHEELWRIGHT
C D WHELT
Hugh W WHITE
John L WHITE
John M WHITE
John W WHITE
Meade F WHITE
W B WHITE
B F WHITESCARVER
D L WHITESCARVER
George A WHITESCARVER
William R WHITESCARVER
Charles F WHITING
A J WHITLOW
Charles H WHITTLEY
Jeremiah — WIGHT
Henry A WILBURN
J — WILCHER
John — WILD
John Terrell WILKES

James — WILLETT
Addison — WILLIAMS
Adolphus — WILLIAMS
David — WILLIAMS
Edwin — WILLIAMS
Francis — WILLIAMS
Franklin — WILLIAMS
H W WILLIAMS
James T WILLIAMS
John J WILLIAMS
J T WILLIAMS
Sewell T WILLIAMS
James J WILLIAMSON
John — WILLINGHAM
A C WILLIS
A S WILSON
James W WILSON
Jeremiah D WILSON
John T WILSON
M — WILSON
Stephen H WILSON
W C WILSON
William H WILSON
Charles — WILTSHIRE
James G WILTSHIRE
G W WIMMS
J S WIMSATT
— — WINDER
Armsted L WINES
George S WINES
T S WINES
A F WINZELLE
Henry M WITHERS
John B WITHERS
R T WOLFE
Charles F WOLLARD
C F WOOD
G G WOOD
H K WOOD
William S WOOD
Edgar S WOODEN
Peter — WOODEN
William W WOODHOUSE
Harvey K WOODS
Luke E WOODWARD
T A WOODWARD
W S WOODWARD

★

Louis/Lewis — WOODYARD
Francis M WOOLF
Charles — WORSAM
Albert — WRENN
JAMES W WRENN
Daniel Giraud WRIGHT
S B WRIGHT
Thomas S WYNE
Charles N YAGER
Frank W YAGER
— — YATES

Francis Marion YATES
J Y YATES
George — YELLOTT
Albert F YERBY
T — YERBY
William M YERBY
Jacob — YOUNG
Lewis — YOUNG
Charles — YOWELL
James G YOWELL

NOTES

Works cited by author and short titles will be found in full in the Bibliography. The following abbreviations are used in the Notes:

B & L	*Battles and Leaders of the Civil War*
BOM	*Baltimore and Ohio Magazine*
CCHA	Clarke County Historical Association
CMH	*Confederate Military History*
CSR/NA	Compiled Service Records/National Archives
CV	*Confederate Veteran*
CWTI	*Civil War Times Illustrated*
DU	Duke University
EU	Emory University
GAS	*Grand Army Scout and Mail*
HANDL	Handley Library
HFNHP	Harpers Ferry National Historic Park
HL	Huntington Library
LC	Library of Congress
MA	*Military Affairs*
MHS	Maryland Historical Society
MOLLUS	*Military Order Loyal Legion of the United States*
MR	*Military Review*
MRF/ WHS	Mosby's Rangers File/Warren Heritage Society
MSHS	Massachusetts Historical Society
OR	*The War of the Rebellion: A Compilation of the Official Records of the Union and Confederate Armies*

★

PCCHA	*Proceedings of the Clarke County Historical Association*
PSU	The Pennsylvania State University
PWCL	Prince William County Library
SB	*Southern Bivouac*
SHSP	*Southern Historical Society Papers*
SMM	Stuart-Mosby Museum
SMSP	Sky Meadows State Park
TBL	Thomas Balch Library
UMICH	University of Michigan
USAMHI	United States Army Military History Institute
USC	United States Census, Seventh, 1860
USSM	*United States Service Magazine*
UVA	University of Virginia
VHS	Virginia Historical Society
VMI	Virginia Military Institute
WRCM	Warren Rifles Confederate Museum

PROLOGUE

1. Mosby, *B & L* III, p. 149; Mosby, *"Stealing A General,"* p. 2, VHS; Williamson, *Mosby's Rangers*, p. 33.
2. Williamson, *Mosby's Rangers*, p. 35; Mosby, *Memoirs*, pp. 151, 152.
3. Williamson, *Mosby's Rangers*, pp. 34, 35; Mosby, *B & L* III, p. 148; Mosby, *Memoirs*, p. 172; *Spies, Scouts*, p. 117.
4. Mosby, *"Stealing A General,"* p. 2, VHS; Richards, "Capture," *SB*, p. 251; Williamson, *Mosby's Rangers*, p. 36.
5. Williamson, *Mosby's Rangers*, pp. 37, 39; *OR*, 25, pt. 1, pp. 1121, 1122; pt. 2, p. 30, all references hereafter are to Series I unless otherwise cited; Scott, *Partisan Life*, pp. 43, 45; Washington *Evening Star*, March 14, 1863; Richards, "Capture," *SB*, pp. 251, 252.
6. Williamson, *Mosby's Rangers*, p. 39; Glazier, *Three Years*, p. 151; *Fairfax County*, p. 69.
7. Plum, *Military Telegraph* I, p. 360; Williamson, *Mosby's Rangers*, p. 39; Geddes, *Fairfax County*, p. 95.
8. Williamson, *Mosby's Rangers*, p. 39.
9. Ibid., pp. 39, 40; *Fairfax County*, p. 66; *Spies, Scouts*, p. 177; Faust, *Encyclopedia*, p. 724; Mosby, Letter, C. W. Misc. Coll., USAMHI.
10. Mosby, *Memoirs*, pp. 173, 175; Williamson, *Mosby's Rangers*, 40.
11. Mosby, *B & L* III, p. 151; Williamson, *Mosby's Rangers*, pp. 40, 41.
12. Williamson, *Mosby's Rangers*, p. 41; *OR*, 25, pt. 1, p. 1122.
13. Jones, *Gray Ghosts*, pp. 156, 175; Williamson, *Mosby's Rangers*, p. 41, 42; *OR*, 25, pt. 1, p. 43.
14. Williamson, *Mosby's Rangers*, pp. 37, 41, 42; Mosby, *"Stealing A General,"* p. 5, VHS.

15. Richards, "Capture," *SB*, p. 252; Williamson, *Mosby's Rangers*, p. 44; Rodenbaugh, *History*, p. 36; J. R. Morey to Cousin Will, March 5, 1863, Morey, Letters, UMICH.
16. Mosby, *B & L* III, p. 151; Williamson, *Mosby's Rangers*, p. 44; Mosby, *Memoirs*, pp. 180, 181.
17. Mosby, *B & L* III, p. 151; Williamson, *Mosby's Rangers*, p. 44.
18. Williamson, *Mosby's Rangers*, p. 46; *OR*, pt. 1, p. 1122.

CHAPTER ONE

1. Mosby, *Memoirs*, p. 28.
2. Ibid., pp. 1, 5; Siepel, *Rebel*, p. 21; Jones, *Ranger Mosby*, p. 16.
3. Mosby, *Memoirs*, p. 6; Jones, *Ranger Mosby*, pp. 18, 19.
4. Siepel, *Rebel*, p. 25; Jones, *Ranger Mosby*, pp. 20, 21.
5. Jones, *Ranger Mosby*, pp. 21, 22.
6. Ibid., p. 21; Siepel, *Rebel*, pp. 25, 26, 27.
7. Jones, *Ranger Mosby*, pp. 22, 23; Siepel, *Rebel*, p. 27; Mosby, *Memoirs*, pp. 7, 8.
8. Jones, *Ranger Mosby*, pp. 23, 24; Mosby, *Memoirs*, pp. 8, 9.
9. Jones, *Ranger Mosby*, pp. 23, 24; Siepel, *Rebel*, p. 27; Mosby, *Memoirs*, p. 9.
10. Jones, *Ranger Mosby*, pp. 25, 26; Siepel, *Rebel*, p. 29.
11. Jones, *Ranger Mosby*, pp. 27, 28; Siepel, *Rebel*, pp. 5, 6; *CMH* III, p. 1057; Mosby, Papers, UVA.
12. Siepel, *Rebel*, p. 13; Jones, *Ranger Mosby*, pp. 29, 33.
13. Wallace, *Guide*, p. 40; Jones, *Ranger Mosby*, p. 39; *CMH* III, p. 1057.
14. Mosby, *Memoirs*, pp. 48, 49; *CMH* III, p. 1057.
15. Blackford, *War Years*, p. 14.
16. Mosby, *Memoirs*, p. 23.
17. Mosby, Papers, UVA; Cooke, *Wearing*, p. 104; Jones, *Ranger Mosby*, p. 57.
18. Mosby to Pauline Mosby, February 14, 1862, Mosby, Papers, UVA; Mosby, *Memoirs*, p. 102; Jones, *Ranger Mosby*, p. 57.
19. Mosby to Marcus J. Wright, February 22, 1896, Mosby, Papers, USAMHI; Mitchell, *Letters*, p. 73; Mosby, *Memoirs*, p. 102.
20. Mosby to Pauline Mosby, June 16, 1862, Mosby, Papers, UVA; Mosby, *Memoirs*, pp. 110, 111.
21. *OR*, 25, pt. 2, p. 594.
22. Bakeless, *Spies*, pp. 103, 104; Collins, *Mosby*, p. 5; *OR*, Series II, 4, p. 442.
23. Jones, *Ranger Mosby*, pp. 67, 68; Faust, *Encyclopedia*, p. 229.
24. Mosby, *B & L* III, p. 148; Divine, interview, October 19, 1988; Scheel, *Civil War*, p. 84; Jones, *Ranger Mosby*, p. 68.
25. Mosby, *Memoirs*, p. 216; Mosby, *B & L* III, p. 148.
26. Williamson, *Mosby's Rangers*, p. 15.
27. Munson, *Reminiscences*, pp. 15–16.
28. Ibid., pp. 15, 17; Mosby, *Memoirs*, p. 23; Schubert, Papers, USAMHI; Bryan, *Joseph Bryan*, p. 123.
29. New York *Times*, August 2, 1865; Bryan, *Joseph Bryan*, p. 123; Cooke,

    Wearing, p. 104; Schubert, Papers, USAMHI; Munson, *Reminiscences*, p. 17; Jones, *Ranger Mosby*, p. 14.

30. Cooke, *Wearing*, p. 104; Munson, *Reminiscences*, p. 17; Garrett, *Raiders*, p. 63; Williamson, *Mosby's Rangers*, p. 96.

31. Williamson, *Mosby's Rangers*, p. 96; Schubert, Papers, USAMHI; MRF/WHS.

32. Garrett, *Raiders*, p. 63; Klonis, *Guerrilla Warfare*, p. 21; Siepel, *Rebel*, pp. xvii, xix; MRF/WHS.

33. Williamson, *Mosby's Rangers*, p. 97; Siepel, *Rebel*, xvii.

34. Cooke, *Wearing*, pp. 110–111; Monteiro, *War Reminiscences*, p. 195.

35. Cooke, *Wearing*, pp. 104, 111; *CMH* III, p. 1058.

36. Siepel, *Rebel*, pp. xiv, xvii.

37. Mosby, *B & L* III, p. 148.

38. Ibid., p. 148; Mosby, "Mosby," *GAS* V, No. 5, p. 8; Scott, *Partisan Life*, p. 20.

39. Emerson, *Life*, p. 298; Head, *History*, p. 15n.

40. Mosby, "Mosby," *GAS* V, No. 45, p. 8; Cooke, *Wearing*, p. 109.

CHAPTER TWO

1. Edmonds, *Journals*, p. 130.

2. Broun, "Family Events," UVA.

3. Dulany, Diary, VHS.

4. Hotchkiss, "Map of Fauquier & Loudoun Co's VA.," LC; Scheel, *Civil War*, p. 2.

5. Scheel, *Civil War*, pp. 2, 3; Poland, *From Frontier*, pp. 74, 75; Marsh, "Water Mills," MSS, TBL; Kirkby, "Partisan," p. 3.

6. Scheel, *Civil War*, p. 2; Poland, *From Frontier*, p. 65; Turner, *Loudoun County*, p. 11; Kirkby, "Partisan," p. 3; Goodhart, *History*, p. 4.

7. Scheel, *Civil War,* pp. 2, 5; Hotchkiss, "Map of Fauquier & Loudoun Co's VA.," LC.

8. Poland, *From Frontier*, p. 68; Goodhart, *History*, pp. 3, 107; Head, *History*, pp. 71, 72, 75, 76.

9. Williams, *Legends*, p. 199.

10. Jones, *Ranger Mosby*, pp. 69, 70.

11. Ibid., p. 71; Scott, *Partisan Life*, p. 63; Mosby to F. F. Bowen, July 25, 1898, Bowen, Papers, VHS; Munson, *Reminiscences*, p. 4.

12. Jones, *Ranger Mosby*, pp. 71, 72; Williamson, *Mosby's Rangers*, p. 18n, 495; *CMH*, III, p. 415; Mosby to F. F. Bowen, July 25, 1898, Bowen, Papers, VHS; CSR/NA.

13. Scott, *Partisan Life*, p. 25; Klonis, *Guerrilla Warfare*, p. 20; Mosby, *B & L* III, p. 149.

14. Mosby, *B & L* III, p. 149; *OR*, 25, pt. 2, pp. 29–3l; Rowe, "Camp Tales," UMICH.

15. Mosby, *Memoirs*, p. 162; Munson, *Reminiscences*, p. 42; Scott, *Partisan Life*, pp. 25, 26; Jones, *Ranger Mosby*, p. 74; Broun, "Family Events," UVA.

16. Jones, *Ranger Mosby*, p. 75; Scott, *Partisan Life*, p. 26.

17. *OR*, 25, pt. 1, p. 5; Scott, *Partisan Life*, p. 26; CSR/NA; Mosby to J. E. B. Stuart, February 4, 1863, Mosby, Papers, LC.
18. *OR*, 25, pt. 1, p. 5; Scott, *Partisan Life*, pp. 21, 27.
19. *OR*, 25, pt. 1, p. 5.
20. Ibid., p. 6; J. E. B. Stuart to Mosby, February 8, 1863, Mosby, Papers, LC.
21. Mitchell, *Letters*, p. 29; Jones, *Ranger Mosby*, p. 78.
22. Broun, "Family Events," UVA; Scott, *Partisan Life*, p. 30; *OR*, 25, pt. 1, p. 37.
23. Munson, *Reminiscences*, pp. 41, 42, 52; Scott, *Partisan Life*, pp. 33, 54.
24. Williamson, *Mosby's Rangers*, pp. 27, 28; Scott, *Partisan Life*, pp. 38, 48, 62, 142; Munson, *Reminiscences*, pp. 42, 43; Gott, *Years*, p. xix; CSR/NA.
25. Mosby, *Memoirs*, pp. 168–169; Scott, *Partisan Life*, pp. 33, 34.
26. Munson, *Reminiscences*, p. 46; Williamson, *Mosby's Rangers*, pp. 30, 31.
27. Crawford, *Mosby*, pp. 76, 77.
28. *OR*, 25, pt. 1, p. 37.
29. Benedict, *Vermont*, II, p. 582; Broun, "Family Events," UVA.
30. Benedict, *Vermont*, II, p. 582; Divine, interview, October 19, 1988; Poland, *From Frontier*, p. 98.
31. Scott, *Partisan Life*, p. 42; Benedict, *Vermont*, II, p. 582; Broun, "Family Events," UVA.
32. Williamson, *Mosby's Rangers*, p. 33.
33. Mosby, *B & L* III, p. 149.
34. Mosby, *"Stealing A General,"* p. 6 VHS; Mosby, *Memoirs*, p. 45.
35. Mosby, *Memoirs*, p. 45; Mitchell, Letters, pp. 126–127.
36. Mosby, *Memoirs*, p. 183.
37. *OR*, 25, pt. 2, pp. 664, 856.
38. "Special Order #82," Mosby, Papers, LC; CSR/NA.
39. *OR*, 25, pt. 2, p. 857.
40. Munson, *Reminiscences*, p. 43.
41. Thomson and Rauch, *History*, p. 246; Boudrye, *Historic Records*, p. 52.
42. William Hamilton to Mother, March 17, 1863, Hamilton, Papers, LC; Richards, "Capture," *SB*, p. 252; Thayer, *Guerrilla*, p. 180; Faust, *Encyclopedia*, p. 711.
43. Kirkby, "Partisan," p. 32.
44. Washington *Evening Star*, March 9, 1863; Boudrye, *Historic Records*, p. 52.
45. Jones, *Gray Ghosts*, pp. 150, 151, 158; Mitchell, *Letters*, pp. 105; *Fairfax County*, p. 66; Bakeless, *Spies*, p. 61.
46. Jones, *Gray Ghosts*, p. 158; Mosby, Papers, LC.
47. *OR*, 25, 1, pp. 65, 66, 71, 72.
48. Munson, *Reminiscences*, pp. 52–54; Williamson, *Mosby's Rangers*, pp. 50, 51; Wright, Letter, USAMHI; "Record of Actions," USAMHI; *OR*, 25, pt. 2, p. 857.
49. Mosby, *Memoirs*, pp. 149, 185; *OR*, 25, pt. 2, p. 667; Scott, *Partisan Life*, p. 53.
50. Jones, *Ranger Mosby*, p. 101; USC, 1860; Divine, interview, October 19, 1988.

CHAPTER THREE

1. USC, 1860; Divine, interview, October 19, 1988; Poland, *From Frontier*, p. 211.
2. *OR*, 25, pt. 1, p. 72; Munson, *Reminiscences*, p. 55; Scott, *Partisan Life*, pp. 62, 63; Williamson, *Mosby's Rangers*, pp. 51, 52.
3. Scott, *Partisan Life*, pp. 63, 64; Williamson, *Mosby's Rangers*, p. 52.
4. *OR*, 25, pt. 1, p. 77; Benedict, *Vermont* II, p. 585.
5. Benedict, *Vermont* II, pp. 585, 586; *OR*, 25, pt. 1, pp. 77, 78.
6. Cochran, Journal, VHS; Williamson, *Mosby's Rangers*, p. 52; Scott, *Partisan Life*, p. 65; Munson, *Reminiscences*, p. 56.
7. Scott, *Partisan Life*, p. 65; Williamson, *Mosby's Rangers*, pp. 52–54; *OR*, 25, pt. 1, p. 78.
8. Munson, *Reminiscences*, p. 56; *OR*, 25, pt. 1, p. 78.
9. Scott, *Partisan Life*, pp. 66–67; Benedict, *Vermont* II, p. 586; Williamson, *Mosby's Rangers*, p. 54; Munson, *Reminiscences*, pp. 57–59; Jones, Ledgerbook, SMM.
10. *OR*, 25, pt. 1, p. 72; Williamson, *Mosby's Rangers*, p. 54; CSR/NA; Scott, *Partisan Life*, p. 68.
11. *OR*, 25, pt. 1, p. 72; Benedict, *Vermont* II, pp. 586, 587; Williamson, *Mosby's Rangers*, p. 54; Cochran, Journal, VHS; Munson, *Reminiscences*, p. 63; Broun, "Family Events," UVA.
12. *OR*, 25, pt. 1, 72; Scott, *Partisan Life*, pp. 67–79; Munson, *Reminiscences*, p. 59.
13. *OR*, 25, pt. 1, pp. 73, 78; R. E. Lee to Jefferson Davis, April 4, 1863, Mosby, Papers, VHS; CSR/NA.
14. Benedict, *Vermont* II, p. 587; *OR*, 25, pt. 1, p. 78.
15. *OR*, 25, pt. 1, p. 80; Broun, "Family Events," UVA; CSR/NA.
16. Broun, "Family Events," UVA; Gott, *Years*, p. 39.
17. Gott, *Years*, pp. 39, 40, 44; Williamson, *Mosby's Rangers*, p. 231; Scott, *Partisan Life*, p. 73.
18. Gott, *Years*, pp. 39–40.
19. Broun, "Family Events," UVA; Dulany, Diary, VHS.
20. Dulany, Diary, VHS; Edmonds, *Journals*, pp. 142, 258, 259; *OR*, 25, pt. 2, p. 738; Williamson, *Mosby's Rangers*, pp. 13, 14n.
21. *OR*, 25, pt. 2, p. 860.
22. Long, *Civil War*, pp. 342–349.
23. Ibid., pp. 342–350; *OR*, 25, pt. 1, pp. 1057, 1058.
24. White, "Civil War Journal," LC; *OR*, 25, pt. 2, p. 321; Black; *Railroads*, pp. 93, 146; Williamson, *Mosby's Rangers*, p. 63.
25. Broun, "Family Events," UVA.
26. Scott, *Partisan Life*, p. 84; Williamson, *Mosby's Rangers*, p. 56.
27. Scott, *Partisan Life*, p. 85; Munson, *Reminiscences*, pp. 64, 66; Williamson, *Mosby's Rangers*, p. 57; *OR*, 25, pt. 1, p. 1104; pt. 2, p. 861.
28. Scott, *Partisan Life*, pp. 86, 88; Williamson, *Mosby's Rangers*, p. 57; *OR*, 25, pt. 2, p. 861.

29. Scott, *Partisan Life*, pp. 86, 88; Munson, *Reminiscences*, p. 65; *OR*, 25, pt. 1, p. 1104; pt. 2, p. 861; Williamson, *Mosby's Rangers*, p. 57.

30. *OR*, 25, pt. 1, p. 1105, 1106; Benedict, *Army Life*, p. 145; Scott, *Partisan Life*, p. 88; Munson, *Reminiscences*, pp. 65, 67.

31. Edmonds, *Journal*, p. 143; Benedict, *Army Life*, p. 143; Williamson, *Mosby's Rangers*, p. 58; *OR*, 25, pt. 2, p. 861.

32. CSR/NA; Munson, *Reminiscences*, p. 65; Scott, *Partisan Life*, p. 391; Williamson, *Mosby's Rangers*, p. 58; Jones, *Ranger Mosby*, p. 116.

33. CSR/NA; Krick, Collection; Scott, *Partisan Life*, p. 320; Munson, *Reminiscences*, p. 202; Williamson, *Mosby's Rangers*, p. 538.

34. Glazier, *Three Years*, p. 152; Scott, *Partisan Life*, p. 78; Williamson, *Mosby's Rangers*, pp. 60, 61.

35. Beach, *First New York*, p. 321; Glazier, *Three Years*, p. 149; Williamson, *Mosby's Rangers*, p. 442; Leech, *Reveille*, p. 269; Lee, *Personal*, pp. 106, 129; Denison, *Sabres*, p. 228.

36. Stevenson, *Boots*, p. 166; Beach, *First New York*, p. 222.

37. Stevenson, *Boots*, p. 166; Beach, *First New York*, p. 222; Williamson, *Mosby's Rangers*, p. 63.

38. Stevenson, *Boots*, pp. 167–169; Beach, *First New York*, pp. 222–223; Williamson, *Mosby's Rangers*, p. 63.

39. Stevenson, *Boots*, pp. 169, 170; CSR/NA.

40. Stevenson, *Boots*, pp. 170–171; CSR/NA; Scott, *Partisan Life*, p. 78; Dulany, Diary, VHS.

41. Mosby, Papers, VHS; Mosby, Papers, UVA; CSR/NA.

42. *OR*, Series III, 5, pp. 632, 633.

43. *OR*, 25, pt. 2, pp. 861, 862.

44. Munson, *Reminiscences*, p. 68; Scott, *Partisan Life*, p. 92; MRF/WHS; Hotchkiss, "Map of Fauquier Co.," LC.

45. Hotchkiss, "Map of Fauquier Co.," LC: MRF/WHS; Williamson, *Mosby's Rangers*, p. 64; Scott, *Partisan Life*, p. 92; Washington *Evening Star*, June 1, 1863.

46. MRF/WHS; Williamson, *Mosby's Rangers*, pp. 64, 65; Scott, *Partisan Life*, p. 92; Denison, *Sabres*, p. 227; New York *Times*, May 31, 1863; Washington *Evening Star*, June 1, 1863.

47. Munson, *Reminiscences*, p. 71; Lee, *Personal*, pp. 91, 92; "Record of Actions," USAMHI; Scott, *Partisan Life*, p. 93; Williamson, *Mosby's Rangers*, p. 65.

48. Munson, *Reminiscences*, p. 71.

49. Ibid., p. 72; MRF/WHS; "Appraisal," *CWTI* IV, No. 7, p. 5; Scheel, *Civil War*, p. 55.

50. Munson, *Reminiscences*, pp. 72, 73; Alexander, *Mosby's Men*, p. 170; "Record of Actions," USAMHI; MRF/WHS.

51. Alexander, *Mosby's Men*, p. 170; Krick, Collection; CSR/NA; Scott, *Partisan Life*, p. 159.

52. Scott, *Partisan Life*, p. 93; Williamson, *Mosby's Rangers*, p. 65; Munson, *Reminiscences*, p. 73; "Record of Actions," USAMHI.

53. Benedict, *Vermont* II, p. 591; Munson, *Reminiscences*, p. 73; Williamson, *Mosby's Rangers*, p. 65.

54. Munson, *Reminiscences*, pp. 70, 71; Williamson, *Mosby's Rangers*, pp. 65–68; Lee, *Personal*, pp. 93, 95; Isham, *Historical*, p. 19; Benedict, *Vermont* II, p. 591.
55. Jones, *Ranger Mosby*, p. 106; Williamson, *Mosby's Rangers*, p. 66; Krick, Collection; MRF/WHS.
56. *OR*, 46, pt. 1, p. 1043.
57. Bowen, *Massachusetts*, p. 759; Cochran, Journal, VHS.
58. Crawford, *Mosby*, pp. 79–80.
59. Ibid., p. 80.
60. Mosby, *"Stealing A General,"* pp. 1–2, VHS.

CHAPTER FOUR

1. Scheel, *Civil War*, p. 56; Divine, interview, October 19, 1988; Smith, *Middleburg*, p. 229; Jones, *Ranger Mosby*, pp. 83, 132–133; Williamson, *Mosby's Rangers*, p. 69.
2. Smith, *Middleburg*, p. 229; Wallace, *Guide*, p. 71.
3. *OR*, 25, pt. 2, p. 857.
4. Ibid., p. 857.
5. Grant, "Partisan Warfare," *MR*, p. 42; Castel, "Guerrilla War," *CWTI*, p. 9.
6. Grant, "Partisan Warfare," *MR*, pp. 46, 47; *OR*, 51, pt. 2, p. 526.
7. Grant, "Partisan Warfare," *MR*, p. 47; Richmond *Dispatch*, May 8, 1862; Castel, "Guerrilla War," *CWTI*, p. 9.
8. *OR*, Series 4, I, p. 532.
9. Grant, "Partisan Warfare," *MR*, pp. 43, 44, 49.
10. Ibid., pp. 44–46, 52; Wallace, *Guide*, pp. 73–79.
11. CSR/NA; Jones, *Ranger Mosby*, pp. 105, 133; Scott, *Partisan Life*, pp. 97, 101; Williamson, *Mosby's Rangers*, p. 70; Gott, *Years*, p. xxiii.
12. Jones, *Ranger Mosby*, pp. 71, 112, 116; Scott, *Partisan Life*, p. 97; Goldsborough, *Maryland*, p. 256; CSR/NA.
13. CSR/NA; Jones, *Ranger Mosby*, pp. 71, 133; Scott, *Partisan Life*, p. 73.
14. CSR/NA; Gott, *Years*, p. xix; Scott, *Partisan Life*, p. 38; Jones, *Ranger Mosby*, pp. 84, 133, 134.
15. CSR/NA; Scott, *Partisan Life*, p. 97; Scheel, *Civil War*, p. 56.
16. *Famous Adventures*, p. 104; Williamson, *Mosby's Rangers*, p. 69.
17. CSR/NA; Williamson, *Mosby's Rangers*, pp. 532–543; Krick, Collection; Smith, *CV*, 31, p. 356.
18. Munson, *Reminiscences*, p. 238.
19. The antebellum residences of Mosby's Rangers are not complete in the records. My research has established that 797 Rangers definitely were Virginians. Of that figure 189 lived in Fauquier, eighty in Fairfax, eighty-nine in Loudoun, forty-two in Rappahannock and twenty-two in Prince William. From the four nearby Shenandoah Valley counties of Frederick, Jefferson, Clarke and Warren, sixty-four identified recruits joined the battalion. Out-of-state residences of 141 Rangers can be established—seventy-eight from Maryland; sixteen from District of Columbia. The prewar homes of 964 of the 1,902 listed members cannot be definitely ascertained. But by extrap-

olating the numbers, at least 86 percent of the command were Virginians, CSR/NA.

20. Munson, *Reminiscences*, pp. 13, 14, 259.
21. Mosby, "Mosby," *GAS* V, No. 45, p. 8; Hunter, *Women*, p. 25; Munson, *Reminiscences*, p. 5; Jones, *Ranger Mosby*, p. 15.
22. Munson, *Reminiscences*, p. 8; Alexander, *Mosby's Men*, p. 24; *CMH* III, p. 866; CSR/NA; Jones, Ledgerbook, SMM.
23. The records indicate that at least 102 Rangers had prior service, CSR/NA; Alexander, *Mosby's Men*, p. 26; Munson, *Reminiscences*, p. 8; Scott, *Partisan Life*, p. 34.
24. Munson, *Reminiscences*, pp. 25–27; CSR/NA; Jones, Ledgerbook, SMM.
25. Monteiro, *War Reminiscences*, pp. 133–134.
26. Munson, *Reminiscences*, pp. 27, 28; Jones, *Ranger Mosby*, p. 13.
27. Mitchell, *Letters*, p. 105; Williamson, *Mosby's Rangers*, p. 23; *OR*, pt. 1, p. 1108.
28. Munson, *Reminiscences*, pp. 259–260, 261; Alexander, *Mosby's Men*, p. 27; CSR/NA.
29. Alexander, *Mosby's Men*, pp. 27–28; Scott, *Partisan Life*, p. 396; Williamson, *Mosby's Rangers*, pp. 443, 445.
30. Monteiro, *War Reminiscences*, p. 61; Cooke, *Wearing*, p. 104; Jones, *Ranger Mosby*, p. 80; WFR/WHS.
31. Hunter, *CV*, 15, p. 258.
32. Alexander, *Mosby's Men*, pp. 19, 24.
33. Fitts, "Mosby," *Galaxy* II, p. 646.
34. Munson, *Reminiscences*, pp. 233, 234; MRF/WHS.
35. CSR/NA.
36. Gott, *High*, p. 43; Klonis, *Guerrilla Warfare*, p. 20; Alexander, *Mosby's Men*, pp. 29, 31; Williamson, *Mosby's Rangers*, p. 272; Munson, *Reminiscences*, p. 30.
37. Williamson, *Mosby's Rangers*, p. 272; Munson, *Reminiscences*, p. 30; Alexander, *Mosby's Men*, pp. 29–30; Jones, *Ranger Mosby*, p. 105.
38. Munson, *Reminiscences*, p. 30; "Appraisal," *CWTI* IV, No. 7, pp. 4, 5; Williamson, *Mosby's Rangers*, p. 18; Alexander, *Mosby's Men*, p. 29.
39. Alexander, *Mosby's Men*, pp. 29, 43; Scott, *Partisan Life*, p. 395; Munson, *Reminiscences*, p. 38.
40. Williamson, *Mosby's Rangers*, p. 18, 19; Munson, *Reminiscences*, pp. 30, 31, 35; *National Tribune*, August 10, 1910.
41. Munson, *Reminiscences*, p. 31; Mosby, *Memoirs*, pp. 30–31; Siepel, *Rebel*, p. 24; Fitts, "Mosby," *Galaxy* II, p. 647; Williamson, *Mosby's Rangers*, p. 22; "Appraisal," *CWTI* IV, NO. 7, p. 6.
42. Mosby, *Memoirs*, pp. 30, 284, 285; Williamson, *Mosby's Rangers*, p. 21; Munson, *Reminiscences*, pp. 22, 23.
43. Mosby, *Memoirs*, p. 285; WRCM, Collection; Faust, *Encyclopedia*, p. 152; Patterson and DeMarco, *Civil War*, p. 3.
44. Patterson and DeMarco, *Civil War*, p. 3; Faust, *Encyclopedia*, p. 152; Marks, interview, September 14, 1988.
45. Munson, *Reminiscences*, pp. 22, 23, 24; Alexander, *Mosby's Men*, p. 21.

46. Alexander, *Mosby's Men*, pp. 30, 31.
47. Ibid., pp. 19, 130.
48. Ibid., pp. 32, 44; Munson, *Reminiscences*, pp. 10, 36; Jones, *Ranger Mosby*, pp. 105, 106; Jones, Ledgerbook, SMM.
49. Munson, *Reminiscences*, p. 7.
50. Bryan, *Joseph Bryan*, p. 126n; Mosby to John S. Russell, April 5, 1905, Russell, Papers, CCHA; Alexander, *Mosby's Men*, p. 18.
51. Williamson, *Mosby's Rangers*, p. 21; Crawford, *Mosby*, p. 198.
52. Munson, *Reminiscences*, p. 39; Alexander, *Mosby's Men*, p. 16.
53. Alexander, *Mosby's Men*, pp. 17–20; Munson, *Reminiscences*, p. 158; Gott, *Years*, p. 62.
54. Alexander, *Mosby's Men*, pp. 17, 20; Gott, *Years*, p. 62; Monteiro, *War Reminiscences*, p. 96.
55. MRF/WHS.
56. Munson, *Reminiscences*, pp. 37, 38; Jones, *Ranger Mosby*, p. 75; *Famous Adventures*, p. 112; Scott, *Partisan Life*, p. 324.
57. Mosby, "Mosby," *GAS* V, No. 45, p. 8; Mosby, *Memoirs*, p. 216.

CHAPTER FIVE

1. *OR*, 27, pt. 2, p. 787; Mitchell, *Letters*, p. 148.
2. *OR*, 27, pt. 2, p. 787; Williamson, *Mosby's Rangers*, p. 69; Scott, *Partisan Life*, p. 100; *Prince William*, p. 52.
3. Williamson, *Mosby's Rangers*, p. 532; Scott, *Partisan Life*, p. 211; Wallace, *Guide*, p. 57.
4. Beach, *First New York*, p. 228; Stevenson, *Boots*, p. 181; Washington *Evening Star*, June 12, 1863.
5. Beach, *First New York*, p. 228; Stevenson, *Boots*, p. 181; *Old Homes*, p. 454.
6. Beach, *First New York*, p. 228; Stevenson, *Boots*, pp. 181, 182; Washington *Evening Star*, June 12, 1863.
7. Stevenson, *Boots*, p. 182; Divine, interview, October 19, 1988.
8. Beach, *First New York*, p. 228; Stevenson, *Boots*, p. 182; Jones, *Gray Ghosts*, p. 179; Munson, *Reminiscences*, p. 78; CSR/NA.
9. Thomas, *Bold Dragoon*, pp. 233–235.
10. Ibid., p. 235; Williamson, *Mosby's Rangers*, pp. 71–73.
11. *OR*, 27, pt. 3, p. 72.
12. Williamson, *Mosby's Rangers*, pp. 76–79.
13. Mosby, *Memoirs*, p. 216; Bakeless, *Spies*, p. 317; Thomas, *Bold Dragoon*, p. 240; Mitchell, *Letters*, p. 148.
14. Thomas, *Bold Dragoon*, pp. 239–240.
15. Ibid., pp. 241–246.
16. Ibid., pp. 252–253; Mosby, *Stuart's Cavalry*, passim.
17. *OR*, 27, pt. 2, p. 229; CSR/NA.
18. Williamson, *Mosby's Rangers*, pp. 79–80.
19. Munson, *Reminiscences*, p. 215; Faust, *Encyclopedia*, p. 738.
20. Munson, *Reminiscences*, p. 76; Long, *Civil War*, pp. 388–390, 408.

21. Williamson, *Mosby's Rangers*, p. 83; Munson, *Reminiscences*, p. 76; Scott, *Partisan Life*, pp. 109, 111, 112.
22. Williamson, *Mosby's Rangers*, p. 83; Bachman, "Experiences," USAMHI; Watrous, "Mosby," *MOLLUS*, p. 305; *OR*, 27, pt. 2, p. 991.
23. Munson, *Reminiscences*, p. 217; Carter, *Four Brothers*, p. 285; *OR*, 29, pt. 1, pp. 69, 70; pt. 2, p. 992; Baltimore *American*, August 10, 1863.
24. *OR*, 27, pt. 2, p. 992.
25. Ibid., p. 652.
26. Ibid., pp. 991, 992.
27. CSR/NA; *CMH*, III, p. 922; *OR*, 27, pt. 2, p. 979.
28. *OR*, 29, 2, pp. 131, 134; Crowninshield to Mammy, August 21, 1863, Crowninshield, Papers, MSHS.
29. Warner, *Generals In Blue*, p. 284.
30. Crowninshield to Mammy, August 25, 1863, Crowninshield, Papers, MSHS.
31. Emerson, *Life*, pp. 35, 294, 295, 296.
32. Crowninshield to Mammy, August 21, 25, 1863, Crowninshield, Papers, MSHS; *Spies, Scouts*, p. 121.
33. Crowninshield to Mammy, August 25, 1863, Crowninshield, Papers, MSHS; Bowen, *Massachusetts*, p. 759; *OR*, 29, pt. 1, p. 80; Crawford, *Mosby*, pp. 99, 100.
34. *OR*, 29, pt. 1, p. 80; Orton, *Records*, p. 848.
35. Crawford, *Mosby*, p. 100; Munson, *Reminiscences*, p. 34; Williamson, *Mosby's Rangers*, pp. 88, 89; Gott, *Years*, p. xviii; *OR*, 29, pt. 1, p. 80; CSR/NA.
36. *OR*, 29, pt. 1, p. 80; Williamson, *Mosby's Rangers*, pp. 89, 91; Mitchell, *Letters*, p. 62; Crowninshield to Mammy, August 25, 1863, Crowninshield, Papers, MSHS; Scott, *Partisan Life*, p. 121.
37. *OR*, 29, pt. 1, pp. 80, 81; Crowninshield to Mammy, August 25, 1863, Crowninshield, Papers, MSHS; Humphreys, *Field*, p. 371.
38. Munson, *Reminiscences*, p. 209; Crawford, *Mosby*, p. 101.
39. Crawford, *Mosby*, p. 102; Long, *Civil War*, pp. 408–418.
40. Crawford, *Mosby*, p. 102; Munson, *Reminiscences*, pp. 209–211.
41. Bevan to Sister, September 12, 1863, Bevan, Letters, USAMHI; CSR/NA.
42. Mosby to Pauline Mosby, October 1, 1863, Mosby, Papers, UVA; *OR*, 29, pt. 2, p. 653.
43. Williamson, *Mosby's Rangers*, pp. 92, 93; CSR/NA.
44. Mosby to Pauline Mosby, October 1, 1863, Mosby, Papers, UVA; Crawford, *Mosby*, p. 128; Faust, *Encyclopedia*, pp. 584–585.

CHAPTER SIX

1. Mosby to Pauline Mosby, October 1, 1863, Mosby, Papers, UVA.
2. Alexander, *Mosby's Men*, p. 62.
3. Mosby to Pauline Mosby, October 1, 1863, Mosby, Papers, UVA.
4. *OR*, 29, pt. 1, p. 81.
5. Williamson, *Mosby's Rangers*, p. 94n; Scott, *Partisan Life*, p. 141; Wallace, *Guide*, p. 71.

6. Scott, *Partisan Life*, p. 141; Crawford, *Mosby*, pp. 120, 121.
7. Williamson, *Mosby's Rangers*, p. 94; Scott, *Partisan Life*, p. 141; Munson, *Reminiscences*, p. 34; CSR/NA.
8. Williamson, *Mosby's Rangers*, p. 534; Scott, *Partisan Life*, pp. 48, 142; Krick, Collection; CSR/NA.
9. Williamson, *Mosby's Rangers*, pp. 532–542; CSR/NA.
10. Crawford, *Mosby*, pp. 121, 122.
11. Ibid., pp. 122, 123, 124.
12. Ibid., pp. 124, 125, 126; Alexander, *Mosby's Men*, p. 50.
13. Crawford, *Mosby*, pp. 110–111; Munson, *Reminiscences*, p. 216.
14. Crawford, *Mosby*, pp. 111–112; Munson, *Reminiscences*, p. 216.
15. Crawford, *Mosby*, pp. 112, 114, 116; Munson, *Reminiscences*, p. 216.
16. Long, *Civil War*, pp. 419–424.
17. Edmonds, *Journal*, p. 173.
18. CSR/NA; Mosby, *Memoirs*, p. 334.
19. Edmonds, *Journal*, p. 170; Emerson, *Life*, pp. 312, 313.
20. *OR*, 29, pt. 1, p. 494; pt. 2, pp. 350, 369; Williamson, *Mosby's Rangers*, p. 100; CSR/NA.
21. Hoadley, *Memorial*, pp. 27, 28, 149, 153.
22. *OR*, 29, pt. 1, p. 495; Williamson, *Mosby's Rangers*, pp. 105–106; Corselius, Letters, UMICH.
23. Crowninshield to Mammy, November 9, 1863, Crowninshield, Papers, MSHS.
24. Warner, *Generals In Blue*, p. 12.
25. Munson, *Reminiscences*, p. 214.
26. Ibid., pp. 214–215.
27. Crowninshield to Mammy, November 9, 1863, Crowninshield, Papers, MSHS.
28. Ibid., November 23, 1863; Williamson, *Mosby's Rangers*, pp. 110–111.
29. Williamson, *Mosby's Rangers*, pp. 107–108.
30. Ibid., pp. 108–109; Crawford, *Mosby*, pp. 128–130; Denison, *Sabres*, p. 327.
31. Williamson, *Mosby's Rangers*, pp. 109–110; Crawford, *Mosby*, p. 131.
32. Williamson, *Mosby's Rangers*, p. 110; Crawford, *Mosby*, pp. 131, 133.
33. Williamson, *Mosby's Rangers*, p. 111; Long, *Civil War*, pp. 438–441.
34. Williamson, *Mosby's Rangers*, pp. 111–113; Crawford, *Mosby*, pp. 134, 135.
35. Williamson, *Mosby's Rangers*, pp. 105, 115; Wallace, *Guide*, p. 71; CSR/NA.
36. Williamson, *Mosby's Rangers*, p. 115; Scott, *Partisan Life*, p. 159; Jones, *Ranger Mosby*, p. 112; Krick, *Lee's Colonels*, p. 78; CSR/NA.
37. Krick, *Lee's Colonels*, p. 78; CSR/NA; Jones, Ledgerbook, SMM.
38. Krick, *Lee's Colonels*, p. 294; CSR/NA; Williamson, *Mosby's Rangers*, p. 115.
39. Bryan, *Joseph Bryan*, p. 127; Kidd, *Personal*, p. 448; Opie, *Rebel*, p. 292; CSR/NA.
40. Monteiro, *War Reminiscences*, pp. 68, 70; Scheel, *Middleburg*, p. 49; Divine, interview, October 19, 1988.
41. Williamson, *Mosby's Rangers*, p. 115; Scott, *Partisan Life*, p. 159; CSR/NA.
42. *OR*, 29, pt. 1, p. 552.
43. Crawford, *Mosby*, pp. 135–139.

44. Ibid., p. 140.
45. *OR*, 29, pt. 2, p. 585; *History Third Pennsylvania*, p. 384; Gott, *High*, pp. 44–45; CSR/NA.
46. Scheel, *Civil War*, p. 72.
47. *OR*, 29, pt. 1, p. 995; CSR/NA.

CHAPTER SEVEN

1. *OR*, 29, pt. 2, p. 397.
2. Starr, *Union Cavalry*, pp. 50, 51.
3. Williamson, *Mosby's Rangers*, p. 175.
4. Scheel, *Civil War*, p. 62; Corselius, Letters, UMICH.
5. Edmonds, *Journal*, p. 195; Bevan to Sister, July 25, 1863, Bevan, Letters, USAMHI; Humphreys, *Field*, p. 105; Scheel, *Civil War*, p. 61; Fitts, "Mosby," *Galaxy* II, p. 644.
6. Hunter, *Women*, p. 40; Mosby, Papers, DU.
7. Williamson, *Mosby's Rangers*, p. 18; Schubert, Papers, pp. 5–6, USAMHI.
8. *Famous Adventures*, p. 106.
9. Williamson, *Mosby's Rangers*, pp. 18, 28, 157; Crawford, *Mosby*, pp. 101, 319, 322, 323; Scott, *Partisan Life*, p. 57; Jones, *Ranger Mosby*, p. 116; Scheel, *Civil War*, p. 78; Divine, interview, October 19, 1988; USC, 1860.
10. Scheel, *Civil War*, p. 5; Edmonds, *Journal*, p. xix; USC, 1860.
11. Edmonds, *Journal*, pp. viii, ix, xxiii, 151; "Sky Meadows"; Williamson, *Mosby's Rangers*, p. 136; Munson, *Reminiscences*, p. 15; *Old Homes*, pp. 30–31; Hotchkiss, "Map of Fauquier Co.," LC: Scheel, *Civil War*, p. 76.
12. *Old Homes*, p. 49; USC, 1860; Williamson, *Mosby's Rangers*, p. 61; Scheel, *Civil War*, p. 78; Divine, interview, October 19, 1988, Hotchkiss, "Map of Fauquier Co.," LC.
13. Hotchkiss, "Map of Fauquier Co.," LC; Munson, *Reminiscences*, p. 243; Chappelear, *PCCHA* VIII, p. 1; Divine, interview, October 19, 1988.
14. Munson, *Reminiscences*, pp. 90, 244–246; Monteiro, *War Reminiscences*, pp. 82, 83; USC, 1860.
15. Scheel, *Civil War*, pp. 4, 5; Hotchkiss, "Map of Fauquier Co.," LC.
16. *Old Homes*, p. 570.
17. *Fauquier County*, p. 251; Hotchkiss, "Map of Fauquier Co.," LC.
18. *Fauquier County*, pp. 251, 252; Hotchkiss, "Map of Fauquier Co.," LC; *Old Homes*, p. 160; Scheel, *Civil War*, p. 78.
19. *Old Homes*, p. 162; Hotchkiss, "Map of Fauquier Co.," LC; Divine, interview, October 19, 1988; Scheel, *Civil War*, p. 78.
20. Scheel, *Civil War*, p. 78; Divine, interview, October 19, 1988; Hotchkiss, "Map of Fauquier Co.," LC; USC, 1860.
21. *Fauquier County*, pp. 232, 233; *Old Homes*, pp. 4, 5; Scott, *Partisan Life*, p. 153; Williamson, *Mosby's Rangers*, p. 109; Hotchkiss, "Map of Fauquier Co.," LC.
22. Crawford, *Mosby*, pp. 131, 335; Monteiro, *War Reminiscences*, pp. 67, 74; Gott, *Years*, p. 53; Baird, *CV*, 31, p. 357; Edmonds, *Journal*, p. ix; Cochran, Journal, VHS; Broun, "Family Events," UVA.

23. Cochran, Journal, VHS; Hunter, *CV*, 15, p. 262.
24. Crawford, *Mosby*, p. 185; Moore, "Through the Shadow," p. 118, CCHA.
25. Jones, Ledgerbook, SMM; Moore, "Through the Shadow," pp. 118–119, CCHA.
26. Hunter, *Women*, pp. 51, 57, 58, 111, 137–138; Crowninshield, *History*, p. 189; Gott, *Years*, p. 55.
27. Bakeless, *Spies*, p. 62; MRF/WHS; Jones, Ledgerbook, SMM.
28. Alexander, *Mosby's Men*, p. 33.
29. Edmonds, *Journal*, pp. 168, 169, 171, 173, 178, 179, 187.
30. Alexander, *Mosby's Men*, p. 33.
31. Ibid., pp. 31–32; Scott, *Partisan Life*, pp. 394, 395.
32. Poland, *From Frontier*, pp. 214–216; Scott, *Partisan Life*, p. 398; Williamson, *Mosby's Rangers*, p. 105.
33. Scott, *Partisan Life*, p. 398; Monteiro, *War Reminiscences*, pp. 93, 94; Kidd *Personal*, p. 445.
34. Scott, *Partisan Life*, pp. 398, 399; Williamson, *Mosby's Rangers*, p. 105; *Famous Adventures*, p. 107.
35. Williamson, *Mosby's Rangers*, p. 152.
36. Hunter, *Women*, pp. 41–42; Scott, *Partisan Life*, p. 398.
37. Gott, *Years*, p. 55.
38. Bevan to Sister, November 19, 1863, Bevan, Letters, USAMHI; Ramsey, letter, August 8, 1863, Ramsey, Letters, USAMHI; Scheel, *Civil War*, pp. 62, 67.
39. Hunter, *Women*, p. 33; "Sky Meadows"; Hunter, *CV*, 15, pp. 259, 260.
40. Baylor, *Bull Run*, p. 321; Mosby, Papers, DU; Broun, "Family Events," UVA; Mosby, Papers, UVA; "Sky Meadows."
41. "Sky Meadows"; Broun, "Family Events," UVA.
42. Bevan to Sister, December 12, 1863, Bevan, Letters, USAMHI.

CHAPTER EIGHT

1. Starr, *Union Cavalry*, pp. 35, 40, 41, 43; *OR*, 33, p. 470.
2. Starr, *Union Cavalry*, pp. 40–43; *OR*, 33, pp. 365, 470.
3. *OR*, 33, p. 365; Starr, *Union Cavalry*, p. 43; Crawford, *Mosby*, p. 186; Crowninshield, *History*, p. 191.
4. *History Third Pennsylvania*, p. 388; Holmes, *Horse Soldiers*, p. 124.
5. Tompkins to Mother, January 14, 1864, Tompkins, Letters, LC.
6. Holmes, *Horse Soldiers*, p. 121; Crawford, *Mosby*, pp. 148–150.
7. *History Third Pennsylvania*, pp. 385, 393, 394, 396.
8. Scott, *Partisan Life*, pp. 150, 152; Thomson and Rauch, *History*, p. 286; Williamson, *Mosby's Rangers*, p. 133.
9. Williamson, *Mosby's Rangers*, pp. 116, 117.
10. Ibid., pp. 116, 117.
11. Newcomer, *Cole's Cavalry*, p. 11.
12. Ibid., pp. 11, 19, 24, 57.
13. Ibid., pp. 57; *OR*, 29, pt. 2, pp. 614–615.

14. Williamson, *Mosby's Rangers*, p. 118; Crawford, *Mosby*, pp. 140–145; *OR*, 33, p. 9.

15. Brown, *Stringfellow*, pp. 3, 4, 15; McClellan, *I Rode*, p. 336.

16. Williamson, *Mosby's Rangers*, pp. 124, 125, 485; Scott, *Partisan Life*, p. 179; Munson, *Reminiscences*, p. 241; Crawford, *Mosby*, p. 156; *OR*, 33, p. 15.

17. Williamson, *Mosby's Rangers*, pp. 125, 126 485; Crawford, *Mosby*, p. 156.

18. Brown, *Stringfellow*, pp. 238–239; Williamson, *Mosby's Rangers*, pp. 126, 486; *OR*, 33, p. 15.

19. Williamson, *Mosby's Rangers*, pp. 126, 485; Scott, *Partisan Life*, p. 179; Crawford, *Mosby*, p. 157; *OR*, 33, p. 15.

20. *OR*, 33, p. 15; Williamson, *Mosby's Rangers*, pp. 126, 485; Munson, *Reminiscences*, 241; Washington *Evening Star*, January 13, 1864.

21. *OR*, 33, p. 15; Williamson, *Mosby's Rangers*, pp. 126, 486; Munson, *Reminiscences*, pp. 241–242; Brown, *Stringfellow*, p. 241.

22. Newcomer, *Cole's Cavalry*, p. 94; Drickamer and Drickamer, *Fort Lyon*, p. 161.

23. Newcomer, *Cole's Cavalry*, p. 95; Drickamer and Drickamer, *Fort Lyon*, p. 161.

24. Williamson, *Mosby's Rangers*, p. 126; Crawford, *Mosby*, p. 163; CSR/NA; McIlhenny, Diary, p. 20, USAMHI.

25. Williamson, *Mosby's Rangers*, pp. 127, 534; Jones, *Ranger Mosby*, p. 169; CSR/NA.

26. Brown, *Stringfellow*, p. 241; Scott, *Partisan Life*, pp. 180, 182; Jones, *Ranger Mosby*, p. 169; Williamson, *Mosby's Rangers*, p. 128; CSR/NA.

27. Williamson, *Mosby's Rangers*, p. 127; Munson, *Reminiscences*, p. 33; Crawford, *Mosby*, p. 162.

28. Williamson, *Mosby's Rangers*, pp. 127, 130, 534; Howard, *Recollections*, p. 209; Goldsborough, *Maryland*, pp. 80, 358.

29. *OR*, 33, p. 16; Crawford, *Mosby*, pp. 163, 164; Scott, *Partisan Life*, p. 181.

30. Williamson, *Mosby's Rangers*, pp. 486, 487; Crawford, *Mosby*, p. 165.

31. *OR*, 33, p. 16; Williamson, *Mosby's Rangers*, pp. 127, 128, *CMH* III, p. 1059; CSR/NA; Scott, *Partisan Life*, p. 182.

32. Williamson, *Mosby's Rangers*, p. 128.

33. Ibid., p. 128; Crawford, *Mosby*, p. 163; *OR*, 33, p. 16.

34. Munson, *Reminiscences*, pp. 241, 242; Crawford, *Mosby*, p. 167; Scott, *Partisan Life*, p. 182; CSR/NA.

35. Ball, Letters, HFNHP; Drickamer and Drickamer, *Fort Lyon*, pp. 161, 162, 163; McIlhenny, Diary, p. 20, USAMHI; Newcomer, *Cole's Cavalry*, pp. 102, 103.

36. Drickamer and Drickamer, *Fort Lyon*, p. 163; Crawford, *Mosby*, p. 165; McIlhenny, Diary, pp. 20, 21, USAMHI.

37. Crawford, *Mosby*, pp. 168, 172, 173; Scheel, *Civil War*, p. 54; CSR/NA.

38. Crawford, *Mosby*, p. 173; *OR*, 33, p. 1113; CSR/NA.

39. *OR*, 33, p. 16.

40. Grant, "Partisan Warfare," *MR*, p. 52.

41. *OR*, 33, p. 1081.

42. Ibid., pp. 1081–1082.

43. Ibid., p. 1082.
44. Ibid., p. 1082.
45. Ibid., pp. 1083, 1252; Grant, "Partisan Warfare," *MR*, p. 53; Delauter, *McNeill's Rangers*, 63.
46. *OR*, 33, pp. 113, 113n, 385, 411; Diezelski, "An Episode," pp. 1, 7, 9, USAMHI; Denison, *Sabres*, p. 336; Crowninshield to Mammy, February 2, 1864, Crowninshield, Papers, MSHS.
47. Crawford, *Mosby*, p. 173.
48. *OR*, 33, p. 568.
49. Pyne, *History*, p. 216; *History Third Pennsylvania*, p. 399; Crawford, *Mosby*, p. 174.
50. Pyne, *History*, pp. 216, 217; Lloyd, *History*, p. 84.
51. Crawford, *Mosby*, pp. 174–177; *History Third Pennsylvania*, p. 386; Williamson, *Mosby's Rangers*, p. 135.
52. Williamson, *Mosby's Rangers*, p. 134; Edmonds, *Journal*, p. 180.
53. *History Third Pennsylvania*, p. 386.
54. Crawford, *Mosby*, pp. 177, 179; Pyne, *History*, p. 219; CSR/NA; *OR*, 33, p. 570.
55. Lloyd, *History*, p. 84; Pyne, *History*, p. 219; *History Third Pennsylvania*, p. 386; Crawford, *Mosby*, p. 177.
56. Crawford, *Mosby*, p. 179.

CHAPTER NINE

1. Munson, *Reminiscences*, p. 83; CSR/NA; Jones, Ledgerbook, SMM.
2. Williamson, *Mosby's Rangers*, pp. 137, 138; *OR*, 33, p. 175; CSR/NA; Jones, Ledgerbook, SMM.
3. Scott, *Partisan Life*, pp. 198, 199; Munson, *Reminiscences*, p. 80; *OR*, 33, p. 157.
4. Munson, *Reminiscences*, pp. 80–82; *OR*, 33, p. 157.
5. *OR*, 33, p. 157; Munson, *Reminiscences*, p. 83.
6. *OR*, 33, p. 157; Scott, *Partisan Life*, pp. 198, 199; Williamson, *Mosby's Rangers*, p. 139; Scheel, *Civil War*, p. 75.
7. *OR*, 33, pp. 156, 157; Scott, *Partisan Life*, p. 199.
8. *OR*, 33, p. 157; Scott, *Partisan Life*, p. 199; Williamson, *Mosby's Rangers*, p. 140; CSR/NA.
9. *OR*, 33, p. 159; Munson, *Reminiscences*, p. 83; Scott, *Partisan Life*, p. 200; Williamson, *Mosby's Rangers*, p. 140; *OR Atlas*, Plate VII.
10. *National Tribune*, August 10, 1910, October 8, 1931; Jones, Ledgerbook, SMM; Munson, *Reminiscences*, p. 90; Williamson, *Mosby's Rangers*, pp. 110–111; CSR/NA.
11. *National Tribune*, August 10, 1910; Williamson, *Mosby's Rangers*, p. 141; *OR*, 33, p. 159; *OR Atlas*, Plate VII; Jones, Ledgerbook, SMM.
12. *OR*, 33, p. 159; Munson, *Reminiscences*, p. 84; Williamson, *Mosby's Rangers*, p. 141; Scott, *Partisan Life*, p. 200.
13. *OR*, 33, pp. 159, 160; Munson, *Reminiscences*, pp. 84–85; Williamson, *Mos-*

by's Rangers, pp. 141–142; Scott, Partisan Life, p. 201; OR Atlas, Plate VII.

14. National Tribune, August 10, 1910; Scott, Partisan Life, p. 201.

15. National Tribune, August 10, 1910; Crowninshield to Mammy, February 27, 1864, Crowninshield, Papers, MSHS.

16. OR, 33, p. 160; Williamson, Mosby's Rangers, pp. 142–143; Crawford, Mosby, p. 182; Munson, Reminiscences, p. 85; Scott, Partisan Life, pp. 201–202.

17. OR, 33, p. 160; Scott, Partisan Life, p. 202; Munson, Reminiscences, pp. 85–86; Williamson, Mosby's Rangers, p. 144, National Tribune, August 10, 1910.

18. Munson, Reminiscences, p. 86; National Tribune, August 10, 1910.

19. Munson, Reminiscences, p. 87.

20. Ibid., pp. 33, 34.

21. Ibid., pp. 89–91.

22. Krick, Collection; Jones, Ledgerbook, SMM.

23. Munson, Reminiscences, pp. 87–88; Krick, Collection; Bowen, Massachusetts, p. 760.

24. Crowninshield to Mammy, February 27, 1864, Crowninshield, Papers, MSHS; OR, 33, p. 158; Munson, Reminiscences, p. 90; National Tribune, August 10, 1910.

25. Jones, Ranger Mosby, p. 176; Gott, Years, p. xiii; Edmonds, Journal, p. 264n; CSR/NA; Jones, Ledgerbook, SMM; OR, 33, p. 158.

26. Crowninshield to Mammy, February 27, 1864, Crowninshield, Papers, MSHS; Humphreys, Field, p. 392.

27. OR, 33, p. 158; 51, pt. 2, p. 823.

28. Crowninshield to Mammy, February 27, 1864, Crowninshield, Papers, MSHS: OR, 33, p. 249; Crawford, Mosby, p. 183.

29. OR, 33, pp. 236, 248, 249, 779; Williamson, Mosby's Rangers, pp. 150–151; Scott, Partisan Life, p. 206.

30. CSR/NA; Krick, Lee's Colonels, p. 294; Williamson, Mosby's Rangers, p. 231.

31. OR, 33, p. 1241.

32. Bryan, Joseph Bryan, p. 124n; Scott, Partisan Life, p. 209; Williamson, Mosby's Rangers, p. 154; Jones, Ranger Mosby, p. 179.

33. Scott, Partisan Life, p. 209; Bryan, Joseph Bryan, p. 124n.

34. Williamson, Mosby's Rangers, p. 154; Munson, Reminiscences, p. 140; Jones, Ranger Mosby, p. 129; Wallace, Guide, p. 71; Lee, Personal, p. 93.

35. Munson, Reminiscences, p. 141; Jones, Ranger Mosby, p. 179; CSR/NA; Hunter, Women, pp. 137, 138; Bryan, Joseph Bryan, p. 124n.

36. Scott, Partisan Life, pp. 85, 100, 209, 210; Williamson, Mosby's Rangers, p. 154; Gott, Years, p. xxii; CSR/NA.

37. Scott, Partisan Life, pp. 209, 211; Williamson, Mosby's Rangers, p. 154; Howard, Recollections, p. 64; CSR/NA.

38. Scott, Partisan Life, pp. 209, 211, 212; Williamson, Mosby's Rangers, pp. 155, 533, 537; CSR/NA.

39. Munson, Reminiscences, p. 141; Bryan, Joseph Bryan, pp. 124n, 125n; Scott, Partisan Life, p. 211; Hunter, Women, pp. 196, 197.

40. *OR*, 33, pp. 1240, 1241, 1268.
41. Ibid., p. 1241; 51, pt. 2, pp. 856, 878, 880l; Crawford, *Mosby*, pp. 186–187.
42. Williamson, *Mosby's Rangers*, pp. 155, 156; Edmonds, *Journal*, pp. 191, 192.
43. *OR*, 33, pp. 306, 847, 1275; Goodhart, *History*, p. 128.
44. *OR*, 33, p. 306; Goodhart, *History*, p. 128; Forty-third Battalion, Items, EU.
45. Forty-third Battalion, Items, EU; Janney Family, Letters, USAMHI.
46. *OR*, 33, p. 1275.
47. MRF/WHS; Williamson, *Mosby's Rangers*, p. 153.
48. *OR*, 33, p. 259; CSR/NA.
49. Humphreys, *Field*, p. 393; CSR/NA.
50. Humphreys, *Field*, pp. 24–33; Divine, interview, October 19, 1988; Scott, *Partisan Life*, pp. 211, 213; CSR/NA; Hoadley, *Memorial*, p. 158.
51. Divine, interview, October 19, 1988; Williamson, *Mosby's Rangers*, pp. 158, 159; CSR/NA.
52. *OR*, 33 p. 315; Williamson, *Mosby's Rangers*, pp. 158, 159.
53. Williamson, *Mosby's Rangers*, p. 159; *OR*, 33, p. 316.
54. *OR*, 33, pp. 315, 316; Williamson, *Mosby's Rangers*, pp. 161, 534; CSR/NA; Crowninshield to Mammy, May 2, 1864, Crowninshield, Papers, MSHS.
55. CSR/NA.
56. Dowdey and Manarin, *Wartime Papers*, p. 689.
57. Ibid., p. 689.
58. Bakeless, *Spies*, p. 356.

CHAPTER TEN

1. Catton, *Grant Moves South*, p. 389; Catton, *Grant Takes Command*, pp. 160, 161.
2. Williamson, *Mosby's Rangers*, pp. 148–149.
3. Ibid., pp. 162–164.
4. Ibid., pp. 164–165.
5. Scott, *Partisan Life*, pp. 207, 214, 215; Stevenson, *Boots*, pp. 162, 260, 261; Krick, *Lee's Colonels*, p. 78.
6. Stevenson, *Boots*, pp. 261, 263, 264; Beach, *First New York*, p. 322.
7. Munson, *Reminiscences*, pp. 202–204; CSR/NA.
8. Thomas, *Bold Dragoon*, pp. 291–292, 295; Mosby, "Memoir," VHS.
9. Munson, *Reminiscences*, pp. 191–193.
10. Ibid., pp. 194–195.
11. Alexander, *Mosby's Men*, pp. 56–58; MRF/WHS.
12. MRF/WHS; Alexander, *Mosby's Men*, pp. 59–60.
13. MRF/WHS; Alexander, *Mosby's Men*, pp. 60–62.
14. Williamson, *Mosby's Rangers*, pp. 171–173.
15. Ibid., pp. 171–173; Plater, "Civil War Diary," *PCCHA*, XXII, p. 74; Scott, *Partisan Life*, p. 227.
16. Crawford, *Mosby*, pp. 204–206.
17. Ibid., p. 199; Weatherby, *Lovettsville*, p. 34; Alexander, *Mosby's Men*, pp. 87, 88.

18. CSR/NA; Williamson, *Mosby's Rangers*, p. 535; Jones, Ledgerbook, SMM; *OR*, 37, pt. 1, p. 593.
19. Hoadley, *Memorial*, p. 160; *OR*, 37, pt. 1, p. 611; CSR/NA.
20. Crawford, *Mosby*, p. 206; Williamson, *Mosby's Rangers*, pp. 175, 178n.
21. Crawford, *Mosby*, p. 206; *OR*, 37, pt. 1, pp. 168, 169; Collins, *John S. Mosby*, pp. 13, 14.
22. Scott, *Partisan Life*, p. 233; Crawford, *Mosby*, p. 207; Williamson, *Mosby's Rangers*, p. 178.
23. Jones, *Ranger Mosby*, p. 185; Russell, Papers, CCHA; CSR/NA.
24. Scott, *Partisan Life*, pp. 233–234; *OR Atlas*, Plate LXIX.
25. Scott, *Partisan Life*, p. 234; Williamson, *Mosby's Rangers*, p. 178.
26. Scott, *Partisan Life*, p. 234; Williamson, *Mosby's Rangers*, p. 178.
27. Scott, *Partisan Life*, pp. 234–235; Crawford, *Mosby*, p. 207.
28. Scott, *Partisan Life*, pp. 235–236; Crawford, *Mosby*, p. 208.
29. Scott, *Partisan Life*, pp. 235–236; Crawford, *Mosby*, p. 208.
30. Williamson, *Mosby's Rangers*, pp. 179–181; Scott, *Partisan Life*, p. 236; Crawford, *Mosby*, p. 209; CSR/NA.
31. Williamson, *Mosby's Rangers*, pp. 181–182; Crawford, *Mosby*, p. 209; Scott, *Partisan Life*, pp. 237, 238; Alexander, *Mosby's Men*, p. 103.
32. Williamson, *Mosby's Rangers*, p. 183n; Vandiver, *Jubal's Raid*, pp. 74–80.
33. Vandiver, *Jubal's Raid*, pp. 6–8.
34. Ibid., pp. 6–7, 10–13.
35. Wert, *From Winchester*, pp. 6–7.
36. Ibid., pp. 7–8; Vandiver, *Jubal's Raid*, pp. 11, 18–20.
37. Wert, *From Winchester*, pp. 7–8; Vandiver, *Jubal's Raid*, pp. 80–87.
38. Mosby to F. F. Bowen, June 12, 1895 [?], Bowen, Papers, VHS: Scott, *Partisan Life*, pp. 238, 239; Crawford, *Mosby*, p. 210; Williamson, *Mosby's Rangers*, p. 184.
39. Crawford, *Mosby*, pp. 210, 211; Williamson, *Mosby's Rangers*, p. 184; Munson, *Reminiscences*, p. 93; Mosby to F. F. Bowen, June 12, 1895 [?], Bowen, Papers, VHS.
40. Crawford, *Mosby*, pp. 211, 212; Williamson, *Mosby's Rangers*, p. 184; Alexander, *Mosby's Men*, pp. 76, 77; Scott, *Partisan Life*, p. 239.
41. Alexander, *Mosby's Men*, p. 77; Williamson, *Mosby's Rangers*, pp. 184, 185; Crawford, *Mosby*, p. 212.
42. Goodhart, *History*, pp. viii, 1, 9; Crawford, *Mosby*, pp. 200–202, 204, 212; Alexander, *Mosby's Men*, p. 81.
43. Alexander, *Mosby's Men*, pp. 77–78; Williamson, *Mosby's Rangers*, pp. 184–185; Crawford, *Mosby*, p. 212; Scott, *Partisan Life*, p. 239; Munson, *Reminiscences*, p. 93.
44. Scott, *Partisan Life*, p. 239; Crawford, *Mosby*, p. 214; Williamson, *Mosby's Rangers*, p. 185; Munson, *Reminiscences*, p. 94; Alexander, *Mosby's Men*, p. 79.
45. Williamson, *Mosby's Rangers*, p. 185; Munson, *Reminiscences*, p. 94; Crawford, *Mosby*, p. 214; Scott, *Partisan Life*, p. 239; Alexander, *Mosby's Men*, p. 79.
46. Scott, *Partisan Life*, pp. 241, 242, 244; Alexander, *Mosby's Men*, p. 80; Craw-

ford, *Mosby*, pp. 215, 217, 219; Williamson, *Mosby's Rangers*, pp. 185, 186.

47. Alexander, *Mosby's Men*, pp. 83, 84; Crawford, *Mosby*, pp. 217, 220.

48. Alexander, *Mosby's Men*, p. 97; Crawford, *Mosby*, p. 221; Scott, *Partisan Life*, p. 492; Mosby to F. F. Bowen, June 12, 1895 [?], Bowen, Papers, VHS.

49. Scott, *Partisan Life*, pp. 244–246; Munson, *Reminiscences*, p. 94; *OR*, 37, pt. 1, pp. 219, 358; Crawford, *Mosby*, pp. 224, 225.

50. Humphreys, *Field*, pp. 93–95; *OR*, 37, pt. 1, p. 358.

51. Humphreys, *Field*, pp. 95, 96; Divine, interview, October 19, 1988; *OR*, 37, pt. 1, p. 359; Alexander, *Mosby's Men*, p. 95; Williamson, *Mosby's Rangers*, p. 187.

52. Alexander, *Mosby's Men*, pp. 91, 92; Crawford, *Mosby*, pp. 225, 226; Munson, *Reminiscences*, p. 95; Scott, *Partisan Life*, p. 247; Williamson, *Mosby's Rangers*, p. 187; Divine, interview, October 19, 1988.

53. Humphreys, *Field*, p. 96; Alexander, *Mosby's Men*, p. 92; Scott, *Partisan Life*, p. 247; Crawford, *Mosby*, p. 226, *OR*, 37, pt. 1, p. 359.

54. Alexander, *Mosby's Men*, p. 92; Scott, *Partisan Life*, p. 247; Munson, *Reminiscences*, p. 96; Williamson, *Mosby's Rangers*, p. 187; Humphreys, *Field*, p. 96; *OR*, 37, l, p. 359.

55. Humphreys, *Field*, p. 96; Munson, *Reminiscences*, p. 96.

56. Humphreys, *Field*, p. 97.

57. Ibid., pp. 97–98; Munson, *Reminiscences*, p. 97; Alexander, *Mosby's Men*, p. 94.

58. Munson, *Reminiscences*, p. 96; Scott, *Partisan Life*, p. 212; Orton, *Records*, p. 850.

59. Humphreys, *Field*, p. 98; Williamson, *Mosby's Rangers*, p. 188; Munson, *Reminiscences*, p. 97; Alexander, *Mosby's Men*, p. 94.

60. Scott, *Partisan Life*, p. 244; Humphreys, *Field*, pp. 99, 100; Munson, *Reminiscences*, p. 98; Divine, interview, October 19, 1988; Crawford, *Mosby*, p. 227.

61. *OR*, 37, pt. 1, p. 359; Crowninshield to Mammy, July 7, 1864, Crowninshield, Papers, MSHS.

62. Williamson, *Mosby's Rangers*, p. 188; Alexander, *Mosby's Men*, pp. 94, 95; Scott, *Partisan Life*, p. 248; Jones, Ledgerbook, SMM.

63. Williamson, *Mosby's Rangers*, p. 188; Alexander, *Mosby's Men*, pp. 54, 95; Divine, interview, October 19, 1988; Mitchell, *Letters*, p. 229.

64. Washington *Evening Star*, July 9, 1864.

65. Ibid.; Alexander, *Mosby's Men*, p. 95; Crowninshield to Mammy, July 7, 1864, Crowninshield, Papers, MSHS.

66. Munson, *Reminiscences*, pp. 99–101; Scott, *Partisan Life*, p. 250.

67. Alexander, *Mosby's Men*, pp. 97–99; Munson, *Reminiscences*, pp. 217, 218.

68. Alexander, *Mosby's Men*, pp. 100, 101.

69. Ibid., p. 101.

70. Ibid., pp. 101–102.

71. Mosby to F. F. Bowen, June 12, 1895 [?], Bowen, Papers, VHS; Scott, *Partisan Life*, p. 492; Jones, *Ranger Mosby*, p. 189.

72. Mosby to F. F. Bowen, June 12, 1895 [?], Bowen, Papers, VHS; Mitchell, *Letters*, pp. 64, 74.
73. Mosby to F. F. Bowen, June 12, 1895 [?], Bowen, Papers, VHS.
74. *OR*, 37, pt. 1, p. 5; Scott, *Partisan Life*, pp. 251, 492; Williamson, *Mosby's Rangers*, pp. 189–191; Crawford, *Mosby*, p. 230.

CHAPTER ELEVEN

1. Douglas, *I Rode*, p. 296.
2. Mosby to F. F. Bowen, April 29, 1895, June 12, 1895 [?], Bowen, Papers, VHS.
3. Wert, *From Winchester*, pp. 23–26.
4. Mosby to F. F. Bowen, April 29, 1895, June 12, 1895 [?], Bowen, Papers, VHS.
5. Ibid., June 16, 1895, July 25, 1898; Williamson, *Mosby's Rangers*, p. 202.
6. Elwood, *Elwood's Stories*, pp. 215–216.
7. Crawford, *Mosby*, pp. 232–233.
8. Ibid., pp. 233, 234; Edmonds, *Journal*, p. 202; Scott, *Partisan Life*, p. 351; Williamson, *Mosby's Rangers*, p. 194.
9. Meaney, *Civil War*, Chaps. 8 and 9; Crawford, *Mosby*, p. 236.
10. Williamson, *Mosby's Rangers*, p. 197; Wallace, *Guide*, p. 71.
11. CSR/NA.
12. Ibid.; Williamson, *Mosby's Rangers*, pp. 197, 198; Scott, *Partisan Life*, p. 271; Krick, Collection.
13. Jones, Ledgerbook, SMM; Mosby, *Memoirs*, p. 356; Alexander, *Mosby's Men*, p. 170; *Old Homes*, p. 33.
14. Williamson, *Mosby's Rangers*, p. 538; Krick, Collection; Mosby, *Memoirs*, p. 152; CSR/NA; Jones, Ledgerbook, SMM.
15. Munson, *Reminiscences*, pp. 201, 202; Williamson, *Mosby's Rangers*, p. 197; Scott, *Partisan Life*, p. 271; CSR/NA.
16. Munson, *Reminiscences*, p. 7; Scott, *Partisan Life*, p. 222; CSR/NA; Alexander, *Mosby's Men*, p. 17.
17. Williamson, *Mosby's Rangers*, p. 538; Krick, Collection; CSR/NA.
18. CSR/NA; Wallace, *Guide*, p. 72; Williamson, *Mosby's Rangers*, p. 543.
19. Williamson, *Mosby's Rangers*, p. 543; Krick, Collection; CSR/NA.
20. Williamson, *Mosby's Rangers*, p. 197; *CMH*, III, p. 1205; CSR/NA; Monteiro, *War Reminiscences*, p. 115.
21. Crawford, *Mosby*, pp. 235, 236.
22. Ibid., p. 235; Hard, *History*, p. 307.
23. Wert, *From Winchester*, p. 8.
24. Ibid., pp. 8–10; New York *Times*, July 11, 1864.
25. Wert, *From Winchester*, pp. 9–13, 15, 16, 22.
26. Ibid., pp. 12, 16.
27. Ibid., pp. 12, 16–18; *OR*, 37, pt. 2, pp. 558, 572.
28. Wert, *From Winchester*, pp. 26–28.
29. Munson, *Reminiscences*, p. 200; Mosby, *Memoirs*, pp. 284, 286, 290; Mosby

to F. F. Bowen, June 12, 1895 [?], Bowen Papers, VHS.

30. Mosby to F. F. Bowen, June 12, 1895 [?], Bowen, Papers, VHS; Munson, *Reminiscences*, pp. 199–200.

31. Crawford, *Mosby*, p. 238.

32. Ibid., p. 238; Stevens, *Three Years*, p. 390; Brown, *Annals* I, pp. 34, 40.

33. Alexander, *Mosby's Men*, pp. 166, 167; Scott, *Partisan Life*, p. 284; Opie, *Rebel*, p. 293; Mosby to John S. Russell, August 28, 1899, Mosby, Letters, CCHA.

34. Alexander, *Mosby's Men*, pp. 163, 165, 166; Russell, Papers, CCHA; Crawford, *Mosby*, p. 260.

35. Scott, *Partisan Life*, pp. 271–272; Williamson, *Mosby's Rangers*, p. 231.

36. Wert, *From Winchester*, pp. 30–32.

37. Mosby, *Memoirs*, p. 290; Munson, *Reminiscences*, pp. 102, 104; Crawford, *Mosby*, p. 238; Mosby to John S. Russell, August 28, 1899, Mosby, Letters, CCHA.

38. Mosby, *Memoirs*, p. 290; Munson, *Reminiscences*, p. 103; Crawford, *Mosby*, p. 238; Mosby to John S. Russell, August 28, 1899, Mosby, Letters, CCHA: Kathy Grachen to Bob Ewing, June 6, 1973, Grachen, CCHA; William Thompson to Eliza, August 14, 1864, Thompson, Letters, PSU; Gold, *History*, p. 123.

39. Mosby, *Memoirs*, p. 291; Scott, *Partisan Life*, p. 276; Gold, *History*, p. 123.

40. Mosby, *Memoirs*, p. 291, 367; Munson, *Reminiscences*, p. 105; Crawford, *Mosby*, p. 239; Williamson, *Mosby's Rangers*, pp. 208, 209.

41. *OR*, 43, pt. 1, pp. 619–629; Moore, "Through the Shadow," p. 146, CCHA.

42. *OR*, 43, pt. 1, pp. 628, 629, 632; New York *Times*, August 21, 1864; Perkins, *Summer*, p. 34; *National Tribune*, October 28, 1909.

43. Mosby, *Memoirs*, p. 291; Crawford, *Mosby*, p. 240; Perkins, *Summer*, p. 34; *OR*, 43, pt. 1, p. 621.

44. Scott, *Partisan Life*, pp. 239, 240; Munson, *Reminiscences*, p. 105; Perkins, *Summer*, p. 34; William Thompson to Eliza, August 14, 1864, Thompson, Letters, PSU.

45. Perkins, *Summer*, p. 34; Williamson, *Mosby's Rangers*, p. 209; Mosby, *Memoirs*, p. 366; *CMH* III, p. 1205; Mitchell, *Letters*, p. 208; Alumni Files, VMI.

46. Perkins, *Summer*, p. 34; Kathy Grachen to Bob Ewing, June 6, 1973, Grachen, CCHA; Crawford, *Mosby*, p. 240; *OR*, 43, pt. 1, p. 484.

47. Crawford, *Mosby*, pp. 240, 241; Williamson, *Mosby's Rangers*, p. 210; Munson, *Reminiscences*, p. 109; Scott, *Partisan Life*, p. 279; Mosby, *Memoirs*, p. 292.

48. *OR*, 43, pt. 1, pp. 485, 634, 836; Moore, "Through the Shadow," p. 148, CCHA; New York *Times*, August 21, 1864; Munson, *Reminiscences*, p. 198; Mosby, *Memoirs*, p. 367.

49. Moore, "Through the Shadow," pp. 114–115, 151, CCHA; Mosby, *Memoirs*, p. 241.

50. *OR*, 43, pt. 1, pp. 623, 634; Munson, *Reminiscences*, pp. 107–109; Scott, *Partisan Life*, p. 279; Mosby to John S. Russell, August 28, 1899, Mosby, Letters, CCHA; Smith, Diary, CCHA.

51. Denison, *Sabres*, pp. 375, 376; Hall, *History*, p. 212; Barnard, Deposition,

USAMHI; Emmons, "Affidavit," USAMHI; Moore, "Through the Shadow," pp. 160, 162, 163, CCHA.

52. *OR*, 43, pt. 1, pp. 619–632.

53. Ibid., p. 842; Wert, *From Winchester*, pp. 32, 35; Hall, *History*, p. 212; Gracey, *Annals*, pp. 283, 284.

54. *OR*, 43, pt. 1, p. 698.

55. Crawford, *Mosby*, pp. 242, 243; Munson, *Reminiscences*, pp. 113, 114, 198, 199; Wert, *From Winchester*, p. 35.

56. Jones, *Gray Ghosts*, pp. 280, 405n.

57. Scott, *Partisan Life*, p. 280; *OR*, 43, pt. 1, p. 634; Denison, *Sabres*, p. 381; New York *Times*, August 25, 1864.

58. Gold, *History*, pp. 157, 158; Jones, *Gray Ghosts*, p. 281; New York *Times*, August 25, 1864.

59. Patterson, *CV*, 12, p. 472; New York *Times*, August 25, 1864; Williamson, *Mosby's Rangers*, pp. 450, 451; McGuire, *Diary*, pp. 293, 294; Cochran, Journal, VHS.

60. *OR*, 43, pt. 1, p. 634; Mosby, "Memoirs," VHS; Peyton, "Diaries," p. 122, PWCL.

61. Gracey, *Annals*, p. 287; Denison, *Sabres*, p. 382.

62. *OR*, 43, pt. 1, pp. 826, 828, 865.

63. Ibid., p. 811.

64. Ibid.

65. Ibid., pp. 822, 842.

66. Ibid., p. 843.

67. Ibid., p. 909.

68. Schneider, Letter, USAMHI; Williamson, *Mosby's Rangers*, pp. 218–220.

69. *OR*, 43, pt. 1, p. 909.

70. Ibid., pp. 831, 870, 942; Janney, *Memoirs*, pp. 218, 219.

71. Hard, *History*, p. 311; *National Tribune*, July 23, 1891; Munson, *Reminiscences*, p. 256; Russell, Papers, CCHA.

72. Hard, *History*, pp. 311, 312.

73. CSR/NA; Munson, *Reminiscences*, pp. 201, 202; Williamson, *Mosby's Rangers*, p. 217; Jones, Ledgerbook, SMM.

CHAPTER TWELVE

1. William Thompson to Eliza, August 22, 1864, Thompson, Letters, PSU.

2. *National Tribune*, February 16, 1911.

3. *OR*, 43, pt. 2, pp. 31–32.

4. Hewitt, *History*, p. 192; Rowe, "Camp Tales," UMICH; William Thompson to Eliza, September 25, 1864, Thompson, Letters, PSU; *History Third Pennsylvania*, p. 330.

5. Williams, *Diary*, pp. 501–502.

6. *OR*, 43, pt. 1, pp. 860; Scott, *Partisan Life*, pp. 364, 365.

7. *OR*, 43, pt. 1, p. 860.

8. Scott, *Partisan Life*, p. 364; Williamson, *Mosby's Rangers*, p. 300.

9. Scott, *Partisan Life*, p. 365; *National Tribune*, October 31, 1889.

10. *OR*, 43, pt. 1, pp. 615, 616; pt. 2, p. 11.

11. Ibid., pt. 1, p. 616; Williamson, *Mosby's Rangers*, p. 223; Wert, *From Winchester*, p. 38.

12. *OR*, 43, pt. 1, p. 634; Williamson, *Mosby's Rangers*, p. 223; Scott, *Partisan Life*, p. 286.

13. *OR*, 43, pt. 1, p. 634; Williamson, *Mosby's Rangers*, p. 224; Crawford, *Mosby*, p. 225; Scott, *Partisan Life*, p. 287.

14. Hall, *History*, pp. 220, 351, 352; Scott, *Partisan Life*, p. 288.

15. Williamson, *Mosby's Rangers*, pp. 223, 224; Hall, *History*, p. 351.

16. Hall, *History*, p. 352; Scott, *Partisan Life*, p. 288; Williamson, *Mosby's Rangers*, p. 244; Jones, Ledgerbook, SMM.

17. Hall, *History*, pp. 221, 352, 357, 358; Williamson, *Mosby's Rangers*, p. 224.

18. Hall, *History*, p. 352; Crawford, *Mosby*, pp. 190, 191.

19. Scott, *Partisan Life*, pp. 159, 288; Mosby, "Memoirs," VHS; Williamson, *Mosby's Rangers*, p. 225; Krick, Collection.

20. Williamson, *Mosby's Rangers*, p. 226; *OR*, 43, pt. 1, p. 634.

21. Williamson, *Mosby's Rangers*, p. 226.

22. Ibid., p. 226; *OR*, 43, pt. 1, p. 616.

23. *OR*, 43, pt. 1, pp. 615, 616; Williamson, *Mosby's Rangers*, pp. 226, 227.

24. Williamson, *Mosby's Rangers*, pp. 227, 228; *OR*, 43, pt. 1, pp. 615, 634.

25. *OR*, 43, pt. 1, p. 615.

26. James Kidd to Father and Mother, September 9, 1864, Kidd, Letters, UM-ICH; Wert, *From Winchester*, pp. 38–39.

27. Crawford, *Mosby*, p. 258; Scott, *Partisan Life,* p. 293; Williamson, *Mosby's Rangers*, pp. 234–236; CSR/NA.

28. Williamson, *Mosby's Rangers*, p. 231; CSR/NA.

29. Williamson, *Mosby's Rangers*, pp. 27, 231, 540; Scott, *Partisan Life*, pp. 38, 305; CSR/NA; Jones, Ledgerbook, SMM.

30. Munson, *Reminiscences*, p. 168; CSR/NA.

31. Munson, *Reminiscences*, p. 47; Williamson, *Mosby's Rangers*, pp. 532, 540; CSR/NA.

32. Scott, *Partisan Life*, pp. 305, 306; Williamson, *Mosby's Rangers*, pp. 48, 474, 540; CSR/NA.

33. Scott, *Partisan Life*, pp. 305, 306; Williamson, *Mosby's Rangers*, p. 206; CSR/NA; Tidwell, *Come Retribution,* p. 140.

34. Williamson, *Mosby's Rangers*, pp. 331, 333n, 540; Gott, *Years*, p. xviii; Krick, Collection; CSR/NA.

35. Mosby, *Memoirs*, p. 298; New York *Herald*, October 9, 1864; *OR*, 43, pt. 2, p. 112; Hoadley, *Memorial*, pp. 183n, 184n.

36. Mosby, *Memoirs*, p. 298; Crawford, *Mosby*, p. 257; New York *Herald*, October 9, 1864; Mitchell, *Letters*, p. 62; *OR*, 43, pt. 2, pp. 132, 146.

37. *OR*, 43, pt. 2, pp. 876–877.

38. Ibid., pt. 1, p. 635; pt. 2, p. 877.

39. Wert, *From Winchester*, Chapters Four and Five.

40. Ibid., Chapters Six and Seven.

41. Mosby, "Retaliation," *SHSP*, 27, p. 314; Scott, *Partisan Life*, pp. 317, 318.

★

42. Scott, *Partisan Life*, p. 318; Richards, *CV*, 7, p. 510.
43. Scott, *Partisan Life*, p. 318; Hale, *Four Valiant Years*, p. 429; "Hanging," *SHSP*, 24, p. 108; Fagan, "Custer," p. 24.
44. Scott, *Partisan Life*, p. 318; Fagan, "Custer," p. 24; Hale, *Four Valiant Years*, p. 429.
45. Scott, *Partisan Life*, pp. 318–319; Jones, *Ranger Mosby*, pp. 207, 208; Hale, *Four Valiant Years*, p. 429.
46. Scott, *Partisan Life*, p. 319; Jones, *Ranger Mosby*, p. 208; Ashby, *Valley Campaigns*, p. 291; Fagan, "Custer," p. 24.
47. Scott, *Partisan Life*, p. 319; Hale, *Four Valiant Years*, pp. 429, 431; MRF/WHS; "Honor," *SHSP*, 25, pp. 239, 240.
48. Jones, *Ranger Mosby*, p. 208; Veil, "Old Boy's," p. 68, USAMHI; Scott, *Partisan Life*, p. 319; Fagan, "Custer," p. 24; "Honor," *SHSP*, p. 240; "Hanging," *SHSP*, 24, p. 109.
49. MRF/WHS; Bruce, *Virginia*, IV, p. 199; Williamson, *Mosby's Rangers*, pp. 242n, 243n; Hale, *Four Valiant Years*, p. 429.
50. Scott, *Partisan Life*, p. 318; Williamson, *Mosby's Rangers*, p. 240.
51. Fagan, "Custer," pp. 24, 42, 45; Moyer, *History*, p. 217; Scott, *Partisan Life*, p. 319; Williamson, *Mosby's Rangers*, p. 240; Heitman, *Historical Register*, p. 677.
52. Mosby, "Retaliation," *SHSP*, 27, pp. 315, 316; Mosby, "Memoir," VHS.
53. Scott, *Partisan Life*, p. 319.
54. Edmonds, *Journal*, p. 206; Cochran, Journal, VHS.
55. Starr, *Union Cavalry*, p. 346; Heitman, *Historical Register*, p. 677.
56. Fagan, "Custer," p. 42; Barbour, Diary, UMICH; *National Tribune*, October 8, 1903.
57. Emerson, *Life*, p. 353; Fagan, "Custer," pp. 42, 43, 46.
58. Scott, *Partisan Life*, p. 320; Williamson, *Mosby's Rangers*, pp. 454, 533; Krick, Collection; CSR/NA.
59. Ashby, *Valley Campaigns*, p. 293; Hale, *Four Valiant Years*, p. 431; Scott, *Partisan Life*, p. 320.
60. Ashby, *Valley Campaigns*, pp. 292, 293; Williamson, *Mosby's Rangers*, p. 240; Hale, *Four Valiant Years*, p. 431; Edmonds, *Journal*, p. 206.
61. Hale, *Four Valiant Years*, p. 431; Ashby, *Valley Campaigns*, p. 293; Mosby, *Memoirs*, p. 301.
62. Hale, *Four Valiant Years*, p. 433; Jones, *Ranger Mosby*, p. 210; Mosby, *Memoirs*, p. 301; "Hanging," *SHSP*, 24, p. 109.
63. Hale, *Four Valiant Years*, p. 433; "Hanging," *SHSP*, 24, p. 109; *Northern Virginia Daily*, September 24, 1964; Moyer, *History*, p. 217.
64. "Hanging," *SHSP*, 24, p. 109; Fagan, "Custer," p. 45.
65. Hale, *Four Valiant Years*, p. 433.
66. Williamson, *Mosby's Rangers*, p. 242n; Scott, *Partisan Life*, p. 320; Overby, Items, EU; MRF/WHS.
67. Williamson, *Mosby's Rangers*, p. 242n; Fagan, "Custer," pp. 43, 44, 46; Moyer, *History*, p. 218.
68. MRF/WHS; Cartmell, *Shenandoah Valley*, p. 234; Hale, *Four Valiant Years*, p. 431; Jones, *Ranger Mosby*; "Hanging," *SHSP*, 25, p. 240.

69. Fagan, "Custer," p. 43; Denison, *Sabres*, p. 392; MRF/WHS; Jones, *Ranger Mosby*, p. 211; Hale, *Four Valiant Years*, p. 433.
70. Williamson, *Mosby's Rangers*, p. 503; Overby, Items, EU; Crowninshield to Mammy, c. October 1, 1864, Crowninshield, Papers, MSHS.
71. Hale, *Four Valiant Years*, p. 433; Jones, *Ranger Mosby*, p. 211; Wert, *From Winchester*, pp. 132, 134.
72. MRF/WHS; Munson, *Reminiscences*, p. 149; Jones, Ledgerbook, SMM.
73. Ashby, *Valley Campaigns*, p. 294; Jones, *Ranger Mosby*, p. 209.
74. Mosby, "Retaliation," *SHSP*, 27, p. 314; Hale, *Four Valiant Years*, p. 432; *Warren Sentinel*, December 7, 1954; "Monument," *SHSP*, 27, pp. 250–253.
75. Cochran, *Journal*, VHS.

CHAPTER THIRTEEN

1. Mosby, *Memoirs*, p. 307; Jones, *Ranger Mosby*, p. 212; Scott, *Partisan Life*, p. 321; Collins, *Mosby*, p. 8; Mitchell, *Letters*, p. 98.
2. Mitchell, *Letters*, p. 98.
3. "Hanging," *SHSP*, 24, p. 109.
4. Mosby, "Memoirs," VHS.
5. Mosby, "Retaliation," *SHSP*, 27, p. 316; Mosby, *Memoirs*, p. 372.
6. Mosby, *Memoirs*, p. 24.
7. Mitchell, *Letters*, pp. 97–98.
8. *OR*, 43, pt. 2, pp. 22, 29.
9. Ibid., p. 198; CSR/NA.
10. *OR*, 43, pt. 1, p. 618; Williamson, *Mosby's Rangers*, p. 245; Hoadley, *Memorial*, pp. 182, 183.
11. Edmonds, *Journal*, p. 207; Monteiro, *War Reminiscences*, p. 82.
12. *OR*, 43, pt. 2, p. 155.
13. Wert, *From Winchester*, pp. 142, 143.
14. Ibid., p. 142.
15. The correspondence between the Union generals and authorities can be found in *OR*, 43, pt. 1, pp. 28, 29, 30, 50; pt. 2, pp. 152, 177, 187, 210, 249, 258; analysis of the dispute is in Wert, *From Winchester*, pp. 141–143.
16. Harrison, *Landmarks*, pp. 588, 589; Black, *Railroads*, pp. 57, 103.
17. *OR*, 43, pts. 2, pp. 259, 268, 275, 290.
18. Ibid., p. 290; Mosby, *Memoirs*, p. 307.
19. *OR*, 43, pt. 2, p. 273.
20. Mosby, *Memoirs*, pp. 307, 308; Scott, *Partisan Life*, pp. 322, 324; Mosby to F. F. Bowen, July 25, 1898, Bowen, Papers, VHS.
21. Gott, *High*, pp. 45, 47; Mosby, *Memoirs*, pp. 307–309; Scott, *Partisan Life*, pp. 324, 325; Williamson, *Mosby's Rangers*, pp. 250, 251; Crawford, *Mosby*, p. 264.
22. *OR*, 43, pt. 2, p. 290; Crawford, *Mosby*, p. 265; Mosby, *Memoirs*, p. 308.
23. Scott, *Partisan Life*, pp. 325, 326; Williamson, *Mosby's Rangers*, p. 253; Crawford, *Mosby*, p. 265; *OR*, 43, pt. 2, pp. 298, 299.
24. Crawford, *Mosby*, pp. 265, 266; Williamson, *Mosby's Rangers*, p. 254;

Mosby, *Memoirs*, p. 309; Scott, *Partisan Life*, p. 327; *OR*, 43, pt. 2, p. 310.

25. *OR*, 43, pt. 2, pp. 298, 299, 301.

26. Ibid., pp. 310, 311, 312; Leech, *Reveille*, p. 350; Cochran, Journal, VHS.

27. *OR*, 43, pt. 2, p. 319; Edmonds, *Journal*, p. 207.

28. Alexander, *Mosby's Men*, pp. 104, 105; Divine, interview, October 19, 1988; Gott, interview, October 20, 1988; Crawford, *Mosby*, p. 267.

29. Scott, *Partisan Life*, pp. 327–329; Hotchkiss, "Map of Fauquier & Loudoun Co's.," LC.

30. Scott, *Partisan Life*, p. 327; Williamson, *Mosby's Rangers*, p. 256; *OR*, 43, pt. 2, pp. 334, 335; Sober, Diary, USAMHI; New York *Herald*, October 11, 1864.

31. *OR*, 43, pt. 2, pp. 334, 335.

32. Ibid., pp. 335, 341; Cochran, Journal, VHS.

33. *OR*, 43, pt. 2, pp. 341, 347; Crawford, *Mosby*, pp. 274, 275; Gott, *Years*, p. 183.

34. *OR*, 43, pt. 2, pp. 345, 348.

35. Ibid., pp. 347, 364; Scott, *Partisan Life*, pp. 329, 334; Munson, *Reminiscences*, pp. 231–233; Sober, Diary, USAMHI.

36. Williamson, *Mosby's Rangers*, pp. 273–274.

37. Mosby to Pauline Mosby, October 12, 1864, Mosby, Papers, UVA; Scott, *Partisan Life*, p. 327.

38. Tidwell, *Come Retribution*, pp. 140–143; Krick, Collection.

39. Tidwell, *Come Retribution*, p. 140; Williamson, *Mosby's Rangers*, p. 256.

40. Tidwell, *Come Retribution*, p. 141; Williamson, *Mosby's Rangers*, p. 256; Scott, *Partisan Life*, p. 311.

41. Tidwell, *Come Retribution*, pp. 141–142; Krick, Collection; Williamson, *Mosby's Rangers*, p. 256; Scott, *Partisan Life*, p. 313.

42. Tidwell, *Come Retribution*, p. 142; Krick Collection; Jones, Ledgerbook, SSM; Williamson, *Mosby's Rangers*, pp. 256, 477.

43. Lufkin, *History*, p. 110; Walker, *History*, p. 165; Nichols, *Soldier's Story*, p. 170; Tyler, *Recollections*, p. 290.

44. Burkholder, "Barn-Burners," *SHSP*, 28, p. 98; J. S. Lloyd to Sister, September 21, 1864, Lloyd, H. L; *OR*, 43, pt. 2, p. 304; Bowen, *History*, p. 382; Lynch, *Civil War Diary*, p. 128.

45. Williamson, *Mosby's Rangers*, p. 259; Crawford, *Mosby*, pp. 268–269; Haines, *History*, p. 273; Alexander Neil to friends, October 13, 1864, Neil, Letters, UVA; Stevens, *Three Years*, p. 410; Putnam, *Memories*, p. 351.

46. Mosby, *Memoirs*, pp. 312, 313; Bushong, *Historic*, p. 241.

47. Williamson, *Mosby's Rangers*, p. 260; Munson, *Reminiscences*, p. 221; Corbin, "Memorandum," VHS.

48. Mosby, *Memoirs*, pp. 313, 314; Scott, *Partisan Life*, p. 335; Williamson, *Mosby's Rangers*, p. 261; Munson, *Reminiscences*, p. 222.

49. Jones, *Ranger Mosby*, p. 216; *OR*, 43, pt. 2, p. 368; New York *Herald*, October 17, 1864; *OR Atlas*, Plate C.

50. Williamson, *Mosby's Rangers*, p. 261; Mosby, *Memoirs*, p. 314; "Drums," *BOM*, p. 10; New York *Herald*, October 17, 1864.

51. Williamson, *Mosby's Rangers*, p. 261; Alexander, *Mosby's Men*, pp. 110, 112; Munson, *Reminiscences*, p. 223; "Drums," *BOM*, p. 10; New York *Herald*, October 17, 1864; *CMH* III, p. 405.

52. Mosby, *Memoirs*, pp. 315, 321; Jones, *Ranger Mosby*, p. 218; Scott, *Partisan Life*, p. 336.

53. Mosby, *Memoirs*, pp. 316, 317.

54. Ibid., p. 317; Crawford, *Mosby*, p. 271; Williamson, *Mosby's Rangers*, p. 263; Alexander, *Mosby's Men*, p. 113; Mosby, Papers, UVA; "Drums," *BOM*, p. 10.

55. *OR*, 43, pt. 2, p. 368; "Drums," *BOM*, p. 10; New York *Herald*, October 17, 1864; Jones, Ledgerbook, SMM.

56. Mosby, *Memoirs*, pp. 319, 320; Alexander, *Mosby's Men*, p. 114.

57. Divine, interview, October 19, 1988; Scott, *Partisan Life*, p. 337; Williamson, *Mosby's Rangers*, p. 263; Mosby, Papers, UVA; *Spies, Scouts*, p. 131; Jones, *Ranger Mosby*, p. 219.

58. *OR*, 43, pt. 2, p. 378; Williamson, *Mosby's Rangers*, p. 266; Monteiro, *War Reminiscences*, p. 210; Hoadley, *Memorial*, p. 186; CSR/NA.

59. *OR*, 43, pt. 1, p. 635.

60. Wert, *From Winchester*, pp. 157–166.

61. Ibid., pp. 165–173.

62. Ibid., Chapters Eleven–Thirteen.

63. *OR*, 43, pt. 2, p. 466.

64. Mosby to F. F. Bowen, April 29, 1895, Bowen, Papers, VHS.

65. Williamson, *Mosby's Rangers*, pp. 280, 281; Crawford, *Mosby*, pp. 278, 279.

66. *OR*, 43, pt. 1, p. 186; pt. 2, p. 475; Warner, *Generals In Blue*, p. 132; Scott, *Partisan Life*, p. 350.

67. Munson, *Reminiscences*, pp. 135–136.

68. Ibid., p. 136; Crawford, *Mosby*, p. 279; Williamson, *Mosby's Rangers*, p. 283.

69. Williamson, *Mosby's Rangers*, p. 284; Crawford, *Mosby*, p. 279.

70. *OR*, 43, pt. 2, p. 488; CSR/NA; Hard, *History*, p. 315.

71. Mosby to F. F. Bowen, June 15 [?], Bowen, Papers, VHS.

72. Alexander, *Mosby's Men*, pp. 129, 130; Williamson, *Mosby's Rangers*, pp. 284, 285; Scott, *Partisan Life*, p. 353; Divine, interview, October 19, 1988.

73. Scott, *Partisan Life*, p. 354; Mosby to F. F. Bowen, June 15 [?], Bowen, Papers, VHS.

74. Williamson, *Mosby's Rangers*, p. 285; Scott, *Partisan Life*, p. 354; Alexander, *Mosby's Men*, pp. 131, 132.

75. Alexander, *Mosby's Men*, p. 132; Williamson, *Mosby's Rangers*, p. 285; Crawford, *Mosby*, pp. 283–284; Scott, *Partisan Life*, p. 354.

76. Alexander, *Mosby's Men*, pp. 132, 133, 136; Williamson, *Mosby's Rangers*, p. 285; *Old Homes*, p. 417.

77. Alexander, *Mosby's Men*, p. 135; Scott, *Partisan Life*, p. 354; Mosby to F. F. Bowen, June 15 [?], Bowen, Papers, VHS; Crawford, *Mosby*, p. 283.

78. Alexander, *Mosby's Men*, pp. 136, 137; Williamson, *Mosby's Rangers*, p. 285; *OR*, 43, pt. 1, p. 646; Scott, *Partisan Life*, p. 354; CSR/NA.

79. Mosby to F. F. Bowen, June 15 [?], Bowen, Papers, VHS.

80. Ibid.

81. *OR*, 43, pt. 2, pp. 405, 494, 528, 537, 583.
82. Mosby, *Memoirs*, p. 328; Mitchell, *Letters*, p. 75.
83. Mitchell, *Letters*, p. 99; Fount Beattie to John S. Russell, March 18, 1920, Russell, Papers, CCHA.

CHAPTER FOURTEEN

1. Brewster, *MOLLUS*, pp. 85, 86; Gott, *Years*, p. 128.
2. "Honor," *SHSP*, 25, p. 242; Mosby to Landon Mason, March 29, 1912, Mosby, Papers, DU; Alexander, *Mosby's Men*, p. 143.
3. Mason, *CV*, 14, p. 68.
4. *OR*, 43, pt. 2, p. 910.
5. Williamson, *Mosby's Rangers*, p. 288; Crawford, *Mosby*, p. 288; Scheel, *Civil War*, p. 80; "Mosby," *CV*, 7, p. 389; Mosby, "Retaliation," *SHSP*, 27, pp. 320, 321; Beach, *First New York*, p. 441.
6. Mosby, "Retaliation," *SHSP*, 27, p. 316.
7. Ibid., p. 316; Alexander, *Mosby's Men*, pp. 144, 145; Brewster, *MOLLUS*, p. 90.
8. Brewster, *MOLLUS*, pp. 74, 77, 78, 91.
9. Ibid., p. 91; New York *Times*, November 10, 1864; Richmond *Dispatch*, December 1, 1864; Alexander, *Mosby's Men*, pp. 144, 145.
10. Mosby, "Retaliation," *SHSP*, 27, p. 319; Mosby to Landon Mason, March 29, 1912, Mosby, Papers, DU.
11. New York *Times*, November 10, 1864; Fagan, "Custer," pp. 35, 36; Brewster, *MOLLUS*, p. 92; *OR*, 43, pt. 2, p. 566.
12. Alexander, *Mosby's Men*, p. 147.
13. New York *Times*, November 10, 1864; Fagan, "Custer," pp. 35, 36; Jones, Ledgerbook, SMM; Brewster, *MOLLUS*, p. 92; *OR*, 43, pt. 2, p. 566.
14. Williamson, *Mosby's Rangers*, pp. 293, 294, 364, 533; CSR/NA; Munson, *Reminiscences*, p. 149.
15. Williamson, *Mosby's Rangers*, p. 294; Kathy Gracher to Bob Ewing, June 6, 1973, Gracher, CCHA; Gold, *History*, p. 128; New York *Times*, November 10, 1864.
16. Munson, *Reminiscences*, pp. 150, 151; New York *Times*, November 10, 1864; *OR*, 43, pt. 2, p. 566; Scott, *Partisan Life*, p. 358.
17. New York *Times*, November 10, 1864; Fagan, "Custer," pp. 35, 36; *OR*, 43, pt. 2, p. 566.
18. *OR*, 43, pt. 2, p. 566; Fagan, "Custer," pp. 35, 36.
19. Mosby to Landon Mason, March 29, 1912, Mosby, Papers, DU; Mitchell, *Letters*, p. 179.
20. *OR*, 43, pt. 2, p. 920; Williamson, *Mosby's Rangers*, p. 294; Jones, Ledgerbook, SMM.
21. New York *Times*, November 24, 1864.
22. Williamson, *Mosby's Rangers*, p. 299; Crawford, *Mosby*, pp. 294, 295; Divine, interview, October 19, 1988; Carpenter, "One For One Hundred," *PCCHA*, V, pp. 60–62.
23. *OR*, 43, pt. 2, p. 315; F. F. Bowen to Charlie, October 15, 1864, Bowen,

Papers, VHS; Williamson, *Mosby's Rangers*, p. 299; Crawford, *Mosby*, p. 294.

24. Williamson, *Mosby's Rangers*, p. 299; *OR*, 43, pt. 2, p. 593.

25. Munson, *Reminiscences*, p. 118; Williamson, *Mosby's Rangers*, p. 300; Scott, *Partisan Life*, pp. 363, 364.

26. *OR*, 43, pt. 1, p. 616.

27. Williamson, *Mosby's Rangers*, p. 301.

28. Ibid., p. 153; Munson, *Reminiscences*, p. 118; Scott, *Partisan Life*, p. 366; Crawford, *Mosby*, p. 307; Chappelear, *Maps*, p. 2; Divine, interview, October 19, 1988.

29. Scott, *Partisan Life*, p. 366; Munson, *Reminiscences*, p. 119; Alexander, *Mosby's Men*, pp. 119, 120.

30. Munson, *Reminiscences*, p. 119; Scott, *Partisan Life*, p. 366; Williamson, *Mosby's Rangers*, p. 303.

31. Scott, *Partisan Life*, p. 367; Munson, *Reminiscences*, pp. 78, 79.

32. Munson, *Reminiscences*, p. 9; CSR/NA.

33. Scott, *Partisan Life*, p. 367.

34. Ibid., p. 367; Munson, *Reminiscences*, p. 119.

35. Williamson, *Mosby's Rangers*, p. 303; Scott, *Partisan Life*, p. 368; Munson, *Reminiscences*, p. 122.

36. Bushong, *Historic*, p. 243; Scott, *Partisan Life*, p. 367; Williamson, *Mosby's Rangers*, p. 303.

37. Williamson, *Mosby's Rangers*, p. 304.

38. Ibid., p. 304; Scott, *Partisan Life*, pp. 367, 368; Munson, *Reminiscences*, p. 120; Bushong, *Historic*, p. 243.

39. Munson, *Reminiscences*, p. 120.

40. Ibid., p. 120; Scott, *Partisan Life*, p. 368; Williamson, *Mosby's Rangers*, p. 305; Opie, *Rebel*, p. 276.

41. Scott, *Partisan Life*, pp. 369, 370; Munson, *Reminiscences*, p. 120; "History of the War," CCHA; *Military Operations*, p. 118; Jones, Ledgerbook, SMM; CSR/NA; Bushong, *Historic*, p. 244; USC, 1860.

42. Scott, *Partisan Life*, pp. 368, 369; Alexander, *Mosby's Men*, p. 126; Munson, *Reminiscences*, p. 123.

43. Munson, *Reminiscences*, p. 121; Williamson, *Mosby's Rangers*, p. 305; *OR*, 43, pt. 2, pp. 648, 654; *National Tribune*, October 31, 1889; Opie, *Rebel*, p. 278; Mosby to W. H. Chapman, April 29, 1891, Mosby, Papers, DU.

44. Williamson, *Mosby's Rangers*, pp. 305, 305n; Munson, *Reminiscences*, p. 124; Bryan, *Joseph Bryan*, p. 138; McCarty, *Foothills*, p. 118.

45. Scott, *Partisan Life*, pp. 370, 371; Williamson, *Mosby's Rangers*, p. 306; Alexander, *Mosby's Men*, p. 119; *National Tribune*, October 31, 1889.

46. Crawford, *Mosby*, pp. 302–304; Scott, *Partisan Life*, p. 374.

47. Crawford, *Mosby*, p. 306; Munson, *Reminiscences*, p. 141; *OR*, 43, pt. 1, p. 670.

48. Crawford, *Mosby*, p. 306; Hunter, *Women*, pp. 137, 138; Jones, Ledgerbook, SMM.

49. Williamson, *Mosby's Rangers*, p. 313; CSR/NA.

50. Williamson, *Mosby's Rangers*, p. 313; Munson, *Reminiscences*, p. 65; Scott, *Partisan Life*, pp. 248, 391; Gott, *Years*, p. 111.

51. Scott, *Partisan Life*, pp. 391, 392; Williamson, *Mosby's Rangers*, pp. 287, 533, 541; Jones, *Ranger Mosby*, p. 231; Munson, *Reminiscences*, p. 9; Gott, interview, October 20, 1988; Krick, Collection; CSR/NA.

CHAPTER FIFTEEN

1. *OR*, 43, pt. 2, pp. 671–672.
2. Ibid., p. 672.
3. Ibid., p. 581.
4. Ibid., pt. 1, pp. 55–56.
5. Ibid., p. 671; Edmonds, *Journal*, p. 209; Hotchkiss, "Map of Fauquier & Loudoun Co's," LC.
6. *OR*, 43, pt. 1, p. 671; Chappelear, *Maps*, p. 3.
7. *OR*, 43, pt. 1, p. 671; pt. 2, p. 685; Cheney, *History*, p. 241; Moyer, *History*, p. 143; "Sky Meadows"; Divine, interview, October 19, 1988.
8. Broun, "Family Events," UVA.
9. Ibid.; *OR*, 43, pt. 1, pp. 671, 672; Moyer, *History*, p. 143.
10. *OR*, 43, pt. 1, p. 671; pt. 2, p. 702; Humphreys, *Field*, pp. 191, 192; Poland, *From Frontier*, p. 2.
11. Carrie Taylor to Mrs. Hannah Stabler, December 3, 1864, TBL; Marsh, "Purcellville," TBL; Janney, *Memoirs*, p. 230; Weatherby, *Lovettsville*, p. 34; *Blue Ridge Herald*, January 9, 1941; *OR*, 43, pp. 2, 712; Turner, *Loudoun*, p. 56.
12. Hall, *History*, pp. 392, 393; Janney, *Memoirs*, p. 230.
13. Broun, "Family Events," UVA; *OR*, 43, pt. 1, pp. 671, 672; Moyer, *History*, p. 144.
14. Crawford, *Mosby*, p. 310; Turner, *Loudoun*, p. 56; *OR*, 43, pt. 1, p. 673; Poland, *From Frontier*, pp. 221, 223, 228; Loudoun County, Manuscripts, VHS.
15. Gott, *Years*, p. 55; Scheel, *Civil War*, pp. 81, 83; Myers, *Comanches*, p. 356.
16. *OR*, 43, pt. 1, p. 672; Broun, "Family Events," UVA; Crawford, *Mosby*, p. 311; Williamson, *Mosby's Rangers*, p. 312; Scott, *Partisan Life*, pp. 376, 378; Alexander, *Mosby's Men*, p. 154; Hall, *History*, p. 242; CSR/NA.
17. Crawford, *Mosby*, pp. 313–315; Mosby, Papers, UVA; *OR*, 43, pt. 2, pp. 744, 752.
18. Mosby to Joseph Bryan, November 25, 1903, Bryan, Papers, VHS; Mosby, *Memoirs*, p. 334; Scott, *Partisan Life*, p. 381.
19. *OR*, 43, pt. 2, p. 937.
20. CSR/NA; Wallace, *Guide*, p. 71; Krick, *Lee's Colonels*, pp. 78, 294.
21. Jones, *Ranger Mosby*, p. 251; Williamson, *Mosby's Rangers*, p. 489; Scott, *Partisan Life*, pp. 387, 388.
22. Mosby, Papers, DU; Gott, interview, October 20, 1988; Munson, *Reminiscences*, p. 249.

23. Gott, interview, October 20, 1988; Mosby, Papers, DU; Munson, *Reminiscences*, p. 249; Mosby, *Memoirs*, p. 335.

24. Mosby, *Memoirs*, p. 336; *Fauquier County*, pp. 255, 256; *Old Homes*, p. 188; Divine, interview, October 19, 1988; Gott, interview, October 20, 1988.

25. Gott, interview, October 20, 1988; Mosby, *Memoirs*, pp. 336, 338; *Fauquier County*, p. 256.

26. Gott, interview, October 20, 1988; Mosby, *Memoirs*, p. 337.

27. Gott, interview, October 20, 1988; Mosby, *Memoirs*, p. 338; *Spies, Scouts*, p. 131.

28. Gott, interview, October 20, 1988; Mosby, *Memoirs*, pp. 340, 341; Williamson, *Mosby's Rangers*, p. 331; *OR*, 43, pt. 2, p. 843.

29. Gott, interview, October 20, 1988; Crawford, *Mosby*, p. 316; Mosby, *Memoirs*, p. 340.

30. *OR*, 43, pt. 2, p. 843; Warrenton *Virginian*, February 18, 1904.

31. *OR*, 43, pt. 2, pp. 831, 843; Mosby, *Memoirs*, pp. 342, 343; Jones, *Ranger Mosby*, pp. 246–248.

32. Divine, interview, October 19, 1988; Gott, interview, October 20, 1988; Mosby, Papers, UVA; Monteiro, *War Reminiscences*, p. 35; New York *Times*, January 2, 1865.

33. Divine, interview, October 19, 1988; Jones, Ledgerbook, SMM; *Fauquier County*, p. 251; Crawford, *Mosby*, p. 320.

34. *OR*, 43, pt. 2, pp. 831, 834, 838, 843, 844.

35. Ibid., p. 834; Peyton, "Diaries," PWCL; New York *Times*, January 1, 1865.

36. Mosby, *Memoirs*, p. 354; Crawford, *Mosby*, pp. 320, 321; Broun, "Family Events," UVA; Jones, *Ranger Mosby*, pp. 251, 252; Monteiro, *War Reminiscences*, pp. 34, 36.

37. Broun, "Family Events," UVA; Myers, *Comanches*, pp. 343, 357, 359.

38. Williamson, *Mosby's Rangers*, pp. 489, 490; Jones, *Ranger Mosby*, p. 244.

39. Williamson, *Mosby's Rangers*, pp. 339, 340, 490; Crawford, *Mosby*, p. 325; Scott, *Partisan Life*, p. 464; Mosby, *Memoirs*, p. 354; Monteiro, *War Reminiscences*, p. 125; *OR*, 46, p. 2, p. 386.

40. Williamson, *Mosby's Rangers*, pp. 490–492; *OR*, 46, pt. 2, p. 1283.

41. Mosby, Papers, UVA; Warner, *Generals In Gray*, pp. 170, 178.

42. Munson, *Reminiscences*, p. 204; Crawford, *Mosby*, p. 330.

43. Munson, *Reminiscences*, pp. 205–207.

44. Crawford, *Mosby*, pp. 332–333.

45. Ibid., p. 333; *OR*, 46, pt. 1, p. 463; CSR/NA.

46. *OR*, 46, pt. 1, pp. 463, 464, 467; Crawford, *Mosby*, pp. 334, 335.

47. *OR*, 46, pt. 1, pp. 464, 467.

48. Scott, *Partisan Life*, pp. 448, 449.

49. Ibid., pp. 449–452; *OR*, 46, pt. 1, p. 464–467; Crawford, *Mosby*, pp. 336–340; Mitchell, *Letters*, p. 144.

50. Broun, "Family Events," UVA.

CHAPTER SIXTEEN

1. Mosby to Pauline Mosby, February 3, 1865, Mosby, Papers, UVA; another copy in Mosby, Papers, VHS.
2. OR, 46, pt. 2, p. 666.
3. Ibid., pt. 1, p. 1308; Monteiro, War Reminiscences, pp. 100, 116.
4. OR, 46, pt. 1, p. 552; pt. 2, p. 898; Crawford, Mosby, p. 344; Williamson, Mosby's Rangers, pp. 352–354; CSR/NA; Janney, Memoirs, pp. 232, 235.
5. Williamson, Mosby's Rangers, p. 355; Crawford, Mosby, p. 346; OR, 46, pt. 1, p. 535.
6. Janney, Memoirs, p. 233; Williamson, Mosby's Rangers, pp. 356, 503; Alexander, Mosby's Men, p. 157; Wiltshire, CV, 8, p. 74.
7. Williamson, Mosby's Rangers, pp. 357, 358, 358n; CMH,III, p. 727.
8. Monteiro, War Reminiscences, p. 123.
9. Williamson, Mosby's Rangers, pp. 358n, 504; OR, 46, pt. 3, p. 82; Crawford, Mosby, pp. 348, 349.
10. Williamson, Mosby's Rangers, p. 359; OR, 46, pt. 1, pp. 535, 536; pt. 3, p. 82; Crawford, Mosby, pp. 349, 350.
11. Munson, Reminiscences, pp. 253, 254; Williamson, Mosby's Rangers, pp. 361, 362; Scott, Partisan Life, p. 460; Chappelear, "Early Grants," PCCHA VIII, pp. 27, 28
12. Munson, Reminiscences, p. 254; Williamson, Mosby's Rangers, p. 362; Scott, Partisan Life, p. 460.
13. Williamson, Mosby's Rangers, p. 362; Scott, Partisan Life, p. 461.
14. Munson, Reminiscences, pp. 253–255; Wiltshire, CV, 8, p. 74; Edmonds, Journal, p. 205.
15. OR, 46, pt. 3, p. 1359.
16. Jones, Ranger Mosby, p. 258.
17. Ibid., p. 258; Prince William, p. 234; Scott, Partisan Life, p. 462, Williamson, Mosby's Rangers, p. 364.
18. Baylor, Bull Run, p. 310.
19. Scott, Partisan Life, p. 462; CSR/NA; Crawford, Mosby, p. 364.
20. Wallace, Guide, p. 72; Williamson, Mosby's Rangers, p. 364; Scott, Partisan Life, p. 462; Krick, Collection; CSR/NA; CMH III, p. 443.
21. Crawford, Mosby, p. 354; OR, 46, pt. 3, p. 617.
22. Williamson, Mosby's Rangers, p. 367; Munson, Reminiscences, pp. 256, 257; Hard, History, pp. 316, 317; OR,46, pt. 3, p. 715.
23. OR, 46, pt. 1, p. 1310; pt. 2, p. 595; Munson Reminiscences, pp. 257, 258; Williamson, Mosby's Rangers, pp. 492.
24. Monteiro, War Reminiscences, p. 126; Munson, Reminiscences, p. 261; Williamson, Mosby's Rangers, p. 492.
25. OR, 46, pt. 3, pp. 684, 685, 697; Warner,Generals In Blue, p. 549.
26. Warner, Generals In Blue, pp. 202–204; OR, 46, pt. 1, p. 525.
27. OR, 46, pt. 3, p. 661.
28. Ibid., p. 699.
29. Ibid., p. 714.

30. Ibid., p. 742; Scott, *Partisan Life,* p. 470; Carpenter, "One," *PCCHA* V, p. 57; Monteiro, *War Reminiscences,* p. 145; Washington *Evening Star,* April 13, 1865.

31. *OR,* 46, pt. 1, p. 526; pt. 3, p. 725.

32. Monteiro, *War Reminiscences,* pp. 147, 153, 155, 157, 167; Williamson, *Mosby's Rangers,* p. 377; Scott, *Partisan Life,* pp. 470, 471.

33. *OR,* 46, pt. 3. pp. 765–766; Mosby, *Memoirs,* p. 360.

34. *OR,* 46, pt. 3, pp. 799, 800; Monteiro, *War Reminiscences,* p. 182.

35. *OR,* 46, pt. 3, p. 800.

36. Ibid., p. 800.

37. Ibid., pp. 817, 838.

38. Tidwell, *Come Retribution,* pp. 339, 340, 470.

39. Ibid., pp. 418–421.

40. Ibid., p. 469; Williamson, *Mosby's Rangers,* p. 217; CSR/NA; Kidd, *Personal,* p. 449; Bakeless, *Spies,* p. 391.

41. Monteiro, *War Reminiscences,* pp. 202, 203; Kidd, *Personal,* pp. 447, 448.

42. Mosby to H. C. Jordan, August 23, 1909, Mosby, Papers, DU; Kidd, *Personal,* pp. 448, 449.

43. *OR,* 46, pt. 3, pp. 774, 830.

44. Ibid., pp. 830, 831; Kidd, *Personal,* p. 452; Williamson, *Mosby's Rangers,* p. 384.

45. *OR,* 46, pt. 3, p. 839.

46. Monteiro, *War Reminiscences,* p. 203.

47. *Clarke Courier,* March 7, 1940; *OR,* 46, pt. 3, p. 868; Munson, *Reminiscences,* pp. 266, 267; Monteiro, *War Reminiscences,* p. 204; Jones, *Ranger Mosby,* p. 264.

48. Munson, *Reminiscences,* pp. 267–268; Monteiro, *War Reminiscences,* pp. 133, 139.

49. Monteiro, *War Reminiscences,* p. 207.

50. Ibid., p. 207; Munson, *Reminiscences,* p. 268.

EPILOGUE

1. Williamson, *Mosby's Rangers,* p. 392; Munson, *Reminiscences,* p. 270.

2. Williamson, *Mosby's Rangers,* p. 392; Mosby to H. C. Jordan, August 23, 1909, Mosby, Papers, DU.

3. Divine, interview, October 19, 1988; Scheel, *Civil War,* p. 87; Williamson, *Mosby's Rangers,* p. 392; Jones, *Ranger Mosby,* p. 270.

4. Copy of Farewell Address in Mosby, Papers, USAMHI; Williamson, *Mosby's Rangers,* p. 392; Jones, *Ranger Mosby,* pp. 270, 271.

5. Williamson, *Mosby's Rangers,* pp. 393, 394; Edmonds, *Journal,* pp. 221, 222; Munson, *Reminiscences,* pp. 269, 271; Monteiro, *War Reminiscences,* p. 55.

6. Mitchell, *Letters,* p. 63; Divine, interview, October 19, 1988.

7. Williamson, *Mosby's Rangers,* pp. 393, 394; Munson, *Reminiscences,* pp. 271, 272; *OR,* 46, pt. 3, pp. 897, 1141; CSR/NA; Jones, Ledgerbook, SMM.

8. Munson, *Reminiscences,* pp. 272, 273; Bakeless, *Spies,* p. 391; *OR,* 46, pt. 3,

pp. 897, 1003, 1080, 1082; Mosby to H. C. Jordan, August 23, 1909, Mosby, Papers, DU.

9. Munson, *Reminiscences*, pp. 272, 273; Palmer, *CV*, 5, p. 195.
10. Jones, *Ranger Mosby*, pp. 272–275; Leesburg *Mirror*, June 29, 1865.
11. New York *Times*, August 2, 1865.
12. Alexander, *Mosby's Men*, p. 28.
13. Scott, *Partisan Life*, p. 387; Fitts, "Mosby," *Galaxy* II, p. 644; Hagemann, *Fighting Rebels*, p. 261; Glazier, *Three Years*, p. 153; Grant, *Personal Memoirs*, 2, p. 142.
14. Foster, *Ghosts*, pp. 4, 5–8.
15. Jones, *Gray Ghosts*, p. 41n.
16. These figures were extracted from various sources, particularly Ranger memoirs and CSR/NA, and then were compiled by a computer.
17. Starr, *Union Cavalry*, pp. 53, 54; Jones, *Ranger Mosby*, p. 12; Mosby, *Memoirs*, p. 126.
18. Jones, *Gray Ghosts*, p. viii; Grant, "Partisan Warfare,"*MR*, p. 55.
19. Jones, *Gray Ghosts*, p. viii; Grant, "Partisan Warfare," *MR*, p. 55; Asprey, *War*, p. 181; Starr, *Union Cavalry*, pp. 55–56.
20. Williamson, *Mosby's Rangers*, pp. 529–530.
21. Ibid., p. 307n; Munson, *Reminiscences*, p. 78.
22. Jones, *Ranger Mosby*, Chapter 25; Siepel, *Rebel*, pp. 187–189.
23. Williamson, *Mosby's Rangers*, pp. 520–528.
24. Mosby, *Memoirs*, p. xxviii.

BIBLIOGRAPHY

UNPUBLISHED SOURCES

Clarke County Historical Association, Museum, Berryville, VA:
  Kathy Gracher, Letter to Bob Ewing, June 6, 1973
  "History of the War between the States Compiled by The Stonewall Chapter
    of the Daughters of the Confederacy, Berryville, Virginia," United
    Daughters of the Confederacy Collection
  Samuel Scolloy Moore, "Through The Shadow: A boy's memories," type-
    script
  John S. Mosby, Letter to John S. Russell, August 28, 1899
  John S. Russell Collection
  Treadwell Smith Diary

Divine, John. Interview with author, October 19, 1988

Duke University, William R. Perkins Library, Durham, NC:
  John S. Mosby Papers
  John S. Russell Papers

Emory University, Robert W. Woodruff Library, Atlanta, GA:
  Forty-third Battalion, Virginia Cavalry Items, Confederate Miscellany I
  William Thomas Overby Items, Confederate Miscellany II

General Stuart–Colonel Mosby Museum, American Historical Foundation, Richmond, VA:
  Virgil Carrington Jones, Ledgerbook, Mosby's Rangers

Gott, John K. Interview with author, October 20, 1988

Handley Library, Archives Room, Winchester, VA:
  John S. Mosby Letter, E. E. Bayliss, Jr. Collection

John S. Russell Papers
United Confederate Veterans, Turner Ashby Comp, Membership Applications
United Daughters of the Confederacy, Turner Ashby Chapter #54, Records

Harpers Ferry National Historic Park, Harpers Ferry, WV:
Horace Ball Civil War Letters

The Huntington Library, San Marino, CA:
J. S. Lloyd, Letter to Sister, September 21, 1864, Americana Collection

Jones, Virgil Carrington. Interview with author, June 12, 1989

Kirkby, Michael Ross, "Partisan And Counterpartisan Activity in Northern Virginia." Master's Thesis, University of Georgia, 1977

Krick, Robert K. Collection, Fredericksburg, VA

Library of Congress, Washington, DC:
William Hamilton Papers
Jedediah Hotchkiss, "Map of Fauquier & Loudoun Co.'s Va.," Jedediah Hotchkiss Collection
———, "A Map of Fauquier Co. Virginia," Jedediah Hotchkiss Collection
———, Untitled Map of Fauquier County, Virginia, Jedediah Hotchkiss Collection
John S. Mosby Papers
Aaron B. Tompkins Letters
John Chester White, "Civil War Journal of John Chester White"

Marks, David. Interview with author, September 14, 1988

Maryland Historical Society, Baltimore, MD:
Augustus W. Bradford Papers

Massachusetts Historical Society, Boston, MA:
Caspar Crowninshield Letters, Crowninshield-Magnus Collection

Middleburg Library, Middleburg, VA:
"Loudoun Chapter of the Grand Division of Daughters of Confederacy in Virginia (Secretary's Book) 1896"

National Archives, Washington, DC:
Compiled Service Records, Mosby's Regiment, Record Group 109

The Pennsylvania State University, Pattee Library, University Park, PA:
William Thompson Letters, The Baldridge Collection of Civil War Letters

Prince William County Library, Manassas, VA:
  John William Peyton, "The Diaries of John William Peyton 1862–1865," Transcribed by Robert A. Hodge, 1978, typescript copy

Sky Meadows State Park, Paris, VA:
  Photograph, No. G 457, 1895 Reunion of Mosby's Rangers
  "Sky Meadows State Park: A History"

Thomas Balch Library, Leesburg, VA:
  Helen Hirst Marsh, "Purcellville, Virginia, 1852–1952"
  ———, "Water Mills of Loudoun County"
  Carrie Taylor, Letter to Mrs. Hannah Stabler, December 3, 1864

United States Army Military History Institute, Carlisle Barracks, PA:
  John W. Barnard, Deposition made before Regimental Quartermaster, September 1, 1864, The Earl W. Hess Collection
  Civil War Miscellaneous Collection:
    John H. Bevan Letters
    Ernst V. Diezelski, "An Episode of our late War"
    John S. Mosby Letters
    Will Ramsey Letters
    David Sober Diary, September 3, 1864–January 8, 1865
    Charles H. Veil, "An Old Boy's Personal Recollections and Reminiscences of the Civil War"
  Civil War Times Illustrated Collection:
    William A. McIlhenny Diary
    John S. Mosby, "Farewell to His Command"
    Silas D. Wesson Diary
  William H. H. Emmous, "Affadavit on Destruction of Wagon Train, August 13, 1864," Keith R. Keller Collection
  Harrisburg Civil War Round Table Collection:
    Aaron E. Bachman, "My Experiences As A Union Soldier in the Civil War"
    Richard J. DelVecchio, "With The First New Dragoons: From The Letters Of Jared L. Ainsworth," 1971
    Joseph Schneider, Letter of July 24, 1864
  Janney Family, Loudoun County, Virginia, Letters, Michael P. Musick Collection
  Lewis Leigh Collection:
    "Record of Actions, Engagements etc. of 5th New York Cavalry"
    Marion Wright, Letter of March 29, 1863
  John S. Mosby Papers
  Joseph Schubert Papers

University of Michigan, Bentley Historical Library, Ann Arbor MI:
  George W. Barbour Diary, Michigan Historical Collections
  Fred Corselius Letters, George Corselius Papers

James Kidd Letters
John Rising Morey Letters
James D. Rowe, "Camp Tales of a Union Soldier"

University of Virginia, Alderman Library, Charlottesville, VA:
 Catherine Barbara Broun, "Family Events, 1862 to 1865"
 John S. Mosby Papers
 Alexander Neil Letters

Virginia Historical Society, Richmond, VA:
 Frederick Fillison Bowen Papers
 Joseph Bryan Papers
 Catherine Mary Powell (Noland) Cochran Journal
 Lemuel Armistead Corbin, "Memorandum [1864 October] 13, of skirmish at
  Adamstown, Md."
 Ida Dulany Diary, Mary Eliza Dulany Papers
 Loudoun County, Manuscripts, 21-A
 John S. Mosby, "Memoir," Joseph Bryan Papers
 John S. Mosby, "*Stealing A General*," As told to James F. Breazeale, John S.
  Mosby Papers

Virginia Military Institute, Archives, Preston Library, Lexington, VA:
 Alumni Files

Warren Heritage Society, Laura Virginia Hale Archives, Front Royal,
 VA:
 Mosby's Rangers File, Hale Historical Collection

Warren Rifles Confederate Museum, Front Royal, VA:
 Collection

NEWSPAPERS

Baltimore *American & Commercial Advertiser*
Blue Ridge Herald
Clarke Courier
Fauquier Democrat
Leesburg *Mirror*
Loudoun Times-Mirror
National Tribune
New York *Herald*
New York *Times*
Northern Virginia Daily
Richmond *Dispatch*
Warren Sentinel
Warrenton *Virginian*
Washington *Evening Star*

PUBLISHED SOURCES

Alexander, John H. *Mosby's Men*. New York and Washington: The Neale Publishing Company, 1907.

Angelo, F. M. "Reunion Of Mosby's Men." *Confederate Veteran* XXXIII (1925).

"An Appraisal Of: John S. Mosby," *Civil War Times Illustrated*, Volume 4, Number 7 (November 1965).

Ashby, Thomas A. *The Valley Campaigns. Being the Reminiscences of a Non-Combatant While Between the Lines in the Shenandoah Valley During the War of the States.* New York: The Neale Publishing Company, 1914.

Asprey, Robert B. *War In The Shadows: The Guerrilla in History, Volume I.* Garden City, NY: Doubleday & Company, Inc., 1975.

Badger, W. W. "My Capture And Escape From Mosby." *United States Service Magazine, June 1865.*

Baird, Charles J. "Mosby's Territory," *Confederate Veteran* XXXI (1923).

Bakeless, John. *Spies of the Confederacy*. Philadelphia & New York: J. B. Lippincott Company, 1970.

Baylor, George. *Bull Run to Bull Run: Or. Four Years in the Army of Northern Virginia.* Richmond, VA: B. F. Johnson Publishing Company, 1900.

Beach, William H. *The First New York (Lincoln) Cavalry, From April 19, 1861 to July 7, 1865.* Reprint edition. Annandale, VA: Bacon Race Books, 1988.

Benedict, George G. *Army Life In Virginia*. Burlington, VT: Free Press Association, 1895.

Benedict, G. G. *Vermont In The Civil War, Volume II.* Burlington, VT: The Free Press Association, 1888.

Black, Robert C. III. *The Railroads of the Confederacy*. Chapel Hill: The University of North Carolina Press, 1952.

Blackford, W. W. *War Years with Jeb Stuart*. New York: Charles Scribner's Sons, 1945.

Boudrye, Louis N. *Historic Records of the Fifth New York Cavalry, First Ira Harris Guard.* Albany, NY: S. R. Gray, 1865.

Bowen, James L. *History of the Thirty-Seventh Regiment Mass. Volunteers. In the Civil War of 1861–1865.* Holyoke, MA and New York: Clark W. Bryan & Company, Publishers, 1884.

Bowen, James L. *Massachusetts In The War 1861–1865.* Springfield, MA: Clark W. Bryan & Co., 1899.

Brewster, Charles. "Captured By Mosby's Guerrillas," *War Papers And Personal Reminiscences, 1861–1865. Military Order of the Loyal Legion of the United States. Missouri. Volume I.* St. Louis, MO: Becktold & Co., 1892.

Brown, R. Shepard. *Stringfellow of the Fourth*. New York: Crown Publishers, Inc., 1960.

Brown, Stuart E., Jr. *Annals of Clarke County Virginia, Volume I.* Berryville, VA: Virginia Book Company, 1983.

Bruce, Philip Alexander. *Virginia: Rebirth Of The Old Dominion.* Chicago and New York: The Lewis Publishing Company, 1929.

Bryan, John Stewart. *Joseph Bryan: His Times, His Family, His Friends, A Memoir.* Richmond, VA: Whittet & Shepperson, 1935.

Burkholder, N. M. "The Barn-Burners: A Chapter of Sheridan's Raid up the Valley." *Southern Historical Society Papers* XXVIII (1900).

Bushong, Millard Kessler. *Historic Jefferson County.* Boyce, VA: Can Publishing Company, Inc., 1972.

Carpenter, Henry W. "One For One Hundred," *Proceedings of the Clarke County Historical Association* V (1945).

Carter, Robert Goldthwaite. *Four Brothers In Blue.* Austin and London: University of Texas Press, 1978.

Cartmell, T. K. *Shenandoah Valley Pioneers and Their Descendants: A History of Frederick County, Virginia From its Formation in 1738 to 1908.* Reprint edition. Berryville, VA: Chesapeake Book Company, 1963.

Castel, Albert. "The Guerrilla War 1861–1865," *Civil War Times Illustrated,* October 1974.

Catton, Bruce. *Grant Moves South.* Boston and Toronto: Little, Brown and Company, 1960.

———. *Grant Takes Command.* Boston and Toronto: Little, Brown and Company, 1969.

Chappelear, B. Curtis. *Maps and Notes Pertaining to the Upper Section of Fauquier County, Virginia.* Warrenton, VA: The Warrenton Antiquarian Society, 1954.

Chappelear, Curtis. "Early Grants Of The Site Of Berryville And Its Northern Vicinity." *Proceedings of The Clarke County Historical Association* VIII, 1948.

Cheney, Newell. *History of the Ninth Regiment, New York Volunteer Cavalry, War Of 1861 to 1865.* Poland Center, NY: n.p., 1901.

Coates, M. C. F. "Mosby's Rangers." *Confederate Veteran* XL (1932).

Collins, John C. *John S. Mosby.* Gaithersburg, MD: Olde Soldiers Books, Inc., 1988.

Cooke, John Esten. *Wearing Of The Gray.* Bloomington: Indiana University Press, 1959.

Cooling, Benjamin Franklin. *Symbol, Sword, and Shield: Defending Washington during the Civil War.* Hamden, CT: Archon Book, 1975.

Crawford, J. Marshall. *Mosby And His Men: A Record Of The Adventures Of That Renowned Partisan Ranger, John S. Mosby.* New York: G. W. Carleton & Co., Publishers, 1867.

Crowninshield, Benjamin W. *A History Of The First Regiment Of Massachusetts Cavalry Volunteers.* Boston and New York: Houghton, Mifflin And Company, 1891.

Delauter, Roger U., Jr. *McNeill's Rangers.* Lynchburg, VA: H. E. Howard, Inc., 1986.

Denison, Frederic. *Sabres And Spurs: The First Rhode Island Cavalry in the Civil War. 1861–1865.* Central Falls, RI: Press of E. L. Freeman & Co., 1876.

Doak, H. M. "Mosby As A Soldier and Patriot," *Confederate Veteran* XII (1904).

Donnelly, Ralph W. "Mosby Re-activated In 1951," *Military Affairs* VX, Number 2 (Summer 1951).

Douglas, Henry Kyd. *I Rode With Stonewall.* Chapel Hill: The University of North Carolina Press, 1940.

Dowdey, Clifford, Ed., and Manarin, Louis H., Ass. Ed. *The Wartime Papers of R. E. Lee.* Boston and Toronto: Little, Brown and Company, 1961.

Drickamer, Lee C. and Karen D., Compilers and Eds. *Fort Lyon To Harper's Ferry: On the Border of North and South with "Rambling Jour.''* Shippensburg, PA: White Mane Publishing Co., Inc., 1989.

"Drums for Little Rebels and a Beaver Hat for Sallie.'' *Baltimore and Ohio Magazine*, May 1936.

Early, Jubal A. *Autobiographical Sketch And Narrative Of The War Between The States.* With Notes by R. H. Early. Introduction by Gary Gallagher, Reprint edition. Wilmington, NC: Broadfoot Publishing Company, 1989.

Edmonds, Amanda Virginia. *Journals Of Amanda Virginia Edmonds: Lass of the Mosby Confederacy.* Edited by Nancy Chappelear Baird. Stephens City, VA: Commercial Press, 1984.

Ellis, John. *A Short History Of Guerrilla Warfare.* New York: St. Martin's Press, 1976.

Elwood, John W. *Elwood's Stories of the Old Ringgold Cavalry 1847–1865.* Coal Center, PA: John W. Elwood, 1914.

Emerson, Edward W. *Life And Letters of Charles Russell Lowell.* Reprint edition. Port Washington, NY and London: Kennikat Press, 1971.

Evans, Clement A., Ed. *Confederate Military History, Extended Edition.* Reprint edition. Wilmington, NC: Broadfoot Publishing Company, 1987.

Fagan, Roberta E. "Custer at Front Royal: 'A Horror of the War,' '' Urwin, Gregory J. W., Ed. *Custer And His Times: Book Three.* n.p.: University of Central Arkansas Press and the Little Big Horn Associates, Inc., 1987.

Fairfax County and the War Between the States. Vienna, VA: Stenger Typographic Service, 1961.

Famous Adventures And Prison Escapes Of The Civil War. New York: The Century Co., 1911.

Fauquier County, Virginia, 1759–1959. Warrenton, VA: Virginia Publishing, 1959.

Faust, Patricia L., Ed. *Historical Times Illustrated Encyclopedia of the Civil War.* New York: Harper & Row, Publishers, 1986.

Fitts, James F. "Mosby And His Men.'' *Galaxy* II (1866).

Forsythe, John William. Edited by Melvin Lee Steadman, Jr. *Guerrilla Warfare And Life In Libby Prison.* Reprint edition. Annandale, VA: Turnpike Press, 1967.

Foster, Alonzo. *Reminiscences and Record of the 6th New York V.V. Cavalry.* n.p.: Alonzo Foster, 1892.

Foster, Gaines M. *Ghosts of the Confederacy: Defeat, The Lost Cause, And The Emergence Of The New South 1865 To 1913.* New York and Oxford: Oxford University Press, 1987.

Freeman, Douglas Southall, Ed. *Lee's Dispatches: Unpublished Letters of General Robert E. Lee. C. S. A. to Jefferson Davis and the War Department of The Confederate States of America 1862–65.* New York: G. P. Putnam's Sons, 1957.

Garrett, Richard. *The Raiders: The Elite Strike Forces that Altered the Course of War and History.* New York: Van Nostrand Reinhold Company, 1980.

Geddes, Jean. *Fairfax County: Historical Highlights From 1607.* Middleburg, VA: Denlingers, 1967.

Glazier, Willard. *Three Years in the Federal Cavalry*. New York: R. H. Ferguson & Company, Publishers, 1873.

Gold, Thomas D. *History of Clarke County Virginia And Its Connection With The War Between The States*. Reprint edition. Berryville, VA: Chesapeake Book Company, 1962.

Goldsborough, W. W. *The Maryland Line in the Confederate Army, 1861–1865*. Reprint edition. Gaithersburg, MD: Butternut Press, 1983.

Goodhart, Briscoe. *History of the Independent Loudoun Virginia Rangers. U.S. Vol. Cav. (Scouts) 1862–65*. Reprint edition. Gaithersburg, MD: Butternut Press, Inc., 1985.

Gott, John K. *High In Old Virginia's Piedmont: A History of Marshall (formerly Salem), Fauquier County, Virginia*. Marshall, VA: Marshall National Bank & Trust Company, 1987.

———, Ed. *The Years of Anguish: Fauquier County, Virginia 1861–1865*. Reprint edition. Annandale, VA: Bacon Race Books, 1987.

Gracey, Samuel L. *Annals of the Sixth Pennsylvania Cavalry*. n.p.: E. H. Butler & Co., 1868.

Grant, Carl E. "Partisan Warfare, Model 1861–65." *Military Review*, November 1958.

Grant, Ulysses S. *Personal Memoirs of U. S. Grant*. New York: Charles L. Webster & Company, 1886.

Hagemann, E. R., Ed. with an Introduction. *Fighting Rebels And Redskins: Experiences In Army Life Of Colonel George B. Sanford 1861–1892*. Norman: University of Oklahoma Press, 1969.

Haines, Alanson A. *History Of The Fifteenth Regiment New Jersey Volunteers*. New York: Jenkins & Thomas, Printers, 1883.

Hale, Laura Virginia. *Four Valiant Years: In The Lower Shenandoah Valley 1861–1865*. Strasburg, VA: Shenandoah Publishing House, Inc., 1968.

Hall, Hillman A., et al, Compilers. *History of the Sixth New York Cavalry (Second Ira Harris Guard), Second Brigade-First Division-Cavalry Corps, Army Of The Potomac 1861–1865*. Worcester, MA: The Blanchard Press, 1908.

"Hanging Of Mosby's Men in 1864." *Southern Historical Society Papers* XXIV (1896).

Hard, Abner. *History of the Eighth Cavalry Regiment Illinois Volunteers, During The Great Rebellion*. Aurora, IL: [Abner Hard], 1868.

Harrison, Fairfax. *Landmarks of Old Prince William*, Reprint edition, Berryville, VA: Chesapeake Book Company, 1964.

Head, James W. *History and Comprehensive Description of Loudoun County Virginia*. n.p.: Park View Press, 1908.

Heitmann, Francis B. *Historical Register and Dictionary of the United States Army*. Washington, DC: Government Printing Office, 1903.

Hewitt, William. *History of the Twelfth West Virginia Volunteer Infantry: The Part It Took in the War of the Rebellion 1861–1865*. n.p.: Published by the Twelfth West Virginia Infantry Association (1892).

History of the Third Pennsylvania Cavalry, Sixtieth Regiment Pennsylvania Volunteers In the American Civil War 1861–1865. Philadelphia: Franklin Printing Company, 1905.

History of Virginia: Virginia Biography. Chicago and New York: The American Historical Society, 1924.

Hoadley, J. C. Memorial of Henry Sanford Gansevoort. Boston: Franklin Press: Rand, Avery, & Co., 1875.

Holmes, Torlief. Horse Soldiers In Blue. Gaithersburg, MD: Butternut Press, 1985.

"A Honor Of the War: How General Custer Hung Some Of Mosby's Men." Southern Historical Society Papers XXV (1897).

Howard, McHenry. Recollections of a Maryland Confederate Soldier And Staff Officer Under Johnston, Jackson and Lee. Introduction, Correction And Notes by James I. Robertson, Jr. Dayton, OH: Press of Morningside Bookshop, 1975.

Humphreys, Charles A. Field, Camp, Hospital and Prison In The Civil War, 1863–1865. Freeport, NY: Books For Libraries Press, 1971.

Hunter, Alexander. "The Women Of Mosby's Confederacy." Confederate Veteran XV (1907).

———. The Women of the Debatable Land. Washington, DC: Corden Publishing Company, 1912.

Isham, Asa B. An Historical Sketch of the Seventh Regiment Michigan Volunteer Cavalry From Its Organization, In 1862, To Its Muster Out, In 1865. New York: Town Topics Publishing Company, 1893.

Janney, Samuel M. Memoirs of Samuel M. Janney. Philadelphia: Friends' Book Association, 1881.

Johnson, Robert Underwood, and Bull, Clarence Clough, eds. Battles and Leaders of the Civil War. Reprint edition. New York and London: Thomas Yoseloff, 1956.

Jones, Virgil Carrington. Gray Ghosts And Rebel Raiders. With An Introduction By Bruce Catton. New York: Henry Holt and Company, 1956.

———. Ranger Mosby. Chapel Hill: The University of North Carolina Press, 1944.

Joyce, Elizabeth Moore. "Colonel Mosby's Henry." Confederate Veteran XXXII (1924).

Kidd, James H. Personal Recollections Of a Cavalryman With Custer's Michigan Cavalry Brigade In The Civil War. Ionia, MI: Sentinel Publishing Company, 1908.

Klonis, N. I. Guerrilla Warfare: Analysis and Projections. New York: Robert Speller & Sons, Publications, Inc., 1972.

Krick, Robert K. Lee's Colonels: A Biographical Register of the Field Officers of the Army of Northern Virginia. Dayton, OH: Press of Morningside Bookshop, 1979.

Laquer, Walter. Guerrilla: A Historical and Critical Study. Boston and Toronto: Little, Brown and Company, 1976.

Lee, William O., Compiler. Personal and Historical Sketches And Facial History Of And By Members Of The Seventh Regiment Michigan Volunteer Cavalry 1862–1865. Detroit, MI: 7th Michigan Cavalry Association, 1902.

Leech, Margaret. Reveille in Washington 1860–1865. New York and London: Harper & Brothers Publishers, 1941.

Lloyd, William P. History of the First Reg't Pennsylvania Reserve Cavalry. Philadelphia: King & Baird, Printers, 1864.

Long, E. B. with Barbara Long. The Civil War Day by Day: An Almanac 1861–

1865. Foreword by Bruce Catton. Garden City, NY: Doubleday & Company, Inc., 1971.

Lufkin, Edwin B. *History of the Thirteenth Maine Regiment From Its Organization in 1861 To Its Muster-Out In 1865*. Bridgton, ME: H. A. Shorey & Son, Publishers, 1898.

Lynch, Charles H. *The Civil War Diary 1862–1865 of Charles H. Lynch, 18th Conn. Vol's*. Hartford, CT: The Case, Lockwood & Brainard Co., 1915.

Mason, J. Stevens. "Retaliation by Col. J. S. Mosby," *Confederate Veteran* XIV (1906).

McCarty, Clara S., Compiler and Ed. *The Foothills Of The Blue Ridge in Fauquier County, Virginia*. Warrenton, VA: The Fauquier Democrat, 1974.

McClellan, H. B. *I Rode with Jeb Stuart: The Life And Campaigns of Major General J. E. B. Stuart*. Bloomington: Indiana University Press, 1958.

McGuire, Judith W. *Diary of a Southern Refugee During The War*. New York: E. J. Hale & Son, 1867.

Meaney, Peter J., O.S.B. *The Civil War Engagement At Cool Spring July 18, 1864*. Morristown, NJ: Peter J. Meaney, O.S.B., 1979.

Military Operations in Jefferson County Virginia (And West VA.) 1861–1865. Reprint edition. n.p.: Whitney & White, 1960.

Mitchell, Adele H., Ed. *The Letters of John S. Mosby*. n.p.: Stuart-Mosby Historical Society, 1986.

"The Monument to Mosby's Men," *Southern Historical Society Papers* XXVII (1899).

Monteiro, Aristides. *War Reminiscences by the Surgeon of Mosby's Command*. Reprint edition. Gaithersburg, MD: Butternut Press, n.d.

"Mosby And His Men," *Confederate Veteran* VII (1899).

Mosby, John S. *The Memoirs of Colonel John S. Mosby*. Edited by Charles Wells Russell. Reprint edition. Gaithersburg, MD: Olde Soldier Books, Inc., 1987.

———. "Mosby And His Cavalry." *Grand Army Scout And Mail* V, No. 45, October 16, 1886.

———. "Retaliation: The Execution of Seven Prisoners By Col. John S. Mosby—A Self-Protective Necessity." *Southern Historical Society Papers* XXVII (1899).

———. *Stuart's Cavalry in the Gettysburg Campaign*. New York: Moffat, Yard and Company, 1908.

Moyer, H. P., Compiler. *History of the Seventeenth Regiment Pennsylvania Volunteer Cavalry or One Hundred And Sixty-Second In The Line of Pennsylvania Volunteer Regiments. War to Suppress the Rebellion, 1861–1865*. Lebanon, PA: Sowers Printing Company, 1911.

Munson, John W. *Reminiscences Of A Mosby Guerrilla*. Reprint edition. Washington, DC: Zenger Publishing Co., Inc., 1983.

Myers, Frank A. *The Comanches: A History Of White's Battalion. Virginia Cavalry. Laurel Brig., Hampton Div., A.N.V., C.S.A.* Introduction and Notes by Lee A. Wallace, Jr. Reprint edition. Gaithersburg, MD: Butternut Press, Inc., 1987.

Newcomer, C. Armour. *Cole's Cavalry: or Three Years In The Saddle in the Shenandoah Valley*. Reprint edition. Freeport, NY: Books For Libraries Press, 1970.

Nichols, G. W. *A Soldier's Story Of His Regiment (61st Georgia) and Incidentally of the Lawton-Gordon-Evans Brigade Army Northern Virginia.* Kennesaw, GA: Continental Book Company, 1961.

Norton, Henry. *Deeds Of Daring. Or History of the Eighth N. Y. Volunteer Cavalry.* Norwich, NY: Chenango Telegraph Printing House, 1889.

Old Homes And Families of Fauquier County Virginia (The W. P. A. Records). Berryville, VA: Virginia Book Company, 1978.

Opie, John N. *A Rebel Cavalryman With Lee Stuart And Jackson.* Reprint edition. Dayton, OH: The Press of Morningside Bookshop, 1972.

Orton, Richard H., Compiler. *Records Of California Men in the War Of The Rebellion 1861 To 1867.* Sacramento: State Printing Office, 1890.

Palmer, W. Ben. "One of Mosby's Bravest Men," *Confederate Veteran* V (1897).

Patterson, C. Meade, and DeMarco, Cuddy J. "Civil War Revolvers." *Civil War Small Arms.* Washington, DC: The National Rifle Association, n.d.

Patterson, W. W. "Swift Retribution for House-Burning." *Confederate Veteran* XII (1904).

Perkins, George. *A Summer In Maryland and Virginia, Or Campaigning with the 149th Ohio Volunteer Infantry.* Chillicothe, OH: The Scholl Printing Company, n.d.

Plater, Richard D., Jr., Ed. "Civil War Diary of Miss Mattella Cory Page Harrison of Clarke County, Virginia 1835–1898." *Proceedings of The Clarke County Historical Association* XXII, 1982–1983.

Plum, William Rattle. *The Military Telegraph During The Civil War In The United States.* Introduction by Paul J. Scheips. Vols. I & II. New York: Arno Press, 1974.

Poland, Charles Preston, Jr. *From Frontier To Suburbia.* Marceline, MS: Walsworth Publishing Company, 1976.

Prince William: The Story of Its People and Its Places. Manassas, VA: The Bethlehem Good Housekeeping Club, 1976.

Putnam, George Haven. *Memories of My Youth, 1844–1865.* New York and London: G. P. Putnam's Sons, The Knickerbocker Press, 1914.

Pyne, Henry R. *The History of the First New Jersey Cavalry (Sixteenth Regiment, New Jersey Volunteers).* Trenton, NJ: J. A. Belcher, Publisher, 1871.

Richards, A. E. "The Capture Of General Stoughton." *Southern Bivouac,* 1885–1886.

———. "Mosby And His Men—The Seven Martyrs," *Confederate Veteran* VII (1899).

Rodenbough, Theodore F., Compiler and Ed. *History of the Eighteenth Regiment of Cavalry Pennsylvania Volunteers (163d Regiment of the Line) 1862–1865.* New York: Wignkoop Hallenbeck Crawford Co., 1899.

Scheel, Eugene M. *The Civil War in Fauquier County Virginia.* Warrenton, VA: The Fauquier National Bank, 1985.

———. *The History of Middleburg and Vicinity.* Warrenton, VA: Piedmont Press, 1987.

Scott, John. *Partisan Life With Col. John S. Mosby.* Reprint edition. Gaithersburg, MD: Butternut Press, Inc., 1985.

Siepel, Kevin H. *Rebel: The Life And Times of John Singleton Mosby*. New York: St. Martin's Press, 1983.

Sinnott, Harry T. "Annual Reunion Of Mosby's Men," *Confederate Veteran* XIII (1905).

Smith, Channing M. "Survivors Of Mosby's Command." *Confederate Veteran* XXXI (1923).

Smith, Jean Herron. *Snickersville: The Biography of a Village*. Miamisburg, OH: The Miamisburg News, 1970.

Smith, Vme Edom. *Middleburg and Nearby*. Leesburg, VA: Potomac Press, 1986.

Spies, Scouts and Raiders: Irregular Operations. Alexandria, VA: Time-Life Books, Inc., 1985.

Starr, Stephen Z. *The Union Cavalry in the Civil War: Volume II, the War in the East From Gettysburg to Appomattox*. Baton Rouge and London: Louisiana State University Press, 1981.

Stevens, George T. *Three Years in the Sixth Corps: A Concise Narrative of Events in the Army of the Potomac, From 1861 To the Close of the Rebellion, April, 1865*. Albany: S. R. Gray, Publisher, 1866.

Stevenson, James H. *Boots And Saddles: A History of the First Volunteer Cavalry of the War, Known as the First New York (Lincoln) Cavalry*. Harrisburg, PA: Patriot Publishing Company, 1879.

Sutton, Joseph J. *History of the Second Regiment West Virginia Cavalry Volunteers During the War Of The Rebellion*. Portsmouth, OH: n.p., 1892.

Swinfen, David B. *Ruggles' Regiment: The 122nd New Volunteers in the American Civil War*. Hanover and London: University Press of New England, 1982.

Thayer, Charles W. *Guerrilla*. New York: Harper & Row, Publishers, 1963.

Thomas, Emory M. *Bold Dragoon: The Life Of J. E. B. Stuart*. New York: Harper & Row, Publishers, 1986.

Thomson, O. R. Howard, and Rauch, William H. *History of the "Bucktails": Kane Rifle Regiment Of The Pennsylvania Reserve Corps*. Reprint edition. Dayton, OH: Morningside, 1988.

Tidwell, William A., with James O. Hall and David Winfred Gaddy. *Come Retribution: The Confederate Secret Service and the Assassination of Lincoln*. Paperback edition. Jackson and London: University Press of Mississippi, 1988.

Turner, Fitzhugh, Ed. *Loudoun County and the Civil War*. Leesburg, VA: Loudoun County Civil War Centennial Commission, 1961.

Tyler, Mason Whiting. *Recollections of the Civil War*. Edited by William S. Tyler. New York and London: G. P. Putnam's Sons, The Knickerbocker Press, 1912.

U.S. Department of Commerce. Bureau of the Census. *Seventh Census of the United States, 1860: Population. Fauquier and Loudoun Counties, Virginia*.

U.S. War Department. *Atlas To Accompany The Official Records of the Union And Confederate Armies*. Reprint edition, Gettysburg, PA: The National Historical Society, 1974.

————. *The War Of The Rebellion: A Compilation of the Official Records of the Union and Confederate Armies*. 128 Volumes. Washington, DC: U.S. Government Printing Office, 1880–1901.

Vandiver, Frank E. *Jubal's Raid: General Early's Famous Attack On Washington in 1864*. Reprint edition. Westport, CT: Greenwood Press, Publishers, 1974.

The 1984 VMI Register Of Former Cadets, Fifth Edition. Lexington, VA: The VMI Alumni Association, Inc., 1984.

Walker, William C. *History of The Eighteenth Regiment Conn. Volunteers in The War For The Union.* Norwich, CT: Published By The Committee, 1885.

Wallace, Lee A., Jr. *A Guide To Virginia Military Organizations 1861–1865.* Revised 2nd Edition. Lynchburg, VA: H. E. Howard, Inc., 1986.

Warner, Ezra J. *Generals In Blue: Lives of the Union Commanders.* Baton Rouge and London: Louisiana State University Press, 1981.

————. *Generals In Gray: Lives of the Confederate Commanders.* Baton Rouge: Louisiana State University Press, 1970.

Watrous, J. A. "Mosby and His Men," *War Papers Read Before The Commandery Of The State Of Wisconsin, Military Order Of The Loyal Legion Of The United States, Volume II.* Milwaukee: Burdick, Armitage & Allen, 1896.

Weatherly, Yetive Rockefeller. *Lovettsville: The German Settlement.* Lovettsville, VA: Lovettsville Bicentennial Committee, 1976.

Wert, Jeffry D. *From Winchester to Cedar Creek: The Shenandoah Campaign of 1864.* Carlisle, PA: South Mountain Press, 1987.

Williams, Charles Richard, Ed. *Diary And Letters of Rutherford Birchard Hayes, Vol. II.* Columbus: The Ohio State Archaeological and Historical Society, 1922.

Williams, Harrison. *Legends Of Loudoun: An Account of the history and homes of a border county of Virginia's Northern Neck.* Richmond, VA: Garrett And Massie, Inc., 1938.

Williamson, James J. *Mosby's Rangers: A Record of the Operations of the Forty-third Battalion of Virginia Cavalry from its Organization to the Surrender.* Second Edition. New York: Sturgis & Walton Company, 1909.

Wiltshire, J. G. "Mosby's Men—Charles B. Wiltshire," *Confederate Veteran* VIII (1900).

Index